MODERN HUMANITIES RESEARCH ASSOCIATION
TEXTS AND DISSERTATIONS
VOLUME 70

INSTITUTE OF GERMANIC AND ROMANCE STUDIES
(UNIVERSITY OF LONDON)
BITHELL SERIES OF DISSERTATIONS
VOLUME 32

ART AND ITS USES IN THOMAS MANN'S *FELIX KRULL*

Art and its Uses in Thomas Mann's *Felix Krull*

by
ERNEST SCHONFIELD

MANEY PUBLISHING
for the
MODERN HUMANITIES RESEARCH ASSOCIATION
2008

Maney Publishing
for the
Modern Humanities Research Association
1 Carlton House Terrace
London SW1Y 5AF
United Kingdom

ISBN 978-1-905981-05-2
ISSN (Bithell Series of Dissertations) 0266–7932
ISSN (MHRA Texts and Dissertations) 0957–0322

Maney Publishing is the trading name of W. S. Maney & Son Ltd,
whose registered office is at Suite 1C, Joseph's Well, Hanover Walk, Leeds LS3 1AB

Copy-Editor: Nigel Hope

Copies may be ordered from Publications Sales, Maney Publishing, Suite 1C, Joseph's Well, Hanover Walk, Leeds LS3 1AB; email mhra@maney.co.uk. Further information about the publications, activities, and membership of the MHRA can be obtained from the website at www.mhra.org.uk.

CONTENTS

PREFACE

The purpose of this book is to demonstrate why and how *Felix Krull* is a great novel. Many of Thomas Mann's readers cherish *Felix Krull* and regard it as one of his best works, but relatively few critics have formulated an adequate account of its greatness. It seems that *Krull* occupies a unique position in Thomas Mann criticism — not quite first rank, not quite second rank. Some critics, such as T. J. Reed, have found *Krull* to be charming and intriguing, but lightweight.[1] Others, like Hans Wysling, have tried to make it heavyweight by elaborating complex mythical structures, which at times seem far removed from the work itself.[2] This book seeks to redress the balance, to show that *Krull* is both entertaining *and* intellectually challenging — and that it possesses formal and conceptual richness on a grand scale. The title, 'Art and its Uses', expresses my firm conviction that *Felix Krull* is far from being a manifesto of unbridled aestheticism (i.e., of 'art for art's sake'). In my view, the novel adopts a much more conciliatory position, seeing art as an essential sphere of human endeavour, but as being related to many other spheres of activity.

At the centre of this book is the idea that identity and society are permeated with aesthetics on a number of levels. In particular, I maintain that social interaction involves an aesthetic dimension, and that all communication relies upon mutually agreed conventions. Every work of art implies a community of people. The Müller-Rosé episode in *Felix Krull* shows that the artist relies upon an unspoken agreement with the audience. Although Krull is nominally a confidence man, in fact he is more of a 'Lebenskünstler', an artist whose mission in life is to charm people; not for financial gain, but because it gratifies him. Krull seems to think that he provides a valuable service to society by beautifying it a little, and I shall argue that, in a way, he does. The crucial point here is that Krull needs the consent of his audience in order to succeed. In short, *Krull* is not so much about illusion as about agreed pretence and knowing collusion.

This book also explores the profound implications which a study of *Felix Krull* can have for our understanding of Thomas Mann's work as a whole. In my view, knowledge of *Krull* is absolutely central to an understanding of Mann's literary ambitions. In chronological terms, it nearly brackets Mann's entire oeuvre. The first written mention of a planned *Novelle* called *Der Hochstapler* occurs in late 1905 (in Mann's seventh notebook),[3] but the dossier of material which Mann collected in order to write the work was begun even earlier, in 1902.[4] The version of the novel we have today was completed in 1954, although a continuation was planned. In other words, the composition of *Krull* stretches (on and off) over a period of more than fifty years, spanning most of Mann's creative life. But it spans his creative achievement thematically as well as chronologically. Because it is an early and a late work, it forms a unique summation of Mann's career, revealing the remarkable continuity of his thought about art. *Krull* is the culmination of a lifelong meditation on the figure of the artist and on the place of art in society. It is a major work, one that addresses the experience of modernity with grace and with wisdom.

Notes

1. According to T. J. Reed the novel lacks substance: 'Mann had the "psychological material", [. . .] but lacked a plot' (Reed, *Thomas Mann: The Uses of Tradition* [1974] (Oxford: Oxford University Press, 1996), p. 113). Reed justifies his appraisal of the novel by quoting letters written in 1951 and 1952 in which Mann expresses the odd doubt about it (ibid., p. 403). However, it is possible to quote texts of 1954 in which Mann defends the work, e.g. 'Rückkehr' (XI, 530–31), and a letter of 17 November 1954 to Fritz Martini (Br III, 360).
2. Hans Wysling, *Narzißmus und illusionäre Existenzform. Zu den Bekenntnissen des Hochstaplers Felix Krull*, TMS 5 (Bern: Francke, 1982). Wysling's study remains the standard work on the novel. However, Wysling's emphasis upon myth, illusion, narcissism, and intertextuality set the agenda for most subsequent critical enquiry. As I seek to demonstrate, this has tended to attract attention away from the text itself and away from some of *Krull*'s wider social implications.
3. N II, 124: '<u>Zum Hochstapler</u> Er markirt in gefährlichen Augenblicken Husten-Anfälle, aus dem Instinkt: der Leidende ist unschuldig, über einen Kranken geht der Verdacht hinweg' [underlining by Mann].
4. The two earliest documents in the dossier tell of Johann Biller, a burglar who escaped from prison by scaling the wall. The two documents are held in the TMA, Mat. 3/260 and 3/261.

ACKNOWLEDGEMENTS

I would like to thank the following organizations and people:

The Arts and Humanities Research Council for financing my research during the years 2003–05, and for a travel grant which enabled me to research at the Thomas Mann Archive in Zurich. The staff of the Thomas Mann Archive, for their hospitality and support. The staff of the Institute of Germanic and Romance Studies, London, for their help and encouragement, for their fine lecture programme and for the use of their library. Professor Rüdiger Görner and Dr Angus Nicholls, for their excellent research colloquium. Professors Matthew Bell and Robert Weninger of King's College London, for some teaching experience. My PhD examiners, Professors T. J. Reed and John J. White, for some valuable pointers. Professor Ritchie Robertson, for his kind words and careful editing. Dr Graham Nelson of the MHRA for his patient editorial guidance. Dr Kevin Hilliard, for a helpful hint. Susan Reynolds, for allowing me to read her unpublished essay on Thomas Mann and Ibsen. Professor Susanne Kord, for her help and for allowing me to participate in her seminar on Goethe. Dr Judith Beniston, Dr Mererid Puw Davies, Professor Mary Fulbrook, Dr Mark Hewitson, Sue Jones, and Dr Adrian Stevens of University College London for their help and support. My secondary supervisor, Dr Stephanie Bird, for her helpful advice, unremitting support, and for our many stimulating discussions. My undergraduate tutors at Sussex University, Dr Daniel Steuer, Dr Margarete Köhlenbach, and Dr Ladislaus Löb, for getting me on the right track. Dr Ruth Martin, for her scrupulous proofreading. Dr Marielle Sutherland, for practical advice. Dr Daniel Wilton, Frank Reinicke MA, Dr Esther von Richthofen, Dr Charlotte Ryland, and Dr George Last, for being there. My family and friends, for their support. Anne-Marie Thornell, for being great. My supervisor, Professor Martin Swales, for his continual encouragement, attention, kindness, and generosity, his thoughtful criticism and inspirational guidance, without which I should never have been able either to undertake or to complete this piece of work.

E. S., April 2008

ABBREVIATIONS

Unless otherwise noted, references to Thomas Mann's works are to the *Gesammelte Werke* in 13 volumes (Frankfurt a.M.: Fischer, 1974). Roman numerals refer to the volume, and arabic numerals refer to the page number. Arabic numerals alone and in brackets refer to *Bekenntnisse des Hochstaplers Felix Krull* in volume VII of the *Gesammelte Werke*.

Br I–III	*Briefe 1889–1955*, 3 vols, ed. Erika Mann
Br A	*Briefe an Paul Amann 1915–1952*, ed. Herbert Wegener
Br B	*Thomas Mann an Ernst Bertram. Briefe aus den Jahren 1910–1955*
Br H	Thomas Mann–Heinrich Mann, *Briefwechsel 1900–1949*, ed. Wysling
Br Hs	Hermann Hesse–Thomas Mann, *Briefwechsel*, ed. Anni Carlsson
Br K	Thomas Mann–Karl Kerényi, *Gespräch in Briefen*, ed. Karl Kerényi
DüD I–III	*Dichter über ihre Dichtungen*, 3 vols, ed. Wysling and Fischer
FAZ	*Frankfurter Allgemeine Zeitung*
GKFA	Thomas Mann, *Große Kommentierte Frankfurter Ausgabe*
GS	Walter Benjamin, *Gesammelte Schriften*, ed. Rolf Tiedemann
HA	Goethe, *Werke, Hamburger Ausgabe*, 14 vols, ed. Erich Trunz
HF	Fontane, *Werke, Schriften und Briefe*, 5 vols, ed. Keitel and Nürnberger
KGA	Nietzsche, *Werke, Kritische Gesamtausgabe*, ed. Colli and Montinari
LRB	*London Review of Books*
MLR	*Modern Language Review*
N	Notes for 'Geist und Kunst', in TMS 1, ed. Scherrer and Wysling, 123–233
N I–II	*Notizbücher*, 2 vols, ed. Hans Wysling and Yvonne Schmidlin
NA	Schiller, *Werke, Nationalausgabe*, ed. Julius Petersen et al.
OC	Roland Barthes, *Œuvres complètes*, 1942–80, 3 vols, ed. Eric Marty
OGS	*Oxford German Studies*
SA	Freud, *Studienausgabe*, 12 vols, ed. Alexander Mitscherlich et al.
Tb	*Tagebücher*, 10 vols, ed. Peter de Mendelssohn and Inge Jens
TMA	Thomas Mann Archive, Zurich
TMJ	*Thomas-Mann-Jahrbuch*
TMS	Thomas-Mann-Studien
WA	Heinrich Mann, *Werkauswahl in 10 Bänden* (Düsseldorf: Claassen, 1976)

INTRODUCTION

In his study *The Age of Empire*, Eric Hobsbawm describes the period between 1875 and 1914 as a time of profound identity crisis for the upper and middle classes, one in which social mobility reached unprecedented levels.[1] As a result, there arose a confusion about 'who was who', and it was in this period that reference volumes about persons of status in the nation, such as the British *Who's Who* (1897), first appeared.[2] The growth of the modern city added to the confusion about identity. As Georg Simmel remarked in his essay 'Die Großstädte und das Geistesleben' (1903), the dominance of the money economy granted to the individual new, unheard-of freedoms. For the first time, identity ceased to be defined by one's social background; from now on, one was free to project whichever persona one wished.[3] This background of social upheaval made the turn of the century a boom period for confidence tricksters. There were a number of celebrated cases. In 1902, one of the most influential ladies in Parisian high society, Thérèse Humbert, was exposed as a penniless fraud.[4] Then there was the famous 'Hauptmann von Köpenick' incident. On 16 October 1906, Wilhelm Voigt, a 56-year-old unemployed shoemaker and ex-convict, disguised himself as a Prussian officer. Wearing a second-hand uniform, he commandeered a division of soldiers, occupied the town hall in Köpenick, had the mayor arrested, stole the cash box, and drove away in a carriage.[5] But it was above all the adventures of Georges Manolescu which made the headlines. Manolescu, a Romanian confidence man, disguised himself as an aristocrat. He visited the grand hotels and spas of Europe, stealing jewellery and committing various frauds. The German publication of his memoirs in 1905 was a huge commercial success.[6]

When Thomas Mann decided to write a story about a confidence man around 1905, he was therefore addressing a well-known phenomenon. The first written mention of *Der Hochstapler* occurs in 1905, in Mann's seventh notebook (N 11, 124). Mann had been planning a work on the link between art and criminality from as early as 1902, as the newspaper cuttings about Johann Biller testify.[7] The discovery of Manolescu's memoirs in 1905, however, gave a new impetus to the project.[8] The influence of these memoirs upon the developing *Hochstapler* project was central, as Hans Wysling[9] and Thomas Sprecher[10] have shown. Even so, Mann studied other confidence men apart from Manolescu. One case which particularly interested him was that of the jewel thief Carlsson. Arrested in 1907, Carlsson claimed to be an aristocrat and operated in Munich and in the spas of central Europe. Mann collected a number of newspaper cuttings about Carlsson, often underlining sentences which appealed to him:

> Carlsson führte ein Manuskript über die Académie Française mit sich, so daß es
> den Anschein machte, er sei Literat oder gehöre gar der Akademie an. [. . .] [Er]

benahm sich stets sehr taktvoll, errötete, wenn irgendein zweifelhafter Witz gemacht wurde. Er erzählte immer: er sei der Sohn eines englischen Barons, seine Mutter sei Schwedin und er würde einst 80 Millionen Mark erben. Als Monatwechsel sende ihm sein Vater 10 000 Mark. Niemand vermutete, er sei Millionendieb.[11]

Another article, this time undated, contains photographs of a number of notorious confidence men, including Manolescu, Major Schiemangk, von Tschernatieff, Graf von Ostrowski, and Margulin.[12] By November 1909, Mann's collection of newspaper cuttings about confidence men had grown to a considerable size, but at this point he still planned *Der Hochstapler* as a short story.[13] Only in January 1910 did work on the text begin in earnest.[14]

Now, as soon as Mann began actually to write *Felix Krull* in early 1910, his choice of documentary material altered radically. Up to that point, Mann had focused almost exclusively upon newspaper reports about criminals. From now on, his selection of material was determined mainly by sociological concerns, and only rarely by criminology.[15] Increasingly, Mann shifted his attention from newspapers to popular illustrated journals such as *Die Woche*. The bulk of the documentary material that Mann collected for *Felix Krull* comes from *Die Woche* and was gathered between 1910 and 1913. It does not deal with crime at all, but with the universe in which Krull was to operate: the worlds of high society and the grand hotel; the worlds of leisure, tourism, and sport.[16] This is evident from the titles Mann selected for the sections of the dossier. While the earlier material went into folders entitled 'Coups Carlsson', 'Streiche', 'Gefangenschaft', the later material was filed under the following headings: 'Kur- und Lustorte', 'Hôtel. Reise (Dandy. Gartenarbeit) Heimat. Zuchthausaufseher', 'Intérieurs', 'Elegante Festlichkeiten', 'Weiblichkeit', 'Sport', and 'Reisen'.[17]

In other words, the principal focus of Mann's dossier for *Felix Krull* is on the aesthetics of society, and not on crime. If he began by underlining sentences in articles about confidence men, soon he was underlining sections in articles with titles like 'Der moderne Dandy', 'Der Beruf eines Hotelkellners', 'Die Dame im Hotel', and 'Beim Fünfuhrtee'.[18] One of the longest texts in the dossier is a memoir by the Russian ballerina Anna Pavlova entitled 'Aus meinem Leben'.[19] The text has many similarities to *Krull*. In it, Pavlova talks about her first visit to the theatre, and the great impression which it made upon her. She goes on to recount her meetings with the crowned heads of Europe, including the Tsar of Russia, the King of Sweden, and Edward VII of England. She describes the time in Stockholm when a crowd appears under her balcony and applauds her. Her maid tells her that she has brought a ray of sunshine into the lives of these people, and Pavlova realizes that this is the true meaning of her art: she helps people briefly to forget life's sorrows ('eine Stunde lang die Trübsal des Lebens vergessen').[20] This is highly relevant to *Krull*, since Krull and Müller-Rosé too bring a touch of beauty into the lives of the people they encounter. It seems that during the composition of the novel, the criminal theme faded more and more into the background, to be replaced by an exploration of the public nature of art.

This becomes clear when one considers the final published version of *Felix Krull*. In it, details of actual criminal activity have been kept to a minimum. This discrepancy between Mann's initial plans for the novel and the finished result is all-important. Mann's original idea was to explore the analogy between artistry and criminality, as Ignace Feuerlicht points out.[21] But Feuerlicht demonstrates that Krull is far from being a *pícaro* in the traditional sense of the word. No *pícaro* worthy of the name would refuse Diane Houpflé's entreaties to call her a 'süße Hure' (443), or so nobly refuse the generosity of Lord Kilmarnock. And what sort of rogue would turn down the passionate advances of Eleanor Twentyman, telling her to overcome her confusion for the sake of decency ('so müssen Sie sie doch um des gesellschaftlichen Naturgesetzes und der guten Sitten willen überwinden' (487))?[22] In other words, if Krull begins life as a rogue in the manner of Manolescu, he soon finds that he prefers good form to criminality. The direction of the work changes: the initial theme of deception and illusion slowly alters, and is largely replaced by the study of aesthetics in society.[23] The most sublime expression of Krull's art is not the epileptic fit with which he escapes military service — it is his activity as a waiter in a grand hotel. He is an artist first and foremost and a rogue second.

Felix Krull begins life as a sceptical attack on the figure of the artist, but it does not remain so. It begins by transposing the artist into the criminal, but it ends by transposing the artist into the social world in general. This pattern of development is perfectly in line with one of the basic premises of the novel, namely, that Krull is one of the happy few who have been blessed by fate. As his first name indicates, Felix Krull is 'ein Sonntagskind', 'ein Vorzugskind des Himmels' (271). There is an allusion here to an operetta that had a special place in Thomas Mann's affections: *Das Sonntagskind*, composed by Carl Millöcker, with a libretto by Hugo Wittmann and Julius Bauer. Mann attended a performance of it on 24 May 1893, and his review of this operetta was one of the very first pieces he ever published. It appeared under the pseudonym 'Paul Thomas' in *Der Frühlingssturm* in Lübeck in June/July 1893. In the review, Mann praises the lightness of *Das Sonntagskind*, appreciating it as a welcome antidote to the heaviness of the recent Wagner-season:

> Nach den schweren Kunstgenüssen, die uns das Stadttheater im vergangenen Winter brachte, wirken die kleine Tivoli- und Wilhelmtheater-Amusements etwa wie ein Glas Selters nach einem großen Diner. — Die gewaltigen Wagner-Gerhäuser-Abende der Saison lagen mir — um im Bilde zu bleiben — noch schwer im Magen; so tat mir Millöckers Kohlensäure-Musik wirklich ganz ausgezeichnet gut. Wenn schon Blödsinn — dann schon gehörig. Das ist ein unstreitbar richtiges Prinzip. Daher geh' ich auch nicht gern zur Schule. Das ist halber Kram. Im 'Sonntagskind' aber ist der Blödsinn mit reizender Konsequenz durchgeführt, und darum ist es ein durchaus lobenswertes und ästhetisch völlig unanfechtbares Stück. (XIII, 245)[24]

This brief text anticipates *Felix Krull* in two important ways. Firstly, there is the metaphorical description of art as carbonated mineral water. This view of art as something effervescent and light-hearted paves the way for the dominant metaphor of sparkling wine ('Sekt') in the opening section of *Krull*. Secondly, there is the dislike of the drudgery of school, a trait shared by both Hanno Buddenbrook and the young Felix Krull. The early provenance of this text (1893) and its humour should not prevent us from taking it seriously. Mann is suggesting that an alternative aesthetic, an aesthetic of lightness, may sometimes have its place alongside the epic grandeur of Wagner. Mann is speaking of opera, but the lesson for literature is clear. Here, in miniature, is the idea that Mann will later formulate in terms of 'doppelte Optik'. This is the idea that at times art can express intense feeling, intense philosophical speculation, and that at other times it can be light-hearted and entertaining.[25] Art, in other words, can speak to the educated elite, but it can also speak to a wider public. This early review shows very clearly Mann's awareness that art takes place in a social context, and that artists create products for public consumption. And when Mann alludes to *Das Sonntagskind* in the early *Felix Krull*, he does so in the belief that comedy, just as much as tragedy, has a key place in the scheme of things.

Much of the secondary literature has portrayed Krull as a mythologist and as an illusionist. In doing so, it has failed to explore the highly socialized and sociable nature of Krull's performances. This relative absence in the secondary literature is, in my view, related to a paucity of research on the collection of documentary material which Mann assembled mainly between 1910 and 1913, and which is held in the Thomas Mann Archive in Zurich. Examination of the dossier reveals an inordinate interest in the aesthetics of society. A study of the genesis of *Felix Krull* shows that it starts as an exploration of the artist as criminal and then tends more and more towards a study of art's involvement in the formation of the self and the community. For example, it is highly significant that the first section of the novel that Mann chose to publish was the Müller Rosé episode.[26]

Part of the object of this thesis is to rescue *Felix Krull* from readings which place too much emphasis on the mythological aspect of the novel.[27] The problem with such readings is that they are reductive. As John J. White has shown, modern novels tend to use mythological motifs in order to inflect the plot in a certain way or to make specific comments, but not to provide an overall structure.[28] *Felix Krull* may contain allusions to Hermes, but it does not recapitulate Greek myths about Hermes. Instead, the remarks about Hermes being a prefiguration of Felix Krull are made in an ironic, secular context. The myth functions as a point of reference, adding a further dimension to the narrative — without, however, providing an overarching meta-narrative. Indeed, references to Hermes make up only a fraction of the novel. Krull is a Hermes figure, but he is many other things as well: he is a Ganymede and a Casanova, a Lazarillo de Tormes and an Egmont, a butterfly and a glow-worm. The insistence upon Hermes in the secondary literature has diverted discussion away from the text itself and how it operates. This is also true for the view of Krull as a Narcissus. First introduced by Hans Wysling in his impressive study of 1982, and taken up by Hermann Kurzke[29] and most of the subsequent secondary literature, this idea has dominated the research on *Krull*. In my view, this is a pity, since the text itself contains no explicit reference to narcissism whatsoever. It is certainly true that at times the novel resembles a wish-fulfilment fantasy, as Kurzke claims.[30] The world does indeed welcome Krull with open arms, and Benno von Wiese is correct to discern fairy-tale elements in the novel.[31] But an element of wish-fulfilment does not necessarily equal narcissism. In fact, Krull's principal aim in life is to please other people — not what one usually associates with narcissism. Kurzke overstates his case when he claims that Krull wants applause rather than love.[32] In my opinion, Krull wants both. After all, this is the Krull who decides early on that it is better to regard other people as 'voll und wichtig' (275), and who explicitly states that his attraction to Genovefa is unselfish ('nicht eigenütziges Wesen war meine Lust' (314)). This is the Krull who delights in Professor Kuckuck's description of 'Allsympathie', because it confirms what he already sensed as a youth ('die große Freude' (312, 547)). As Jürgen Scharfschwerdt points out, Krull's yearning *for* the world is a vitally important part of his character and must be taken into consideration along with his other, more selfish tendencies.[33] The narcissistic reading of *Krull* is one-sided; it ignores the subtle ambivalence of the novel, the way in which Krull is continually drawn out into the world. The whole point of the conversation about 'Allsympathie' with Kuckuck is that Krull may imaginatively expand his being in order to recognize his relatedness to other forms of life.

Felix Krull is an important novel to get right because, as we have already noted, its composition spans almost all of Thomas Mann's creative life, from the first years of the twentieth century to 1954. Indeed, if one includes the 1893 text 'Das Sonntagskind', *Krull* goes back even further. This is what Hans Wysling means when he asserts that Krull's confessions form a summation of Thomas Mann's entire oeuvre, leading thematically to the very heart of his creative endeavour:

> Seit 1905 geplant, mit ihren tiefsten Wurzeln aber in die Vor-*Buddenbrooks*-Zeit zurückreichend, nach jahrzehntelangem Unterbruch in den fünfziger Jahren abgeschlossen, bilden sie [die *Bekenntnisse*] einen Rahmen um Thomas Manns gesamtes Werk [. . .]. Sie führen thematisch und motivisch ins Zentrum von Thomas Manns Schaffen.[34]

Jürgen Scharfschwerdt offers a similar evaluation of *Krull*, reading it as evidence for the overall thematic unity of Mann's work.[35] However, while Scharfschwerdt analyses the continuity of Mann's engagement with the tradition of the Bildungsroman, this book will investigate other continuities, such as the theme of 'Sympathie' and the treatment of art as a social phenomenon.

The principal aims of this book are threefold: (i) to provide a balanced and synthetic reading of *Felix Krull*, one which analyses its full philosophical and social implications, but without becoming so heavyweight that one loses sight of its stylistic elation and levity, (ii) to show how the novel portrays art and aesthetics as constitutive elements of both social life and the life of the mind, and (iii) to explore the profound implications which a study of the novel can have for the understanding of Thomas Mann's work as a whole.

This book contains three main thematic sections. The first, 'Art and the Notation of Identity', studies the involvement of art in the articulation and cultivation of the self. Arising from Mann's early theoretical deliberations, *Felix Krull* is shown to elaborate a fluid and experimentally open model of identity. The second section, 'Art and the Notation of Community', analyses the way in which *Felix Krull* explores interaction and complicity between *Bürger* and *Künstler*. It reflects upon the novel's affinities with developments in the social sciences in the early twentieth century, and maintains that social interaction in *Krull* involves a series of aesthetically modulated negotiations. The third section, 'Narrative Performance in *Felix Krull*', explores narrative features including play of genres, interaction with the reader, and polyvalent realism, showing that the novel's form operates as a meta-commentary upon the thematics of the work as a whole. In particular, the direct form of narrative address seeks to cultivate a community of highly self-conscious readers. Each of these three chapters concludes with a discussion of how these features relate to Mann's other major works. In this way, the thesis seeks to demonstrate the overall continuity of Mann's literary achievement.

Notes to the Introduction

1. Eric Hobsbawm, *The Age of Empire 1875–1914* (London: Abacus, 1994), pp. 10, 170.
2. Hobsbawm, *Age of Empire*, p. 174. Hobsbawm distinguishes such guides from the already established directories of aristocratic lineage, such as the *Almanach de Gotha*.
3. Georg Simmel, 'Die Großstädte und das Geistesleben' [1903], in Georg Simmel, *Soziologische Ästhetik* (Bodenheim: Philo, 1998), pp. 119–33.
4. Hilary Spurling, *La Grande Thérèse or The Greatest Swindle of the Century* (London: Profile, 1999).
5. Voigt's memoirs appeared in 1909. Voigt, *Wie ich Hauptmann von Köpenick wurde* (Leipzig and Berlin: Püttmann, 1909). The incident was later dramatized by Carl Zuckmayer in 1931.
6. Georges Manolescu, *Ein Fürst der Diebe* and *Gescheitert. Aus dem Seelenleben eines Verbrechers* (Berlin/Lichterfelde: Langenscheidt, 1905). Mann's own copies are not to be found in the TMA.
7. TMA, Mat. 3/260 and 3/261.
8. Mann seems to have been sent the two volumes of Manolescu's memoirs by the publisher, Langenscheidt, since a quotation from Mann appeared on some advertising for the books. Cf. Wysling, TMS 5, p. 344. Manolescu's memoirs also inspired a popular French novel of the time, Maurice Leblanc's *Arsène Lupin, gentleman-cambrioleur* (Paris: Lafitte, 1907).
9. For Wysling's analysis of the influence of Manolescu on *Krull*, see TMS 5, pp. 153–70. Wysling also notes the influence of other contemporary works on the *Krull* project, including Heinrich Mann's *Im Schlaraffenland* (1900), Frank Wedekind's *Der Marquis von Keith* (1901), Herman Bang's *Exzentrische Novellen* (1905), and Otto Julius Bierbaum's *Prinz Kuckuck* (1907/08), (TMS 5, pp. 36–53).
10. Thomas Sprecher, 'Das grobe Muster. Georges Manolescu und Felix Krull', *TMJ* 19 (2006), 175–200.
11. 'Von dem Juwelendieb und Hochstapler Carlsson', *Münchener Neueste Nachrichten*, October 1907, no. 507; cf. TMA, Mat. 3/306. [Underlinings by Mann].
12. TMA, Mat. 3/510–11.
13. Cf. undated letter to the *Saale-Zeitung*, published 2 November 1909, quoted in Scherrer and Wysling, TMS 1, p. 234: 'Ich arbeite jetzt an einem Essay, der den Titel "Geist und Kunst" führen wird. Ferner beschäftige ich mich mit einer kleineren Erzählung "Der Hochstapler", die psychologisch eine gewisse Ergänzung zu meinem Fürstenroman bedeuten wird'.
14. Cf. letter of 10 January 1910 to Heinrich Mann: 'Ich sammle, notiere und studiere für die Bekenntnisse des Hochstaplers, die wohl mein Sonderbarstes werden' (Br H, 104). For a more detailed account of the work's genesis, see Wysling, 'Archivalisches Gewühle', in Scherrer and Wysling, TMS 1, pp. 234–57.
15. The sociological significance of the confidence man also forms the basis for a book written in the late 1920s: the Dadaist Walter Serner's book *Letzte Lockerung. Ein Handbrevier für Hochstapler und solche, die es werden wollen* [1927] (Munich: Renner, 1981). For a discussion of this work, see Helmut Lethen, *Cool Conduct: The Culture of Distance in Weimar Germany* (Berkeley, CA: University of California Press, 2002), pp. 115–27. A confidence man named Stefan Zannowitch also crops up at the beginning of Alfred Döblin's novel *Berlin Alexanderplatz: Die Geschichte vom Franz Biberkopf* [1929], in *Ausgewählte Werke in Einzelbänden*, ed. by Walter Muschg (Olten, Breisgau: Walter, 1961), pp. 21–28.
16. The dossiers for *Felix Krull* comprise 102 double-sided pages of notes, and 521 cuttings from newspapers and illustrated journals, and are held in the Thomas Mann Archive (TMA) in

Zurich. They are described in Wysling, TMS 5, pp. 395–97, 476–81. Wysling has published the bulk of the notes in TMS 5 and many of the images from the dossier in *Bild und Text bei Thomas Mann. Eine Dokumentation*, ed. by Hans Wysling and Yvonne Schmidlin (Bern and Munich: Francke, 1975). Even so, much of the documentary material still remains unpublished.

17. Cf. Wysling, TMS 5, pp. 395–97, 476–81. Wysling fails to comment on the chronological shift in the nature of the documentary material.

18. Paul von Szczepanski, 'Der moderne Dandy', *Die Woche*, vol. 14, no. 27, 6 July 1912, pp. 1111–13, TMA: Mat. 3/132–33; 'Der Beruf eines Hotelkellners', source unknown, TMA: Mat. 3/381; Ola Alsen, 'Die Dame im Hotel', *Die Woche*, vol. 12, no. 28, 9 July 1910, pp. 1181 87, TMA: Mat. 3/135–38; Ola Alsen, 'Beim Fünfuhrtee', *Die Woche*, 12. 50, 10 December 1910, pp. 2129–32. TMA: Mat. 3/140–41.

19. Anna Pawlowa [English: Pavlova], 'Aus meinem Leben', *Die Woche*, vol. 14, no. 27, 6 July 1912, pp.1128–33, TMA: Mat. 3/25–26, 43–44.

20. Anna Pawlowa, 'Aus meinem Leben', p. 1130: Als sich die Menge danach nicht zurückzog, fragte ich mein Mädchen, womit ich ihnen wohl die Köpfe verdreht hätte. Sie antwortete mir: 'Madame, Sie machten sie eine Stunde lang die Trübsal des Lebens vergessen.' Ich vergaß diese Antwort niemals. Das einfache russische Mädchen, das sie mir gab, wies meiner Kunst ein neues Ziel.

21. Ignace Feuerlicht, *Thomas Mann und die Grenzen des Ich* (Heidelberg: Carl Winter, 1966), p. 98.

22. Feuerlicht, *Thomas Mann*, p. 97: Krull ist, obwohl Mann und die Kritiker dies behaupten, kein *pícaro*. [. . .] Kein Schelm, der etwas auf sich hält, [. . .] würde es ablehnen, das Wort "Hure" in den Mund zu nehmen, wie es Felix in der Episode mit Diane tut. [. . .] Was für ein *pícaro*, der ein liebestolles Mädchen beschwört, sich 'um des gesellschaftlichen Naturgesetzes und der guten Sitten willen zu überwinden'! Das ist ja förmlich eine Parodie oder Negation des Schelmenromans.

23. In the later *Krull*, the theme of deception does not disappear entirely, but, in Professor Kuckuck's speech, it is modulated into a celebration of the transitory nature of all things.

24. And the piece continues in the same insouciant style: 'In den Couplets wird sogar Ibsen zitiert. Ich meine, mehr kann man doch nicht verlangen!' (XIII, 245).

25. Letter to Hermann Hesse, 1 April 1910 (Br Hs, 6). Cf. XII, 109–10. For a more detailed discussion of 'doppelte Optik', see Chapter III(vi).

26. The first fragment, 'Bekenntnisse des Hochstaplers Felix Krull: Bruchstück aus einem Roman', consists exclusively of the Müller-Rosé episode. It was published in *Das fünfundzwanzigste Jahr. Almanach des S. Fischer Verlages* (Berlin: Fischer, 1911), pp. 273–88.

27. For mythological and Jungian readings of *Krull*, see Donald F. Nelson, *Portrait of the Artist as Hermes: A Study of Myth and Psychology in Thomas Mann's 'Felix Krull'* (Chapel Hill: University of North Carolina Press, 1971) and Frederick A. Lubich, 'The Confessions of Felix Krull, Confidence Man', in *The Cambridge Companion to Thomas Mann*, ed. by Ritchie Robertson (Cambridge: Cambridge University Press, 2002), pp. 199–212.

28. John J. White, *Mythology in the Modern Novel: A Study of Prefigurative Techniques* (Princeton, NJ: Princeton University Press, 1971), pp. 13–15, 21–22.

29. Kurzke, *Thomas Mann* (1985), pp. 289–92.

30. Kurzke, *Thomas Mann* (1985), p. 290.

31. Benno von Wiese, '"Die Bekenntnisse des Hochstaplers Felix Krull" als utopischer Roman', in *Thomas Mann 1875–1975. Vorträge in München-Zürich-Lübeck*, ed. by Beatrix Bludau, Eckhard Heftrich, and Helmut Koopmann (Frankfurt a.M.: Fischer, 1977), pp. 189–206.

32. Kurzke, *Thomas Mann* (1985), p. 289.

33. Jürgen Scharfschwerdt, *Thomas Mann und der deutsche Bildungsroman: Eine Untersuchung zu den Problemen einer literarischen Tradition* (Stuttgart: Kohlhammer, 1967), p. 251: 'Ist die von der Welt distanzierende Phantasie die eine Hauptkomponente, die das Hochstaplerdasein der Hauptfigur ermöglicht, so [ist] die Sehnsucht zur Welt, der ausdrückliche Weltbezug die andere Komponente'.

34. Wysling, TMS 5, p. 10.

35. Scharfschwerdt, *Thomas Mann*, pp. 246–69.

CHAPTER 1

ART AND THE NOTATION OF IDENTITY

> Masks are arrested expressions and admirable echoes of feeling, at once faithful, discreet, and superlative. Living things in contact with the air must acquire a cuticle, and it is not yet urged against cuticles that they are not hearts; yet some philosophers seem to be angry with images for not being things, and with words for not being feelings. Words and images are like shells, no less integral parts of nature than are the substances they cover, but better addressed to the eye and more open to observation. I would not say that substance exists for the sake of appearance, or faces for the sake of masks, or the passions for the sake of poetry and virtue. Nothing arises in nature for the sake of anything else; all these phases and products are involved equally in the round of existence . . .
>
> GEORGE SANTAYANA
> *Soliloquies in England and Later Soliloquies* (London: Constable, 1922)

In this chapter I will argue that the early work on *Felix Krull* represents a creative watershed in Mann's career. It marks the moment when Mann realized that he could imaginatively expand his identity to the extent that he could identify with persons and characters far removed from his own experience and disposition. I will seek to show that *Felix Krull* offers a creatively adaptable model of identity, and that it presents art and aesthetics as being central to the development of the individual subject.

(i) The Articulation of the Self: Theatre as Metaphor

The debate about the formation and cultivation of the self goes back to classical antiquity; it resurfaces in the humanism of the Renaissance and is a principal concern of the Enlightenment. Art has often been a key term in this debate, and the German Enlightenment in particular viewed the cultivation of an aesthetic sensibility as a vital condition for the development of a mature selfhood. Goethe and Schiller regard the project of self-realization as a task of the highest order, one in which art and nature would complement each other. Art and education are even related etymologically through the German word 'bilden', which can mean, variously, 'to form', 'to educate', 'to create'. The increasing industrialization and secularization of the late nineteenth century brought a new urgency to these questions. For Marx, the subject is under threat from the forces of ideology and alienation. Nietzsche, too, writes from an embattled perspective: he views the subject as agonistic, fragmented, and contradictory, and prone to the dangers of nihilism and decadence. By the early twentieth century, modernism and the crisis of the subject had reached a new peak. The new psychologies of Freud, Jung, and Mach boldly proclaimed the division of the subject, giving rise to a modernist literature which revelled in the exploration of the divided self.[1] Living in turn-of-the-century Munich, Thomas Mann was well placed to take stock of these cultural shifts and their effect on the perception of individuality. In 1918, in the preface to the *Betrachtungen*, he even defined the essence of his writing as a moral and intellectual effort about a problematic self:

> Schriftstellertum selbst erschien mir vielmehr von jeher als ein Erzeugnis und Ausdruck der Problematik, des Da und Dort, des Ja und Nein, der zwei Seelen in einer Brust, des schlimmen Reichtums an inneren Konflikten, Gegensätzen und Widersprüchen. Wozu, woher überhaupt Schriftstellertum, wenn es nicht geistig-sittliche Bemühung ist um ein problematisches Ich? (XII, 20)[2]

Mann's writings of the first decade of the twentieth century bear witness to a complex meditation on his own identity. The role of his imaginative life — most particularly his existence as an artist — was central to this meditation. Time and time again, art is seen as both problematizing and articulating the self. In my view, these early texts form the theoretical background to *Felix Krull*, and so a thorough interpretation of the novel must take them into account. By examining these early texts I hope to demonstrate that *Felix Krull* occupies a key position in the development of Mann's thinking about identity and the self. The novel is, after all, the first of Mann's works to be narrated in the autobiographical first person; whilst it adopts the problems and antitheses of the previous years, it also aims toward a more conciliatory position.[3]

The Krullian themes of acting and the conciliation between art and life can be traced back to 'Bilse und ich' (1906), Mann's polemical response to the charge that *Buddenbrooks* was a *roman-à-clef*. In 'Bilse und ich', Mann sets out to justify himself by defining what kind of an artist he really is. At the heart of his creativity is a process which he calls 'Beseelung' (X, 15) or 'subjektive Vertiefung' (X, 16): a mixture of identification, empathy, and projection which is described as 'das innere Einswerden des Dichters mit seinem Modell' (X, 17). This kind of sympathetic identification will later reappear as the basis for Felix Krull's chameleon-like ability to empathize with those he meets. In 'Bilse und ich', this capacity for identification is seen as essential to great art, and Mann cites Goethe and Shakespeare as examples. But 'Beseelung' involves projection as well as identification: the creative artist imbues the model with his own feelings. Mann's creative writer is a multi-faceted composite, a kind of supercharged subject who creates art from the contradictions and tensions within his own being:

> Es ist bekannt, daß jeder echte Dichter sich bis zu einem gewissen Grade mit seinen Geschöpfen identifiziert. Alle Gestalten einer Dichtung, mögen sie noch so feindlich gegeneinander gestellt sind, sind Emanationen des dichtenden Ich, und Goethe ist zugleich in Antonio und Tasso lebendig [. . .] (X, 16)

This is a vision of the great artist as somehow having multiple aspects or personalities, acting every part of the play in turn — and Mann now extends the theatrical metaphor even further. Like an actor, the poet assumes different personae or 'masks' ('Masken') which he then 'makes his own' ('Aneignung') (X, 16). And Mann contrasts the objective exteriority ('Äußerlichkeit') of the mask (x, 16–17) with the rich subjective inner life of the poet. He is also careful to point out that the enmity between poet and reality is only apparent and is based on a misunderstanding (x, 18–19). The underlying implication is that art is born from a meeting of subject and reality, and if the artist wishes to create substantial works then he must adopt the forms of exterior reality. In other words, self-expression requires a borrowed persona or a mask. This is hardly surprising. As long as subjective inner life is not expressed, it remains ethereal; only when it has taken on a concrete form can it be known. In its exploration of these issues, 'Bilse und ich' sets out the terms of a debate about artistic identity which will continue for the rest of the decade.

'Bilse und ich' was soon followed by Mann's first extended essay on literary theory, 'Versuch über das Theater' (written 1906, published 1908). The occasion was harmless enough: a survey on the 'value of the theatre' was being carried out by the journal *Nord und Süd*, and Mann was invited to contribute. He thought the article would be finished in a couple of days, but it kept growing and ended up taking weeks to complete. Added impetus for the essay doubtless came from Mann's abortive experience with *Fiorenza* (finished 1905, performed 1907). But it went deeper than that. In a letter to Moritz Heimann, Mann complains of the trouble which the essay had caused him, saying: 'die Theaterfrage saß mir wie ein Widerhaken im Fleisch'.[4] The urgency of the 'Theaterfrage' and its implications somehow seem to go beyond a discussion of the theatre; it becomes a question of Mann's own identity and principles as an artist. The guiding context here is that of Nietzsche, and Mann cites an aphorism in which Nietzsche throws doubt upon the notion of 'character', calling it a superficial generalization resembling the stage 'characters' invented by a dramatist. According to Nietzsche, we credit stage characters with reality because in real life we remain content with a superficial impression of other people; we lack true insight (x, 28). Mann uses Nietzsche's aphorism to assert the superficiality of drama compared to the psychological insight of the novel. But there is an ambivalence here. Despite Mann's repeated polemical assertions that the theatre is fundamentally distinct from serious literature, he is forced to admit the primal, fundamental unity between the actor and the author ('der erste Theaterdichter war der Schauspieler') (x, 42). And Mann is even more explicit a couple of years later, in a note for the unfinished essay 'Geist und Kunst', where he describes the actor as 'the artist in the raw state' ('[der] Künstler im Urzustand, gewissermaßen').[5] It seems that in spite of his Nietzschean denunciations, Thomas Mann is fascinated by the figure of the actor, since he recognizes in him a vital component of his own self.

Now, what is Felix Krull if not an actor, an 'artist in the raw'? As a youth, his favourite activity is dressing up in costumes provided by his godfather, an occupation which earns him the nickname of 'Kostümkopf' (284). His first visit to an operetta begins a lifelong love affair with the theatre, and once installed in Paris he becomes a keen opera- and theatregoer (498). There are numerous references to the theatre ('wie im Theater' (300); 'Theatersaison' (499); 'Szene' (301, 368, 376); 'das riesige Theater' (649)). One of Felix Krull's favourite words is the carnivalesque 'Darbietung' (which can be variously translated as 'routine', 'rendition', 'offering', or 'show'). The repetition of this word — it is used on several important occasions in the novel, often in the plural — tends to increase the general feeling of illusion, in particular the formulation '[die] Welt und ihren Darbietungen' (292).[6]

Felix Krull uses 'Darbietung[en]' to describe both his own performances (300, 323, 414) and the 'scientific performances' of Professor Kuckuck ('dessen wissenschaftlichen Darbietungen' (596), 'seine[r] Darbietungen' (606)). Further use of theatrical vocabulary includes Felix Krull's description of his love affairs as 'die Stückchen meines Lebens' (385) and his first appearance in the hotel dining hall as a kind of 'début' ('debütieren') before 'the eating public' ('das Speisepublikum' (470)). And the care with which he prepares his 'Toilette' resembles that of an actor applying his make-up ('Maske-Machen des Schauspielers' (553)).

Felix Krull is essentially a performer, and he views existence in theatrical terms, as Donald F. Nelson has shown.[7] For Krull, the old saying 'All the world's a stage' represents a universal truth, one which he will consistently apply in his dealings with the world.[8] As a consequence, he tends to perceive identity as being constructed through a process of role-playing. But while most people act out the roles assigned to them by their social status, he feels able to improvise new roles for himself. In 'Versuch über das Theater', Mann had quoted Nietzsche to the effect that, in general, we relate to other people on a superficial level as if they were actors in a play (x, 28). Felix Krull develops the idea further in order to show that social interaction relies upon the performance of prearranged, conventional roles. Crucial here is Krull's description of his train journey to Paris and the conductors who check his ticket. The highly formal, ritualized nature of these encounters requires both parties to appear uninterested in the other. Both parties must behave artificially, almost like marionettes:

> Ich mußte mich stellen, als ob mir der Gedanke an seine menschlichen Bewandt-
> nisse völlig fernliege, und jede Erkundigung danach, die verraten hätte, daß ich
> ihn nicht nur als dienstliche Marionette betrachtete, wäre höchst unangebracht
> gewesen. Umgekehrt [. . .] Die Richtigkeit meines Fahrscheins war alles, was
> ihn anging von meiner ebenfalls marionettenhaften Passagierperson [. . .].
> Etwas seltsam Unnatürliches und eigentlich Künstliches liegt ja in diesem
> Gebaren [. . .] (387)

In this carefully defined interaction, Felix Krull exceeds his role by introducing a more personal dimension. Having noticed the guard's wedding ring, he asks the guard to give his regards to his wife and children. The guard is so embarrassed by this incongruity that he nearly falls over ('so sehr hatte die Menschlichkeit ihn aus dem Tritt gebracht' (387)). The implicit suggestion is that people are expected to play different roles in different social spheres; an official transaction will proceed along different lines from more personal interaction. This is a dynamic model of identity as something site-specific and related to social context. The text does not claim that people are always conscious of their role-playing; it implies, on the contrary, that such role-playing is usually unconscious. The only characters apart from Felix Krull who manage to achieve such a conscious level of role-playing are Madame Houpflé, Professor Kuckuck, and perhaps the Marquis de Venosta with his affectation of melancholy (493)[9] and his 'theatralische Verzweiflungsgebärde' (496). By and large, however, it appears that social context is a major factor in determining identity. This truth appears self-evident: people behave differently according to the different social contexts in which they find themselves.

Felix Krull develops this idea even further during his time as a waiter in the Saint James and Albany Hotel. There, he imagines that the rich hotel guests might just as easily be waiters, and vice versa. Wealth here is the deciding factor in determining one's identity, but this factor is based on 'pure chance' and can easily change. This leads to Felix Krull's idea of what he calls the interchangeability ('Vertauschbarkeit') of social roles:

> Es war der Gedanke der *Vertauschbarkeit*. Den Anzug, die Aufmachung gewech-selt, hätten sehr vielfach die Bedienenden ebensogut Herrschaft sein und hätte so mancher von denen, welche, die Zigarette im Mundwinkel, in den tiefen Korbstühlen sich rekelten — den Kellner abgeben können. Es war der reine Zufall, daß es sich umgekehrt verhielt — der Zufall des Reichtums; denn eine Aristokratie des Geldes ist eine vertauschbare Zufallsaristokratie. (491–92)[10]

This passage connects the problem of identity to that of modernity. It implies that late capitalism has led to an unprecedented degree of social mobility, and that this has led in turn to a more fluid — and superficial — notion of identity as being dependent upon wealth. But Felix Krull immediately qualifies his own analysis: in fact, identity is not always interchangeable, since some of the hotel guests possess an innate elegance which is independent of wealth. Krull is the only waiter with enough skill to impersonate the most elegant guests. The fact that his thought experiments ('Gedankenexperimente') only work sometimes suggests that personal characteristics are not always interchangeable after all:

> Darum gelangen mir diese Gedankenexperimente öfters recht gut, wenn auch nicht immer, da [. . .] in den polierten Pöbel der Hotel-Sozietät immer auch eigentliche, vom Gelde unabhängige [. . .] Vornehmheit eingesprengt war. Zuweilen mußte ich geradezu mich selbst einsetzen und konnte niemanden sonst vom Kellner-Corps dazu brauchen, wenn der Rollentausch phantasieweise gelingen sollte. (492)

In other words, identity is fluid, but not that fluid. Some roles demand enormous natural talent if they are to be performed successfully. Here, the (Goethean) notion of a natural aristocracy rules out the possibility of identity being entirely open-ended.

Felix Krull, then, takes the theatre as a metaphor for human interaction and exploits it to the full. In doing so, it offers a dynamic model of identity. This model does not view the self as being completely defined by social context. Neither, however, does it see identity as completely fluid or malleable. It is remarkable how much the novel anticipates the ideas of the Canadian sociologist Erving Goffman. In his influential book *The Presentation of Self in Everyday Life* (1959), Goffman uses the theatre as an analogy for human interaction. In doing so, he elaborates a model of the self based upon performance, aided by the use of 'fixed props' and 'settings' such as houses, clothes, and institutions.[11] For Goffman, however, 'performance' is less about deception than it is about the pressure to conform to certain social norms. Deliberate deception is much rarer since, in general, people will tend to notice inconsistencies in another person's behaviour.[12] It is worth bearing in mind, however, that Goffman's book ends with a disclaimer in which he admits that the analogy of the theatre was a rhetorical manoeuvre which he has pushed to its limits.[13] In other words, Goffman's use of the theatrical metaphor has its limitations. The metaphor provides a compelling model for understanding the self, but as Jenny Diski points out, this model is not to be absolutized,[14] just as we should beware of absolutizing any other theoretical tool (such as psychoanalysis, Marxism, etc). Even Felix Krull stops short of a totalizing, Schopenhauerian model of illusion. If he is an actor, he is a method actor who draws upon his own potentialities, his own latent truths, in order to create his effects. In other words, he still believes in the notion of reality ('das Wirkliche'):

> Nur der Betrug hat Aussicht auf Erfolg und lebensvolle Wirkung unter den Menschen, der den Namen des Betrugs nicht durchaus verdient, sondern nichts ist als die Ausstattung einer lebendigen, aber nicht völlig ins Reich des Wirklichen eingetretenen Wahrheit. (298)

Michael Beddow points out that despite Krull's predilection for theatrical metaphors, he only ever chooses roles which require an elegant bearing (whether as servant or master). Krull's 'Bedürfnis [. . .] nach schöner Form' (593) means that he does not have the range of determinability of the true actor, who can assume a much wider range of roles than Krull wishes to.[15] In other words, Thomas Mann and Erving Goffman do not offer free-floating, postmodern views of the self. What they do offer is ways of looking at how identity is articulated through instances of interaction. This functionalist approach to identity is similar to Wittgenstein's approach to meaning and truth through context-related language games ('Sprachspiele'). In trying to understand a difficult concept like 'identity', it seems that the best method is to look at identity in the contexts in which it is articulated. Life is not art, but that should not blind us to the fact that life and art often interact. Of course, the theatrical metaphor can only be taken so far, but it certainly is one compelling way of looking at human identity. And there are benefits to be had from a model which does not consider the personality as static and absolute, but rather as dynamic and evolving within a network of social interaction.

(ii) Identification and Self-development

> [. . .] daß aber ein junger Mensch ohne Bedeutung und Namen sich einfallen läßt, aus dem Inkognito einiges Vergnügen zu ziehen, möchte mancher für einen unverzeihlichen Hochmut auslegen. [Aber] so wollen wir für diesmal, unserer Unterhaltung zu Liebe, dem Jüngling seinen Dünkel verzeihen, um so mehr, als ich anführen muß, daß von Jugend auf in mir eine Lust mich zu verkleiden selbst durch den ernsten Vater erregt worden.
>
> GOETHE, *Dichtung und Wahrheit* (HA IX, 431)

The first decade of the twentieth century was a time of urgent self-analysis for Thomas Mann, a period of deliberation about his own identity as an artist which culminated in the mass of notes for the essay 'Geist und Kunst'. Although this essay was left unfinished, it provided a wealth of material and laid the theoretical groundwork for later works such as *Der Tod in Venedig* and *Doktor Faustus*, as T. J. Reed has shown.[16] In this section I intend to demonstrate that the notes for 'Geist und Kunst' also had a direct bearing on the work which was most contemporaneous with them: namely, *Felix Krull*. The periods of composition of the two works overlap; they were written almost consecutively. The initial idea for *Krull* was noted in 1905, in Mann's seventh notebook.[17] 'Geist und Kunst' was begun in the spring of 1909 and abandoned in early 1910. In November 1909, while still working on 'Geist und Kunst', Mann planned his next two works: a short story entitled 'Der Hochstapler', and a novel about Frederick the Great.[18] Mann began writing *Felix Krull* in January 1910.[19] By the middle of 1911, the plan of the novel and most of Book I was complete.[20] In other words, the theoretical wranglings of the planned 'Geist und Kunst' would first bear fruit in *Felix Krull*. In my view, both 'Geist und Kunst' and the early *Krull* are bold experiments which point the way towards the controlled mastery of the later works. I will therefore begin by examining the relevance of 'Geist und Kunst' for an understanding of *Krull*.[21]

The notes for 'Geist und Kunst' reflect Mann's attempt to justify himself as a moral and intellectual novelist in the face of the aestheticism which was dominant in the Munich literary circles of the time. Mann is concerned with legitimizing himself as a critical writer ('Schriftsteller'/'Literat') representing the intellect ('Geist') — after the model of Nietzsche — in opposition to the instinctively creative, unreflecting poet ('Dichter') representing 'pure', naïve art ('Kunst') — and here Wagner is the example. Thus N 40 asserts the primal affinity between criticism and the lyric mode, claiming that the intellectual writer is the true artist ('der Dichter par excellence').[22] In N 49, however, Mann begins to alter the terms of his opposition. He now reflects upon two different conceptions of art, one Christian and Platonic, and one sensual and pagan. Mann then reformulates the dichotomy in Schillerian terms. Schiller, in his essay *Über naive und sentimentalische Dichtung*, had described two modalities of artistic creation: the *naiv* mode, represented by Goethe, was close to nature and experience, while the *sentimentalisch* (or 'reflective') mode was represented by Schiller himself. But rather as the final phase of Schiller's essay seeks a reconciliation between the two modes, so Mann's adoption of Schiller's terminology points the way towards the possibility of reconciliation:

> Der Gegensatz schillerisch formuliert: 'Naiv und sentimentalisch.' Dieser Gegensatz in Goethe und Schiller nicht rein ausgedrückt. Goethe Spinoza-Schüler. Schiller besitzt eine gute Portion sinnlicher Naivetät. (N 49)[23]

The implication is clear: if Goethe and Schiller possessed characteristics of both types, then perhaps the modalities are not mutually exclusive after all; perhaps they may be complementary. Just two notes later (N 51) we have arrived at the kernel of *Felix Krull*: 'Wedekind und Manolesku. ("Ein *wirklicher* Schelmenroman!") Aber doch nur ein menschliches Dokument, ein Stoff und Material nichtwahr?'. This is soon followed by a rush of Krullian motifs: 'Nacktkultur', 'Kokotten-Talent' (N 57); the hotel industry (N 58); 'Variété' and the actor as 'Künstler im Urzustand' (N 59). Then there is a tentative shift in favour of the 'naiv' mode, accompanied by a more tolerant attitude towards the theatre: 'Herr Fuchs soll [. . .] uns untheoretischen Theaterfreunden, die wir gern einmal einfältig sind, uns gern einmal blenden lassen' (N 61). But Mann is quickly drawn back towards the more moral figure of the critical writer: 'Vornehmste Entwicklungsstufe des Typus [des Literaten]: der Heilige' (N 62). In N 103, on the other hand, Mann considers the modern trend towards a new immediacy with nature, and decides that he must somehow take account of it in his own work. 'Geist und Kunst' is unfinished, its tensions unresolved, but it remains a vital testimony to the evolution of Mann's own identity as an artist. The antitheses in 'Geist und Kunst' are not part of some abstract debate, but form part of Mann's own attempt at self-definition. As Hans-Joachim Sandberg puts it: 'Diese [. . .] Begriffspaare bildeten das Vexierbild, das der Autor in seinen essayistischen Bemühungen hin- und herdrehte, um in ihm die Konturen des Künstlers zu finden, mit dem er sich identifizieren konnte'.[24] If 'Geist und Kunst' is a theoretical attempt at self-definition, then it is interesting to note that the names Goethe and Schiller occur with greater frequency in the latter portion of the notes. Goethe is increasingly viewed as an acceptable alternative to Wagner. Thus, in N 97, Goethe's decision to set Shakespeare above himself as an ideal is said to reveal a noble sensibility that contrasts favourably with Wagner's arrogance ('Wagner hat niemals emporgeblickt').[25] Of course, the interest in Schiller is also evident in the story *Schwere Stunde* (1905), in which Mann's Schiller experiences an envious admiration of, and longing for, Goethean form ('der Sehnsucht nach Form' (VIII, 377)).[26] The problem of form returns in 'Geist und Kunst' under the rubric of 'Plastik' (plasticity). Here, the word is used to denote the boldly realistic effects achieved by the 'naiv' artist. Thomas Mann considered his own novel *Buddenbrooks* to be a good example of 'Plastik'.[27] In 'Geist und Kunst', however, Mann attempts to claim an equal status for the intellectual artist, even broadening the definition of 'Plastik' to include the modulations of theoretical discourse (N 104). Mann quotes Schopenhauer to the effect that words are misleading and comments: 'Gerade der Schriftsteller, der dies nie vergißt, der also *bewußt spielt*, ist ein Künstler so gut wie der Plastiker' (N 68). In other words, the intellectual artist's conscious scepticism about language enables him to manipulate ideas and concepts with the grace and beauty of a poet.[28] The formulation 'who *plays consciously*' ('der *bewußt spielt*') is another movement towards synthesis, since it unites both the spontaneity of the 'naiv' artist and the consciousness of the intellectual ('sentimentalisch') one. This movement towards conciliation goes, in my view, to the heart of *Felix Krull*.[29] Mann's insight was that plasticity did not have to be exclusively the preserve of unselfconscious, visceral, divinely inspired nature. He understood that plasticity could also have aspects which were performed consciously and intellectually. In other words, great art could arise from an admixture of unconscious and self-conscious elements: *techne* (craft), self-consciousness, even scepticism were not obstacles to making great art.

From this perspective, *Felix Krull* can be viewed as a deliberately playful approach to Goethe, a conscious experiment ('bewußt spielen' (N 68)) in classical plasticity and form which takes Manolescu's memoirs as raw material ('Stoff' (N 51)) and lends them a classical, Goethean form. The juxtaposition is not as jarring as it first seems; after all, the trickster has been a central figure of the classical repertoire ever since Homer wrote the *Odyssey*. The engagement with Goethe in *Felix Krull*, however, is more than just a stylistic exercise. More than an approach to Goethe, it is in my view a deliberate attempt at *rapprochement*, a willed identification.[30] The first significant evidence for this is perhaps N 22 for 'Geist und Kunst'. In it, Mann considers Hugo von Hofmannsthal's identification with Goethe, quoting Nietzsche approvingly, and calling such a project a great undertaking: 'Hofmannsthal betrachtet sich ohne Weiteres als eine Art Goethe. Wir haben das "Bewusstsein der grossen Meister gewonnen" (Nietzsche). Sympathisches daran. Grössere Verpflichtung. Höheres, strengeres, ernsteres Leben'.[31]

And Mann is even more explicit six years later, in a letter to Paul Amann on the subject of *Der Tod in Venedig*. Here, Mann describes the basic purpose of his whole work as an attempt to acquire the consciousness of the great masters:[32]

> [Nietzsche] nennt die lebenden Künstler wärmeleitende Medien, deren Thun dazu diene, 'das Bewusstsein der grossen Meister zu gewinnen'. Wenn ich mich genau prüfe, so war dies und nichts anderes immer der Zweck meines 'Schaffens': das Bewusstsein der Meister zu gewinnen. Indem ich künstlerisch arbeitete, gewann ich Wissenszugänge zur Existenz des Künstlers, ja des großen Künstlers, und kann davon etwas sagen.[33]

Book I of *Felix Krull*, then, was composed at a crucial juncture. Written in 1910–11, in the period between 'Geist und Kunst' and *Der Tod in Venedig*, it is an imaginative approach to Goethe, the apparent frivolity of which conceals a serious dialogue with the classical tradition. It is perhaps no accident that Mann decided to visit Weimar for the very first time in 1910. This visit may well have formed part of Mann's attempt to acquire 'das Bewusstsein der Meister'.[34]

In taking Goethe as a model, Thomas Mann was writing himself ironically into the classical tradition of the Bildungsroman. In effect, this strategic move meant selecting and acknowledging Goethe as a literary father, just as Felix Krull develops himself by imitating the signature of his own father, Engelbert. In the following passage, Felix Krull employs the scientific vocabulary of his day, defining identification as a precondition for development:

> Ein Vater ist stets das natürlichste und nächste Muster für den sich bildenden [. . .] Knaben. Unterstützt durch geheimnisvolle Verwandtschaft und Ähnlichkeit der Körperbildung, setzt der Halbwüchsige seinen Stolz darein, sich von dem Gehaben des Erzeugers anzueignen, was die eigene Unfertigkeit ihn zu bewundern nötigt — oder, um genauer zu sein: Diese Bewunderung ist es, die halb unbewußt zu der Aneignung und Ausbildung dessen führt, was erblicherweise in uns vorgebildet liegt. (296)[35]

The key word in this passage is 'Aneignung' ('making one's own'): through a process of deliberate imitation and identification, Felix Krull is entering into the possession of his inherited potential and making it his own. The book's comment upon itself is clear: Thomas Mann, in a bold act of literary hubris, is accessing and appropriating elements of the classical, Goethean tradition. The early *Felix Krull* is thus arguably the beginning of Thomas Mann's conscious imitation of Goethe, an identification which was to sustain him throughout the later crises in his life.[36] *Felix Krull*, begun in 1910, is already moving towards what Thomas Mann, in 1911, will call 'eine neue Klassizität' (x, 842). It is his first approach towards a more healthily balanced and classical style, one that would keep his earlier 'Erkenntnisekel' firmly in check.

If the work remains deeply ironic, this reflects Mann's persistent ambivalence and his refusal to adopt a facile synthesis. This new affirmation was always going to be reticent. Nevertheless, an affirmation it is — the sign of a new exuberant grace, one which had not been seen since the character of Antonie (Tony) in *Buddenbrooks*. *Felix Krull* thus manages to achieve a new proximity, ease, and informality with respect to tradition. In 'Lebensabriß' (1930) he described this approach as forming the essence of his mission as a writer:

> Es [*Krull*] mag in gewissem Sinn das Persönlichste sein, denn es gestaltet mein Verhältnis zur Tradition, das zugleich liebevoll und auflösend ist und meine schriftstellerische 'Sendung' bestimmt. Die inneren Gesetze, nach denen später der 'Bildungsroman' des 'Zauberbergs' sich herstellte, waren ja verwandter Natur. (XI, 122–23; cf. XIII, 147)

To conclude: *Felix Krull* was a necessary act of hubris. It represents a bold imaginative leap which enabled Mann to relate to classical writers and themes on far more intimate terms than ever before. Thus it sets the scene and paves the way for Mann's new experiments with the classical tradition.

(iii) Goethe and *Felix Krull*

From the beginning of *Felix Krull*, there is a conscious attempt to relate to the world in a Goethean way. Goethe, famous for his love of nature, had placed experience at the centre of his art. In 1809 Goethe said in conversation that his genius would always be subordinate to the world's own genius: 'Das Benutzen der Erlebnisse ist mir immer Alles gewesen; das Erfinden aus der Luft war nie meine Sache: ich habe die Welt stets für genialer gehalten, als mein Genie'.[37] Thomas Mann copied this sentence into his ninth notebook, which he kept between 1905 and 1908 (N II, 169), and, in 1910, he incorporated the idea into Felix Krull's own *Weltanschauung*.[38] In Chapter 2, the young Felix asks himself whether it is better to consider the world as being small or large ('"Was ist förderlicher", fragte ich mich, "daß man die Welt klein oder daß man sie groß sehe?"' (274)). The choice is essentially between a Schopenhauerian world-view and a Goethean one. After carefully weighing up the pros and cons, he finally decides that it is more productive to view the world as something great:

> Eine solche Gläubigkeit und Weltfrömmigkeit [bietet] doch auch große Vorteile. Denn wer alle Dinge und Menschen für voll und wichtig nimmt, wird ihnen nicht nur dadurch schmeicheln und sich sogar mancher Förderung versichern, sondern er wird sein ganzes Denken und Gebaren mit einem Ernst, einer Leidenschaft, einer Verantwortlichkeit erfüllen, die, indem sie ihn zugleich liebenswürdig und bedeutend macht, zu den höchsten Erfolgen und Wirkungen führen kann. (275)

Goethe is deeply implicated in this passage: the term 'Weltfrömmigkeit' (respect for the world) immediately suggests as much.[39] While the mention of flattery ('schmeicheln') adds a sceptical note, the use of the word 'Verantwortlichkeit' (responsibility) here is highly significant. It implies moral feeling — surprising in such an apparently frivolous character. Felix Krull, then, is no ordinary con man. His conscious decision to respect the world makes him much more than an unashamed narcissist. Furthermore, this new attitude of respect and admiration for the world shows that Mann, in 1910, is seeking — experimentally, at least — to distance himself from his previous Schopenhauerian distaste for the world. But to what extent does he believe in his recently acquired Goethean attitude? This is uncertain. It is clear at any rate that, in the years leading up to 1910, Goethe is increasingly taken as a point of reference. In his ninth notebook, Mann quotes *Tasso* ('Vergleiche Dich! Erkenne, was du bist!'),[40] and cites Goethe's remark that the highest poetry appears to be completely external.[41] Mann's 1908 essay 'Versuch über das Theater' concludes by privileging the German Bildungsroman above all other genres, defining it in moral terms as 'persönliches Ethos, Bekenntnis, Gewissen, Protestantismus, Autobiographie, individualistische Moral-Problematik, Erziehung, Entwicklung, Bildung . . .' (x, 61). This definition implies the recognition that the intellectual German novel owes its existence to the supposedly 'naiv' Goethe.

So far, I have shown that Mann's principal concern in the period leading up to *Felix Krull* (and especially during the composition of the notes for 'Geist und Kunst') was with his own self-definition as an artist, and that this concern with personal development had led to an interest in the Goethean notion of *Bildung* and in Goethe himself as a potential model. In light of this it is hardly surprising that Mann should have turned to Goethe's own autobiography, *Dichtung und Wahrheit*. *Felix Krull* owes much to Goethe's autobiography. Both texts begin with highly self-conscious justifications to the reader, and this is only the first of a long list of resemblances, both stylistic and thematic.[42] Mann himself called his novel 'eine Parodie auf "Dichtung und Wahrheit", aber positiv endlich doch in seiner verzerrten Lyrik'.[43] A parody it certainly is, but for Thomas Mann it was more than that: it was also a thoroughgoing apprenticeship in the Goethean *Weltanschauung*. I shall discuss the use of Goethean style in *Krull* later on.[44] What I intend to do here, however, is demonstrate how certain key thematic elements of *Dichtung und Wahrheit* found their way into *Krull*, and in so doing transformed Mann's own understanding of himself as an artist.

Dichtung und Wahrheit is a book about education and the formation of Goethe's own character. It focuses on Goethe's early years in Frankfurt, Strasbourg, and Leipzig, and describes his youthful adventures and misadventures from the comfortable perspective of middle age.[45] The autobiography is remarkable for its sunny disposition, but this is by no means the only aspect that it has in common with *Felix Krull*. Goethe's description of his own *Bildung* is a fascinating account of how he sought out those persons and influences which would best be able to help him develop his own unique potential. Much as Goethe's first contacts with art are through the painters in his father's employ, Felix Krull is introduced to painting by Schimmelpreester. Identification often forms an important part of this process, and Goethe regards the impulse to identify with one's superiors as a valid means of self-development. He even views the impulse to compare oneself with characters in novels as permissible: 'Unter die läßlichsten Versuche, sich etwas Höheres anzubilden, sich einem Höheren gleich zu stellen, gehört wohl der jugendliche Trieb, sich mit Romanenfiguren zu vergleichen. Er ist höchst unschuldig, und, was man auch dagegen eifern mag, höchst unschädlich' (HA IX, 463). In other words, Thomas Mann receives the sanction for his imitation of the Olympian Goethe from no less an authority than Goethe himself. Goethe, who presented himself in his own autobiographical fictions, himself becomes the raw material for fiction.

In *Dichtung und Wahrheit*, Goethe talks of how he loves to disguise himself, most notably in Book X when he visits the family of Friedrike Brion in Sesenheim. There he first appears as a 'lateinische[r] Reiter' (HA IX, 431), and then later dresses up as the innkeeper's son (HA IX, 438). Goethe, then, delights in playing roles — a characteristic which he shares with Felix Krull. But if Goethe demands this licence for himself, he is also very willing to extend it to others. It is characteristic of his generosity that he will take other people at face value, and allow them to pass for whatever they wish:

> Bei meiner Art zu empfinden und zu denken kostete es mich gar nichts, einen jeden gelten zu lassen für das, was er war, ja sogar für das, was er gelten wollte, und so machte die Offenheit eines frischen jugendlichen Mutes, der sich zum erstenmal in seiner vollen Blüte hervortat, mir sehr viele Freunde und Anhänger. (HA IX, 369–70)

The key phrase in this sentence is 'gelten lassen' ('let be', 'accept as valid'). In other words, Goethe is willing to accept appearances, and this candid approach to life wins him friends. Felix Krull, too, makes it a point of honour to take seriously everyone he meets ('wer alle Dinge und Menschen für voll und wichtig nimmt' (275)); and it is precisely this attitude which makes him so appealing to others ('[die] ihn zugleich liebenswürdig und bedeutend macht' (275)). The attitudes of Goethe and Felix Krull contrast sharply with the beliefs of Goethe's friend Merck, nicknamed 'Mephistopheles' (HA X, 21; X, 72). Merck detests having to live and let live: 'das ewige Geltenlassen, das Leben und Lebenlassen war ihm ein Greuel' (HA X, 128). Merck thus fails to realize an important truth, one that Goethe has instinctively grasped: namely, that trust is a vital element of all human interaction.[46] It is true that Goethe's trusting character sometimes gets him into trouble, as in Book V where he falls into bad company. On the other hand, it is often precisely his faith in nature — and in his own nature — that sees him through. In the passage dealing with the necessary renunciations of life, Goethe states that nature preserves humanity by granting it the gift of frivolity ('Leichtsinn'): 'Diese schwere Aufgabe zu lösen, hat die Natur den Menschen mit reichlicher Kraft, Tätigkeit und Zähigkeit ausgestattet. Besonders aber kommt ihm der Leichtsinn zu Hülfe, der ihm unzerstörlich verliehen ist' (HA X, 77). 'Leichtsinn', then, figures in Goethe's thought as an antidote to the strenuousness of life: it softens the blows of fate by permitting us to transfer our attention to something new. Perhaps it was this very mercurial quality which enabled him to sense his own inner necessity in 1786 and flee to Italy in order to develop his full potential. 'Leichtsinn' is, in any case, one of the principal attributes of Goethe's hero Egmont.

Egmont is important here. It seems that Mann had not only *Dichtung und Wahrheit* but also *Egmont* in mind while writing the early *Krull*. The first evidence for this is Mann's essay in praise of sleep, 'Süßer Schlaf' (XI, 333–39), first published in the *Neue Freie Presse* on 30 May 1909, half a year before he began work on *Krull*. The title of the essay alludes to Egmont's soliloquy in Act V, where sleep comes to Egmont like a blessing after everything he has endured ('Süßer Schlaf! Du kommst wie ein reines Glück ungebeten, unerfleht am willigsten' (HA IV, 452)). Egmont's gift of sleep and his prophetic vision prove beyond a shadow of a doubt that he is a favourite son of mother-nature. Similarly, Mann in 1909 regards the ability to sleep as evidence of mankind's connection with the natural world (XI, 334–35).[47] Sleep, for Mann, signifies a relation with infinite being:

> Mir ist dann, als sei alles individuelle Dasein als Folge zu begreifen eines übersinnlichen Willensaktes und Entschlusses zur Konzentration, zur Begrenzung und zur Gestaltung, zur Sammlung aus dem Nichts, zur Absage an die Freiheit, die Unendlichkeit, an das Schlummern. (XI, 337)

Remarkably, in this early text, Mann has already developed an understanding of the individual's ontological connection with the rest of the universe — an idea that will be expressed in the later *Krull* under the rubric of 'Allsympathie'.[48] It is therefore most significant that the youthful Krull, like Egmont and Mann himself, is a gifted sleeper: he possesses '[eine] außerordentliche[n] Neigung und Begabung zum Schlafe, die mir von klein auf eigentümlich war' (270). There are a number of other connections between *Krull* and *Egmont*. *Egmont*, after all, forms the keynote and conclusion to Goethe's own presentation of himself in *Dichtung und Wahrheit*. In the play, Egmont's charm arises from his insouciance and his desire to live in the moment (*carpe diem*). This same carefree nature means that Egmont falls victim to Alba's treacherous plot, and he becomes a political martyr. If one compares *Egmont* and *Krull*, at first glance, the two works seem very different. It is true that *Krull* lacks the overtly political dimension of *Egmont*. Nevertheless, Krull's existential attitude to life appears very similar to Egmont's. Perhaps the key feature of both characters is their *Lebenslust*, their *joie de vivre*. In a late monologue, Egmont talks of how he used to dislike the long political discussions at court. As soon as he could, he would rush out of doors, into the fresh air, and jump onto his horse:

> Da eilte ich fort, sobald es möglich war, und rasch aufs Pferd mit tiefem Atemzuge! Und frisch hinaus, da wo wir hingehören! Ins Feld, wo aus der Erde dampfend jede nächste Wohltat der Natur, und durch die Himmel wehend alle Segen der Gestirne einhüllend uns umwittern [. . .] (HA IV, 438)

The young Felix Krull feels much the same way about school. In order to avoid it, he composes sick notes in his father's handwriting excusing him from school. When this strategy succeeds, he heads straight for the open fields around town:

> War dies gelungen, so hinderte nichts mich mehr, die Schulstunden eines Tages oder mehrerer frei [. . .] zu verbringen, auf grünem Anger, im Schatten der flüsternden Blätter hingestreckt, den eigenartigen Gedanken meines jungen Herzens nachzuhängen. (297)

This type of idyllic description of nature is on the whole rare in Mann's work, and it seems reasonable to link this new lyrical tone to Mann's interest in Goethe, and to his desire to cultivate a Goethean sensuality.

Another quality which Egmont and Krull share is their commitment to freedom. Even so, each character understands freedom differently. Egmont takes freedom to mean his own political autonomy and his right to express himself freely, no matter what the cost. Krull, for his part, regards freedom as an existential or metaphysical category, asserting that it is the fundamental condition of his existence ('so beruhte es [mein Leben] doch in erster Linie auf der Vor- und Grundbedingung der Freiheit' (372)).[49] In both cases, this commitment entails a defence of free-thinking, of fantasy. Warned by his secretary that his servants' new uniforms might offend the authorities, Egmont contends that such play is harmless and should be permissible:

> Ist ein Faßnachtspiel gleich Hochverrat? Sind uns die kurzen bunten Lumpen zu mißgönnen, die ein jugendlicher Mut, eine angefrischte Phantasie um unsers Lebens arme Blöße hängen mag? Wenn ihr das Leben gar zu ernsthaft nehmt, was ist denn dran? (HA IV, 400)

Such sentiments are also shared by Felix Krull. His defence of fantasy is hardly less passionate: 'Welch eine herrliche Gabe ist nicht die Phantasie, und welchen Genuß vermag sie zu gewähren!' (272). Furthermore, both characters love dressing up. Krull is a 'Kostümkopf' (284), and Egmont impresses Klärchen by wearing his court regalia, the Golden Fleece.[50] As critics of *Egmont* from Schiller onwards have pointed out, such behaviour is ill-suited to a politician, and even irresponsible. Nevertheless, this very insouciance is an integral part of Egmont's charm. Both Egmont and Krull charm all they meet: not only women, but men too (in Egmont's case, this charisma even extends to Ferdinand, the son of his enemy, Alba). Indeed, the attractiveness of both figures borders on the supernatural. Mann knew Goethe's discussion of 'das Dämonische' at the end of *Dichtung und Wahrheit*. There, Goethe defines the Daemonic as a force in nature which can express itself in a variety of ways. If it manifests itself in people, these individuals become irresistible:

> Eine ungeheure Kraft geht von ihnen aus, und sie üben eine unglaubliche Gewalt über alle Geschöpfe [. . .]. Alle vereinten sittlichen Kräfte vermögen nichts gegen sie; vergebens, daß der hellere Teil der Menschen sie als Betrogene oder als Betrüger verdächtig machen will, die Masse wird von ihnen angezogen. (HA X, 177)

Much has been written on the subject of the Daemonic. For an excellent summary, I refer the reader to a recent study by Angus Nicholls, who relates the genesis of the concept to Goethe's engagement with the philosophies of Kant and Schelling, arguing that Goethe uses the term 'daemonic' in order to distinguish the epistemological limits of rational philosophy.[51] Thomas Mann's reading of the term, like that of Friedrich Gundolf, relies more heavily on Goethe's later presentation of the Daemonic (in the autobiography and in the *Gespräche mit Eckermann*) as a vital force, linked to fate and expressed through great individuals. It seems that even the later, classical Goethe was not beyond a touch of nature mysticism. There is a sort of joyful fatalism about this attitude which appealed to Nietzsche, and it appealed to Thomas Mann as well.

It seems to me that, for Mann, writing *Felix Krull* was a kind of thought experiment: the hypothetical attempt to replace Schopenhauerian pessimism with a Goethean faith in nature. Of course, the natural world *per se* barely features in *Krull*. One aspect of 'nature' is, however, frequently discussed: sexuality. The novel is remarkable for its celebration of sexuality, which, at the time (1910), was something quite new in

Mann's work. I will discuss gender and sexuality later on in section vi; the point here is that the novel's relatively positive treatment of sexuality may well be a result of Mann's new preoccupation with Goethe. Goethe's emphasis on nature as a key to development could well have given Mann a new confidence in himself. For Goethe, education had to be guided by nature to be considered valid. *Bildung* as portrayed in *Wilhelm Meister* is something elusive which is acquired by living, and not through reason alone. Felix Krull, too, views *Bildung* as an organic process, one which cannot be forced, and which requires a light touch:

> Bildung wird nicht in stumpfer Fron und Plackerei gewonnen, sondern ist ein Geschenk der Freiheit und des äußeren Müßigganges; man erringt sie nicht, man atmet sie ein; verborgene Werkzeuge sind ihretwegen tätig, ein geheimer Fleiß der Sinne und des Geistes, welcher sich mit scheinbar völliger Tagediebenerei gar wohl verträgt [. . .] (339)

At the same time, a precondition for successful development is to have a happy nature. Felix Krull's own native confidence in himself, the belief that he is 'ein Sonntagskind', 'ein Vorzugskind des Himmels' (271), is accompanied by the belief that there is such a thing as natural aristocracy, and that he is 'aus feinerem Holz geschnitzt' (273). Such an attitude implies faith in a providential, divine order: 'Vorsehung' (271). Seen from this Goethean perspective, a healthy dose of confidence is an essential condition for a happy life. Later on, however, Krull has an inkling that this blithely fatalistic attitude could be portrayed as morally irresponsible. When the town priest Chateau praises him for the natural, innate quality of his voice, he realizes that such praise sits uneasily with the Protestant work ethic of the bourgeoisie, even implying paganism:

> Denn Lob oder Tadel gebührt nach der Meinung unserer bürgerlichen Welt nur dem Moralischen, nicht dem Natürlichen: dieses zu loben, würde ihr als ungerecht und leichtfertig erscheinen. Daß nun Stadtpfarrer Chateau es ganz einfach anders hielt, mutete mich wie etwas völlig Neues und Kühnes an, [. . .] die zugleich etwas heidnisch Einfältiges an sich hatte und mich zu einem glücklichen Nachsinnen anregte. (329–30)

What the narrative touches upon here is the old crux of faith versus works. Faith, since it leaves everything up to the gods, flies in the face of admonishments to work: there is something subversive, even irresponsible, in the idea of leaving everything up to nature (again, one thinks of *Egmont*). In Goethe, this tension is never quite resolved. *Felix Krull* signals the problem as Goethean by using the phrase 'angeborene Vorzüge' (328) — a deliberate allusion to the Goethean phrase 'angeborene Verdienste' ('innate merits').[52] Here Mann prefigures his great essay of the early 1920s, 'Goethe und Tolstoi' (1921/25), which features a detailed discussion of the problem. The basic question, according to Mann, is whether merit lies in being (*esse*) or in works (*operari*). Goethe's phrase 'angeborene Verdienste' pronounces judgement in favour of *esse*, to the detriment of *operari* (ix, 101). The problem is already there in the pre-war *Felix Krull*, gently touched upon in the encounter with the priest and left unresolved (330). Later, it is mentioned again and still left open (339–40).[53] To leave the question open means to sit on the fence and allow that *both* works and faith may be valid. This is roughly the same happy conclusion that Goethe drew. In his early *Sturm und Drang* period, Goethe's violent attachment to nature produced ecstatic works of art, but threatened to destroy him (*Werther*). Later, in his classical period, he was able to achieve a harmonious equilibrium between faith and works, nature and intellect. In other words, in Goethe, the pagan affirmation of life and the protestant affirmation of hard work coexist in a harmonious balance. And so Mann's formula for *Felix Krull*, 'Protestantismus plus "Griechentum"',[54] has a distinctly Goethean quality.

Felix Krull allowed Thomas Mann to experience a hypothetical intimacy with Goethe for the first time in his career — but not for the last. Indeed, the novel seems to have laid the groundwork for much of Mann's subsequent engagement with Goethe. The connections between Goethe and *Felix Krull* are particularly evident in Mann's short piece on the writer Erich von Mendelssohn, 'Vorwort zu einem Roman', which he wrote in 1913 for the *Süddeutsche Monatshefte* (x, 559–65). The opening section deals with autobigraphy, Goethe, and Manolescu, and Mann used the text again on 5 November 1916 in order to introduce a reading of *Felix Krull* at the Berliner Sezession ('Der autobiographische Roman' (xi, 700)). Already in this 1913 text we have the presentation of Goethe as 'Götterliebling' and the phrase 'angeborene[r] Verdienste' (x, 559); we have a description of *Dichtung und Wahrheit* as the formation of a genius thanks to the guidance of beneficent fate. Goethe's autobiography announces: 'wie ein Genie sich bildet, Glück und Verdienst nach irgendwelchem Gnadenschlusse sich unauflöslich verketten' (x, 559). Thirty-five years later, Mann was to use exactly the same phraseology in 'Phantasie über Goethe' (1948): ' "Dichtung und Wahrheit" [. . .] darüber unterrichtet, wie ein Genie sich bildet, Glück und Verdienst nach irgendwelchem Gnadenschlusse sich unauflöslich verketten' (ix, 716). And the 1913 text talks of the importance of real life, again alluding to Goethe's saying that 'ich habe die Welt stets für genialer gehalten, als mein Genie' — an echo of which had already found its way into *Felix Krull* (274–75).

It is evident that the themes addressed for the first time in *Felix Krull* inform much of Mann's subsequent treatment of Goethe. Indeed, much of 'Goethe und Tolstoi' (1921/25) already exists *in nuce* in *Krull*. The presentation of Goethe in 'Goethe und Tolstoi' as a 'Götterliebling' (ix, 71), 'ein Glücksfall' (ix, 73), as a 'Persönlichkeit' (ix, 76) resonates with *Krull*, as does the theme of sympathy — 'die wissende Sympathie der Naturgesegneten mit dem organischen Leben' (ix, 144).[55] Some critics have tried to present the mood of social responsibility in 'Goethe und Tolstoi' as something completely new in Mann's work. But these stirrings go back to *Felix Krull* and Mann's interest in the moral tradition of autobiography. Thus as early as 1913 Mann suggests that autobiography may have an objective — that is to say, exemplary — function: 'Der Trieb eines Menschen, sein Leben zu fixieren [. . . vermag . . .] ein Leben nicht nur subjektiv zum Roman zu stempeln, sondern auch objektiv ins Interessante und Bedeutende zu erheben' (x, 559). This movement from subjective to objective becomes an important theme in 'Goethe und Tolstoi'. There, Mann shows how the focus on the self in Goethe's early works slowly widens in perspective to encompass the moral and social world: *Wilhelm Meister* becomes an exemplary case. The movement here is from autobiography to pedagogy: 'Das pädagogische Element lebt [. . .] bereits in dem autobiographischen, es ergibt sich daraus, es wächst daraus hervor' (IX, 149). The implication is clear: autobiography is an inherently moral genre. Even *Felix Krull*, for all its show of vanity, is motivated by a humanitarian impulse.

The celebration of Goethean charm in *Felix Krull* also has major repercussions for later works. The novel is Mann's first attempt to work through the problem of Goethean charisma, that 'Daemonic' which he found in *Egmont* and *Dichtung und Wahrheit*. Charisma is an essentially religious concept; to be charismatic is to have divine grace, 'something bestowed on man by God' as Donald MacRae points out in his study of Max Weber.[56] From the Krullian charisma there is a direct line leading to the 'große Persönlichkeit' of Mynheer Peeperkorn in *Der Zauberberg*, the personality that sweeps all before it and leaves Naphta and Settembrini looking like pygmies. Hans Castorp, too, has a similar charm, but in his case it is more muted, more balanced. The insistent dialogue with the Goethean tradition of *Bildung* also continues in *Der Zauberberg*. And from here, Mann's Goethean trajectory takes us, via *Joseph* and *Lotte in Weimar*, back to *Felix Krull*. It is fascinating to observe the periodicity of these themes. In 1948, having finished *Doktor Faustus* and 'Nietzsches Philosophie im Lichte unserer Erfahrung', Mann turns once more to Goethe. The time of great reckoning is over: it is time to breathe again (systole, diastole). 'Phantasie über Goethe' (1948), written shortly before Mann resumed work on *Felix Krull* in 1950, restates the same configuration of themes as insistently as ever. Goethe is described as a 'Glückskind' (IX, 735), a son of mother-nature (IX, 736). We hear once more of the ambiguities of his 'Persönlichkeit' (IX, 716), his belief in natural aristocracy and in innate merits ('angeborenen Verdiensten' (IX, 735)). In fact, the density of Krullian motifs in 'Phantasie über Goethe' is remarkable. Goethe's desire to know led him into Protean metamorphoses: 'die Freiheit des Proteus, der in alle Formen schlüpft, alles zu wissen, alles zu verstehen, alles zu sein, in jeder Haut zu leben verlangt' (IX, 740). Felix Krull, though not mentioned here, arrogates the same freedom to himself. What motivates him is a Goethean desire for experience. 'Phantasie über Goethe' also contains familiar references to *Dichtung und Wahrheit* (IX, 716) and to *Egmont*. Egmont, for Mann, represents the culmination of Goethean charm: ' "Egmont", ein Stück, [. . .] in welchem für mich die spezifisch goethische Liebenswürdigkeit kulminiert' (IX, 744). Reading between the lines of Mann's Goethe *imitatio*, one might add: Felix Krull, 'liebenswürdig' (275) as he is, represents the culmination of Mann's charm as an engaging and polished narrator. By 1950, Thomas Mann had come a long way, but he came back to *Felix Krull*. Why? One possible answer is that writing the first part of *Felix Krull* had enabled him to assimilate Goethean elements into his own identity. The early identification with Goethe had acted as a guide, setting Mann on a humanistic course, and sustaining him through the trauma of two world wars. For Mann, *Felix Krull* implied an intimate bond with the most sacred figure in German literature.

(iv) Identity as Experiment

Felix Krull comes at the end of a decade in which Mann thought more deeply than ever before about identity. The exuberance with which it is written suggests a newfound confidence, a new willingness to experiment. Felix Krull has a flexibility, an adaptability about him which Mann's earlier characters had lacked. Thomas Buddenbrook's unbending rigidity, his inability to reconcile the warring sides of his own character, proves his downfall. As for Tonio Kröger, when he tries to decide what sort of person he wants to become, all he can imagine is possibilities which somehow seem impossibilities:

> Fragte man ihn, was in aller Welt er zu werden gedachte, so erteilte er wechselnde Auskunft, denn er pflegte zu sagen [. . .], daß er die Möglichkeiten zu tausend Daseinsformen in sich trage, zusammen mit dem heimlichen Bewußtsein, daß es im Grunde lauter Unmöglichkeiten seien. (VIII, 288–89)

What is implied here is that it will be impossible for Tonio Kröger to attain a true identity, because for him such a fixed idea of selfhood appears inauthentic. Hans Hansen may be secure in his own identity, but Tonio Kröger has such a high degree of consciousness that what is natural in the case of Hans can only seem artificial when applied to himself.[57] This is the dilemma of the modern subject who knows himself to be contingent and conditional and is thus haunted by a feeling of inauthenticity. Crucial here is Thomas Mann's reception of Nietzsche. Nietzsche, having announced the death of God, proclaimed that henceforth man would have to create his own values. Identity could no longer be taken as a given; indeed, for Nietzsche, 'becoming who you are' takes on the dimensions of a heroic struggle (*Ecce Homo* is subtitled 'Wie man wird, was man ist').[58] An important dimension of this struggle is aesthetic: in *Die Geburt der Tragödie*, Nietzsche announces that the world can only be justified as an aesthetic phenomenon.[59] Even identity becomes aesthetic: one must give style to one's character ('Eins ist noth. — Seinem Charakter "Stil geben" — eine grosse und seltne Kunst!').[60] This is where *Felix Krull* comes in. Whereas Tonio Kröger perceives all his possibilities as inauthentic and artificial, Krull revels in his own aesthetic being. No longer haunted by questions of authenticity, he is free to experiment with whatever identity he chooses, and longs to change his name: 'Welche Wohltat, welche Anregung, welche Erquickung des Daseins, sich mit einem neuen Namen vorzustellen und anreden zu hören!' (317). There is an incongruity here, however: Krull is no prophet. Unlike Nietzsche's Zarathustra, he has no interest in creating new values. There is an insouciance about him that would have shocked Nietzsche. Sometimes he even echoes Nietzsche's critique of the decadent artist, as Wysling has shown.[61] Certainly, the work notes for *Felix Krull* employ Nietzschean terms such as 'Anpassungsfähigkeit': 'Seine Unwirklichkeit und Wesenslosigkeit bewirkt eine enorme Anpassungsfähigkeit'.[62] But Wysling's comparison only works up to a point. Felix Krull combines *joie de vivre*, 'Lebenslust', a sense of self-preservation, and a capacity for organization and hard work: a set of traits which are the opposite of decadent. If there is something unreal about him, it is the high level of reflectivity that makes him unwilling to commit fully to the roles which he adopts in life. At any given moment, Felix Krull has an identity, but one which is experimental, provisional, and liable to change. The only thing which remains consistent is his commitment to freedom and flexibility.

In this respect, the key passage in the novel on the theme of identity is the *Musterungsszene* in Book II, when Krull evades conscription by pretending to have epilepsy. In this scene, Krull succeeds in tricking the medical board by thinking his way into the soldierly mindset. He does not become a soldier, but his entire mental activity becomes focused upon thinking in a military way. As the scene progresses, Krull as narrator uses a number of military metaphors. He prepares himself for his appearance before the medical board as if it is a matter of life or death. He is 'vollkommen entschlossen, bis zum Äußersten zu gehen, ja, wenn es nötig sein sollte, alle Grundkräfte des Leibes und der Seele daranzusetzen' (352). It will be a test of nerves requiring exceptional courage ('mit dem äußersten, der gemeinen Menge unglaubhaftesten Wagemut' (350)); it is a serious business which must be attacked ('eine ernste Sache [. . .] in Angriff zu nehmen' (350)) if he is to avoid defeat ('Niederlage' (350)). It requires months of careful preparation ('lange[r] Vorübungen' (357)), until he becomes like a man armed to the teeth ('der bis an die Zähne gerüstet in einen Kampf geht' (357)). By the time he appears before the medical board, he has adopted the manner of military personnel: he has an impersonal, bureaucratic way of speaking ('ich beabsichtige [. . .] die Hotelkarriere einzuschlagen' (359)) and a subservient attitude to his superiors — for example, he continually addresses the examining doctor as 'Herr Generalarzt' (358). Krull's eagerness to join the army appears so genuine that it is hard to attribute any deception to him: his soldierly eagerness guarantees his sincerity. When his 'epileptic fit' finally occurs, it is violent enough to shock even the most hardened officers. And when Krull is declared unfit for service, he is, ironically, full of regret ('so wollte fast Bedauern mich anwandeln' (371)). After all, access to the army means 'Zugang zu einer so kleidsamen Daseinsform' (371), and its innate sense of hierarchy appeals to him. The *Musterungsszene* is remarkable because it shows the innate flexibility of the Krullian intellect. In it, Krull thinks his way into being a soldier and then thinks his way out again. At the end of the chapter, he carefully distances himself from the army. He concludes that it would have been a mistake for him to enlist, since this would have interfered with the basic condition of his life, which is freedom:

> War ich doch nicht im Zeichen des Mars geboren, wenigstens nicht im besonderen und im wirklichen Sinn! Denn wenn freilich kriegerische Strenge, Selbstbeherrschung und Gefahr die hervorstechendsten Merkmale meines seltsamen Lebens bildeten, so beruhte es doch in erster Linie auf der Vor- und Grundbedingung der Freiheit, — einer Bedingung also, welche mit irgendwelcher Einspannung in ein plump tatsächliches Verhältnis schlechterdings unvereinbar gewesen wäre. (371–72)

What prevents Felix Krull from ever committing too fully to anything, then, is his need for freedom. His imagination requires room to manoeuvre ('Spielraum' (334)); his consciousness demands an escape clause. Put simply, he refuses to 'be' anything in a straightforwardly literal sense; he insists on viewing his identity as something hypothetical. There is a cognitive dimension to his experience which implies a distance from empirical immediacy. The chapter culminates in a rush of subjunctives which underline the distinction between living literally and figuratively, between living *as* a soldier and living *like* a soldier:

> Lebte ich folglich soldatisch, so wäre es doch ein tölpelhaftes Mißverständnis gewesen, wenn ich darum als Soldat leben zu sollen geglaubt hätte; ja, wenn es gälte, ein so erhabenes Gefühlsgut wie dasjenige der Freiheit für die Vernunft zu bestimmen und zuzurichten, so ließe sich sagen, daß dies eben: soldatisch, aber nicht als Soldat, figürlich, aber nicht wörtlich, daß im Gleichnis leben zu dürfen eigentlich Freiheit bedeute. (372)

If Felix Krull chooses to live metaphorically, in the subjunctive mood of the imagination, it is because of his imperious need for freedom. The repetition of the word 'Freiheit' here and the reference to it as 'erhabenes Gefühlsgut' is a clear allusion to the classical aesthetics of Schiller, to that disinterestedness which is the precondition for aesthetic appreciation. The dignity of freedom requires aesthetic detachment, and it is this which Felix Krull seeks to embody ('im Gleichnis leben'). In this respect, the second half of the novel, written over forty years later, shows a great deal of continuity. The reason why Felix Krull refuses Lord Kilmarnock's offer to accompany him back to Scotland and be his butler is that such a role would restrict his possibilities, entailing too great a commitment to reality. Such a role would be 'penible' (485), since his primary allegiance is to the freedom of his own imagination:

> Die Hauptsache war, daß ein Instinkt [. . .] Partei nahm in mir gegen eine mir präsentierte und obendrein schlackenhafte Wirklichkeit — zugunsten des freien Traums und Spieles, selbstgeschaffen und von eigenen Gnaden, will sagen: von Gnaden der Phantasie. Wenn ich als Knabe erwacht war mit dem Beschluß, ein achtzehnjähriger Prinz namens Karl zu sein, und an dieser reinen und reizenden Erdichtung, solange ich wollte, in Freiheit festgehalten hatte — das war das Rechte gewesen [. . .] (489)

Here, as earlier, the emphasis is clearly on freedom ('Freiheit') and on the sovereign imagination of the individual ('des freien Traums'). These are the values which the narrator perceives as giving rise to authenticity ('das Rechte').

J. P. Stern has analysed *Felix Krull* with specific reference to the *Musterungsszene* in a remarkable essay, 'Living in the Metaphor of Fiction'. Stern reads the novel as a critique of Nietzsche, but one which is enacted in Nietzschean terms.[63] He points out that Felix Krull's decision to live in the metaphor ('im Gleichnis leben') closely resembles Nietzsche's programme in the short essay 'Über Wahrheit und Lüge im aussermoralischen Sinn' (1873). According to Nietzsche, metaphors are the only access we have to reality: they form the modality of human experience. Because of this, he views art as the paradigm for all positive activity. For him, the only authentic response to existence is to give free rein to one's fundamental creative impulse, what he calls 'jener Trieb zur Metaphernbildung, jener Fundamentaltrieb des Menschen' (KGA 3.2, 381). Thus both Nietzsche and *Felix Krull* offer a view of the self as being based upon metaphor. And yet Stern shows that there is also something very un-Nietzschean about Felix Krull. Nietzsche subscribes to what Stern calls an 'ideology of strenuousness',[64] the belief that the value of an achievement is directly related to the hardship involved. The tendency to privilege 'das Schwere' — that which is hard, difficult, or costly — is regarded by Stern as a key characteristic of German modernism as a whole. This cast of mind is common to all of Mann's major characters, with the notable exception of Felix Krull. Krull is not haunted by notions of inauthenticity or strenuousness; he perceives the aesthetic dimension of his existence as something to celebrate. This implies a consciousness which accepts its own contingency. Mann's novel is prepared to acknowledge the untidiness of the modern subject: it contains an element of ironic self-critique which is quite absent from the grandiose prophetic visions of Nietzsche's *Zarathustra*.[65] What was the impetus which led Mann to turn away from this Nietzschean doctrine of 'das Schwere' around 1909–10? The clues are to be found, once more, in the notes for 'Geist und Kunst'. Initially, the shift is expressed in Nietzschean terms. Thus N 103 describes the celebration of health and the body in the new generation of writers as posing a challenge to Mann himself. A Krullian motif, 'die Tennispartie', is mentioned for the first time, and Mann observes Gerhart Hauptmann's attempt to keep up with the times. Finally, he decides that it is a question of two different readings of Nietzsche: it is time to favour the life-affirmer (*Nietzsche triumphans*) over the radical psychologist (*Nietzsche militans*). A little later, in N 114, the spirit of *Krull* is definitely in the air, as Mann calls for a new conception of art, one which would be less serious and more playful. Such an art would be liberating and would promote happiness and life.[66] Perhaps we can read the early *Krull*, then, as an experiment in identity: the creation of a type of consciousness that would still be reflective, but less stringent, less masochistic (less Stoic, more Epicurean). N 114 shows the way. 'Verschlagenheit' (cunning) is a key attribute, not only of Felix Krull, but also of Hans Castorp and Joseph. Associated with the mythical Hermes, it implies practical intelligence and accommodation with life. In my view, Stern's essay on *Krull* remains the most convincing interpretation of the novel in Nietzschean terms. Less convincing is Eric Downing's treatment of the novel in his book *Artificial I's*.[67] Downing, inspired by Alexander Nehamas' book *Nietzsche: Life as Literature*, correctly presents 'life as literature' as the central issue at stake in the novel,[68] and his inventive reading makes an impressive case for *Krull* as a supremely self-referential novel. Unfortunately, his reading is distorted by an undue reliance on the *Musterungsszene*, which he uses as the point of departure for a hypertrophied postmodern meditation on mimesis.[69]

If aesthetic identity is a vital aspect of *Felix Krull*, it also has a central role in Robert Musil's masterwork *Der Mann ohne Eigenschaften*. The two novels beg comparison: both are deeply influenced by Nietzsche, but respond to that influence in vastly different ways.[70] Musil's hero Ulrich thinks the subject is constructed from odds and ends, rather like a bird's nest, by what he calls: 'einen Ichbautrieb, der wie der Nestbautrieb der Vögel aus vieler Art Stoff nach ein paar Verfahren sein Ich aufrichtet'.[71] Ulrich even goes so far as to claim that 'unser Dasein ganz und gar aus Literatur bestehen sollte!'.[72] There is, then, a distinct similarity between Felix Krull's attempt at living 'im Gleichnis' (372) and Ulrich's description of 'Gleichnis' as the mechanism of the soul ('die gleitende Logik der Seele').[73] Kerstin Schulz, in her recent extensive study of *Felix Krull*, concludes with a parallel between the two novels.[74] According to Schulz's reading, Felix Krull completely lacks identity in the traditional sense; like Musil's Ulrich, he dwells in a world of 'Möglichkeitssinn' which is opposed to reality.[75] Schulz bases her argument principally upon a passage in the later section of the novel,[76] where Felix Krull talks of the ambiguity of his double life as a gentleman and a waiter, and of the thrill of not knowing which one is the true him:

> Es lief dies, wie man sieht, auf eine Art Doppelleben hinaus, dessen Anmutigkeit darin bestand, daß es ungewiß blieb, in welcher Gestalt ich eigentlich ich selbst und in welcher ich nur verkleidet war [. . .]. Verkleidet war ich also in jedem Fall, und die unmaskierte Wirklichkeit zwischen den beiden Erscheinungsformen, das Ich-selber-Sein, war nicht bestimmbar, weil tatsächlich nicht vorhanden. (498)

As Michael Beddow points out, however, it is mistaken to argue from these remarks that Krull has no real selfhood of his own — a point of view belied by much of the novel.[77] In fact, Krull is denying that he has a 'true' self as distinct from the self that is expressed through his playing of the twin roles, and as distinct from his continual awareness that he can play a number of roles without abandoning his inner freedom. After all, only a little later Krull talks of natural characteristics ('natürlich-überzeugende Anlage' (498)), and he also talks of identity: '[von] meiner Identität — der Identität zwischen dem Kavalier und dem Kellner' (500). It seems that, in spite of his overt denials, Felix Krull does have a working definition of identity after all, but one which is empirically based and flexible. He adopts a working hypothesis by comparing contexts and situations. Identity, for him, is a composite of multiple possibilities: he has several identities ('Viele Ichs').[78] There is certainly something slightly unreal about this, and he twice refers to 'das zart Schwebende meiner Existenz' (584, 632) which prevents him from making too great a commitment to reality:

> Das zart Schwebende meiner Existenz, [. . .] verbot [mir], es solcherart mit der Wirklichkeit aufzunehmen. (584)

> [. . .] weil mir in meiner Unwirklichkeit ja nicht erlaubt war, es mit der Wirklichkeit aufzunehmen. (632)

Schulz is at her most persuasive when she argues that Felix Krull represents freedom from categorical definition ('[die] Freiheit der Uneindeutigkeit').[79] This is indeed the point of Krull, that multiple possibilities may coexist with equal validity. This is the force of the argument in the Müller-Rosé chapter where the reader is told to beware of categorization: 'Wann zeigt der Glühwurm sich in seiner wahren Gestalt [. . .]? Hüte dich, darüber zu entscheiden!' (294). Nevertheless, Schulz is inaccurate when she claims that Felix Krull represents utopian freedom from all responsibility ('Freiheit von allen Bindungen').[80] This is simply untrue. Felix Krull may have a selective memory which allows him to ignore events that he would rather forget,[81] but he also has an excellent sense of practical reality, and he has a 'moralische Veranlagung' to boot.[82] And this is where Schulz's connection between *Felix Krull* and *Mann ohne Eigenschaften* breaks down. Felix Krull, unlike Ulrich, never contemplates a holiday from life. When he accepts the Marquis de Venosta's offer, this is in order to exchange one life for another. It has nothing to do with wanting to disengage from life. While both characters clearly have a utopian sense of human possibility, Krull has an empiricism about him which Ulrich lacks. Ulrich tends to define himself for the most part in opposition to the world of practical concerns; Krull, on the other hand, frequently puts his hypothetical identities to the test: he moves back and forth between possibility and reality. *Der Mann ohne Eigenschaften* is both social satire and philosophical novel, but ultimately its historical analysis gives way to mystic ambiguity. It remains an impressive critique of modernity, but it ultimately evades reality in a way that *Felix Krull*, with its ironic commitment to experience, does not.

So far I have explored how Mann's treatment of identity in *Felix Krull* relates to Nietzsche and Musil. I have shown that there is a considerable degree of overlap between the three writers, but that there are also some significant differences. What emerges from a study of all three writers is a view of identity as something inherently tenuous and experimental, a dynamic model of identity as a kind of literary work in progress, subjected to multiple possibilities. This is remarkably similar to the 'multiple drafts' model of consciousness proposed by the philosopher Daniel C. Dennett.[83] To a certain extent, the aesthetic model of identity which Mann develops in *Felix Krull* also anticipates recent theoretical work which regards the self as being formed and shaped through acts of self-narration. For the philosopher Alisdair MacIntyre, narratives are inextricable from experience: 'we all live out narratives in our lives and [...] we understand our own lives in terms of the narrative we live out'.[84] Anthony Kerby's study *Narrative and the Self* goes even further, arguing that subjects are given content by means the stories they tell about themselves. Kerby proposes 'a model of the human subject that takes acts of *self-narration* not only as descriptive of the self but, more importantly, *as fundamental to the emergence and reality of that subject*'.[85] In an excellent recent article, Julia Schöll applies Kerby's theory (and that of Paul Ricœur) to *Felix Krull*.[86] Schöll argues that although Krull is a master of self-stylization and self-performance, he is by no means a narcissist, because his narrative is intelligent enough to take other people and things into account.[87]

In order to achieve a more precise definition of Thomas Mann's thought on identity, however, we will need to avoid comparison with other thinkers and turn to a closer examination of his own work. *Felix Krull* is something of a watershed because it treats identity with a new experimental flexibility. It does this, however, by putting into practice ideas from the essays of the preceding decade. Indeed, subtle intimations of the change can be found as early as 'Kritik und Schaffen' (1896), an article Mann wrote for the right-wing journal *Das XX. Jahrhundert*. There, Mann contrasts the forceful personality of the artist with the wavering personality of the critic: 'Der Künstler ist einseitig, wie jede starke Persönlichkeit; der Kritiker ist vielseitig, eben weil er keine Persönlichkeit ist, denn er ist jeden Tag eine neue' (XIII, 520). What we have here, in effect, is an early statement of the dichotomy between the naïve *Dichter* and the intellectual *Literat/Schriftsteller*. Especially striking is the admiration that Mann expresses for the Jewish critic Georg Brandes, precisely because of his mercurial ability to play a variety of different roles:

'Georg Brandes, als private Persönlichkeit betrachtet, ist ein ganz uninteressanter freisinniger Jude; aber er vermag, unter Umständen, sich selbst auszulöschen und Heine oder Mérimée oder Tieck oder ein anderer zu *sein* — oder ihn zu *spielen*' (XIII, 521). As Heinrich Detering points out, the fact that Brandes' identity is capable of metamorphosis is viewed positively by Mann.[88] As we have seen, Mann's respect for the theatre tends to increase in the next decade, and, as it does so, a more playful notion of identity begins to emerge. Thus in 'Bilse und ich' (1906) Mann accords the title of 'Dichter' to the writer 'who works upon himself' ('der an sich selbst arbeitet, wenn er arbeitet' (X, 18)). This is a wonderfully ambiguous statement: how, exactly, does the writer 'work upon himself'? Does he critique himself, or is the act of writing perhaps an essential part of his development? The answers will be provided in the years to come. *Königliche Hoheit* deals with the cultivation of the self, and represents another step towards the Bildungsroman. Klaus Heinrich turns to the study of economics with great gusto, prefiguring Hans Castorp's scientific researches in *Der Zauberberg*. The self is increasingly viewed as susceptible to development, and worthy of cultivation. *Königliche Hoheit* therefore represents a turn towards the socio-political domain, but Klaus Heinrich lacks the flexibility of Felix Krull. Krull explores his potential for imaginative self-development, and in doing so he exemplifies a new vision of the self as something that can be moulded and shaped with comparative ease. The novel's keynote is experiment (much as it is, in a different way, for *Der Tod in Venedig*).[89] Krull is constantly testing his limits — and society's limits — to see what he can get away with. If his stunts and tricks generally succeed, this is because he takes care to rehearse them well, as well as to scout out the terrain. Failure is always possible however, and it is worth remembering that the plans for the novel require him to end up in jail. The key word even crops up twice in the second half of the novel: while working in the hotel, Felix Krull busily conducts thought experiments ('Gedankenexperimente' (492, 495)), little suspecting that he himself is a colossal 'Gedankenexperiment' on the part of his creator.[90]

Mann left off work on *Felix Krull* in the summer of 1913 to devote himself to *Der Zauberberg*, but it is clear that the novel was still very much on his mind. In November of that year, Mann's piece on Erich von Mendelssohn, 'Vorwort zu einem Roman', is packed with Krullian motifs: Goethe, *Dichtung und Wahrheit*, Manolescu, and autobiography. The opening section is particularly relevant, since Mann used it again on 5 November 1916 in order to introduce a reading of *Felix Krull* at the Berliner Sezession ('Der autobiographische Roman' (XI, 700)). The text begins with an allusion to Oscar Wilde's 'To love oneself is the beginning of a lifelong romance':[91] 'Liebe zu sich selbst, hat ich weiß nicht mehr welcher Autor gesagt — es war ein geistreicher Autor, soviel ist sicher — Liebe zu sich selbst ist immer der Anfang eines romanhaften Lebens' (X, 559; XI, 700).[92] In fact, as Eric Downing has shown, Mann's formulation is very different from Wilde's.[93] Whereas Wilde talks of a 'lifelong romance', Mann talks of 'eines romanhaften Lebens': a 'novelistic life'. This directly relates to Felix Krull's intention to live in the metaphor ('im Gleichnis leben' (372)), his wish to live life in a literary, self-conscious mode. For him, identity is not a Platonic abstraction, but part of a creative process of becoming, continually inscribed and re-inscribed through autobiographical discourse. In this respect, Mann's comment on Erich von Mendelssohn (in the same 1913 text) is particularly revealing. According to Mann, the source of Mendelssohn's creativity lies in the uncertain status of his identity:

> Ich übersehe nicht das persönliche Problem des jungen Mendelssohn, das ein Problem des Blutes — seines halb jüdischen, halb junkerlichen Blutes — war und das ihn wahrscheinlich zum Schriftsteller machte; denn nur wo das Ich eine Aufgabe ist, hat es einen Sinn, zu schreiben. (x, 564)

Mann's sentence moves swiftly from the particular (Mendelssohn's problem of his own mixed heritage) to the general: now the search for identity is seen as essential to all writing. As Heinrich Detering says, the subject is no longer just Mendelssohn, but Mann himself.[94] The problem of mixed inheritance is an important factor in many of Mann's works, especially *Buddenbrooks* and *Tonio Kröger*. The above citation is important: partly because it sheds light on questions of ethnicity, but mainly because it shows that the indistinctness of his own self-image was, for Thomas Mann, an essential part of his own creativity. Identity, for Mann, was a problem which demanded solutions and which acted as a vital spur to his own artistic endeavours. This dynamic, creative approach to identity is an important feature of the essays of the following years. In the *Betrachtungen*, Mann defines writing as a 'geistig-sittliche Bemühung [. . .] um ein problematisches Ich' (xII, 20), and approvingly cites Dostoevsky's dictum 'Arbeite an dir' (xII, 519). In 'Goethe und Tolstoi', identity is portrayed as a challenge, as a task: 'diese Empfindung des eigenen Ich als einer *Aufgabe*' (ix, 150). A further quotation from 'Goethe und Tolstoi' is even more remarkable. It is perhaps Mann's clearest formulation of his creative approach to identity: 'Mit Geist und Empfindung ist aus jedem Leben alles zu machen, ist aus jedem Leben ein "Roman" zu machen' (ix, 72). What Mann is asserting here is that every life can be shaped, every life can be a novel. The underlying implication is clear: there is a measure of creativity involved in all self-consciousness. Self-consciousness makes artists of us all, since it involves the narration of one's own selfhood. As we grow up, as we live life, we are continually trying out new narratives, new scenarios; we are constantly picturing different aspects of ourselves and others. In other words, art is not simply an option for human beings: every life is, in a sense, a work of art. This does not mean that every transformation is possible, but it does mean that consciousness is a dynamic process, one in which the creative imagination plays a central role. People need art in order to become conscious of who they are, in order to narrate themselves to themselves. Art is what we do, it is necessary to the formation of selfhood.

There is a fascinating moment in 'Lebensabriß' (1930) when Mann describes art as a journey of self-discovery.[95] Mann sees every work as a fragmentary actualization of our essence and the only way we have of finding out what that essence is:

> In Wahrheit ist jede Arbeit eine zwar fragmentarische, aber in sich geschlossene Verwirklichung unseres Wesens, über das Erfahrungen zu machen solche Verwirklichung der einzige, mühsame Weg ist, und es ist kein Wunder, daß es dabei nicht ohne Überraschungen abgeht. (xi, 123)

In this passage, the use of the first person plural ('unseres') has a generalizing effect: this is an experience common to all artists, perhaps common to everyone. As for the word 'Verwirklichung' (actualization, realization), it is somehow ambivalent.

If writing is a process of self-discovery, then that discovery is achieved through a creative, imaginative effort. The fragmentary 'realization' of our being is a work of art. In other words, if writing is self-discovery, then it is also self-*definition*, with all the creativity which that implies. Through writing, through dialogue with ourselves, we create and define ourselves. The physical act of writing becomes a means to achieve self-consciousness, self-definition. Mann expressed this insight even more succinctly in 1930 when he wrote: 'Die Kunst nun gar ist das stärkste Mittel zur Bewußtmachung und Verwirklichung des Ich' (IX, 266). To conclude: identity in *Felix Krull* is composed discursively, becoming an artistic project, a creative experiment. There is a fundamental interaction between art and life, between fiction and truth, between 'Dichtung' and 'Wahrheit'. To quote *The Tempest*: 'we are such stuff as dreams are made on'.

(v) Gender and Sexuality

Felix Krull's sexuality is an important part of his identity, as his references to 'die große Freude' (312, 547) make plain. Like his identity, his sexuality appears mercurial and difficult to define. While most of Krull's sexual encounters are heterosexual ones, the publication of Mann's diaries between 1977 and 1995 has given rise to a number of studies of Mann's work in terms of homosexual allusions, and I will need to take these into account. For example, Karl Werner Böhm interprets many of Mann's early fictions as allegories of homosexuality.[96] Böhm regards the stigmatized outsiders of these years (the sick man, the cripple, the artist, the decadent) as the means through which Mann expressed his own homosexuality.[97] Most recent biographies of Mann take a similar position, viewing Mann's potential homosexuality as one of the wellsprings of his creativity: one of them, Ronald Hayman, reads Mann's works as expressions of his desire in sublimated, often coded form.[98] Böhm claims that in a number of early short stories Mann used a feminine persona in order to convey desire.[99] Between 1900 and 1903 — the period of his infatuation with Paul Ehrenberg — Mann often employs the figure of the suffering woman as a type of feminine alter ego (Baronin Anna in 'Ein Glück', Gabriele Klöterjahn in 'Tristan', and Adelaide in the planned novel *Die Geliebten*). The feminine voice is also the topic of Mann's 1903 essay 'Das Ewig-Weibliche', which features an enthusiastic discussion of *Die Hochzeit der Esther Franzenius* by the lesbian novelist Toni Schwabe.[100] This interest in femininity was, however, relatively short-lived. After the break with Paul Ehrenberg at the end of 1903, and Mann's marriage to Katia Pringsheim in 1905, Mann seems to lose interest in 'woman' as an alter ego. The role of martyr now falls back to male characters. Schiller in 'Schwere Stunde', Savonarola in *Fiorenza* and Klaus Heinrich in *Königliche Hoheit* are — to a certain extent — ascetic, hermit-like figures who have renounced worldly pleasures. Eroticism seems to have been banished from these works; it is alluded to obliquely, if at all. The effect is of a sexual stalemate.

Viewed from this perspective, *Felix Krull* appears to be something of a breakthrough. With this novel, it seems that Mann has had enough of martyrdom. For the first time in his work, we find an explicit celebration of sensuality. The novel has a directness that, in 1910, was quite new. As Böhm points out, when one compares the novel to the works of the fifteen previous years, one could almost speak of a dam bursting, an explosive increase of 'das Anstößige'.[101] *Felix Krull* is centrally about sex: it is a consciously bisexual novel, marked with sexual ambivalence. The ambivalence is there on the very first page: while we hear of his father's amorous interest in the French au pair, the 'Fräulein aus Vevey', Felix Krull himself is closer to his godfather, the painter Schimmelpreester, 'mit dem ich auf sehr innigem Fuße stand' (265). This relationship, apparently innocent, is not without its sexual undertones. As a teenager, between the ages of sixteen and eighteen, Felix Krull often stands naked as model for Schimmelpreester to paint (284). Years earlier, Schimmelpreester was forced to leave his native Cologne because of some scandal, never subsequently explained (283) — another hint. Meanwhile, we hear of the licentious goings-on at the wild parties held at the family villa. The parties last all night and usually culminate in the lights being turned out: 'was jedesmal ein unbeschreibliches Drunter und Drüber zur Folge hatte' (279). The next principal episode, the encounter with Müller-Rosé, also has a cluster of homosexual motifs. As Gerhard Härle points out, the description of Müller-Rosé's stage persona assigns him typical feminine characteristics: his face is 'zart rosafarben', his eyes are almond-shaped, his nose is short, and his mouth is coral-red (288).[102] To this gender ambivalence, one can add the contrast between Müller-Rosé's stage persona and his ugliness backstage. The episode is highly reminiscent of Wilde's *The Picture of Dorian Gray*, which Mann had read some years before.[103] Härle reads Müller-Rosé as an image of Felix Krull's own possible future, as a kind of Aschenbach.[104] A similar doubling does indeed occur in *Der Tod in Venedig*, when the old fop on the boat anticipates what Aschenbach is to become.

In the Genovefa episode, Felix Krull reflects upon his precocious sexuality. Even while sucking at his nurse's breast, he is said to have shown signs of arousal (312). And long before anyone told him about sex, he had developed his own name for sexuality; he calls it simply 'Das Beste' or 'Die große Freude' (312). Significantly, he knows there is something special, something different about him, that he will have to conceal: '[ich hielt] die lebhafte Neigung zu gewissen Vorstellungen [. . .] für eine ganz persönliche und anderen gar nicht verständliche Eigentümlichkeit, über die ihrer Sonderbarkeit halber lieber nicht zu sprechen sei' (312). The narrator even says he must guard his sexuality as a precious secret ('ein köstliches Geheimnis' (312)). Reading these lines, one might think of homosexual desire. In fact, though, Felix Krull's first sexual encounter is typically heterosexual. At the age of sixteen he sleeps with a woman nearly twice his age, the maid Genovefa. The pleasure he experiences with Genovefa seems to be a genuine instance of 'Die große Freude': he describes it as 'das markverzehrende, wahrhaft unerhörte Vergnügen' (314). There is an altruistic dimension to this relationship, since Krull enjoys giving pleasure: 'meine Lust [. . .] entzündete sich [. . .] so recht erst an dem Ergötzen, das Genovefa über die genaue Bekanntschaft mit mir an den Tag legte' (314). As J. P. Stern has said, the erotic here is the pattern of Felix Krull's attitude to the world at large: 'he gives pleasure by taking it, the giving and the taking are inseparable'.[105] When it comes to the problem of trying to define Krull's sexuality, however, one is faced with serious interpretational difficulties. Firstly, the narrative itself is contradictory. Krull claims that his attitude has always been serious and manly (315);[106] a few lines later, he explains that he has always remained a child and a dreamer (315).[107] Secondly, the narrator's own definition stresses lack of specificity. This is a sexuality that appears to elude categorization, one which branches out into polymorphous perversity: 'Das meine ging stets ins Große, Ganze und Weite, es fand feine, würzige Sättigung, wo andere sie nicht suchen würden, es war von jeher wenig spezialisiert oder genau bestimmt' (315). Felix Krull, it seems, is such a sensual person that there is an element of Eros in all his relations with the world. This attitude may be indistinct, but it does not exclude a moral dimension. In the latter portion of the novel, 'Die große Freude' turns out to be a synonym for the concept of 'Allsympathie' (548). In other words, eroticism implies sympathy, implies charity. This argument does not represent a radically new departure, however. It is already implicit in the beginning of the novel, in Felix Krull's decision to love the world, to view all people and things as 'voll und wichtig', an attitude which gives rise to 'Ernst' and 'Leidenschaft' (275). Felix Krull's morally conscious attitude is thus qualitatively different from the infantile polymorphous perversity described by Freud: at times, it seems more of a metaphysical credo than a sexuality. Nevertheless, there is an erotic charge to him, a sensuality about everything he does, as the following work note from 1910 shows: 'Lust, etwas zu oeffnen, ein Paket, einen Brief, hat er immer sehr stark empfunden. Neugierde und Vergnügen beim Öffnen eines gestohlenen Koffers, einer Brieftasche etc. Die erotische Vermischung steht immer dahinter'.[108] Despite this underlying sensuality, however, Felix Krull's sexual attitudes are not as indeterminate as he would like us to believe. This is made quite clear in the Frankfurt section. If Felix Krull is interested in the fine objects on display, this is because of their relatedness to humanity. He is no fetishist, making it quite clear that he prefers people to objects: 'wieviel tiefer doch ins Gefühl greift das Erschauen, das Mit-den-Augen-Verschlingen des Menschlichen' (344). He views the beautiful pair on the balcony as the culmination of his desire (345). This mysterious pair, brother and sister, represent unity in division, androgyny and sexual ambivalence. As Hans-Heinrich Reuter has shown, it is very likely that Mann took the image from one of Theodor Fontane's letters. In a letter of 2 March 1895, Fontane describes an 'englisches Geschwisterpaar', a brother and sister whom he saw on the balcony of a hotel in Thale. The letter was printed in 1909 in a collection of Fontane's letters which, one year later, provided the stimulus for Mann's essay 'Der alte Fontane' (1910).[109] While the scene provided Fontane with the image of Effi Briest, in *Felix Krull* the pair of siblings becomes a structuring principle, one that determines Krull's later attraction to Frau Kuckuck and her daughter.[110] In the early *Felix Krull*, the pair of siblings form a binary image of desire, an image that suggests both heterosexual and homosexual love.[111] Helmut Koopman believes that these double images tend to cancel out the notion of identity,[112] but in my view the purpose of the siblings is to show that sexuality, like identity, is never completely homogeneous. Felix Krull's own tastes appear to be highly ambivalent. He might attract a wide variety of women (Genovefa, Rozsa, Diane Houpflé, Miss Twentyman, Zouzou, Maria Pia), but he also has flirtations

with a long series of men: Schimmelpreester, Geistlicher Rat Chateau, the jeweller Jean-Pierre, Lord Kilmarnock, the Marquis de Venosta (whose name suggests Venus, the goddess of love), Ribeiro. And Mann's work notes are even more explicit. This is especially true of the later work notes, but even the early notes mention the handsome young Argentinian, Panchito Meyer-Novaro, with whom Felix Krull is later to have some sort of affair ('den hübschen Panchito').[113] Indeed, even at this early stage, Mann planned for Felix Krull to fall in love with both Argentinian siblings simultaneously, a double romance prefigured by the pair of siblings in Frankfurt: '*Er liebt Bruder und Schwester fast gleichmäßig*, nur weil [die] [das] [h]Hetero-Erotische aussichtsreicher ist, tritt es mehr hervor. Ebenso ist der Bruder beinahe ebenso in ihn vernarrt wie sie'.[114] This passage marks Felix Krull as consciously bisexual. If, in practice, he tends to favour heterosexual relations, this is not because of an innate preference, but because social convention makes hetero-sexuality simply more viable. In this respect, one may conjecture that Krull's description of his sexuality as indeterminate (315) might be to some extent a cover for his own bisexual inclinations.[115] It is certainly possible to read other incidents in the first part of the novel as allusions to homosexuality. Schimmelpreester's reference to 'Seitenpfaden' (333) might well be a coded reference to homosexuality.[116] As for the *Musterungsszene*, on closer examination, a wealth of meaning appears. Gerhard Härle has produced a fascinating reading of homosexual undertones in this scene. Härle points out that, in 1900, Thomas Mann had himself seen a man exempted from military service for being homosexual, and that Mann later offered this anecdote to Heinrich Mann to use in his novel *Der Untertan*.[117] While Felix Krull chooses a different means to escape conscription, his simulation of epilepsy has a highly sexualized aspect. It is presented as a demonic vision of Dionysian excess: 'so, wie keine menschliche Leidenschaft, sondern nur teuflischer Einfluß und Antrieb ein Menschenantlitz verzerren kann. [. . .] Anbeginn eines wahren Hexensabbats von Fratzenschneiderei [. . .] irrer Wollust' (366). Despite the fact that Krull's epilepsy is a pretence, there is an authenticity about it which borders on the supernatural. After all, we have already been told that every successful deception is based on a truth that has not yet come into being (298). And the narrator even suggests that there is something true about this performance: 'Ist es aber nicht so, daß Affekte, wovon wir die Miene annehmen, sich ahnungsweise und schattenhaft wahrhaftig in unserer Seele herstellen?' (367). In other words, the intensity of the 'performance' seems to suggest the eruption of a repressed, forbidden sexuality. As Härle points out, Felix Krull even describes his condition to the military doctor as a highly personal, even shameful secret.[118] Asked why he has never mentioned this condition to anyone else, he replies:

> 'Weil ich mich schämte [. . .] und es niemandem sagen mochte; denn mir war, als müsse es ein Geheimnis bleiben. Und dann hoffte ich auch im stillen, daß es sich mit der Zeit verlieren werde. Und nie hätte ich gedacht, daß ich zu jemandem so viel Vertrauen fassen könnte, um ihn einzubekennen, wie sehr sonderbar es mir oftmals ergeht'. (364)

And the doctor later claims that this secrecy ('Verschwiegenheit') is typical of this kind of suffering ('Leiden[s]' (369)). Is it possible, then, to read the 'epilepsy' as the

deliberate simulation of a hidden truth, as a metaphorical coming-out of the closet? Härle is careful to say that such a reading would be too simplistic and one-sided. Nevertheless, Felix Krull's excessive spasms do suggest the return of the repressed: the eruption of a highly charged, forbidden sexual desire.[119] Epilepsy is also linked to sexuality in *Der Zauberberg*. In 'Totentanz', the teacher Popów has an epileptic fit at the dinner table (he sits with the Russians). This incident creates mass panic: some diners have seizures, other flee (III, 417). The panic is partly due to the fact that Dr Krokowski has recently claimed that epilepsy is caused by sexual desire, calling it an 'Orgasmus des Gehirns' (III, 418). This causes people to regard Popów's fit as a 'wüste Offenbarung und mysteriösen Skandal' (III, 418). One might read this scene in *Der Zauberberg* as an ironic comment on the earlier *Musterungsszene*. Such an interpretation, if valid, would lend a new meaning to Zouzou's statement: 'Schweigen [ist] nicht gesund' (586).

The latter portion of the novel appears even more suggestive. In the St James and Albany, the washroom is full of naked youths (403), Stanko addresses Krull as 'beauté' (404), and Hector, the Commis de salle, gives him a present of half a packet of cigarettes (405). As for the hotel director, Stürzli, he is so enraptured by Krull's smile that he barely listens to what he is saying: 'Es war schade um diese Artigkeit, denn er hörte gar nicht darauf, sondern sah nur mein Lächeln an' (413). Much more significant still are Lord Kilmarnock and Diane Houpflé. Erika Mann was well aware of the homosexual implications of the Houpflé scene. After a reading of the episode in 1951, Thomas Mann remarks in his diary: 'Erika auf der Heimfahrt über das Erz-Päderastische ("Schwule") der Szene. Soit' (Tb, 31 December 1951). According to this reading, Diane Houpflé would be an autobiographical figure, the literary equivalent of cross-dressing. She bears comparison to other suffering female characters in Mann, including Baronin Anna and Mut-em-enet. Her ecstatic outpourings, however ('Der Geist ist wonnegierig nach dem Nicht-Geistigen, dem Lebendig-Schönen' (443)) seem to caricature the yearning hymns of Gustav von Aschenbach and Tonio Kröger, as Wysling points out.[120] In any case, in terms of gender relations, Houpflé is determined to assume a masculine, dominant posture with respect to Felix Krull. She designates a feminine role for him, calling him 'Mignon in Livree' — a pointedly Goethean reference. My analysis of this scene would be incomplete if I failed to mention Mann's diary entries from the summer of 1950 dealing with his infatuation with Franz Westermeier. Westermeier, nineteen years old at the time, worked as a waiter at the Grand Hotel Dolder in Zurich where Mann was staying. Mann was also attracted to another young man he saw on the tennis courts. One critic in particular, Jens Rieckmann, has used the evidence of the diaries to argue for an autobiographical reading of the Diane Houpflé and Lord Kilmarnock episodes. Rieckmann argues that Mann's own ambivalent feelings about Westermeier are reflected in the two contrasting characters of Houpflé and Kilmarnock.[121] Mann himself was uncertain whether his feelings for Westermeier stemmed from 'eine Zuneigung aus Herzensgrund', from a sensual excitation (Tb, 15 August 1950), or whether it was a question of 'sinnlich–übersinnliche Liebes-krankheit' (Tb, 20 July 1950). While Diane Houpflé is physically direct, revelling in her peculiarity, Lord Kilmarnock's feelings for Krull are nobler, almost Platonic. Kilmarnock is used to renunciation, and bears his suffering with a quiet dignity:

'Sein Wesen war von der melancholisch umflorten Freundlichkeit eines Mannes, der viel gelitten hat' (480). The manuscript shows that Mann intended Felix Krull to have yet another admirer, Mr Twentyman. This scene was perhaps the most blatant yet, but Mann acted according to the advice of his daughter Erika and removed it.[122] What is the origin of this new, more explicit treatment of sexuality? In part, perhaps, from Mann's reading of Gore Vidal's homosexual novel *The City and the Pillar* (1948). Vidal had based his hero, Jim Willard, on Hans Castorp, and had sent a copy of the novel to Mann in 1948.[123] Reading the novel in November 1950, Mann found it an 'interessantes, ja wichtiges menschliches Dokument, von ausgezeichneter und belehrender Wahrhaftigkeit' (Tb, 24 November 1950). It is certainly possible to speak of a sort of kinship between Felix Krull and Jim Willard. Both are aged nineteen, both are physically graceful and adept (as tennis players, for example), both travel the world, and both have older women try to seduce them.[124] Mann was greatly disappointed by the end of Vidal's novel, which he considered tasteless (Tb 29 November 1950). Nevertheless, he used the name of one of the central characters, Bob, in *Felix Krull*. In Mann's novel, Bob is the young anarchist who works in the St James and Albany (396–97, 402, 434).

In this latter section of *Felix Krull*, it often seems as if Mann is deliberately pushing himself to see how far he can go. He writes something extremely bold, and then he goes back and revises it, moderates it. An important case in point is Felix Krull's encounters with rich pederasts on the streets of Frankfurt. The original version of the scene is much longer. According to the manuscript, Felix Krull occasionally responds to the sexual advances of his male admirers: 'Auch leugne ich nicht, daß ich mit der Zeit als meine Liebeserziehung vollendet war, dieser Gefühlssphäre ein gelegentliches leichtes Entgegenkommen erwiesen und mich auch in ihr angenehm zu machen gewußt habe'.[125] The printed version of the scene is much shorter, and the narrator contents himself with a generalization and a classical allusion: 'Ich verschmähe es, die Moral gegen ein Verlangen ins Feld zu führen, das mir in meinem Fall nicht unverständlich erschien. Vielmehr darf ich mit jenem Lateiner sagen, daß ich nichts Menschliches mir fremd erachte' (374).[126] Nevertheless, the final version is still quite radical. As it stands, Felix Krull explains that while rich women ignored him because of his poverty, this did not put off several gentlemen from making advances to him, drawn by his androgynous appearance:

> Die Frau bemerkt nur den 'Herrn' — und ich war keiner. Ganz anders nun aber verhält es sich mit gewissen abseits wandelnden Herren, Schwärmern, welche nicht die Frau suchen, aber auch nicht den Mann, sondern etwas Wunderbares dazwischen. Und das Wunderbare war ich. (374)

Here, the narrator describes himself as being both masculine and feminine, or rather as something in between. So with Felix Krull we have a character who seems to refuse the simple 'either–or' of gender definition.[127] He is to a certain extent a composite of both masculine and feminine characteristics, as in the *Musterungsszene*, where he talks of: 'eine Art Zärtlichkeit also gegen mich selbst, die meinem Charakter von jeher anhaftete und ganz leicht zur Weichlichkeit und Feigheit hätte entarten können, wenn nicht männlichere Eigenschaften ihr berichtigend die Waage gehalten hätten' (352).

How does this relate to contemporary gender theory? *Felix Krull*, like much recent gender theory, owes a great deal to the work of Nietzsche. Nietzsche, in *Zur Genealogie der Moral*, describes the self as a historical construction.[128] Judith Butler draws on Nietzsche in her book *Gender Trouble* (1990) in order to argue that identity and gender are constructed by power relations and social discourse.[129] For Butler, gender is something we perform, but we do not perform it freely. This is because the matrix of gender relations precedes the coming into being of the human subject. We cannot simply choose which gender to perform, as if we were putting on a new suit for the day, because we as agents are already constructed by our performance of gender, a performance which has lasted our entire lives and which has created and formed our own subjectivity. Performativity is more an act of discourse than it is the conscious act of a subject. Thus every person's subjectivity is always already gendered; every identity is formed by what Butler calls a 'sedimentation of gender norms'.[130] Butler's analysis dwells on the coercion and power play which is involved in the construction of identity. This is not something we find in Thomas Mann's novel, since Felix Krull seems relatively free to assume different roles. And yet his sexuality does resist categorization, for he is neither simply straight nor gay. Thus his existence does manage to disrupt, or at least to call into question, the binary model of sexuality which modern gender theory opposes. *Felix Krull* goes a long way towards what Butler calls 'the parodic proliferation and subversive play of gendered meanings'.[131] In the later sections of the novel, for example, the continuing emphasis on the 'Doppelbild' helps to blur identity. The true significance of a person is seen increasingly as resulting from their role as part of a dyad; or, as in the bullfight scene, part of a triad: first the bullfighter Ribeiro merges with the bull, and then Maria Pia somehow merges with both of them, forming a kind of pagan trinity (392). Similarly, although Felix claims he is attracted to Zouzou and her mother because of his interest in 'Doppelbilder', the importance of Professor Kuckuck as a father-figure is clearly also part of the equation. Much has been made of the mythical connotations of these final scenes.[132] It is worth bearing in mind, however, that the cosmic apotheosis of the final scene — Felix Krull's union with Maria Pia — borrows its elements from the standard repertoire of farce. *Felix Krull* is at times highly theoretical; at other times it is the most glorious high camp, a true *comédie humaine*.

(vi) Identity in Context

Felix Krull, especially in its opening sections, is a novel about the development of the creative self. It remains faithful to the genre of autobiography, carefully tracing the early impressions and incidents which determine selfhood. Indeed, it is remarkable how literary modernism's interest in autobiography as a genre complements the modern study of child development.[133] *Felix Krull* is a particularly valuable account of development because it combines both immediacy and reflection, clearly showing the relations between the self and its environment. As a character, Felix Krull is clearly special, gifted with a mimetic ability far above the norm. On the other hand, many aspects of his childhood are instantly recognizable: the dislike of

school, the daydreaming, the love of pranks and practical jokes are typical features of most childhoods. To put it another way: despite his uniqueness, Felix Krull has a representative function. As a general type, he reveals how identity is formed. The family home may be the scene of wild parties, and his father's business may be fraudulent, but it is nonetheless clear that, as a child, Krull is well loved and well cared-for. He carries no visible trauma into his adult life; his greatest fault appears to be his excessive vanity, the result of being spoiled and pampered as a child. In many ways he is antithetical to the figure of the damaged and isolated child. Having been raised in the bosom of the family, he is the opposite of Caspar Hauser, that enigmatic and traumatized figure who haunts German modernism.[134] Caspar Hauser is an interesting test case: the victim of an experiment to determine whether a person could develop in total isolation from language and society. Caspar Hauser's damaged persona and his early death point towards a negative result: i.e. that a human self cannot develop properly in the absence of human contact. The self needs identification; it needs emotional attachment in order to grow. It has to be pieced together from an enormous array of behavioural standards and cultural values. This is what *Felix Krull* shows us: that building of the self takes place through a process of simulation and copying. Children seek attention and they often do this by imitating adults. What appears as idle play in childhood actually has an important socializing function, because it is through such play that a person internalizes and assimilates societal norms. I will now examine two instances in *Krull* where we can see this process at work. The first of these occurs when the character is still a very young child. As his nurse pushes him around in his pram, he entertains members of the household by pretending to be Kaiser Wilhelm I. He does this by extending his lower jaw so that his upper lip becomes huge, and slowly blinking. Everybody is expected to participate in the make-believe, and the performance generates a good deal of mirth:

> Ich glaube mich wohl zu erinnern, und oft ist es mir erzählt worden, daß ich, als ich noch Kleidchen trug, gerne spielte, daß ich der Kaiser sei, und auf dieser Annahme wohl stundenlang mit großer Zähigkeit bestand. In einem kleinen Stuhlwagen sitzend, worin meine Magd mich über die Gartenwege oder auf dem Hausflur umherschob, zog ich aus irgendeinem Grunde meinen Mund so weit wie möglich nach unten, so daß meine Oberlippe sich übermäßig verlängerte, und blinzelte langsam mit den Augen, die sich nicht nur infolge der Verzerrung, sondern auch vermöge meiner inneren Rührung röteten und mit Tränen füllten. Still und ergriffen von meiner Betagtheit und hohen Würde, saß ich im Wägelchen; aber meine Magd war gehalten, jeden Begegnenden von dem Tatbestande zu unterrichten, daß eine Nichtachtung meiner Schrulle mich aufs äußerste erbittert haben würde. 'Ich fahre hier den Kaiser spazieren', meldete sie, indem sie auf unbelehrte Weise die flache Hand salutierend an die Schläfe legte, und jeder erwies mir Reverenz. (271–72)

The first thing to notice about this event is the way in which it is introduced ('oft ist es mir erzählt worden'). In other words, we need not rely solely upon the memory of the narrator, which might be at fault. Instead, the tale is guaranteed through repetition by other members of the household: as an anecdote it has been told, and retold, so many times that it has become legend, part of the family's own mythology. Interestingly, the narrator himself appears not to know what caused him to put on this act: he calls it a quirk ('Schrulle'), and is unable to explain his motivation ('aus irgendeinem Grunde'). While the act appears involuntary to the narrator, his dedication to it shows the importance of the ritual. Significant, too, is the tenacity ('Zähigkeit') with which the young Felix insists upon the illusion. This is not simply a game: it is a matter of proudly asserting his own place as being the centre of attention. The imperious ego proclaims itself as sovereign, and demands to be recognized as such. At the same time, however, the performance restates the social contract: Felix invests great physical effort in his performance, and is deeply moved. In return for his efforts, he demands audience participation. He is only too happy to entertain, provided that he is recognized as a central figure within the household economy. And so this assertion of individuality takes place in a socially conditioned way, via the impersonation of a pillar of society. The toddler aspires to the dignity of an adult, and not just any adult, but the most venerable one: the father of the nation, the Emperor (and one is reminded of the common remark that babies look like Winston Churchill). This is the attitude of the child who has reduced the surrounding adults to willing drones devoted to his care, like servants in a royal household. And yet he himself is deeply affected by his own performance: 'ergriffen von meiner Betagtheit und hohen Würde', he almost seems to have internalized this role that he has adopted. Meanwhile, watching his partners in the game, he learns the rules of comportment, how to relate to authority. In this way, this supposedly innocent game introduces the individual into a historicity: the Prussian authoritarianism and paternalism of the 'Gründerjahre'. It thus becomes apparent that this playful episode in *Felix Krull*, the impersonation of the Kaiser, works on a number of levels. At first glance it is a snapshot of family life, one moment of a happy childhood. On another level, it is mild social satire. On yet another level it is a miniature study in developmental psychology: an exploration of how childhood play is essential to the coming-into-being of the self.

The following chapter contains a scene in which the young Felix Krull visits a spa town with his family, the evocatively named Langenschwalbach. There, he finds a small orchestra playing daily concerts on the promenade. By studying the musicians, he learns how to mime playing the violin, a skill which he uses to great effect. His father persuades the conductor of the orchestra to let Felix mime along to the music. Equipped with a tiny violin, the bow covered with vaseline, Felix cannot fail to please. The 'Komödie' (281) is a great success, and the crowd goes wild.[135] This episode, like the previous one, is multi-layered. On the surface, it is simply a practical joke, a harmless piece of entertainment. At the same time, the episode is rich in psychological insights. Once again, it demonstrates the centrality of mimesis to the development of the subject. As in the previous scene, the young Felix engages with the world by seeking to imitate it. Here, too, he is unsure of what motivates him. All he knows is that the music powerfully attracts him ('Anziehungskraft' (280)), charms and bewitches him. However, it is not simply the music alone which attracts him, but the whole paraphernalia which goes along with it: the smart uniforms of the musicians ('die kleidsam uniformierte Truppe' (280)), the pretty bandstand in the form of a pavilion, which even seems to resemble a Greek temple ('zierliche[s] Kunsttempel' (280)). Context and visual impact are thus intrinsic elements of the musical performance. The narrator's heart may be enchanted by the music, but he is careful to follow every detail of the musicians' movements with his eyes: '[ich] verfolgte zugleich mit eifrig teilnehmenden Augen die Bewegungen, mit denen die ausübenden Musiker ihre verschiedenen Instrumente handhabten' (280). By isolating the visual dimension of the performance, Felix Krull is soon able to reproduce convincingly the gestures of the first violinist, to the great delight of his nearest and dearest:

> Namentlich das Geigenspiel hatte es mir angetan, und zu Hause, im Hotel, ergötzte ich mich und die Meinen damit, daß ich mit Hilfe zweier Stöcke, eines kurzen und eines längeren, das Gebaren des ersten Violinisten aufs getreueste nachzuahmen suchte. Die schwingende Bewegung der linken Hand zur Erzeugung eines seelenvollen Tones, das weiche Hinauf- und Hinabgleiten aus einer Grifflage in die andere, die Fingerläufigkeit bei virtuosenhaften Passagen und Kadenzen, das schlanke und geschmeidige Durchbiegen des rechten Handgelenkes bei der Bogenführung, die versunkene und lauschend-gestaltende Miene bei hingeschmiegter Wange — dies alles wiederzugeben gelang mir mit einer Vollkommenheit, die besonders meinem Vater den heitersten Beifall abnötigte. (280–81)

This performance is incongruous in two ways. Firstly, the purely visual display appears amusing because it lacks the musical stimulus that usually accompanies it. Secondly, while showmanship and serious demeanour are usual qualities in an adult musician, such qualities appear incongruous when displayed by a child. The young Felix brings a level of dedication and commitment to the performance which raises it above mere caricature. He seeks to imitate the violinist as truthfully as possible ('aufs getreueste nachzuahmen'), reproducing facial expression as well as hand and wrist movements. What occurs is a type of method-acting, an investment of emotion in which the performer strives towards a maximum degree of faithfulness.

The opportunistic Engelbert Krull decides that his son's mimetic achievement is worthy of being put on display, and he arranges a public performance, accompanied by the rest of the orchestra. Vaseline on the bow ensures fluidity of movement, and the audience goes into raptures:

> Eine kleine Violine wird billig erstanden und der zugehörige Bogen sorgfältig mit Vaselin bestrichen. [. . .] Und eines Sonntagnachmittags, während der Kurpromenade, stehe ich [. . .] zur Seite des kleinen Kapellmeisters an der Rampe des Musiktempels und beteilige mich an der Ausführung einer ungarischen Tanzpièce, indem ich mit meiner Fiedel und mit meinem Vaselinbogen tue, was ich vordem mit meinem beiden Stöcken getan. Ich darf sagen, daß mein Erfolg vollkommen war. (281)

If the performance is a runaway success, this is due to a number of factors. First of all, the visual dimension is complete: Felix has been equipped with a violin, and given a fine costume to wear. His position at the side of the conductor is a powerful indication to the audience that he is the star of the show, the centre of attention. The framing pavilion indicates that this is an aesthetic space, worthy of respect. The fact that he is eight years old adds sentimentality to the equation: such seriousness appears poignant in one so young. Essentially, this is a child acting like an adult.

But in fact this happens all the time: this is how children grow up. Finally, there is the audience itself to consider. The narrator dwells at some length on the audience reaction. The keynote here is not pleasure in deception, however, but the narrator's joy at being accepted into high society. What really makes his day is being invited by the sons of Graf Siebenklingen to play a game of croquet. Looking back on the incident, the narrator reflects that this was one of the best days of his life: 'Es war einer der schönsten Tage meines Lebens, vielleicht der unbedingt schönste' (282). The statement may be triumphant, but this is triumph at having found willing partners, not triumph at having fooled people. Overall, what emerges from the description is a vision of the audience, not as gullible pawns, but rather as willing participants in the festival atmosphere, contributors to the sense of occasion. Mann had depicted a similar phenomenon in the short story 'Das Wunderkind', which he alludes to here: 'Man sah ein Wunderkind'. (281).[136] This episode in *Krull*, like 'Das Wunderkind', focuses upon the audience's reaction. Once more, the public is very much involved in what is going on. Indeed, the cheers of the audience constitute a reciprocal performance, an answering musical chorus: 'Als ich mit einem vollen und energischen Bogenstrich über alle Saiten geendigt hatte, erfüllte das Geprassel des Beifalls, untermischt mit hohen und tiefen Bravorufen, die Kuranlagen' (281). Does the crowd really believe in the phenomenon, or is it just playing along? Perhaps the audience's display of good will towards Krull is part of a group affirmation: an expression of their good will towards themselves as a community. If we accept this reading, then art becomes a locus for the statement of a group identity. I will examine the connections between art and society in the next chapter. What I want to stress here is that these early episodes in *Krull* show that art is central to the formation of the subject, deeply implicated in the development of the self. The young Felix Krull's attempts to relate to the world of adults continually involve mimesis. When he imitates the Kaiser, or when he imitates a virtuoso musician, what is happening is not so much the imposition of a wilful temperament upon a gullible world but a collusion whereby adults allow children to act in a grown-up way, to copy adult gestures. If this is entertaining, this is not because of deception, but because such play tends to affirm and restate interpersonal relationships. It grounds the subject in a social and historical world; it functions as a process of initiation. Through mimesis, the subject learns to relate to the adult world.

Identity cannot exist independently of a social context. Modern philosophy, from Nietzsche onwards, regards identity as an ongoing process based upon interaction with cultural symbols. In the previous section, I mentioned Judith Butler's performative theory of identity. Butler thinks of identity as 'citational': in her view, acts of self-assertion by an individual tend to 'cite' the norms that constitute the social group or community to which that person belongs.[137] According to Butler, identity is a corporate matter; something which is, to a large extent, foisted upon us by the community into which we are born.[138] Butler's work exposes the limits to individual autonomy, showing that identity arises through imitation of group norms. However, she recognizes the possibility of divergence as well. The episodes in *Krull* that I have just discussed seem to corroborate this theory. When Krull 'cites' the Kaiser, when he 'cites' the violinist (and when he later copies his father's signature), he is restating the conditions of his own emergence, quoting from the culture into which he has been born. The tone of Mann's narrative is, however, more conciliatory than Butler's theory. While Butler dwells upon the oppressive dimension of discourse, *Felix Krull* is more optimistic. Mann's novel is aware of the contingent nature of the self, but it also clearly indicates some room to manoeuvre. After all, identity may be built through imitation, but every identity involves degrees of departure. Identity may be given through social context, but each individual puts his or her own inflection onto it. The manner in which a given identity is acted out or enunciated contributes to the meaning of the 'performativity'. This is where Felix Krull excels: he accepts the cards which life has dealt him, but he can play them in a number of different ways. If there is an element of wish-fulfillment in his character, this is because he knows how to inflect his identity better than most people. Even so, he is not radically different from others; it is more a matter of degree. Experimenting with identity is part of growing up. Every life is a matter of inflection within a domain of social norms; it is a question of finding, or carving out, a niche for oneself within a realm of given circumstances. Krull's confessions are valuable because they remind us of how we grow up. This does not mean, however, that we should understand Krull as the representative of a free-floating, endlessly malleable identity. I agree with Ignace Feuerlicht when he asserts that Krull's transformations take place within an intellectual superstructure that ensures a degree of stability.[139] And, finally, even Krull knows that where he comes from is a vital part of his identity, one which exerts a persistent fascination. Early on in Book II he shifts into the third-person present tense in order to pay tribute to his home town. He may have been glad to leave, but his *Heimat* continues to shape his experience of the world:

> Wie leicht [. . .] läßt der ins Weite stürmende Jüngling die kleine Heimat in seinem Rücken [. . .] doch bleibt ihr lächerlich-übervertrautes Bild in den Hintergründen seines Bewußtseins stehen oder taucht nach Jahren tiefer Vergessenheit wunderlich wieder daraus hervor: Das Abgeschmackte wird ehrwürdig, der Mensch nimmt unter den Taten, Wirkungen, Erfolgen seines Lebens dort draußen geheime Rücksicht auf jene Kleinwelt, an jedem Wendepunkt, bei jeder Erhöhung seines Daseins fragt er im stillen, was sie wohl dazu sagen werde oder würde. (335)

The home town provides a frame of reference which never completely disappears: thus, despite the element of wish-fulfilment evident in the novel, Felix Krull is aware that his powers have their limits. He cannot efface his origin, and he cannot escape his birthright as a 'Sonntagskind' (271). Krull's destiny is forever marked by the land of his birth: the Rhineland, with its sparkling wines and Lorelei myths. In spite of his many transformations, Krull remains a creature of his Rhineland home, a man who is built for happiness. In Theodor Fontane's novel *Der Stechlin*, Dubslav remarks that South Germans are more socially advanced because of their naturally happy disposition. In Dubslav's words, a happy nature is the best education: '[eine] glückliche Natur, das ist doch die wahre Bildung' (HF I.V, 206). This is a sentiment which underpins the whole of *Felix Krull*: education is good, but a happy nature is better.

In *Felix Krull*, art is shown to be intimately involved with the formation, cultivation, and expression of identity. The aesthetic element of identity development does not give *carte blanche* to every transformation. But it does help to free up identity. Felix Krull, highly self-conscious, knows that his identity is not something monolithic, but something conditional, experimental, and potentially variable.

(vii) Two Models of Identity: *Faustus* and *Krull*

Felix Krull offers an important model of identity, but it is not the only one. In this section I will argue that Mann's work as a whole presents the reader with two contrasting versions of identity. These two versions of identity correspond to two distinct registers in Mann's work: one rigorous and pessimistic, the other optimistic and conciliatory. Much of the drama in Mann's novels arises from the antagonism between these two registers. On the level of identity, this tension reveals itself in the form of two opposing tendencies: firstly, the tendency towards strict delimitation and conflict; secondly, the tendency towards open-endedness and harmony. One type of identity is based on antipathy, the other on sympathy.

To illustrate what I mean, let us consider the novel which, although temporally close to the last phase of the work on *Felix Krull*, seems most totally opposed to the *Krull* project. I mean, of course, *Doktor Faustus*.[140] In *Doktor Faustus*, Mann takes stock of Germany in the first half of the twentieth century, exploring the cultural crisis which helped to prepare the moral climate for fascism. The novel is also deeply personal: this judgement upon German culture is simultaneously a judgement upon Mann himself, and upon the conservative romanticism which he had embraced during the First World War. In *Doktor Faustus*, the violent tragedy of German politics is embodied in the allegorical figure of the composer Adrian Leverkühn. Leverkühn's view of modern culture as a stalemate causes him to yearn for a new breakthrough in music. He decides that the only remedy is to go to extremes, both artistic and moral: self-destruction through syphilis is a price that he is only too willing to pay. On one level, then, *Doktor Faustus* is a novel about wilful violence to the self, about the divided self. Leverkühn's attempt to deny all human feeling leads to an almost pathological split within his consciousness between the most abstract intellect and the most coarse sensuality. Leverkühn's intellect delights in tormenting itself, and, in a protracted and painful manner, ultimately commits suicide.

What, one might ask, does this have to do with *Felix Krull*? At first glance, Adrian Leverkühn would seem to be the antithesis of Krull. The unbending, uncompromising, sternly self-disciplined Leverkühn appears to be the exact opposite of the compliant, opportunistic, and self-indulgent Krull.[141] While Leverkühn longs for self-sacrifice, Krull prefers easy evasion. And where Krull lives his entire life by illusions, Leverkühn finds fulfillment precisely in destroying them. For example, Leverkühn denounces the work of art as a fraud ('Das Werk! Es ist Trug'. (VI, 241)), claiming that art must turn against itself and purify itself, becoming knowledge: 'Schein und Spiel haben heute schon das Gewissen der Kunst gegen sich. Sie will aufhören, Schein und Spiel zu sein, sie will Erkenntnis werden' (VI, 242). In other words, Leverkühn completely rejects Krull's ludic, playful conception of art, opting instead for an art that strives towards the coldness of interstellar space and the hygienic brutality of a surgeon's scalpel.[142] This seems as far removed from *Felix Krull* as it is possible to be. But appearances can be deceptive. It is worth noting that the initial conceptions of both *Krull* and *Doktor Faustus* date from the same year: 1905.[143] As for Mann himself, he was convinced that there was a secret affinity between *Krull* and *Doktor Faustus*. In *Die Entstehung des Doktor Faustus* (1949), he relates that after the completion of *Joseph* he did not know whether to work on the *Faust* legend or whether, for the sake of completion, to return to *Felix Krull* (XI, 157–58). Then, whilst re-reading his notes for *Krull*, Mann realized with amazement that they shed light on his *Faust* dilemma:

> Ein Tag brachte trotz allem die Auflösung der Materialpakete zum 'Hochstapler', die Wiederlesung der Vorarbeiten — mit wunderlichem Ergebnis. Es war "Einsicht in die innere Verwandtschaft des Faust-Stoffes damit (beruhend auf dem *Einsamkeitsmotiv*, hier tragisch-mystisch, dort humoristisch-kriminell), doch scheint dieser, wenn gestaltungsfähig, der mir heute angemessenere, zeitnähere, dringendere . . ." Die Waage hatte ausgeschlagen. Dem *Joseph*-Theater sollte nicht 'erst noch' der Schelmenroman folgen. (XI, 159–60)

Thus, according to Mann, the thematic link between the two works is the motif of loneliness. Of course, if the root problem of both Leverkühn and Krull is the same — loneliness — then their solutions to it are radically different. Krull seeks to transcend the bounds of his own identity by immersing himself in society and through his technique of experimental identification, or sympathy. Leverkühn deliberately divests himself of human attachments, seeking transcendence on a mystic level: he seeks to articulate the voice of the cosmos itself through music. On this reading, Krull would be Leverkühn's profane counterpart. And yet Krull too is capable of metaphysical speculation, as the Müller-Rosé episode amply testifies. In fact, there are a number of thematic links between the two works. *Doktor Faustus* re-enacts two of *Felix Krull*'s central motifs — the butterfly and the affair with a prostitute — under an altogether more sinister aspect. In *Krull*, the image of the butterfly refers to the discrepancy between Müller-Rosé's onstage persona and his offstage self; it also evokes the libidinally charged relationship between artist and audience. In *Doktor Faustus*, the butterfly once more signifies the erotically charged trumpery of art, but this time with the added element of disease. The butterflies depicted in Jonathan Leverkühn's scientific tomes in Chapter III are pretty, but deadly: 'Insekten, die in phantastisch übertriebener Schönheit ein ephemeres Leben fristen, und von denen einige den Eingeborenen als böse Geister gelten, die die Malaria bringen' (VI, 23). The butterfly *Hetaera esmeralda* is nakedly transparent, but for the pink and violet beauty spot which stands out like a mark of original sin (VI, 23). Felix Krull's time in the Frankfurt brothel with Rozsa is just one episode among many, one stage in his sentimental education. In contrast, Adrian Leverkühn's visit to the brothel becomes his dominant obsession, the secret centre of his music and his career.

In my view, Adrian Leverkühn and Felix Krull represent two conflicting, but related, models of artistic identity.[144] One is uncompromisingly strenuous, and insists upon the fundamental opposition between *Geist* and *Leben*. The other attempts a reconciliation between *Geist* and *Leben*. One of the clues to Leverkühn's essence is the chair in which he works: a 'Savonarola-Sessel' (VI, 343). Leverkühn's all-or-nothing approach to art recalls Savonarola's firebrand approach to morality in Mann's earlier play *Fiorenza*. Leverkühn and Savonarola are natural extremists. Both are gifted with an artistic genius that turns against art, wishing to purify it. Leverkühn seeks absolute art, Savonarola seeks absolute truth. Both are heedless of the cost.[145] Leverkühn sacrifices his life, and the lives of those around him, to his work. In this respect, he resembles two of Ibsen's characters, Brand and Halvard Solness. Felix Krull, on the other hand, is much closer to Ibsen's Peer Gynt, since he regards art as a form of play, rather than an existential struggle. Krull does not shun work, but he refuses to yoke his entire life to the single-minded service of an artistic work. Leverkühn's work is his life; Krull's life is his work. The one instrumentalizes life, while the other celebrates it. Leverkühn's quest for intellectual purity means that his identity becomes constricting. Ultimately, he takes pleasure in tearing himself apart. Krull suffers from the reverse problem: his identity is almost too free, it lacks gravity. While diametrically opposed in this way, however, both characters seem to represent potentialities which Mann was aware of in himself. In other words, Leverkühn and Krull are two sides of the same coin: they are two related approaches to the loneliness of the artist-figure ('Einsamkeitsmotiv', (XI, 159–60)). Leverkühn shocks his friend Zeitblom when he tells him that he wishes to redeem music from the coldness of the intellect, by creating an art that could connect with the people:

> Ist es nicht komisch, daß die Musik [. . .] der Erlösung bedarf, nämlich aus einer feierlichen Isolierung [. . .] so daß also die Kunst bald völlig allein, zum Absterben allein sein wird, es sei denn, sie fände den Weg zum 'Volk', das heißt, um es unromantisch zu sagen: zu den Menschen? (VI, 428–29)

Leverkühn longs for the ease of a Krull, he yearns for an art which would be 'heiter' and 'zutraulich' (VI, 429) — an art that would be on intimate terms with humanity: 'eine Kunst mit der Menschheit auf du und du' (VI, 429). Like Krull, Leverkühn wants to connect with his audience. Of course, the scale of his ambition is far greater — he intends nothing less than a revolution in art. Krull, on the other hand, has more modest ambitions. More importantly, Krull has qualities that Leverkühn signally lacks: a productively unstable identity, and an abundance of sympathy.

Perhaps the profoundest difference between *Faustus* and *Krull* is the way in which they represent two distinct models of identity. Adrian Leverkühn suffers from a selfhood that is rigidly defined. Krull's selfhood, on the other hand, lacks any clear borders. Krull's identity is labile, elastic: 'meine elastische Natur' (473). My analysis here is based in part on Ignace Feuerlicht's study *Thomas Mann und die Grenzen des Ich*. Feuerlicht argues that in Mann's early work (and in *Doktor Faustus*, which draws upon the themes of the early work), the borders of the self are perceived as rigid, even insurmountable.[146] The words of 'Beim Propheten' (1904) — 'Hier herrscht . . . das verzweifelt thronende Ich [. . .] [ein] fieberhaftes und furchtbar gereiztes Ich' (VIII, 362, 368) — could just as well apply to Adrian Leverkühn. By the time we get to 1909 and 'Süßer Schlaf', Mann's view of identity is changing. Now he considers identity formation to be an act of self-delimitation, a deliberate setting of borders ('Begrenzung' (XI, 337)).[147] The implication is clear: if the boundaries of the self are maintained by an act of the will ('Begrenzung'), then it must be possible to release the self from those boundaries ('Entgrenzung'). This is what Felix Krull seems to represent: release from the constrictions of selfhood. There is a similar dichotomy in *Dichtung und Wahrheit*, as Feuerlicht points out. Goethe's terms are different: 'verselbsten' and 'entselbstigen' (HA IX, 353), but the underlying meaning is the same.[148] In this way, it is possible to regard Leverkühn and Krull as the representatives of two opposing tendencies: contraction and expansion, systole and diastole.[149]

In what way, precisely, does *Krull* represent a liberation of, perhaps even from, identity? The early *Krull* was significant for Mann because it allowed him to explore a character with a more flexible identity, a character with elements of both *Bürger* and *Künstler* within his make-up. Although Krull is an artist, he is no stranger to bourgeois society or to the bourgeois values of hard work and self-discipline. Even his libertinism is tempered by a strong moral sense (315),[150] and he even regards himself as a sort of *Leistungsethiker*: 'so daß alles, was mein Leben an tätiger Wirksamkeit aufweist, als Produkt der Selbstüberwindung, ja als eine sittliche Leistung von hohem Range zu würdigen ist' (299).[151] It soon became apparent to Mann, however, that this new synthetic approach to the *Bürger/Künstler* problematic opened up a number of possibilities which could no longer be accommodated within the structure of the *Hochstapler* novel. In July 1911, he interrupted *Krull* in order to write *Der Tod in Venedig*, a work which is in many ways starkly different from the one that preceded it. Despite the contrast between the two works, there are points of contact. Aschenbach, like Krull, conceals his emotions behind a mask of bourgeois respectability, and both of them strive towards classical effect ('ein gewolltes Gepräge der Meisterlichkeit und der Klassizität' (VIII, 455)). Mann had even considered turning Felix Krull into a man of substance. One of his notes presents Krull as a respectable scholar sporting a moustache:

> *Maske*, als er [. . .] ein bürgerlicher Doktor wird: Läßt sich den Schnurrbart länger wachsen, überfallend, ohne ihn aufzudrehen und trägt eine goldene Brille dazu. Zusammen mit der Eleganz seines Anzuges ergiebt das einen Eindruck von disti[n]guierten Gelehrtentums [sic].[152]

And then there is the obvious family resemblance between Aschenbach and Krull's godfather Schimmelpreester, not to mention the parallels between the Müller-Rosé episode and Aschenbach's own use of stage make-up. Despite the radical differences between the two works, I believe they both owe their creation to Mann's brave and unsparing concern for self-analysis. Ibsen's famous statement that art is a Judgement Day upon the self, which Mann refers to in his notes for 'Geist und Kunst', applies to both *Felix Krull* and *Der Tod in Venedig*, as well as to *Doktor Faustus*. As a strict moralist, Mann knew that authentic criticism did not shy away from self-analysis and confession: 'Kritik, die nicht auch Bekenntnis ist, ist wertlos. Die eigentliche tiefe und leidenschaftliche Kritik ist Dichtung im Sinne Ibsens: Gerichtstag über *sich-selbst*'.[153] *Felix Krull* too is a form of self-judgement, and it is even possible that Thomas Mann had Ibsen's *Peer Gynt* in mind whilst writing the early *Krull*.[154] Mann's moral insistence upon self-analysis means that we can read all of his works as fragments of a great spiritual autobiography. Within this autobiography there are different registers: tragedy *and* comedy, elegy *and* idyll. Corresponding to these registers are two models of selfhood. Aschenbach and Leverkühn are masters of the systole, of the insistent concentration of the self. Krull is a master of the diastole and the easy outpouring. I believe that the early *Felix Krull* is profound because the comic element — which had always been there in Mann's work — is, for perhaps the first time, allowed to become the dominant and conciliatory register. Krull excels at finding an accommodation with (and in) the world, and he amuses us because he is so obviously vain. Even so, he is the precursor of other great mediators, paving the way for Hans Castorp and Joseph. If Aschenbach and Leverkühn represent the stern contraction of the systole, then Krull, Castorp, and Joseph represent the welcoming release of the diastole.

Of course, within the individual novels we have both systole and diastole. In *Doktor Faustus*, for example, the figure of Leverkühn is offset by other, more conciliatory characters: the humanist narrator Serenus Zeitblom, and the impresario Saul Fitelberg. From Leverkühn's point of view, Zeitblom's humanism seems weak and ineffective, and Fitelberg's business acumen is only worthy of contempt. Both are presented in an ironic light (especially Fitelberg), but even so they provide an important counterweight to Leverkühn's strenuousness. In *Die Entstehung des Doktor Faustus*, Mann explains that the creation of Serenus Zeitblom was in part influenced by the thought of Felix Krull: 'Gewiß hatte die Erinnerung an die parodistische Autobiographie Felix Krulls dabei mitgewirkt, und überdies war die Maßnahme bitter notwendig, um eine gewisse Durchheiterung des Stoffes zu erzielen' (XI, 164). According to Ruprecht Wimmer, both Krull and Zeitblom are unreliable narrators because they function as autobiographical masks for Mann himself.[155] Wimmer regards Zeitblom's conversation with a Lutheran minister as a pendant to Krull's meeting with the Catholic priest, Geistlicher Rat Chateau.[156] Another affinity between Krull and Zeitblom is that their Christian names ('Felix', 'Serenus') both signify contentment.[157] They also have remarkably similar functions as narrators: each of their narrations can be read as a justification, as an elaborate plea for the defence. Krull pleads persuasively in his own defence, but Zeitblom is hardly less eloquent in his defence of Leverkühn. Like Krull, his sympathetic nature is one of his principal characteristics; only, in Zeitblom's case, most of his sympathy is reserved for Leverkühn. Zeitblom may appear at times ineffectual, but his presence is vital to the economy of the novel. Zeitblom, like Krull, begs the reader for his or her indulgence. Zeitblom wants indulgence for Leverkühn and for Germany; Krull wants indulgence for himself — and also for art. He is pleading not just for himself, but for art as well.

To conclude, then: art can bolster identity by grounding the individual in a network of significations. Art can shape the self, giving it an identity and providing it with a *raison d'être*. But if the system of significations becomes rigid, then what began as individual self-assertion can become a straitjacket that is dangerous to the self. In my view, it is highly fitting that after the reckoning of *Doktor Faustus*, Mann returned once more to a more conciliatory model of identity in *Felix Krull*. In *Faustus*, Mann registered the way in which his culture had fallen under the sway of anti-intellectual atavism. In the later *Krull*, he returns to a more humane and sociable intelligence, one which recognizes the charms of primitivism, but which rejects them. Professor Kuckuck may well be alluding to the fate of Leverkühn when he says: 'oft werde das Feinste müd' seiner selbst, vergaffe sich in das Urtümliche und sinke trunken ins Wilde zurück' (547). And Kuckuck adds pointedly: 'Davon nichts weiter' (547). It is not for him to dwell upon such things. Instead, he would rather reflect upon humanity's connection to the cosmos. *Felix Krull*, Mann's last fictional work, is, in spite of the catastrophe of German history, an affirmation: a last-ditch humanism against all the odds.

(viii) Continuity with Other Works: 'Sympathie'

One of the constants in Thomas Mann's work is his awareness of the complicity of fictional statements in the creation, articulation, and definition of the self. Mann shows us that art shapes identity, both for good and for ill. Mann's early short stories, culminating in *Tonio Kröger*, explore the highly developed self-consciousness of the artist and the pain of that insistent self-consciousness. By the time we get to *Königliche Hoheit* and the early *Felix Krull* in the years 1906–11, we find Mann in search of a broader concept of identity, one which might accommodate an engagement with life. Hans Wysling points out that in these works Mann is striving towards a new relationship with the world: '[es geht] um die Frage, wie der ironische abgeschnürte Geist aus der Isolation heraustreten könne, um ein freundlicheres Verhältnis zum Leben zu gewinnen'.[158] In other words, the keynote of the early *Felix Krull* is already an attempted reconciliation with life: an undertaking which required a new kind of irony. As Wysling puts it: '[Es galt], die kalt-zurückweisende Ironie des décadent durch eine vermittelnd-liebenswürdige abzulösen'.[159] The crucial word here is 'vermittelnd' ('mediating'). This quest for mediation between self and world is the fundamental characteristic of the Bildungsroman, and it is thus by no means a coincidence that *Königliche Hoheit* and *Felix Krull* mark new approaches towards the Bildungsroman in Mann's work.[160]

In order to understand precisely how *Felix Krull* achieves conciliation, we will have to examine the evolution of the concept of 'Sympathie' within Thomas Mann's thought. From 1915 onwards Mann comes to regard 'Sympathie' as a vital function of the human imagination. In *Der Zauberberg*, the term suggests a whole spectrum of attitudes, including both romantic and humanist outlooks ('Sympathie mit dem Tode', 'Sympathie mit dem Organischen'). In my view, the key function of 'Sympathie' is the way in which it effects a conciliation between self and world. The term is central to Mann's later work, and to the later *Krull*, but its origins go back much earlier. As Jochen Bertheau has shown, sympathy first appears in Mann's earliest short stories as a technique, a literary modus operandi. In Mann's early short stories, suffering is often portrayed in a highly objectified manner. Much as in the stories of Guy de Maupassant, this apparently cold and distant treatment of suffering is designed precisely in order to arouse the sympathy of the reader.[161] In Mann's early tales, however, conciliation between self and world still seems impossible. Things start to change by the time we get to *Tonio Kröger* in 1903. Tonio Kröger is painfully aware that his artistic nature somehow distances him from the common run of humanity. He fears that in order to remain true to his artistic calling, he has had to renounce human pleasures and become cold: 'Was aber war gewesen während all der Zeit, in der er das geworden, was er nun war? — Erstarrung; Öde; Eis; und Geist! Und Kunst!...'. (VIII, 336). At the end of the story, however, Kröger realizes that the one quality which might redeem him as an artist is love. If anything is capable of transforming him from a 'Literat' into a 'Dichter', it is his 'Bürgerliebe zum Menschlichen' (VIII, 338). Kröger feels that he must remain unfruitful as long as he lacks love, that love of which it is said 'daß Einer mit Menschen- und Engelszungen reden könnte und ohne sie doch nur ein tönendes Erz und eine klingende Schelle sei' (VIII, 338). In other words, *Tonio Kröger* ends with a programmatic gesture of conciliation between the intellectual self and the world of everyday life.

'Bilse und ich' (1906) is another important step towards 'Sympathie' because it introduces the concept of 'Beseelung' (X, 15), which implies a union between self and other: 'das innere Einswerden des Dichters mit seinem Modell' (X, 17). According to Mann, only the greatest of artists such as Goethe and Shakespeare are capable of such an expansive notion of selfhood, one which could include a multiplicity of roles. This is a vital insight, and one which was soon to bear fruit. The early *Krull* was the next important phase in Mann's attempt to break with solipsism and to develop a new understanding of the relations between self and world. Writing the early *Krull* was a means for him to experience a hypothetical conciliation between self and world in the form of a thought experiment. Felix Krull's principal blessing resides in the fact that he can experience harmony with the world. One of Mann's pre-war work notes for the novel reads thus: 'In einer Rolle geht eine mystische Vereinigung mit einem Stück Welt vor sich'.[162] The 'Beseelung' of 'Bilse und ich' and the early Krull's ability to experience a 'Vereinigung mit einem Stück Welt' are forerunners of the concept of 'Sympathie'.

The term 'Sympathie' does not occur in the early *Krull*.[163] Nevertheless, it is precisely during the first period of work on *Krull*, namely the period from 1910 to 1913, that Mann begins to adopt the term. In 1910, he interrupts the work on *Krull* in order to begin 'Der alte Fontane'. He does this in the hope that reading Fontane's letters will help him to capture the humorous style he needs for *Krull*.[164] Now, if Mann associates *Krull* with Fontane, then he associates Fontane with 'Sympathie'. 'Der alte Fontane', published in October 1910, makes this abundantly clear:

> Mir persönlich wenigstens sei das Bekenntnis erlaubt, daß kein Schriftsteller
> der Vergangenheit oder Gegenwart mir die Sympathie und Dankbarkeit, dies
> unmittelbare und instinktmäßige Entzücken, diese unmittelbare Erheiterung,
> Erwärmung, Befriedigung erweckt, die ich bei jedem Vers, jeder Briefzeile,
> jedem Dialogfetzchen von ihm empfinde. (IX, 23)

At this early stage, 'Sympathie' seems to represent the good humour which Mann finds in Fontane, and which he hopes to achieve in *Krull*. It also implies a measure of bourgeois decency, because it is the principal feature which, in Mann's view, distinguishes Fontane from a writer like Strindberg.[165] The word seems to have stuck, because it crops up a year later in the 'Chamisso' essay (IX, 38). Even more remarkable, however, is the discussion of 'Sympathie' in *Der Tod in Venedig*, written between 1911 and 1912. Here, 'Sympathie' refers to the all-important affinity between the great writer and his public. To be truly significant, the work of art must be representative, it must be based upon a profound 'Sympathie':

> Damit ein bedeutendes Geistesprodukt auf der Stelle eine breite und tiefe Wirkung zu üben vermöge, muss eine geheime Verwandtschaft, ja Übereinstimmung zwischen dem persönlichen Schicksal seines Urhebers und dem allgemeinen des mitlebenden Geschlechtes bestehen. Die Menschen wissen nicht, warum sie einem Kunstwerke Ruhm bereiten [. . .] aber der eigentliche Grund ihres Beifalls ist ein Unwägbares, ist Sympathie. (VIII, 452)

In other words, by the time we get to *Der Tod in Venedig*, 'Sympathie' has ceased to be a stylistic quirk; instead, it has become the secret precondition of great art, the force which motivates Aschenbach to become a *Leistungsethiker*. But these are only the beginnings of Thomas Mann's reflections upon the meaning of 'Sympathie'.

The next significant use of the term occurs in Mann's tenth notebook, written some time between 1914 and 1915. The term 'Sympathie' now appears under the religious and romantic aspect of 'Sympathie mit dem Tode'. It is associated with Christian morality, pity, and the mortification of the flesh:

> Die 'Sympathie mit dem Tode' bringt es mit sich, daß man das Moralische nicht in der Vernunft und Zucht erblickt, sondern in der Hingabe an das Schädliche, sodaß man es als sittlich empfindet, zu verkommen. Christliche Sympathie mit dem Elend, auch dem moralischen. Es steht sittlich höher, als die Tugend. (N II, 228)

It is worth noting, however, that even this manifestation of the term should be understood in the context of Mann's attempts to establish a connection with the world. A few pages later in the same notebook, Mann writes that it is essential to compare oneself to others: 'Nur durch Vergleichen schöpft man Mut. Einsamkeit entmutigt bis zur Ohnmacht und völligen Thatlosigkeit' (N II, 231). In other words, even in 1915, 'Sympathie mit dem Tode' is quite removed from Schopenhauerian resignation: Mann regards it as a moral striving, a willed activity. Soon after this, the phrase 'Sympathie mit dem Tode' crops up again in a letter to Paul Amann dated 3 August 1915, where Mann describes it as the keynote of what will become *Der Zauberberg* (Br A, 29). From now on, the phrase appears with increasing regularity. During the long composition of *Der Zauberberg*, the phrase begins to have much wider ramifications. If 'Sympathie mit dem Tode' enters Mann's writings as a primarily Christian conception, it gradually takes on humanist overtones. In *Betrachtungen eines Unpolitischen*, in a moment harking back to *Tonio Kröger*, Mann defines 'Sympathie' as the essential quality of the plastic artist: 'Ich glaube nicht, daß ohne Sympathie überhaupt Gestalt werden könne' (XII, 144). By the early 1920s, the term 'Sympathie mit dem Tode' appears to have fallen from favour; under the influence of Goethe it has become 'Sympathie mit dem Organischen' (III, 832), or, as Mann puts it in the great essay 'Goethe und Tolstoi' (1921/25), 'die wissende Sympathie der Naturgesegneten mit dem organischen Leben' (IX, 144).

From now on, 'Sympathie' remains a central concept in Mann's thought. 'Sympathie', although primarily a moral value, also has a functional purpose: it opens up the identity of the individual, giving the subject a sense of his or her relations with the world. 'Sympathie' creates relationships for the self. This begins with a relationship to death, but then quickly expands, becoming relationships with all of organic life. In this new conception of self and world, sympathy enables the individual to sense the ties that bind the whole of creation together. In *Der Zauberberg*, 'Sympathie' is linked to both to *eros* and *charitas* (III, 832).[166] It is also part of a scientific-humanist world-view in which nature and mankind are related aspects of being.[167] In other words, Mann has ceased to think in terms of irreconcilable antitheses, and begun to think in terms of underlying relationships. As he puts it in 'Lebensabriß' (1930): 'Ich liebe dies Wort: Beziehung. [. . .] Das Bedeutende, das ist nichts weiter als das Beziehungsreiche' (XI, 123–24). The early *Felix Krull*, written between 1910 and 1913, has not yet arrived at such insights. Nevertheless, it represents an important step on the journey towards them.

An understanding of 'Sympathie' is crucial to the present discussion of art and identity because it differentiates the notion of identity. 'Sympathie', for Mann, is the process which enables the individual to form a creative synthesis, an organic symbiosis with the world. From the early *Felix Krull* onwards, Mann strives to broaden his concept of selfhood. In order to do this, he analyses himself, he compares himself to others, and he tries to understand his place in the world. The fruits of this labour are impressive: *Der Tod in Venedig*, the *Betrachtungen*, *Der Zauberberg*. Like *Felix Krull*, these works show that art can develop the self by giving it a sense of its multiple connections with the world. The practice of literature enlightens the self by showing it how it relates to others. As Mann puts it in 'Kultur und Sozialismus' (1928): 'Erkenntnis aber ist für einen Künstler auf keine andere Weise zu gewinnen als durch Hingabe, durch erlebende Leidenschaft, durch das liebende Aufgehen in seinem Gegenstande' (XII, 640). 'Sympathie' continues to play an important role in *Joseph*, *Lotte in Weimar* and in the later *Krull*. It features in Mann's Schopenhauer essay of 1938.[168] In *Joseph*, it features as the principal lesson which Joseph has to learn. As a youth, Joseph's lack of sympathy for his brothers is his undoing; he has to travel to Egypt to learn that the world consists of coexisting centres of identity ('die Welt hat viele Mitten, eine für jedes Wesen' (IV, 665)). By the time we get to the end of the tetralogy, sympathy is described as Joseph's most essential quality: 'das Tiefste seiner Natur [war] Sympathie' (V, 1508). It is Joseph's imaginative sympathy which makes him so adept at role-play. As Joseph plays with myth, he also plays with identity. The mythical framework of *Joseph* is not fixed, but syncretic: Joseph is able to pick and choose whichever mythical model suits him best.[169] Early on, he identifies with Adonis and Tammuz; later, he associates himself with Hermes.[170] Mann's epic novel asserts that although our actions may be doomed to fall into mythical patterns or types, we are still relatively free to choose which of these types or roles we want to play ('Wechsel der Charakterrolle') (IV, 191–92).[171] The similarity to *Felix Krull* is obvious. Right from the start, Mann conceived Joseph as a sort of Krull. In a letter to Ernst Bertram of 28 December 1926 he announces that Joseph will be a sort of mythical confidence man: 'Ich tue wohl recht, den Joseph zu einer Art von mythischem Hochstapler zu machen' (Br B 155; DüD II, 94). The two works feed into each other, as Kerstin Schulz has shown.[172] Joseph, like Krull, has a sense of critical distance ('Vorbehalt' (V, 964, 966)) which saves him from disaster. Just as Joseph knows where to draw the line with Mut-em-enet, Krull refuses Diane Houpflé's request for him to hit her. Joseph and Felix Krull may flirt with wrongdoing, but they stop short of real evil — saved by their ability to self-reflect.

One of the highlights of Mann's experiments in consciousness is *Lotte in Weimar*, written in exile in the late 1930s — the culmination of the Goethe-*imitatio* begun in the early *Krull*.[173] Hans Wisskirchen regards Mann's identification with Goethe at this time as a means to cope with the trauma of exile by restoring the damaged interplay of self and world.[174] *Lotte in Weimar* alludes to the possibility of containing the whole of nature within oneself: 'Alsobs nicht Alleines wäre, das Alles; alsob nicht nur der was davon verstünde, der Einheit hat, und die Natur sich nicht dem nur vertraute, der selber eine Natur . . .' (GKFA 9.1, 295).[175] Mann's attempt to expand his identity relies once more upon sympathy. In the novel, Riemer considers 'Sympathie' to be one of Goethe's key attributes (GKFA 9.1, 94). And Goethe's meditation upon his own literary technique also revolves around sympathy:

> Kontaktnahme, tiefes Wort, viel aussagend über unsere Art und Weise, dies bohrende Sich vertiefen in Sphäre und Gegenstand, ohne das mans nicht leistete, dies Sich vergraben und Schürfen besessener Sympathie, die dich zum Eingeweihten macht der liebend ergriffenen Welt. (GKFA 9.1, 332)

Sympathy is thus the key to opening up the self; it implies empirical study aided by the imagination, a conjunction of sense and intellect.[176] Such a technique is not only productive, it also contains a moral and metaphysical dimension. It allows the writer to transcend the usual, but sterile obsession with originality ('Ist ja Originalität das Grauenhafte [. . .] ich verachte sie unsäglich, weil ich das Produktive will' (GKFA 9.1, 334)), by demonstrating that certain aspects of human experience are universal and shared.[177]

Joseph and *Lotte in Weimar* both strive towards flexible, conciliatory models of identity. Mann's concept of 'Sympathie' enabled him to redefine himself in a difficult time. He coped with the trauma of exile by drawing on the wellsprings of the classical tradition, and sounding a rallying call against German fascism. This brief synopsis of Mann's work has come full circle, taking us back to *Felix Krull*, and back to the exploration of 'Sympathie'. Krull's genius for sympathy finds expression in his job as a waiter, an activity which he regards as a 'Sympathie-Austausch zwischen mir und der Welt' (472). And the latter part of *Krull* adds a final, cosmic dimension to 'Sympathie'. The great conversation with Professor Kuckuck recalls the scientific and metaphysical speculations of *Der Zauberberg*. Kuckuck, however, goes one step further, inviting Felix Krull to participate in an all-embracing 'Allsympathie' (548). The sources for the Kuckuck episode have been admirably researched by Malte Herwig.[178] What is crucial for our purposes is that the discussion of 'Allsympathie' revokes the negative view of nature expressed in Chapter 3 of *Doktor Faustus*. In that work, the existence of 'Eisblumen' or 'living crystals' — crystals which imitate forms of organic life — was regarded by Jonathan Leverkühn as proof of 'die Einheit der belebten und der sogenannten unbelebten Natur' (VI, 29), an image of life in death ('Und dabei sind sie tot' (VI,

32)). In Zeitblom's view, such things are uncanny apparitions ('Gespenstereien', 'Spuk' (VI, 32)). But while *Doktor Faustus* presents nature's mimicry as something sinister, Professor Kuckuck thinks that 'Eisblumen', too, have an important part to play in the great festival of being. According to Kuckuck, whenever nature cheats and mimics other nature, it is telling us that everything is linked: 'Immer, wenn die Natur uns gaukelnd im Unorganischen das Organische vortäusche, wie in den Schwefel-, den Eisblumen, wolle sie uns lehren, daß sie nur *eines* sei' (545). This vision of cosmic unity is the moral message behind the fakery of Felix Krull. Professor Kuckuck's glad tidings lead Felix Krull to experience what he calls 'die große Freude': a mighty expansion of his being ('diese mächtige Ausdehnung [des Gefühls]' (547)).[179] And Krull listens with awe to Kuckuck because he recognizes that sympathy — like love — is the best kind of magic, because it enables the individual to transcend his or her own identity. Sympathy is a form of love, and love is the ultimate experiment in identity. As Krull later tells Zouzou, a kiss is a miracle because it cancels out the isolation of the individual: '[der Kuss], der doch die Besiegelung ist der wunderbaren Aufhebung der Getrenntheit und des eklen Nichts-wissen-Wollens von allem, was einer nicht selbst ist!' (641).[180] Kuckuck's teachings have made a lasting impression upon his listener, and Krull feels that he has undergone a 'paläontologische Auflockerung' (594).

In this section, I have traced the development of 'Sympathie' in Mann's work, showing how it becomes a codeword for the multifarious connections and relationships which open up the self and ground it in the world. The term 'Sympathie' is immensely rich in connotations, both moral and metaphysical. It is capable of a number of inflections, which we may categorize as follows:

(a) *ethical*: sympathy implies a moral relationship with others, suggesting service, self-sacrifice, and the attempt to make a contribution to the lives of others.

(b) *ontological*: on an ontological and metaphysical level, sympathy suggests a common ground with all organic life and all human experience — including degeneration and decay. Sympathy leads to a love of life understood in all its fleeting transiency and imminent mortality. As Mann puts it in *Der Zauberberg*: 'sie [die Liebe] ist die Sympathie mit dem Organischen, das rührend wollüstige Umfangen des zur Verwesung Bestimmten' (III, 832).[181]

(c) *artistic*: on an artistic level, sympathy refers to the representative quality of the work of art, the fact that it implies an affinity between artist and audience (VIII, 452).[182] Sympathy also enables the artist to form an intimate bond with the canonical figures of tradition. It connects the individual to the matrix of human history, including culture, myth, and religion. (Here I am thinking, in particular, of the Goethe *imitatio* in *Lotte in Weimar* — or the mythological tradition in *Joseph*.)

(d) *social*: sympathy grounds the self in a community, creating a social and political awareness.[183]

(e) *linguistic*: language is an inherently social medium. Every instance of communication, every speech act, sets up a bond between interlocutors. Partners in a discourse must adopt the same conventions in order to communicate successfully. Comprehension requires a certain degree of sympathy.[184]

In Thomas Mann's work, these five categories of 'Sympathie' are profoundly interrelated. Sympathy is inflected in different ways throughout Mann's career, so that different aspects of sympathy come to the fore in different texts. In my view, however, it is *Felix Krull* which explores the different aspects of 'Sympathie' most fully.[185] *Krull* points the way to the opening up ('Entgrenzung') of the self in Mann's work. Because it examines the borders of the self, it remains the paradigmatic text for any discussion of Thomas Mann's use of the term 'Sympathie', which is the agency that both acknowledges and transcends those borders. If we would understand Mann's love for connections ('Beziehung', 'das Beziehungsreiche' (XI, 123–24)), then we must turn to *Krull*.

Notes to Chapter 1

1. For a comprehensive survey of the modernist exploration of identity, see Ritchie Robertson, 'Modernism and the Self 1890–1924', in *Philosophy and German Literature 1700–1990*, ed. by Nicholas Saul (Cambridge: Cambridge University Press, 2002), pp. 150–96.

2. One can trace this back to an earlier remark in 'Bilse und ich' (1906) where Mann accords the title of 'Dichter' to the writer 'who works upon himself' ('der an sich selbst arbeitet, wenn er arbeitet' (X, 18)).

3. In its allegorical equation of prince and artist, *Königliche Hoheit* (1909) is already beginning to tend towards a more conciliatory position. However, Klaus Heinrich still maintains a careful distance from his subjects, while Felix Krull is able to interact with his public in a much less inhibited way.

4. A copy of the missing letter to Heimann is in the notebooks (N II, 169–70); cf. TMS 1, p. 163.

5. Mann, 'Geist und Kunst', N 59, TMS 1, p. 182. For a detailed discussion of the importance of 'Geist und Kunst' to *Felix Krull*, see the following subsection, I(ii).

6. Other instances of the word include: 'Darbietungen der Bühne' (289), 'Darbietungen und Weltergötzungen' (384). The word is also used to describe the bullfight (647).

7. Donald F. Nelson, 'Felix Krull or: "All the World's a Stage"', *The Germanic Review*, 45 (1970), 41–51.

8. One of the texts which influenced *Felix Krull*, Heinrich Mann's *Im Schlaraffenland*, is even more direct in this respect, simply equating society with the theatre: 'Sie haben so etwas Glückliches an sich, daß sie beim Theater, das heißt in der Gesellschaft, ungemein rasch fordern wird' (WA 23). In comparison, *Felix Krull* is more finely nuanced, refusing to absolutize the concept.

9. 'Er hatte zu dicke, gerötete Kinderbacken und kleine, verschmitzte Äuglein darüber, die mir übrigens gut gefielen und deren anschlägige Lustigkeit die Melancholie Lügen strafte, die er manchmal an den Tag zu legen liebte' (493).

10. Although this passage first appeared in 1954, the idea goes back to early 1906, and Mann's ninth notebook (N II, 148), as Hans Wysling points out (TMS 5, pp. 157–58). Wysling traces the idea to J. J. David's short story *Die Weltreise des kleinen Tyrnauer* (1906), in which a bank clerk swaps places with a count. Wysling also points out (ibid., pp. 345–46) that the idea also appears in *Unordnung und frühes Leid*, where the young servant bears an astonishing resemblance to Cornelius's son Bert (VIII, 618–19).

11. Erving Goffman, *The Presentation of Self in Everyday Life* [1959] (London: Penguin, 1990).

12. Goffman, *Presentation*, p. 20: 'The arts of piercing an individual's effort at calculated unintentionality seem better developed than our capacity to manipulate our own behaviour, so that regardless of how many steps have occurred in the information game, the witness is likely to have the advantage over the actor'.

13. Goffman, *Presentation*, p. 246: 'In developing the conceptual framework employed in this report, some language of the stage was used. [. . .] Now it should be admitted that this attempt to press

a mere analogy so far was in part a rhetoric and a manoeuvre. The claim that all the world's a stage is sufficiently commonplace for readers to be familiar with its limitations and tolerant of its presentation, knowing that at any time they will easily be able to demonstrate to themselves that it is not to be taken too seriously.'

14. Jenny Diski, 'Erving Goffman', *LRB*, 4 March 2004, p. 11.

15. Michael Beddow, 'Thomas Mann's "Bekenntnisse des Hochstaplers Felix Krull" and the Traditions of the Picaresque Novel and the Bildungsroman' (unpublished doctoral thesis, University of Cambridge, 1975), p. 280.

16. T. J. Reed, '*Geist und Kunst*: Thomas Mann's Abandoned Essay on Literature', *OGS* 1 (1966), 53–101.

17. N II, 124: '<u>Zum Hochstapler</u> Er markirt in gefährlichen Augenblicken Husten-Anfälle, aus dem Instinkt: der Leidende ist unschuldig, über einen Kranken geht der Verdacht hinweg'. The note first appears in notebook 7, which was completed in 1905, and was then copied into notebook 9 (N II, 147).

18. Cf. undated letter to the *Saale-Zeitung*, published 2 November 1909, quoted in Scherrer and Wysling, TMS 1, p.234: 'Ich arbeite jetzt an einem Essay, der den Titel 'Geist und Kunst' führen wird. Ferner beschäftige ich mich mit einer kleineren Erzählung 'Der Hochstapler', die psychologisch eine gewisse Ergänzung zu meinem Fürstenroman bedeuten wird. Auch mache ich die ersten Studien zu einem geplanten historischen Roman.'

19. Cf. letter of 10 January 1910 to Heinrich Mann (Br H, 104).

20. At this point Mann interrupted his work on the novel to begin *Der Tod in Venedig*, which occupied him between July 1911 and July 1912. After completing the novella, Mann returned to *Felix Krull*, writing Book II — including the *Musterungsszene* — up to the first draft of the Rozsa-episode (Chapter 6). He then abandoned the novel again in the summer of 1913 to begin *Der Zauberberg*. For further details of the composition of *Krull* see Hans Wysling, 'Archivalisches Gewühle', in Scherrer and Wysling, TMS 1, pp. 234–57.

21. As Wysling puts it: 'Diese Notizenmasse ['Geist und Kunst'] gehört zum frühen *Krull* wie etwa Bilse und ich zu den *Buddenbrooks*, der Freud-Vortrag zum *Joseph* oder die Nietzsche-Rede zum *Dr. Faustus*'. Wysling, 'Archivalisches Gewühle. Zur Entstehungsgeschichte des Hochstapler-Romans', *Blätter der Thomas Mann Gesellschaft*, 5 (1965), 23–43 (p. 28). This sentence was omitted when the article was reproduced in TMS 1.

22. Scherrer and Wysling, TMS 1, p. 171.

23. Scherrer and Wysling, TMS 1, pp. 175–76.

24. Hans-Joachim Sandberg, *Thomas Manns Schillerstudien. Eine quellenkritische Untersuchung* (Oslo: Universitets forlaget, 1965), p. 76; cf. also Reed, 'Geist und Kunst', p. 64.

25. Scherrer and Wysling, TMS 1, p. 203.

26. On this point see also Reed, '*Geist und Kunst*', p. 60.

27. See letter of 18 February 1905 to Heinrich Mann on the fiasco of *Fiorenza*: 'Umkehr! Zurück zur Buddenbrook-Naivität!' (Br H 57); cf. Reed, 'Geist und Kunst', p. 81; Sandberg, *Thomas Manns Schillerstudien*, p. 60.

28. For more detailed discussions of *Plastik*, see Reed, 'Geist und Kunst', pp. 80–82; Scherrer and Wysling, TMS 1, pp. 137–41.

29. In Hans Wysling's view, the 'Goethe-Schiller-Komplex' of 'Geist und Kunst' forms the prelude to *Felix Krull*. Commenting on the conciliatory tendency of 'Geist und Kunst', Wysling remarks: [Thomas Mann] möchte zeigen, daß die beiden Kategorien ['naiv'und 'sentimentalisch'] nicht absolut genommen werden dürfen, daß vielmehr der sentimentalische Dichter auch an der Position des naiven teilhabe und umgekehrt. Ein Akt der Selbstverteidigung zunächst: Thomas Mann will nachweisen, daß er nicht einfach unter die Literaten einzureihen sei, daß vielmehr gerade in seinem Falle die Kluft zwischen 'naiv' und 'sentimentalisch' sich überbrücken lasse, weil er durchaus nach eigenem Empfinden und Erleben zu gestalten in der Lage sei. (Wysling, 'Archivalisches Gewühle', *Blätter der Thomas Mann Gesellschaft*, 5 (1965), 23–43; p. 28)

30. Eric Wilson points out that Krull's Goethe *imitatio* immediately precedes and apparently initiates Mann's own. Wilson, 'Felix Krull: Thomas Mann's Comic Artist' (unpublished doctoral thesis, Stanford University, 1966), p. 68.

31. Scherrer and Wysling, TMS 1, p. 165. The Nietzsche quotation is from the Nachlaß of 1876–77

(KGA 4.2, 561). Cf. Reed, *'Geist und Kunst'*, p. 84: 'The relevance to Thomas Mann's later development of "betrachtet sich . . . als eine Art Goethe" and "grössere Verpflichtung" can hardly be overlooked'.

32. Virtually the same note is to be found in Mann's ninth notebook (N II, 178).

33. Letter to Paul Amann, 10 September 1915 (Br A 32); cf. DüD I, 305–06; Reed, *'Geist und Kunst'*, p. 94.

34. Hinrich Siefken certainly thinks so: '1910 besuchte Thomas Mann Weimar, unseres Wissens zum ersten Mal. Es liegt nahe, diesem Besuch eine ähnliche Intensivierung des Interesses an den Klassikern zuzuschreiben'. Siefken, *Thomas Mann. Goethe — 'Ideal der Deutschheit', Wiederholte Spiegelungen, 1893–1949* (Munich: Fink, 1981), p. 72. On Mann's relation to Goethe, cf. also Bernhard Blume, *Thomas Mann und Goethe* (Bern: Francke, 1949).

35. Although this passage was written in 1911, six years after Freud had described the centrality of identification for the development of the self in *Drei Abhandlungen zur Sexualtheorie* (1905), it is unlikely that Mann knew Freudian theory at this point in any great detail. Even though this passage anticipates the Freudian view of the self as being created through a series of identifications, the vocabulary here is much more likely to stem from the vitalist, monistic theory of Ernst Haeckel (1834–1930), the German popularizer of Charles Darwin. For a thorough survey of Mann's scientific knowledge, see Malte Herwig, *Bildungsbürger auf Abwegen: Naturwissenschaften im Werk Thomas Manns*, TMS 32 (Frankfurt a.M.: Klostermann, 2004).

36. A quarter of a century later, Mann uses almost identical terms to describe his 'imitatio Goethe's' in 'Freud und die Zukunft' (1936): 'Vaternachahmung', 'das Bewunderte', 'Bildung' (IX, 498–99). The terms are the same, but ironic fiction has given way to explicit assertion: what began as a playful identification has become a guiding principle of Mann's literary career.

37. *Goethes Gespräche*, II: *1805–1810*, ed. by Woldemar Biedermann (Leipzig: Biedermann, 1889), p. 292

38. Cf. N II, 110: 'Die Welt groß oder klein sehen — was ist das Förderlichere? . . . (auszuführen)'.

39. The term 'Weltfrömmigkeit' appears in *Wilhelm Meisters Wanderjahre* (HA VIII, 243).

40. N II, 187. Mann later used this quotation as the motto for the *Betrachtungen*.

41. N II, 178: '*Moderne Tendenz*. Goethe sagt, daß die Poesie auf ihrem höchsten Gipfel *ganz aeußerlich* erscheine, daß sie aber, je mehr sie sich ins Innere zurückziehe, auf dem Wege sei, zu sinken'. A few pages later, Mann reflects upon universal harmony in Goethean terms: 'Alles löst sich in die denkbar einfachsten harmonischen Verhältnisse auf' (N II, 191).

42. Thomas Sprecher's book on this topic, *Felix Krull und Goethe: Thomas Mann's 'Bekenntnisse' als Parodie auf 'Dichtung und Wahrheit'* (Bern: Peter Lang, 1985), despite being painstakingly researched, is at times distorted by its emphasis upon the more oedipal aspects of *Felix Krull*. While Sprecher accentuates Mann's ambivalence towards Goethe at this stage, I would be more inclined to see a conscious, playful attempt at *rapprochement*.

43. Letter to Paul Amann, 3 August 1915 (Br A, 30; DüD I, 305).

44. In Chapter 3(ii) on intertextuality.

45. Parts I–III of *Dichtung und Wahrheit* were written from 1809 to 1813; Part IV was written from 1816 to 1831.

46. Erving Goffman makes the same point: 'Others are likely to find that they must accept the individual on faith' (Goffman, *Presentation*, p. 14).

47. (XI, 334–35): 'so recht nach meinem Herzen war es zum Beispiel, wenn Mesmer die Möglichkeit betonte, daß der Schlaf, in dem das Leben der Pflanzen besteht [. . .], vielleicht der dem Menschen natürliche, ursprüngliche Zustand sei, dem Zweck des Vegetierens am unmittelbarsten entsprechend'.

48. For a discussion of Mann's development of the term 'Sympathie', see the concluding section of this chapter.

49. Cf. Krull's earlier statement: 'Die Bedingung, unter der ich einzig zu leben vermag, ist Ungebundenheit des Geistes und der Phantasie' (295–96).

50. Egmont had been awarded the Order of the Golden Fleece by the Emperor Charles V, as a mark of his favour. There may be a teasing allusion to this fact in a later section of *Felix Krull*. When Krull, in the guise of the Marquis de Venosta, meets the King of Portugal, he impresses the King so much with his respect for the monarchy that the King awards him the Order of the Red Lion,

Second Class (614). In any case, the preoccupation with the symbols of authority in both texts reveals an interest in the social power of image-making.

51. Angus Nicholls, *Goethe's Concept of the Daemonic: After the Ancients* (Rochester, NY: Camden House, 2006), pp. 210–13.

52. The formula 'angeborene Verdienste' comes from a passage in *Dichtung und Wahrheit* Book III, Ch. XI, where Goethe describes Schöpflin's great natural gifts: 'sein Glück war, ohne daß er sich mühsam angestrengt hätte, die Folge angeborner und ruhig ausgebildeter Verdienste' (HA IX, 475).

53. 'Und sehr schwer ist es hier wiederum, zwischen persönlichem Verdienst und dem, was man als Gunst der Umstände bezeichnet, eine gerechte und scharfe Trennungslinie zu ziehen' (340).

54. Letter of 21 September 1918 to Ernst Bertram: 'Todesromantik plus Lebensja im Zauberberg, Protestantismus plus "Griechentum" im Hochstapler. . .' (Br B, 76).

55. For a discussion of Mann's use of the term 'Sympathie', see the concluding section of this chapter.

56. Donald G. MacRae, *Max Weber* (London: Fontana, 1987), p. 12.

57. Even later on in the *Novelle*, when Tonio Kröger has begun to accept the different sides of his character, he is mistaken for a confidence man (VIII, 316).

58. The injunction 'Werde, der du bist' dates from antiquity; cf. Pindar's second Pythian Ode (v. 71); it is also mentioned in Fontane's *Frau Jenny Treibel* [1892] (HF I.IV, 469).

59. 'Nur als *ästhetisches Phänomen* ist das Dasein und die Welt ewig *gerechtfertigt*' (KGA 3.1, 43).

60. *Die fröhliche Wissenschaft*, para. 290 (KGA 5.2, 210).

61. Wysling, TMS 5, pp. 21–25.

62. Note 249 (TMS 5, 458); compare *Die fröhliche Wissenschaft*, para. 361: 'ein Ueberschuss von Anpassungs-Fähigkeiten aller Art' (KGA 5.2, 290).

63. This paper, first given in 1977, is published in 'Living in the Metaphor of Fiction', in *Comparative Criticism*, 1 (1979), 3–16 and in *Critical Essays on Thomas Mann*, ed. by Inta M. Ezergailis (Boston: G. K. Hall, 1988), pp. 206–18. It was reworked into the penultimate chapter of Stern's last book, *The Dear Purchase: A Theme in German Modernism* (Cambridge: Cambridge University Press, 1995), pp. 382–93. I shall give page references to *Comparative Criticism*, 1 (1979).

64. Stern, 'Living', pp. 4–6.

65. Stern, 'Living', p. 13.

66. Scherrer and Wysling, TMS 1, p. 212: 'Man muß die Kunst nicht zu ernst nehmen. Wir Deutschen neigen dazu, verführt durch die Schwere unseres Nationalcharakters und durch den Ehrgeiz einiger unserer starken Künstler. Aber wieviel heiterer und reicher wäre der Mensch, wenn er nicht darauf bestünde, glauben und ganz ernst nehmen zu können, bevor er liebt. Eine leichtere, skeptischere, ungläubigere, verschlagenere, schalkhaftere und genußfrohere Kunstauffassung, die die Kunst nicht mehr als einen 'Lastwagen nach dem Himmelreich', sondern als ein Spiel, ein Stimulans, einen schönen Rausch, ein erquickliches Blendwerk, hervorgebracht mit den feinsten sinnlichen und intellektuellen Zaubermitteln, — als eine Sache des Lebens und der Verführung zu Leben nimmt, wird vielleicht eine der Befreiungen, Erlösungen, Beglückungen, Erleichterungen sein, die eine nahe Zukunft der Menschheit bringen wird.'

67. Eric Downing, *Artificial I's: The Self as Artwork in Ovid, Kierkegaard, and Thomas Mann* (Tübingen: Niemeyer, 1993).

68. Downing, *Artificial I's*, p. 129. Cf. Alexander Nehamas, *Nietzsche: Life as Literature* (Cambridge, MA: Harvard University Press, 1985).

69. Downing's wordplay with 'conscription' is a case in point: he takes the English word as a starting point for a fantasy that bears little relation to its source. His interpretation of the *Musterungsszene* as an intertextual *Walpurgisnacht* makes interesting reading, but he fails to notice the conciliatory tendency in Mann's dialogue with tradition. Downing's insistence that imitation is 'violent' and 'dehumanizing' is unfortunate; it ignores the fact that imitation can be the sincerest form of flattery. Furthermore, Downing's comparative approach means that he tends to fit the novel into a prearranged schema; what then predominates is a straightforward Nietzschean reading of the text which tends to overlook the subtleties of Mann's engagement with Nietzsche.

70. For a comparison of the two novels, see Martin Swales, *Studies of German Prose Fiction in the Age of European Realism* (Lewiston, NY: Mellen, 1995), pp. 163–64, 170–71.

71. Musil, *Gesammelte Werke in neun Bänden*, ed. by Adolf Frisé (Hamburg: Rowohlt, 1978), I, 252.

72. Musil, *Werke*, II, 365.

73. Musil, *Werke*, II, 593.

74. Kerstin Schulz, *Identitätsfindung und Rollenspiel in Thomas Manns Romanen 'Joseph und seine Brüder' und 'Bekenntnisse des Hochstaplers Felix Krull'* (Frankfurt a.M.: Peter Lang, 2000), pp. 644–50.

75. Schulz, *Identitätsfindung*, p. 650.

76. Schulz, *Identitätsfindung*, p. 631.

77. Beddow, pp. 243–44.

78. See Wysling, TMS 5, work note 571, p. 407.

79. Schulz, *Identitätsfindung*, p. 648.

80. Schulz, *Identitätsfindung*, p. 651.

81. See Wysling, TMS 5, work notes 572–73, p. 408: 'Bei der Erinnerung an Verbrechen etc in anderen Städten, auch an Demütigungen, Blamagen, Infamierungen, die er erlitten, kann er sich ganz vom *Identitäts*gefühl befreien. 'Ob das *ich* war, der ich hier jetzt unter anderem Namen etc bin und lebe, oder ein anderer, Fremder, der mich nichts angeht und dessen Schande nicht die meine ist, davon wissen die Zeugen von damals nichts, und es braucht mich also nicht zu kümmern.'

82. See Wysling, TMS 5, work note 557, p. 404: 'Moralische Veranlagung. Lebensernst.' and note 582, p. 415: '*Moralistische* Veranlagung. Lebensernst'.

83. Using arguments drawn from cognitive psychology, Dennett denies the existence of a unified, Cartesian self. Instead, he regards consciousness as arising from the interaction of multiple narratives, from the parallel processing of perceptual and cognitive subsystems. In his view, the 'self' is a heuristic — an explanatory tool used by subsystems of the brain as they work in tandem to compile consciousness, rather like a team of scriptwriters. According to this theory, every individual is not just a narrator, but a team of narrators. Daniel C. Dennett, *Consciousness Explained* (London: Allen Lane, 1991).

84. Alisdair MacIntyre, *After Virtue: A Study in Moral Theory* (Notre Dame, IN: University of Notre Dame Press, 1984), p. 212.

85. Anthony Kerby, *Narrative and the Self* (Bloomington, IN: Indiana University Press, 1991), p. 4 [his italics].

86. Julia Schöll, '"Verkleidet also war ich in jedem Fall". Zur Identitätskonstruktion in *Joseph und seine Brüder* und *Bekenntnisse des Hochstaplers Felix Krull*', *TMJ* 18 (2005), 9–29.

87. Schöll, '"Verkleidet"', p. 29: '[Krull zeigt], dass er durchaus auf die Befindlichkeiten seiner Umwelt Rücksicht zu nehmen bereit ist'.

88. Cf. Heinrich Detering, 'Juden, Frauen, Literaten. Stigma und Stigma-Bearbeitung in Thomas Manns frühen Essays (1893–1914)', in *Thomas Mann und das Judentum*, TMS 30, ed. by Manfred Dierks and Ruprecht Wimmer (Frankfurt a.M.: Klostermann, 2004), pp. 15–34 (p. 30).

89. T. J. Reed has shown that the keynote of Mann's later comments on *Der Tod in Venedig* is experiment; see Reed, 'Geist und Kunst', p. 95.

90. The writings of the following years only tend to confirm this reading of the novel. In the *Betrachtungen*, Mann discusses the modern striving for culture and form and claims that he has tried to portray this tendency in his fiction: 'novellistisch, das heißt: experimentell und ohne letzte Verbindlichkeit' (XII, 517). The work of fiction that Mann is referring to here is actually *Der Tod in Venedig*. But the statement can also be applied to *Felix Krull*, since the essential quality of Krull's play with different identities is the fact that it is experimental, hypothetical, and not binding.

91. The aphorism comes from Wilde's *Phrases and Philosophies for the Use of the Young*, and also appears in *An Ideal Husband*. Mann underlined the aphorism in his copy of Franz Blei's *In Memoriam Oscar Wilde* (Leipzig: Insel, 1904): 'Selbstliebe ist der Anfang zu einem lebenwährenden Roman'. Cf. GKFA 14.2, p. 552.

92. The same argument is later incorporated into 'Goethe und Tolstoi' (IX, 69–70).

93. Downing, *Artificial I's*, p. 129.

94. Detering, 'Juden, Frauen, Literaten', p. 31.

95. The passage relates to *Der Tod in Venedig* and goes on to describe the novella as a crystalline structure containing a network of relationships. On this point see T. J. Reed, *Death in Venice: Making and Unmaking a Master* (New York: Twayne, 1994), p. 72.

96. Karl Werner Böhm, *Zwischen Selbstzucht und Verlangen. Thomas Mann und das Stigma Homosexualität* (Würzburg: Königshausen & Neumann, 1991).

97. Böhm, *Zwischen Selbstzucht*, p. 187.

98. Ronald Hayman, *Thomas Mann: A Biography* (London: Bloomsbury, 1996), p. 65: 'Mann overcame literary inhibitions by speaking freely about his inner life through characters apparently dissimilar to himself'.

99. Böhm, *Zwischen Selbstzucht*, pp. 176–85.

100. Mann, *Essays I* (1993), pp. 25–30. For a detailed discussion, cf. Heinrich Detering, 'Das Ewig-Weibliche. Thomas Mann über Toni Schwabe, Gabriele Reuter, Ricarda Huch', *TMJ* 12 (1999), 149–69.

101. Böhm, *Zwischen Selbstzucht*, pp. 317–18. Böhm alludes here to a letter of 22 May 1910 to Alexander von Bernus in which Mann writes: 'Ich schreibe an den Memoiren eines Hochstaplers, — einer sehr sonderbaren, auch anstößigen und — für mich — aufwühlenden Sache' (DüD I, 256).

102. Gerhard Härle, 'Simulationen der Wahrheit. Körpersprache und sexuelle Identität im *Zauberberg* und *Felix Krull*', in '*Heimsuchung und süßes Gift.' Erotik und Poetik bei Thomas Mann*, ed. by Gerhard Härle (Frankfurt a.M.: Fischer, 1992), 63–86 (p. 71).

103. Some time between 1901 and 1905, Mann notes that he has read *Dorian Gray* (N II, 35).

104. Härle, 'Simulationen', p. 72.

105. Stern, *Dear Purchase*, p. 387.

106. 'Letzten Endes jedoch und im ganzen genommen war meine Sinnesart ernst und männlich' (315).

107. 'weshalb ich [. . .] ja eigentlich zeit meines Lebens ein Kind und Träumer verblieb' (315).

108. Wysling, TMS 5, n. 587, p. 419.

109. Hans-Heinrich Reuter, *Fontane*, II (Munich: Nymphenburger, 1968), pp. 977–78.

110. As Felix Krull approaches Frau Kuckuck and her daughter, he feigns interest in a 'Fontäne' (558). Reuter suggests that this may be a veiled allusion to Fontane (Reuter, *Fontane*, II, p. 979).

111. For Mann's revisions of this scene, see Wysling, TMS 5, pp. 516–18. Wysling too views Felix Krull as bisexual (p. 89).

112. Helmut Koopmann, *Der schwierige Deutsche. Studien zum Werk Thomas Manns* (Tübingen: Niemeyer, 1988), p. 159.

113. Wysling, TMS 5, note 212, p. 437.

114. Wysling, TMS 5, note 551, p. 465. Editing and correction from 'die' to 'das' by Wysling.

115. On the other hand, it is also possible to read Krull's indeterminate sexuality as forming part of his tendency towards 'Allsympathie'. For a discussion of 'Sympathie'/'Allsympathie', see the concluding section of this chapter, (viii).

116. References to 'Seitenpfaden' continue in the latter section of the novel (452, 474, 515).

117. Härle, 'Simulationen', pp. 67–68; Böhm, *Zwischen Selbstzucht*, p. 320. Cf. letter of 27 April 1912 to Heinrich Mann (Br H 123; DüD I, 300–01). Cf. Heinrich Mann, *Der Untertan* (WA 49).

118. Härle, 'Simulationen', p. 67.

119. Härle, 'Simulationen', p. 72.

120. Wysling, TMS 5, pp. 87–88.

121. Jens Rieckmann, '"In deinem Atem bildet sich mein Wort": Thomas Mann, Franz Westermeier und *Bekenntnisse des Hochstaplers Felix Krull*', *TMJ* 10 (1997), 149–65 (p. 162).

122. Letter of Erika Mann, 10 February 1954, printed in TMS 5, pp.522–27: 'Ich bin in harten inneren Kämpfen zu der Überzeugung gelangt, daß Twentyman *fallen* müssen' (p. 523). The scene with Twentyman was published as 'Thomas Mann: Ein nachgelassenes Kapitel aus "Felix Krull"', in *Die neue Rundschau*, 68.2 (1957), 181–86. There, Mr Twentyman explains that he has a 'weakness for good-looking youngsters'. He offers Felix Krull money and makes bold advances: '"As a matter of fact, I should like us to have dinner together in town some evening and have fun, a lot of it afterwards. How's that?" Und das aufgeschlagene Buch in der Linken, versuchte er, sehr zudringlich zu werden mit der Rechten' (pp. 185–86).

123. Gore Vidal, *The City and the Pillar* [1948] (London: Abacus, 1997). In the 1994 preface, Vidal says: 'I deliberately made Jim Willard a Hans Castorp type' (p. 5). Cf. Rieckmann, 'In deinem Atem', pp. 161–62.

124. Vidal, *City*, p. 41.

125. Wysling, TMS 5, p. 519. The narrator then continues, claiming that his first experience of 'die große Freude', with Genovefa, had a defining effect upon his character. The consequence is: 'daß es mir allezeit ausgesprochen unbequem war, mich mit Herren zur Ruhe zu begeben'.
126. The Latin original is: 'Homo sum, nihil humani a me alienum puto'. Mann may have found the phrase in German in Fontane's *Der Stechlin* (HF I.v, 378). Hans Wysling attributes the phrase to Seneca, TMS 5, p. 519, but in fact it comes from Terence's comedy *The Self-Tormentor* (*Heautontimorumenos*), I, i, 25.
127. Indeed, according to Rolf-Peter Janz, Krull sees androgyny as an ideal. Janz, 'Schwindelnde Männer oder die Liebe zum Betrug. Krull, Schwejk, Gunten, "Rotpeter"', in *Schwindelerfahrungen. Zur kulturhistorischen Diagnose eines vieldeutigen Symptoms*, ed. by Rolf-Peter Janz, Fabian Stoermer, and Andreas Hiepko (Amsterdam: Rodopi, 2003), pp. 99–116 (pp. 101–02).
128. *Zur Genealogie der Moral*, Part I, para. 13: 'es giebt kein "Sein" hinter dem Thun, Wirken, Werden; "der Thäter" ist zum Thun bloss hinzugedichtet, — das Thun ist alles' (KGA 6.2, 293).
129. Judith Butler, *Gender Trouble: Feminism and the Subversion of Identity*, 2nd edn (New York: Routledge, 1999).
130. Butler, *Gender Trouble*, p. 17: 'Consider that a sedimentation of gender norms produces the peculiar phenomenon of a "natural sex" or a "real woman" or any number of prevalent and compelling social fictions'.
131. Butler, *Gender Trouble*, p. 44.
132. For Jungian readings of *Felix Krull*, see Donald F. Nelson, *Portrait of the Artist as Hermes: A Study of Myth and Psychology in Thomas Mann's 'Felix Krull'* (Chapel Hill: University of North Carolina Press, 1971) and Wysling, TMS 5, pp. 238–69.
133. I am thinking of Joyce's *A Portrait of the Artist as a Young Man*, Benjamin's *Berliner Kindheit*, Nathalie Sarraute's *Enfance*, and Christa Wolf's *Kindheitsmuster*, to name but four examples.
134. Caspar Hauser appears in the novel by Jakob Wassermann, the play by Peter Handke, and the film by Werner Herzog.
135. Mann had used a similar idea before, in *Buddenbrooks*, where Christian mimes the gestures of a virtuoso pianist (I, 264).
136. 'Das Wunderkind', written in December 1903, also features a musical child prodigy. Here, too, the vital point is people's willingness to accept aesthetic convention: the audience contributes 'ein bißchen guten Willen [. . .] fünf gerade sein zu lassen' (VIII, 340).
137. Cf. Vicki Bell, *Performativity and Belonging* (London: Sage, 1999), p. 3.
138. Interview with Butler, in Bell, *Performativity*, pp. 165–66.
139. Feuerlicht, *Thomas Mann*, p. 99: 'so muß man sich aber auch vor Augen halten, daß ohne ein bei allem Wechsel und Spiel gleichbleibendes Ich Krull sein Rollenspielen [. . .] nicht genießen könnte. Ein zentrales Koordinatensystem ist immer da'.
140. The possibility that *Felix Krull* might be a pendant to *Doktor Faustus* is also explored by Ruprecht Wimmer in his essay 'Krull I — Doktor Faustus — Krull II. Drei Masken des Autobiographischen', *TMJ* 18 (2005), 31–50.
141. Each character has important geographical associations. Leverkühn hails from the mythical town of Kaisersaschern, which suggests the Teutonic piety of the Middle Ages; Krull hails from the Rhineland, the region of Germany which is closest to France, and is therefore more cosmopolitan in outlook. Of course, *Doktor Faustus* is a political allegory in a way that *Krull* is not.
142. Leverkühn draws on physics in order to justify his anti-humanist world view, claiming that science disrupts the anthropocentric world-view upon which humanism is based (VI, 364).
143. The initial plans for both *Doktor Faustus* and *Felix Krull* both occur towards the end of Mann's seventh notebook, completed in 1905. The two notes occur within a few pages of each other (N II, 121–22, 124)
144. We might seek to understand the difference between Krull and Leverkühn in terms of the Nietzschean distinction between Apollonian and Dionysian. The Apollonian is a primarily visual category; the Dionysian is predominantly aural and musical. These categories determine Leverkühn's own understanding of himself as an *Ohrenmensch* ('ear-man'). While the *Augenmensch* ('eye-man') forms and adapts himself based on what he sees in the external world,

the *Ohrenmensch* listens intently to his own inner voice. Leverkühn denounces the vagaries of the *Augenmensch*: 'Die Unterscheidung zwischen den Typen des Augen- und des Ohrenmenschen hieß er gut und unumstößlich richtig und rechnete sich entschieden zu dem zweiten' (VI, 236). The narrator Serenus Zeitblom, however, has a less categorical mindset, and immediately comments: 'Was mich betrifft, so habe ich diese Einteilung nie für reinlich durchführbar gehalten' (VI, 236). As for Felix Krull, his delight in seeing ('Augenlust', VII, 342) shows him to be an *Augenmensch*. But he loves the opera too (498).

145. Similarly, the watchword of both characters is 'Erkenntnis' (VI, 242; VIII, 986–87).

146. Feuerlicht, *Thomas Mann*, p. 20.

147. 'Mir ist dann, als sei alles individuelle Dasein als Folge zu begreifen eines übersinnlichen Willensaktes und Entschlusses zur Konzentration, zur Begrenzung und zur Gestaltung, zur Sammlung aus dem Nichts, zur Absage an die Freiheit, die Unendlichkeit, an das Schlummern' (XI, 337).

148. Feuerlicht, *Thomas Mann*, p. 24. Feuerlicht finds the same dichotomy in Baudelaire: 'De la vaporisation et de la centralisation du Moi: tout est là' (Feuerlicht, p. 24).

149. As Feuerlicht puts it (p. 139): 'Überbegrenzung des Ich und anscheinend völlige Entgrenzung, entzündetes Selbstbewußtsein und liebende Selbstverwandlung, Narzißmus und Selbstvergessenheit sind also nach Mann die gegensätzlichen Erscheinungsformen des ästhetischen Erlebens und Schaffens'.

150. 'Oft bin ich ausgeschweift, denn mein Fleisch war schwach, und ich fand die Welt nur allzu bereit, mir buhlerisch entgegenzukommen. Letzten Endes jedoch und im ganzen genommen war meine Sinnesart ernst und männlich, und aus erschlaffender Wollust verlangte mich baldigst in eine strenge und angespannte Führung zurück.' (315)

151. In one early work note, Mann muses: 'Er könnte von Frauen leben, sich aushalten lassen, ist aber zu schüchtern und <u>ernst</u> dazu, zieht es vor, zu arbeiten' (Wysling, TMS 5, p. 415).

152. TMS 5, p. 419. [...] signifies an editorial addition by Hans Wysling.

153. Scherrer and Wysling, TMS 1, N 110, p. 211.

154. Although I have been unable to discover any specific references to confirm this hypothesis, there are a number of striking resemblances between Krull and Peer Gynt. Both have fathers who are drunken profligates; both are daydreamers and fabulists who get up to all sorts of tricks; both become outlaws and embark upon round-the-world trips; and both find closure in the arms of women who are mother-figures (this aspect is particularly evident in Peer Gynt's final reunion with Solveig).

155. Wimmer, 'Drei Masken', pp. 37–38.

156. Wimmer, 'Drei Masken', pp. 39–40.

157. Significantly, the name of Zeitblom's father is 'Wohlgemut'. Another feature that Krull and Zeitblom have in common is their Catholic backgrounds (which, for Mann at least, implies sensuality and a love of beautiful images). In Zeitblom's case, his Catholicism suggests a liberal humanism, one that is untouched by the schism of the Reformation and the evangelical fervour of Lutheranism ('eine von der Kirchenspaltung unberührt gebliebene christ-katholische Überlieferung heiterer Bildungsliebe' (VI, 15)).

158. Scherrer and Wysling, TMS 1, p. 234.

159. Scherrer and Wysling, TMS 1, p. 236. Like his creator, Krull wishes to transcend the narrow boundaries of his identity. As Mann put it in his early work notes: '[Krull sehnt] sich inbrünstig nach anderen Wirklichkeiten' (Wysling, TMS 5, p. 414).

160. Cf. Scharfschwerdt, *Thomas Mann*, p. 104. Scharfschwerdt regards *Königliche Hoheit* as the first step towards Mann's later, more substantial engagements with the Bildungsroman, namely *Der Zauberberg* and *Joseph*.

161. Jochen Bertheau, *Eine komplizierte Bewandtnis: Der junge Thomas Mann und die französische Literatur* (Frankfurt a.M.: Peter Lang, 2002), pp. 92–93.

162. Note 579a (Wysling, TMS 5, p. 414).

163. It occurs as an adjective in an early work note: 'Er begegnet dem Beamten mit einer so feinen und sympathischen Leidensmiene' (Wysling, TMS 5, p. 415).

164. Scherrer and Wysling, TMS 1, p. 239.

165. In the same Fontane essay, we find: 'Sein [Fontanes] Sinn für Diskretion, Takt, Sauberkeit,

Liebenswürdigkeit und bürgerlichen Anstand, mußte gegen dies *unsympathische* Genie [Strindbergs] revoltieren' (IX, 28) [my italics].

166. (III, 832): '[Die Liebe] ist die Sympathie mit dem Organischen, das rührend wollüstige Umfangen des zur Verwesung Bestimmten, — Charitas ist gewiß noch in der bewunderungsvollsten oder wütendsten Leidenschaft.'

167. For a more detailed analysis of how Mann's reception of Goethe influenced his understanding of 'Sympathie', see Malte Herwig, TMS 33, pp. 53–59. Herwig also explores the origins of Krullian 'Allsympathie' in his article ' "Nur in der Jugend gestielt". Die langen Wurzeln des *Felix Krull*', *TMJ* 18 (2005), 141–58.

168. In the Schopenhauer essay, Mann asserts that 'der böse Mensch' is one who remains trapped in the *principium individuationis*, one who sees him- or herself as the middle-point of the world (IX, 553). 'Der gute Mensch' is the person who sees through this illusion and realizes that he or she is part of a universal life-force (IX, 554). Mann is subtly altering Schopenhauer's doctrine of quiescent pity ('Mitleid'), replacing it with a more active Goethean notion of 'Sympathie'.

169. For discussions of myth in *Joseph*, see Eckhard Heftrich, 'Joseph', *Thomas-Mann-Handbuch*, ed. by Helmut Koopmann (Stuttgart: Kröner, 1990), 452–61; and Kurzke, *Thomas Mann*, pp. 243–49, 252, 257.

170. Letter of 18 February 1941 to Karl Kerényi (Br K 98): '[Joseph] wechselt aus der ursprünglichen Tammuz-Adonis-Rolle immer mehr in die eines Hermes hinüber'.

171. Cf. Dierk Wolters, *Zwischen Metaphysik und Politik: Thomas Manns Roman 'Joseph und seine Brüder' in seiner Zeit* (Tübingen: Niemeyer, 1998), pp. 156, 246.

172. Schulz, *Identitätsfindung*, pp. 372–91.

173. For detailed studies of Mann's Goethe-*imitatio*, cf. Siefken, *Thomas Mann. Goethe*; Martina Hoffmann, *Von Venedig nach Weimar. Eine Entwicklungsgeschichte paradigmatischen Künstlertums* (Frankfurt a.M.: Peter Lang, 1999).

174. Hans Wisskirchen, *Zeitgeschichte im Roman. Zu Thomas Manns 'Zauberberg' und 'Doktor Faustus'*, TMS 6 (Bern: Francke, 1986), pp. 145, 151.

175. Because of the unreliable quality of earlier editions of *Lotte in Weimar*, quotations from this novel are taken from the GKFA. The *Gesammelte Werke* edition reads: 'Als obs nicht all eines wäre, das alles; als ob nicht nur der was davon verstünde, der Einheit hat, und die Natur sich nicht dem nur vertraute, der selbe eine Natur. . .' (II, 629).

176. Cf. Malte Herwig, TMS 32, pp.56–58. Herwig argues that Mann's understanding of the sciences derives from the phrase 'exakte sinnliche Phantasie' which he underlined in Bielschowsky's study of Goethe. The phrase combines categories of both body ('sinnliche') and mind ('Phantasie').

177. Just as Goethe and Shakespeare adapted the work of others, Mann's works arise from a creative dialogue with what has gone before.

178. Herwig, TMS 32, pp. 210–53.

179. Kuckuck manages to articulate a tendency which already exists in Felix Krull. As Mann puts it in a short text of 1953, 'Einführung in ein Kapitel der "Bekenntnisse des Hochstaplers Felix Krull" ': 'Sein [Krulls] eigentliches Anliegen, sein tiefstes Ungenügen an der eigenen Individualität geht aber weiter. Es ist ein Verlangen aus sich heraus, ins Ganze, eine Welt-Sehnsucht, die, auf ihre kürzeste Formel gebracht, als *Pan-Erotik* anzusprechen wäre' (XI, 704–05).

180. The fact that these words are spoken by a confidence man signals that in love, as in life, there are no guarantees.

181. The same idea informs the 1952 text 'Lob der Vergänglichkeit': 'was ich am höchsten stelle [. . .] ist die *Vergänglichkeit*' (X, 383).

182. I will discuss this bond between artist and audience in Chapter 2(ii) on the Müller-Rosé episode.

183. It is worth noting that Mann's interest in 'Sympathie' during the composition of *Der Zauberberg* coincided with a deepening political commitment. With *Felix Krull*, the case is rather different. Artist that he is, Krull refuses any solid commitment that would endanger his freedom (and that includes politics). Even so, he has a political awareness; at one point he tells the hotel workers that they should unite if they ever want to be respected by anyone (410). I will discuss the treatment of society in *Krull* in Chapter II(i).

184. I will discuss the linguistic relationship between narrator and reader in Chapter 3(iv).

185. We should not reject the novel out of hand because of its concern with surfaces. After all, the surface is the site where the inner and the outer world communicate. Krull's surface is inordinately sensitive: it is a surface which permits osmosis.

CHAPTER 2

ART AND THE NOTATION OF COMMUNITY

> Wenn schon das Bedürfniß den Menschen in die Gesellschaft nöthigt, und die
> Vernunft gesellige Grundsätze in ihm pflanzt, so kann die Schönheit allein
> ihm einen *geselligen Charakter* ertheilen.
>
> SCHILLER (NA 20, 410)

Much has been written about the structural dichotomy of *Bürger* and *Künstler* in the
early works of Thomas Mann. In this early phase, the *Künstler*, as the representative
of *Geist*, finds himself isolated from, and opposed to, the coarse realities of bourgeois
life (*Leben*); and the possibility of conciliation between these two spheres appears
remote. By the time Mann came to write the autobiographical *Tonio Kröger* (1903),
however, he was beginning to realize that this opposition was too simplistic, and
that a person could contain both types within himself. Tonio Kröger is both artist
and 'verirrter Bürger' (VIII, 305), torn between his artistic calling and his longing
for a normal bourgeois life. At the end of the story, Kröger recognizes his duality:
'Ich stehe zwischen zwei Welten' (VIII, 337). This realization that the two tendencies
could coexist signals a new subtlety in Mann's approach to the problem. In the
later works, the relations between *Bürger* and *Künstler*, between *Geist* and *Leben* are
explored from every conceivable angle. This vital aspect of Mann's work was often
ignored by his earliest critics. One notable exception is Pamela Reilly's 1949 thesis,
'Die Synthese des Bürgers und des Künstlers bei Thomas Mann'.[1] Reilly points
out that many of Mann's mature works aim at reconciling the two categories. She
singles out *Betrachtungen eines Unpolitischen* as the first major text in which Mann
successfully combines the two personae, presenting himself simultaneously as artist
and as concerned citizen.[2] In the *Betrachtungen* the two opposing terms *Bürger* and
Künstler are merged together in Mann's description of Wagner, whom Mann regards
as a representative of 'Bürgerliches Künstlertum' (XII, 108).[3]

Since Reilly's contribution, advances in the social sciences and in Thomas
Mann scholarship have enabled us to deepen our understanding of these issues. For
instance, Jürgen Habermas's seminal work *Strukturwandel der Öffentlichkeit* (1962)
demonstrated that the emergence of the bourgeoisie was related to changes in the art
market. In the eighteenth century, the new accessibility of culture as a commodity
— one that everyone could buy — entailed a broadening of the very notion of the
public.[4] According to Habermas, changes in theatre-going habits actually helped to
define the new bourgeoisie.[5] The fact that literature and drama are defining aspects

of bourgeois culture establishes a relation of complicity between *Bürger* and *Künstler*. Thomas Mann, in his mature works, shows a complex understanding of the interrelations between the two. This is particularly true in the case of *Felix Krull*, a novel that subverts the traditional opposition between *Bürger* and *Künstler* at every turn.[6] The following analysis will therefore avoid the *Bürger/Künstler* dichotomy. In terms of methodology, it will be far more productive to pursue the question: What forms does the relationship between *Bürger* and *Künstler* take? *Felix Krull* is a novel that is intimately aware of the way in which aesthetics permeates almost every aspect of our lives. Art is not just part of the fabric of everyday life; in a secular society such as our own, it also performs a metaphysical function. Nietzsche, in *Geburt der Tragödie*, and Benjamin, in his *Kunstwerk* essay, both argue that in the absence of theology, art becomes vitally important in providing a focus for the metaphysical longings of humanity. Art matters, because it provides meaning, emotional outlet, and a sense of community. From this perspective, I intend to analyse *Felix Krull* in terms of the multifarious interactions between art and society which it portrays.

(i) Art as a Social Modality

(a) *Rituals of exchange*

The central thesis of this chapter is that Felix Krull is more of an artist, more of a 'Lebenskünstler' than a confidence man. His primary concern is not to deceive, but to give free rein to what he calls 'meine natürliche Begabung für gute Form' (266). In doing so, he reveals that even the most mundane aspects of social interaction have an aesthetic dimension. In order to analyse the interplay between aesthetics and society in the novel, I will need to refer to certain social and anthropological theories. It is important to stress that many developments in social theory occurred during Thomas Mann's lifetime and that he was far from being unaware of them. Mann was, after all, a contemporary of Max Weber and Georg Simmel, and it was around the turn of the twentieth century that the field of sociology first emerged as a fully-fledged discipline.[7] The early sociologists, like Thomas Mann, emerged from the classical German intellectual tradition. Simmel, for example, wrote studies of Goethe, Nietzsche, and Schopenhauer. It is not insignificant to state that the tradition which produced *Felix Krull* also produced works that are classics of social theory. To begin with, I wish to draw upon the perspective of ethnography, or what the English-speaking world calls anthropology.[8] On one level, *Felix Krull* is clearly an immensely rich anthropological study of pre-war Europe. This is hardly surprising when one considers that Thomas Mann and Bronislaw Malinowski, the Polish founder of modern anthropology, shared a common intellectual background: for both of them, Nietzsche was a formative influence.[9] Nietzsche's attention to aesthetics, his perspectivism, and his wide-ranging studies of world cultures inspired not only Thomas Mann, but also Malinowski and his followers. The work done by Mann on *Felix Krull* in the 1950s displays an even greater understanding of some of these intellectual currents. The conversations with Professor Kuckuck and the palaeontology museum episode reflect Mann's study of the origins of culture in the 1930s and 1940s.[10] The later *Felix Krull* is highly sensitive to cultural specificities.

For example, Felix Krull knows that to do well in Paris one should talk about *jolies femmes*, whereas in Munich one should talk about beer (153).

Anthropological research shows that art has two main functions in society. Firstly, it provides psychological gratification; and secondly, art, like religion, helps to maintain social stability through its embodiment of an ethos and a style of living, thereby reinforcing social structures and institutions.[11] Aesthetics is especially important in rituals of exchange which underpin social structures. The notion of exchange is developed in two founding works of modern anthropology: Malinowski's *Argonauts of the Western Pacific* (1922)[12] and Marcel Mauss's *Essai sur le don* (1925).[13] During his fieldwork among the Trobriand islanders of Melanesia, Malinowski found a system of inter-tribal exchange called 'Kula', carried on within a ring of islands stretching 120 miles in diameter. In the Kula cycle, red-shell necklaces were exchanged for white-shell bracelets; the necklaces always travelling clockwise and the bracelets constantly travelling anti-clockwise around the islands. The shells had prestige value rather than monetary value and could not be bartered for other objects. However, the prestige derived not from owning the shells, but from giving them at public ceremonies, which were regulated by mutual obligation. The giving of the shells was accompanied by feasting, celebration, and magical rites. Malinowski points out that this system, involving the exchange of ornamental objects, binds together a large number of disparate tribes, thus promoting social cohesion and giving a harmless outlet to rivalry, by channelling it into ostentatious displays of gift-giving.[14] More practical trade then takes place alongside the Kula ritual. This, then, is the classic example of a society conditioned by aesthetics.

Inspired by Malinowski, Marcel Mauss synthesized a vast amount of similar data in his essay on the gift. Mauss's essay shows that, among most tribal societies, the main transfer of goods occurs in cyclical form, through cycles of obligatory returns of gifts. Mauss cites the fact that these exchanges are accompanied by magic rituals in order to support his thesis of the religious origin of the notion of economic value.[15] The philosopher Georges Bataille follows Mauss, introducing metaphysics into economics. In his 1949 essay *La notion de dépense*, Bataille attacks utilitarian economics, claiming that sacrificial expenditure precedes, and forms the basis of, monetary acquisition.[16] These notions are not merely archaic — they have a direct bearing on the world described by Mann in *Felix Krull*. Put quite simply, the novel is crammed full of scenes of exchange, feasting, and social ritual.

One might object that the fact that the hero is a confidence man tends to disrupt any sense of fair exchange. But this is not the case, because Felix Krull is a rather unique kind of confidence man: he is one who aims to please, rather than take money. In many ways he is closer to being a travelling performer than a con man. After all, he sings for his supper, and wins admiration with faultless displays of charm. His routines are the result of long and careful preparation. There is only one episode in the novel when Felix Krull steals something from an unknowing victim, and reciprocates nothing: when he steals sweets from the delicatessen (308–11). In every other case, one can justifiably talk of an exchange. For example, when Felix steals a strange woman's jewellery case (389), this is soon 'made good', when he meets her again by chance in Paris and confesses the theft (447–48). It turns out that

Diane Houpflé is only too pleased to be stolen from, in return for sexual favours. Even in his economic transactions, Felix Krull shows himself to be scrupulous, and to be a scrupulous observer of the aesthetic rituals which regulate monetary exchange.

The studies mentioned above describe how the phenomenon of money arose from a context of belief and faith. This aspect of economics is still with us today: modern economics is the result of a process of increasing abstraction and reliance upon confidence. Pre-modern coins were made of gold and silver, metals which were highly prized for their rarity and beauty, despite having little practical or objective use-value. The introduction of paper money represented a further stage of abstraction, leading to financial speculation on a much larger scale.[17] Paper money was supposed to be guaranteed by the gold standard: UK banknotes still bear the Bank of England's promise to 'pay the bearer on demand the sum of . . .' (an unlikely promise, given that the number of banknotes in circulation far exceeds the nation's gold reserves). A brief glance at today's media serves to illustrate the paramount importance of confidence in world financial markets. In fact, confidence underpins every financial transaction. If no confidence exists, people will not enter into the transaction. Every transaction represents a contract between two people, and is the result of negotiation. Indeed, money, like language and art, is a socially negotiated currency. The whole point of the lengthy haggling between Felix Krull, Stanko, and Meister Jean-Pierre in Book II is that the real cash value of an object is only ever what someone is willing to pay at the time. The fact that these transactions take place within a black market economy does not prevent them from being paradigmatic of business deals in general. The features are instantly recognizable and generally applicable, for, although these deals are illegal, — once they are done, all parties concerned stick to the terms: Felix pays Stanko the three thousand francs they agreed upon, even though this leaves him less than half that amount. The agreed price will depend on the practicalities of the situation, and on the quality of the relationship between the two trading partners. This is where the rhetorical element comes into play. Hence the discussion of 'realen Gesamtwert' and '[theoretisches] Risiko' (427) — the risk must be factored in; hence Jean-Pierre's attempts to make much of Felix's lack of experience, by calling him 'Bürschchen' (426), 'Dummkopf' (427), and 'Grünschnabel' (428). Arguments are supported by invoking recognized authorities; hence the appeals to 'Vernunft', 'gemeinsame Grundsätze', and morality: 'Ich kenne den Realwert dieser Dinge, [. . . und] ich [werde] nicht dulden, daß sich die Leistung des Käufers in unmoralischem Grade davon entfernt' (426–27). Each of the pair asserts to the very last that he is the one losing out, that he is being too generous. And, in a moment reminiscent of Malinowski's Trobriand islanders, Jean-Pierre makes an appeal to the idea that a business relationship calls a lasting friendship into being, by throwing in an extra gift, and begging Krull to return:

> Sieh, ich möchte die Verbindung mit dir gern aufrechthalten. [. . .] erweise dich dankbar, indem du wiederkommst! Hier ist deine Uhr. Ich schenke dir diese Kette dazu. [. . .] Komm wieder! Ich habe mich etwas verliebt in dich, bei unseren Geschäften. (429–30)

Felix Krull, too, is keen to show his good faith to Stanko, giving him the agreed amount of money, without trying to renegotiate. Krull is not a miser or a penny-pincher; he prefers to spend his money on fine things. He has little interest in usury. For example, he prefers to pay up front for his waiter's uniform rather than in instalments, 'den aber ich, versteht sich, bar erlegte' (469) — the idea of hanging onto the money for as long as possible, or of making money from the extra interest, does not occur to him. Furthermore, when Felix agrees to impersonate the Marquis de Venosta, he has to stump up an initial sum as his part of the bargain. Felix doesn't haggle here and seems aware that he too must bring something to the table. The momentous nature of the occasion obviously demands a grand gesture on his part, and so he contributes twelve thousand francs, his entire savings — an act which moves the Marquis to tears (521). Felix's sound grasp of the aesthetics of business shows that he does indeed have bourgeois traits which complement his bohemian nature.

(b) *Food and drink*

If business transactions, by the use of aesthetic means, depend upon and establish a community, then so does eating. In what follows I will be drawing on the theories of the sociologist Georg Simmel. We know that Thomas Mann's reception of Nietzsche was in part influenced by Simmel's study *Schopenhauer und Nietzsche* (1908) because Mann cites Simmel in the *Betrachtungen* (XII, 84). It is not known whether Mann was acquainted with Simmel's other works (such as the study of Goethe), but it is clear that he was interested in Simmel. The news of Simmel's death on 26 September 1918 prompted Mann to reflect in his diary about his own mortality,[18] and later, in 'Pariser Rechenschaft', he described Simmel as a leading intellectual light of pre-1914 Berlin (XI, 38). Georg Simmel's groundbreaking essay 'Soziologie der Mahlzeit' (1910) analyses the immense socializing power of eating together, linking it to the religious notion of communion:

> Das gemeinsame Essen und Trinken, das selbst dem Araber den eben noch todfeindlichen Fremden in einen Freund verwandelt, löst eine ungeheure sozialisierende Kraft aus, die [. . .] die primitive Vorstellung erzeugt, man stelle hiermit gemeinsames Fleisch und Blut her.[19]

Simmel describes how the regulation of communal eating and table manners has succeeded in elevating a primitive, selfish event into the sphere of social interaction and interpersonal significance. This standardization of eating has taken place along aesthetic principles. For example, meals take place regularly, at set times, and the courses follow in a set order. The use of cutlery and crockery also helps to transform individual selfishness into the social form of the meal. Simmel describes how all the plates must be identical, in order to cancel out the notion of individuality.[20] Another important aspect of the meal, for Simmel, is the ritualized conversation. Conversation at the dinner table should retain a certain generality and never become too personal, in order to hold the brute fact of eating at an appropriate distance: 'Auch die Tischunterhaltung darf sich, wenn sie im Stil bleiben will, nicht über die allgemeinen, typischen Gegenstände und Behandlungsarten in individuelle Tiefen begeben'.[21] One should not, however, try to obscure the act of eating completely; it is rather a question of sublimating the phenomenon. It is the basic, fundamental nature of eating which calls the polite merriment into being: 'weil erst an dessen festgehaltenem Character die ganze auflösende Leichtigkeit und Anmut ihres Oberflächenspiels sich offenbart'.[22] If successful dining relies on an understanding of this play of surface and depth, if it demands a fine sense of propriety and where to draw the limits, then Felix Krull possesses these qualities in abundance — as his success shows. Scenes of eating recur throughout the novel, and they usually form preludes to scenes of closer intimacy. For example, Krull's success at the dinner table leads to him being invited to play tennis with Zouzou (595). Of course, not all instances of communal eating succeed in establishing a lasting bond. Despite the wild parties held by Engelbert Krull at the beginning of the novel (278–79), which often last all night, none of the guests come to his funeral later on: the deceased is forgotten by those 'Freunde' who had partaken greedily of his hospitality (326). It seems that Krull senior is being punished for his excessive carousing; despite the fact that he is merely conforming to the regional stereotype of the Catholic Rhinelander.[23] If Felix Krull's encounters at the dinner table prove to be more successful than his father's, then this surely derives, not just from his beauty, but from his ability to keep within the bounds of good taste. An obvious example is the way he elegantly sidesteps the rude provocation of Zouzou's 'Patatípatatá!' — he simply parries the outburst with a compliment (588).

Simmel's theory about the socializing power of food is borne out in the scene where the Marquis de Venosta discovers Felix Krull eating on the roof terrace of the Grand Hôtel des Ambassadeurs. The fact that Krull is eating in the same restaurant as the Marquis (moreover, observing the same dress code as him) instantly establishes a relationship of equal footing between the two men (500). The Marquis joins Krull's table at once and launches into a polite, inconsequential, discourse, intended to put him at his ease while he finishes his meal: 'Um Gottes willen, essen Sie weiter und sagen Sie kein Wort! Lassen Sie mich schwatzen' (502). And, although the Marquis has now begun to treat Krull as an equal, he only becomes confident enough to entrust Krull with the job of impersonating him after he has closely observed Krull's table manners: 'Ich sah wohl, daß er meine Art zu essen beobachtete' (503). The Marquis obviously considers table manners to be of paramount importance. He reveals this by his remarks about 'fremde Speisesitten' (503): the disparaging remark about the American method of eating (cutting the food up first, then laying down the knife and eating with the fork in one's right hand) shows only too clearly that table manners act as a badge of cultural belonging. In other words, Felix Krull is allowed to become a marquis because he is the perfect dinner guest. He possesses what the sociologist Pierre Bourdieu calls 'cultural capital': a comprehensive understanding of the modalities and regulations of upper-class society.[24] Krull's wish to become a marquis and his love of fine restaurants is a symptom of modernity's persistent nostalgia for aristocratic forms of conduct.[25]

Felix Krull cuts a fine figure as a marquis, but it is arguably in his capacity as a waiter that he truly shines. In the Saint James and Albany Hotel he becomes the purveyor of excellence at the dinner table. His first appearance in the hotel restaurant is the debut of an artiste ('Der nächste Tag also schon sah mich in voller Parure bei der Mittagsmahlzeit im Saale debütieren' (470)). Felix Krull takes his role as a waiter very seriously. He spends a long time laying the tables, arranging cutlery and menus, setting the stage for his performance: 'Lange bevor die ersten Gäste zum Luncheon sich einfanden, war ich zur Hand gewesen, hatte geholfen, auf einer bestimmten Gruppe von Tischen [. . .] die Couverts zu legen, die Menukarten zu verteilen' (470). When the guests arrive, Krull does his utmost to impress upon them his gracefulness and his pleasure in serving them. Everything must go smoothly. It doesn't matter if the guests are attractive or not, it is a question of satisfaction in a job well done:

> [Ich] ließ es mir dann nicht nehmen, das Speisepublikum [. . .] mit markierter Herzensfreude zu begrüßen, den Damen die Stühle unterzuschieben, ihnen die Karten zu reichen, Wasser einzuschenken, kurz, diesen Pfleglingen, ohne Ansehen ihrer ungleichen Reize, meine Gegenwart artig einprägsam zu machen. (470)

It is evident that Felix Krull enjoys being a waiter. He does not consider it beneath him to wait on tables, on the contrary: for him, it is an opportunity to show off his grace and skill. He makes a brilliant waiter, and quickly impresses his superiors, the hotel director Stürzli and the maître d'hôtel, Machatschek. Although the hotel sequence was written in the early 1950s, Thomas Mann's research for this part of the novel dates back at least as early as 1910. The evidence for this is in the dossier of newspaper cuttings which he gathered between 1910 and 1914. Three documents are particularly significant, since they contain numerous underlinings by Mann. The first two articles are by Ola Alsen and appeared in *Die Woche* in 1910: 'Die Dame im Hotel' and 'Beim Fünfuhrtee'.[26] The third document, 'Der Beruf eines Hotelkellners', is undated but most probably predates 1914.[27] 'Die Dame im Hotel' describes the recent phenomenon of the luxury hotel. In order to cope with increasing numbers of independent female travellers, modern hotels have developed an impressive array of luxuries to pamper their guests. The most splendid of these new features is the five o'clock tea. Mann highlighted the following paragraph:

> Was früher die Kurkonzerte waren, ist heute der Five o'clock tea. Er hat eine gewaltige Karriere gemacht. Er ist das enfant gâté geworden. Jedes größere, erstklassige Hotel hat in seiner Halle einen Nachmittagsempfang, der von der eleganten Welt besucht wird. Leichte Musik, <u>ein wenig Lyrik, von Jünglingen mit bleichem, lockenumrahmten Antlitz vorgetragen</u>, hier und da eine tanz-beflissene junge Dame, die der Ruhm der Duncan nicht ruhen läßt [. . .]. Bei dem Tee und dem Zigarettenduft gedeiht der Flirt wunderbar. Es plaudert sich so schön in dieser Stunde [. . .]. Man schuf sogar besondere Toiletten für diese Nachmittagzeit, die einen solch friedvollen heiteren Uebergang zu dem Abend bildet.[28]

Alsen's article appears to have interested Mann for a number of reasons. It describes the hotel tea hall as a place for coquettish behaviour. More importantly, it presents the five o'clock tea service as an art form in its own right. It has replaced the spa concert as the main social event, and it has developed its own unique aesthetic. Alsen's second article, published a few months later in December 1910, is a variation on the same theme. This time, Alsen depicts the five o'clock tea as the successor to the eighteenth-century salons of Madame d'Epinay and Rahel Varnhagen.[29] The hotel tea room, luxuriously furnished with wicker chairs and Japanese silks, has also replaced the boudoir ('Das Teezimmer ist die Nachfolgerin des Boudoirs. Das Boudoir hat sich überlebt').[30] In these elegant surroundings, women show off the latest fashions and mingle with their male admirers. The five o'clock tea is a triumph of modern civilization: magnificent, yet intimate. Mann highlighted the margin of this passage:

> Der Hoteltee — wie ein Hinausgleiten aus dem Alltag, aus dem Drängen und Haften, aus dem Lärm der Straße. Die Windfänge drehen sich, in der Halle springen die livrierten Boys herbei, die überflüssigen Toilettenstücke in die Garderobe zu tragen. Weit und dennoch intim dehnt sich die Halle, lichtüberströmt, gedämpfte Musik, als ob sie von fern käme, durchklingt den Raum. Eine Atmosphäre des Wohllebens! Eine Geselligkeit ohne Verbindlichkeit, ohne große Ankündigung, ein stets bereitetes Tischlein-deck-dich![31]

The hotel dining hall is the place where love affairs begin, where lovers meet. Alsen ends her article with a quotation from Heine: 'Sie saßen und tranken am Teetisch und sprachen von Liebe viel'.[32]

The influence of these documents on Book II of *Felix Krull* is apparent. In Mann's novel, the hotel is the place of high aesthetics and amorous liaisons. Crucial to all of this Felix Krull's role as a waiter. The position of hotel waiter is highly demanding. Thomas Mann found a newspaper article which points out that a first-class waiter must train for several years and be fluent in at least three languages. This is the kernel of the scene with the hotel director Stürzli:

> Der Laie wird staunen, wenn er hört, daß der tüchtige, es mit seinem Beruf ernst nehmende Hotelkellner eine Lehrzeit machen muß, die an Länge der des studierten Mannes nicht viel nachgibt. [. . .] Studieren muß auch der Hotel-kellner und zwar folgende Disziplinen: Lebende Sprachen, Länder- und Völker-kunde. Der moderne, vorwärtsstrebende Hotelkellner muß mindestens drei Sprachen beherrschen und zwar so, daß er sich geläufig unterhalten kann.[33]

Felix Krull is a superlative waiter, full of professional courtesy. He knows that he has to be sensitively encouraging, and help people to choose their orders with the utmost tact. He is well aware that this performance also has an erotic dimension, and even uses the word 'Liebesdienst':

> Wie wohl verstand ich es doch, Schwankende dabei mit der weichen, diskret zurückhaltenden Stimme, die dem Kellner ansteht, zu beraten, wie wohl, allen Darreichungen und Versehungen den lieblosen Charakter des Vorwerfens fernzuhalten, alle vielmehr auf eine Art zu tätigen, als handle es sich um einen persönlichen Liebesdienst. (473)

This is the artist as waiter, bringing an emotionally charged performance to the simple act of serving food. Krull is, after all, 'zum Liebesdienst geschaffen' (381). Under such circumstances, it is no wonder that Miss Twentyman and Lord Kilmarnock soon fall in love with him. Felix Krull is so charming to both of them that they become addicted to his presence. Both, in their different ways, make advances to him; both are rather pathetic figures — one gets the impression that Felix is the first person who has been really kind to them. Indeed, he has been *too* kind to them; he does too much for Miss Twentyman: 'und tat mit alldem entschieden zuviel' (476); he is too gentle towards Lord Kilmarnock: 'Es war aber nicht gut für ihn' (480). These episodes fit into a long literary tradition which stretches from Greek myths about gods falling in love with their cupbearers, to the amorous poems which Goethe dedicates to his wine-waiter in the 'Schenkenbuch' section of the *West-östlicher Divan*. The point is, though, that mealtimes bring into play a whole series of expectations; they form a complex social ritual, which channels and releases basic drives through an aesthetically mediated festivity.

There is a key moment in the analysis of this phenomenon at the beginning of the book, when Mann describes the sparkling wine ('Sekt') produced by Felix's father Engelbert, the brand known as 'Lorley extra cuvée'. There is a highly comic discrepancy between the ostentatious, luxurious form of the bottle and its unsavoury, diluted contents.[34] By concentrating all of his resources into producing bottles with elegant exteriors, and neglecting to produce a wine of decent quality, Engelbert Krull is operating a confidence trick which plays directly into the demand for highly aestheticized alcoholic drinks. As well as physical drunkenness, the wine is expected to produce feelings of exclusivity and wealth, to intoxicate by its alluring exterior as well as by its interior. One wants a wine label to conjure up images of great chateaux and vast estates; and so Schimmelpreester's design features coats of arms and gold embossed lettering; so too does it feature the image of the 'Lorley', who is of course the central mythical figure of the Rhine valley, thus managing to combine sexual titillation with further cultural acknowledgement of the Rhine. This is a prime example of the role of fiction in social occasions. Engelbert Krull is obviously catering for a real need; the exterior of the bottle fulfils a fantasy and that is why he can say in his defence that: 'kurz, ich gebe dem Publikum, woran es glaubt' (268). In this passage, written in 1910, Mann anticipates the work of the French structuralist Roland Barthes nearly half a century later. In his book *Mythologies* (1957), Barthes points out that there is a whole complex of cultural traditions and ideological clichés associated with wine. Wine, more than any other drink, is a totem drink for the French. For them it has a magical power; it is supposedly capable of transforming almost any situation into its opposite.[35] Barthes insists that the act of drinking wine cannot be reduced to the functional purpose of getting drunk; rather, it is a decorative gesture: 'le vin n'est pas seulement philtre, il est aussi acte durable de boire: le geste a ici une valeur décorative, et le pouvoir du vin n'est jamais séparé de ses modes d'existence'.[36] But it is not just drinking which is infused with decorative value. One of the things which become apparent from reading both Mann and Barthes is that every aspect of modern life is permeated by aesthetics. In the next subsection I will look at the affinity between *Felix Krull* and Barthes's survey of modern culture.

(c) *Structuralism*

> Was jedermann für ausgemacht hält, verdient am meisten,
> untersucht zu werden. — Lichtenberg

Structuralism was an intellectual movement of the 1950s and 1960s, which, starting from the linguistic notions of Charles Sanders Peirce (1839–1914) and Ferdinand de Saussure (1857–1913), applied these notions to various fields of inquiry including anthropology, psychoanalysis, philosophy, and cultural studies.[37] Saussure made the fruitful distinction between *la langue*, the language 'as a whole', existing as a social institution, and *la parole*, a speech-act or instance of usage of the language. *La langue* is an autonomous value-system, which has its own rules. Roland Barthes refers to it as a sort of collective contract, which must be complied with if one wishes to communicate.[38] The anthropologist Claude Levi-Strauss applied this theory to ethnological data. He studied the discourse of tribal societies in order to ascertain the fundamental structures, such as structures of kinship and belief, which provided the basis for individual speech acts.[39] Barthes, in *Mythologies*, applied the same theory to the cultural products of 1950s France, looking at everyday objects, ones which are usually taken for granted, and noting how they express the value-systems of modern bourgeois culture. Barthes later explicitly compared his approach to that of the ethnologist: 'Dans les *Mythologies*, c'est la France elle-même qui est ethnographiée' (OC III, 158). Pursuing the topic of food, Barthes notes how the beefsteak participates in the same sanguine mythology of wine: if it becomes over-cooked, it loses its potency as a national emblem, and becomes morally dubious. Thus the bleeding steak represents a morality.[40]

Barthes claims that social fictions or 'myths' like this one tend to depoliticize an object by concealing its history, the story of its production. The myth makes the object seem 'natural' and ahistorical.[41] One prime example is the new Citroën car, which is seemingly devoid of origin; there are no visible rivets or welded joints which would betray the labour that went into producing it. In this way, the car appears as if it had fallen from the skies.[42] Incidentally, this coincides remarkably with what Nietzsche says about the effect aimed at by the artist, namely that the artwork should look as if it was the product of divine inspiration, rather than hard work.[43] Similarly, Felix Krull prepares for months in order to make his faked epileptic fit seem as natural as possible, in the *Musterungsszene*. Despite the fact that they are working from different perspectives — Barthes from a Marxist one, while Mann's views are closer to those of Nietzsche and Schopenhauer — both writers want to call appearances into question. To call appearances into question, however, is not to dismiss or invalidate them. The minute analysis of cultural ephemera practised by Mann and Barthes is highly ambivalent, and can be seen as affirmation as well as criticism. *Felix Krull* and *Mythologies* can both be read as affectionate, gently ironic tributes to their respective cultural milieux.

Taking his cue from de Saussure, Barthes showed that modern commodities can be considered as part of systems of signification, which may then be analyzed linguistically. Clothes and food (to name but two) are both systems of signification to which Saussure's distinction can be applied. For example, with food, *la langue* is composed of the various rules of food, such as: taboos, oppositions of type (e.g.

savoury/sweet), accepted combinations of foodstuffs and opinions concerning food. *La parole* is then the various instances of food production (OC 1, 1479). The great value of Barthes's work is to show the extent to which societies have an aesthetic coherence that gives them a way of life. Cultural objects which we consider to be natural are in fact the result of a long historical and ideological development. They express social values through aesthetic means.

Thomas Mann's preparation for *Felix Krull* involved the careful study of modern life, as it was portrayed in the popular media of the time. He carried out this research with the thoroughness that we nowadays associate with Roland Barthes or Walter Benjamin. From 1910 to 1914 Mann collected 521 newspaper and magazine cuttings. He arranged the documents under headings such as 'Kur- und Lustorte', 'Intérieurs', 'Elegante Festlichkeiten', and 'Hôtel. Reise'.[44] Just as Roland Barthes's favourite source of cultural data was the glossy magazine *Paris Match*,[45] Thomas Mann's main source, apart from newspapers, was the weekly illustrated journal of high society, *Die Woche*. This is not to claim that Mann somehow anticipated structuralism. The use of montage does not make one a structuralist. Nevertheless, it is clear that Mann had decided to incorporate the study of his own culture into his process of self-analysis as a writer. Felix Krull was thus to inhabit the world of collective fantasy, to live the 'high life' of luxury and celebrity so frequently mythologized by the modern media. And it is hardly surprising that Mann takes his hero to Paris, the city which has, of course, long been mythologized as the most beautiful, most romantic city in Europe, the epitome of high culture. French culture has excelled at turning itself into a sort of universal myth. Long before Felix Krull gets to Paris, he has heard about it at length from his francophile father:

> Paris, diese Stadt, deren bloßes Erinnerungsbild meinen armen Vater zeit seines Lebens vor Vergnügen schwach gemacht hatte (334) [. . .] während der Conducteur Namen anmeldete, die ich so oft aus dem Munde meines armen Vaters in zärtlicher Betonung vernommen, wie 'Place de la Bourse', 'Rue du Quatre Septembre', 'Boulevard des Capucines', 'Place de l'Opéra' und andere mehr. (392)

Of course it is never easy to analyse the everyday. Normally we do not notice it because we are absorbed in it. Analysis requires a perspective, and this is difficult when it comes to dissecting one's own culture. Barthes points out that in order to reveal the discourse embedded in everyday objects, one has to stand outside the community.[46] This implies a tension between the bourgeois who enjoys commodified objects, who revels in their myth, and the outsider who analyses these mythical structures, taking them apart; in other words, another version of Thomas Mann's *Bürger/Künstler* dichotomy. It is an opposition that both Mann and Barthes were starting to unpick. Felix Krull combines both roles: long before he joins high society, he spends ages studying the shop windows of Frankfurt in detail. In fact, the window displays have given him an entire education into the ways of the bourgeoisie and their customs:

> Soll ich noch reden von den Blumenhandlungen, [. . .] hinter deren Fenstern sich mir jene üppigen [. . .] Körbe zeigten, die man den Frauen schickt, um ihnen seine Aufmerksamkeit zu erweisen? Von den Papeterieläden, deren

Auslagen mich lehrten, welcher Papiere man sich kavaliermäßigerweise zu seinen Korrespondenzen bedient [. . .]? (343–44)

Even as Felix Krull falls for these luxury consumer goods, he senses that there is something deeply unreal and fantastical about them: he knows they are fictions. He refers to the precious stones which he sees as 'Phantasiesteine', 'Schätze des Märchenlandes' (343). Thus, while Hermann Kurzke links Felix Krull to the narcissistic phase of psychological development — what Jacques Lacan calls the 'imaginary order' — I would rather see Felix Krull as typifying the next stage of development, involving access to the 'symbolic order' in Lacanian terms. The ease with which he operates in the world of cultural symbols shows that he has a very adult grasp of the customs and paraphernalia of the adult world. Indeed, as Michael Neumann shows, Krull's attitude to the big city is highly analytical, like that of a detective who considers everything to be a sign: 'In der Metropole ist alles Zeichen; es bleiben "bedeutungsfreien" Zwischenräume mehr'.[47]

Despite Krull's critical awareness as a narrator, one of the reasons that Mann abandoned *Felix Krull* in 1913 was that he felt it was too apolitical, or in other words that it was becoming a symptom rather than an analysis. In the introduction to a reading of Krull given on 5 October 1916 he remarks that the novel has 'einen sehr vorkriegerischen u. vorpolitischen Charakter' (N II, 283; DüD I, 307). A few days later, in a letter to Peter Pringsheim, he complains that the novel caters for the current demand 'nach dem "Beziehungslosen"', a demand that he disapproves of (Br III, 465; DüD I, 307). This is why it was interrupted in favour of the ideological complexity of the *Betrachtungen* and *Der Zauberberg*. Even so, my central argument in this chapter is that although *Felix Krull* lacks the direct political references of those other works, it nevertheless represents Mann's fullest examination of the role of aesthetics in society. When Mann went back to writing the novel after the end of the Second World War, he claimed that he was motivated by the desire for completion and the need for some light relief after *Doktor Faustus*. But it seems clear that after his portrayal of the dark consequences of culture for society in that novel, he wished to view the interplay between culture and society again in a more positive light.

In *Felix Krull*, the view of turn-of-the-century Europe is obviously tinted with nostalgia and affection; indeed, it seems to me that one can draw a parallel between the novel and *Brideshead Revisited*, which was written in early 1944. *Brideshead Revisited* raises the question of the value of a 'geistige Lebensform'. Evelyn Waugh explains in the preface that when he wrote the book, he believed that the stately homes of England were to be destroyed. He thus wished to commemorate a way of life destined to vanish forever. Written in a period of privation, the book is 'infused with a kind of gluttony, for food and wine, for the splendours of the recent past'.[48] When Thomas Mann was writing *Felix Krull* a few years later, the post-war reconstruction of Germany still had a long way to go, and no one could foresee the *Wirtschaftswunder* which was to follow. Hence Mann's novel too is imbued with a sort of elegiac longing for the halcyon days of youth, a youth lived out against the elegant backdrop of pre-war Europe. Perhaps it is also true to say that the perspective of time allowed Mann to take stock of that era in a more dispassionate way. It was a time of rigid formality but also of increasing social mobility, and this is exemplified in the meteoric rise of Felix Krull. And throughout the narrative Mann strives to capture the feel of this world. Time and time again, the surface of things comes to the fore; the light touch and ironic style of the first few chapters is wonderfully sustained. The narrative dwells upon appearances: mannerisms, styles, decors. Now, what seemed a mere epiphenomenon is seen as essential, and it becomes clear that the fabric of the social order is formed primarily of aesthetic representations. Just as in the final chapter of *Der Zauberberg*, shadows change places with things, and become more relevant than the things themselves: 'aus der Hochmutsneigung, die Schatten für die Dinge zu nehmen, in diesem aber nur Schatten zu sehen' (III, 985). The texture of society becomes its defining feature: society is made out of things aesthetic.

(d) *Social interaction*

> Bald ist er nicht mehr damit zufrieden, daß ihm die Dinge gefallen; er will selbst gefallen, anfangs zwar nur durch das, was *sein* ist, endlich durch das, was *er* ist. — SCHILLER (NA 20, 408)

Felix Krull considers it a social and moral duty to be pleasing to the eye. As he tells Zouzou in Book III: 'Aus eingeborener Rücksicht auf die Welt, die mich erwartete, habe ich im Werden acht darauf gegeben, daß ich ihr Auge nicht kränkte. Das ist alles. Ich möchte es eine Sache der Selbstdisziplin nennen' (591). Despite the faint irony, this statement invokes humanist notions of courtesy and self-cultivation. It is typical of the playful humanism which pervades much of Book III. In order to understand the philosophical roots of the early *Felix Krull*, however, it will be necessary to consider Thomas Mann's earlier influences: in particular, Friedrich Nietzsche. Mann's Nietzsche reception has been well documented elsewhere by such writers as T. J. Reed and Peter Pütz.[49] I will focus my attention upon Nietzsche's idea that social relations are regulated by aesthetics, and show how this idea finds expression in the early *Felix Krull* and in the contemporaneous works of Georg Simmel. The main point here is that Nietzsche, Simmel, and Mann all see personal interaction as being dominated by aesthetics. In Nietzsche's writing, friendship and closeness form an opposite pole to the rhetoric of distance and solitude. Between these poles, there is, however, a dynamic, dialectical relation, which has sometimes been overlooked. Terry Eagleton is, I believe, too hasty in his discussion of Nietzsche's aesthetics when he says that, for Nietzsche, individual autonomy takes precedence above all else.[50] In fact, there is a strong undercurrent in Nietzsche's writing which undermines such categorical judgements. Although Nietzsche champions the individual, he does not dismiss culture or social consensus out of hand; rather, he strives towards a higher, more exacting culture. Indeed, Nietzsche's work and life reveal a constant search for literary forebears, and for a proper audience. Friendship is obviously of crucial importance to him, as can be seen from the final chapters of *Also sprach Zarathustra*, in which Zarathustra attempts to found a community of equals. In Nietzsche's writings on friendship we can discern a tentative approach to the aesthetic as a mode of social consensus; here, friendship is viewed as a delicate balance between agonistic and consensual urges.

In the paragraph 'Von den Freunden' in *Menschliches, Allzumenschliches*, Nietzsche claims that all friendships are based upon misunderstanding, upon the implicit agreement to conceal the hard truths which would destroy such a relationship: 'denn fast immer beruhen solche menschliche Beziehungen darauf, dass irgend ein paar Dinge nicht gesagt werden, ja dass an sie nie gerührt wird' (KGA 4.2, 269). Later in the same treatise Nietzsche says that friends must create an impression of intimacy which, however, preserves the fundamental differences between them:

> Die gute Freundschaft entsteht [. . .] wenn man endlich, zur Erleichterung des Verkehrs, den zarten Anstrich und Flaum der Intimität hinzuzutun versteht, zugleich aber sich der wirklichen und eigentlichen Intimität und der Verwechslung von Ich und Du weislich enthält. (KGA 4.3, 123)

Thus, to quote Rüdiger Görner, Nietzsche sees friendship as a creative balancing act, as 'Schein von Nähe'.[51] Görner also points out that Nietzsche derives his ideal of friendship from the classical tradition of antiquity, as transmitted by Michel de Montaigne, who considered friendship to be a work of art involving the harmonizing of two wills ('convenance des volontez').[52] In much the same way, the youthful Felix Krull looks for people who will humour him and play along with his intentions. The entire household must accept him as the Kaiser (271–72), and he is glad when his uncle allows him to dress up (284–85). When he feigns illness, it is his mother's turn to play along (300).[53] This sort of game provides the pleasure of an agreed illusion ('einer vereinbarten Illusion' (300)). Nietzsche's view of friendship is remarkably similar, but to say that Nietzsche regards friendship as an elaborate fiction is not to say that he dismisses it as being false. Nietzsche's thought aims at going beyond simple dichotomies such as 'true' and 'false'. For him, aesthetic value is the highest value that exists. If Nietzsche's project aims at an aesthetic justification of the world, as he claims in *Die Geburt der Tragödie*, then it seems clear that his discussion of the poetics of friendship plays an important part within this scheme. This does not preclude, however, an extreme mistrust of friendship and an insistence upon its agonistic element. For example, in *Also sprach Zarathustra*, Nietzsche notes that the man of knowledge must be able not only to love his enemies but to hate his friends (KGA 6.1, 97). Nietzsche does not condemn friendship *per se*, rather, his longing for friendship is directed towards a utopian future. Nietzsche calls himself untimely because he believes that his true equals will exist in the future, i.e. that he is contemporary with the future. When he claims to be a destiny in *Ecce Homo*, he is in effect saying that only in the future will he be truly understood and appreciated. This may seem far removed from the adventures of Felix Krull, who as a character is certainly no adherent of the stoic, Nietzschean ideal of friendship. But in fact Krull admirably performs what Nietzsche demands of art in *Menschliches, Allzumenschliches*, namely, that art should beautify life: 'Sodann soll die Kunst alles Häßliche *verbergen* oder *umdeuten*'. In the same passage, Nietzsche claims that the most important art is the art of living; making works of art is secondary:

> Nach dieser grossen, ja übergrossen Aufgabe der Kunst ist die sogenannte eigentliche Kunst, *die der Kunstwerke*, nur ein *Anhängsel*: ein Mensch, der einen

Ueberschuss von solchen verschönenden, verbergenden und umdeutenden Kräften in sich fühlt, wird sich zuletzt noch in Kunstwerken dieses Ueberschusses zu entladen suchen. (KGA 4.3, 90)

Felix Krull perfectly fulfils this requirement because he is a *Lebenskünstler* first and foremost: his primary concern is to live a beautiful life. He therefore represents the aesthetic sphere, that sphere which, in secular modernity, takes on a sacred function. According to Nietzsche in *Die Geburt der Tragödie*, in the absence of theology, aesthetics must bear the weight of humanity's metaphysical longings. This is because the very superfluity of the aesthetic places it beyond use value and therefore allows it to become a refuge for authentic interpersonal relations, beyond the alienating effects of industrial modernity. At the same time, the ambiguity of art continues to place it under suspicion. Art's freedom and its reliance on semblance make it morally questionable.

Felix Krull as a character neatly encompasses these contradictions within himself. On the one hand he is charming and humane, because he has understood that the essence of sociability is to be found in conversations pursued, like art, for their own sake, and not for some functional purpose. On the other, his duplicity makes him questionable. The imaginative capacity to lie, or to embellish the truth, may be highly suspect; nevertheless, it can also be the spice of life, the lubricant which makes social interaction flow more easily. This is especially true if one conceives of social interaction as an aesthetically mediated construct. Successful communication requires the imaginative ability to identify with the interlocutor, and thus to maintain an imagined community, even when no deeper bond exists.[54] The aesthetic world may be, in a sense, more authentic than the functional world of utilitarianism. This idea is developed most fully by Georg Simmel in his essay 'Soziologie der Geselligkeit', where he introduces the notion of an 'impulse to sociability' ('Geselligkeitstrieb'), which he compares to the creative impulse. According to Simmel, sociability is a form of aesthetic play which takes its form from the competitive realities of life, but which lacks the serious consequences of real life. Sociability is often composed of competitive games and sports, but these have no real consequences and are pursued for their own sake, rather like a work of art. Hence, Simmel calls sociability 'the play form of association' ('die Spielform der Vergesellschaftung').[55] Sociability, for Simmel, is a kind of socially created fictional world in which people put aside their differences and act as if their pleasure depended upon others being pleased: 'Die Geselligkeit schafft, wenn man will, eine ideale soziologische Welt: denn in ihr ist [. . .] die Freude des Einzelnen durchaus daran gebunden, dass auch die anderen froh sind'.[56] Sociability may depart from reality, but that does not make it a lie any more than a work of art is a lie: '[Die Geselligkeit] ist so wenig Lüge, wie das Spiel oder die Kunst mit all ihrer Abweichung von der Realität Lügen sind'.[57]

'Geselligkeit' is thus a sort of ideal semblance of society; it enacts society on another level, and most social interactions make an appeal to this ideal. Thomas Mann comes remarkably close to this notion in the first book of *Joseph und seine Brüder*, when he comments that it is humane and moral to hold a pleasant conversation merely for its own sake. Good form is thus a measure of human worth:

> Ist es doch schlechthin der Luxus der Übersachlichkeit und der Scheinvorrang
> ehrenhalber der schönen Form, eingerechnet den hochherzig unbekümmerten
> Zeitverbrauch um ihretwillen, welche das menschlich Würdige, nämlich das
> mehr als Natürliche und also Gesittete eigentlich ausmachen. (IV, 162)[58]

Simmel's exposition of social interaction provides the link between Nietzsche's
view of friendship as a balancing act, and the 'schöne Form' which is so dear
to Felix Krull (593). For Simmel, social relations are guided above all by tact
('Taktgefühl').[59] Simmel's concept of coquetry, which involves simultaneously
giving and withholding, is a sort of playful struggle, reminiscent of Nietzsche's
artistic balancing act. It is a social game which turns equivocation into an art:

> So ist es das Wesen der weiblichen Koketterie, ein andeutendes Gewähren
> und ein andeutendes Versagen wechselnd gegeneinander zu spannen, den
> Mann anzuziehen, ohne es zu einer Entscheidung kommen zu lassen, ihn
> zurückzuweisen, ohne ihm alle Hoffnung zu nehmen. [. . .] Ihr Verhalten
> pendelt zwischen dem Ja und dem Nein, ohne auf einem haltzumachen.[60]

In reading this description I am reminded of the ambiguous, ironic style which is the
hallmark of Thomas Mann's work. Mann had been schooled in irony by a number
of writers (not only Nietzsche, but Goethe, Heine, and Fontane as well), and he
brought the art of irony to a new level of refinement. Irony is a rhetorical structure
that implies freedom because it suspends judgement: Nietzsche once claimed that
Laurence Sterne, because of his 'Zweideutigkeit', was the freest writer of all (KGA
4.3, 60–61). At the same time, irony is intrinsically coquettish, since it both offers
and withdraws. This is especially true in the case of *Felix Krull*, a seductive work
which Mann himself described as the narrative equivalent of a trapeze act ('ein
heikelstes Balancestück' (XI, 123)). This notion of coquetry applies to both the form
and the content of the novel. Felix Krull is not only an incorrigible flirt, but also
a kind of acrobat, a vocation which he shares with Andromache, *la fille de l'air*. His
sense of balance and measure is vital to his profession as *Lebenskünstler*. It is also
an essential requirement for the job of waiting tables, where he must both arouse
and dampen the enthusiasm of his public: 'Man gab mich ihm preis, diesem mich
umbrodelnden Wohlgefallen, und ließ es mein Kunststück sein, es sowohl durch
schmelzendes Entgegenkommen anzuspornen, als es auch wieder durch sittige
Reserve einzudämmen' (473). Of course this flirting results in heartbreak for Lord
Kilmarnock and Miss Twentyman, but Felix Krull shows amazing tact and reserve
when it comes to letting his admirers down gently. It is worth noting as well that
the narrative here conforms to Simmel's rules of sociability by steering well clear
of tragedy, tacking instead towards farce. Rather than exploit the tragic potential
of these scenes, the rapid juxtapositions serve to accentuate the comedy. Extreme
forms of emotion are simply banished from the narrative. This corresponds to
Simmel's definition of sociable conversation, where talking is an end in itself, and
should thus be light and mercurial:

> Darum gehört zum Wesen der geselligen Unterhaltung, daß sie ihren
> Gegenstand leicht und rasch wechseln könne; [. . .] Die feinste gesellig erzählte
> Geschichte ist die, bei der der Erzählende seine Person völlig zurücktreten
> läßt; die ganz vollendete hält sich in dem glücklichen Gleichgewichtspunkt der

> sozusagen geselligen Ethik, in dem sowohl das subjektiv Individuelle wie das
> objektiv Inhaltliche sich völlig in den Dienst an der reinen Geselligkeitsform
> aufgelöst haben.[61]

Reading this passage, one is struck by the way it captures the bantering, after-dinner-conversational quality of *Felix Krull*. The novel has a lightness of tone which made it one of Mann's favourite texts for reading in public. Furthermore, Simmel's reference to a happy balance ('Gleichgewichtspunkt') calls us back once more to the image of the acrobat, so admired by Felix Krull.

If Mann's final novel is a tribute to the art of living, then it is also a tribute to the art of living socially. It presents the reader with a variety of social milieux, while at the same time articulating philosophical concerns. In fact, *Felix Krull* attempts to negotiate between the two traditions of 'Gesellschaftsroman' and 'Bildungsroman'; it tries to portray a world of social and sexual mores while at the same time retaining a commitment to the interiority ('Innerlichkeit') that is the hallmark of German literature. Mann's novel offers a view of the world in which depth and superficiality, *Leben* and *Geist*, *Bürger* and *Künstler*, are no longer seen as radical opposites, but as dialectically related elements of an organic whole. Felix Krull's obsession with surfaces may be trivial, but it is rooted in the genuine, sociable desire to gladden the eyes of his fellow men and women. Philosophically, the main point here is that aesthetic signification and mediation are vital to the life of *every* society. It is to Thomas Mann's credit that, like Nietzsche and Simmel, he draws out the underlying connections between the metaphysical and the physical realms. As Simmel points out, both art and sociability rely on conventional form, but this does not mean they should be regarded as being 'merely superficial'. Although sociability is only a symbol of life, it still retains a deep and true relation to reality, just as art does:

> Alle Geselligkeit ist nur ein *Symbol* des Lebens [. . .] aber eben doch ein Symbol
> des *Lebens*, dessen Bild [. . .] sich von einem tiefen und treuen Verhältnis zur
> Wirklichkeit nährt. [. . .] Aus diesem Zusammenhang wird ersichtlich, daß die
> Menschen über die *Oberflächlichkeit* des gesellschaftlichen Verkehrs mit Recht
> und mit Unrecht klagen.[62]

Deep and yet superficial; this is the paradox in which art and society are caught. According to Simmel, art and sociability partake of a different order of reality; they turn away from practical life, but only in order to experience life more deeply. In the apparently autonomous forms of art we experience the forces and meaning of reality:

> So offenbart etwa die Kunst das Geheimnis des Lebens: daß wir uns nicht
> durch einfaches Wegsehen von ihm erlösen, sondern gerade indem wir in dem
> scheinbar ganz selbstherrlichen Spiel seiner Formen den Sinn und die Kräfte
> seiner tiefsten Wirklichkeit, aber ohne diese Wirklichkeit selbst, gestalten und
> erleben.[63]

It seems, then, that the work of art is fated to be both profound and superficial at the same time. In Nietzsche's aesthetics, however, the dominance of the cheerful surface represents a triumph of Apollonian will, an affirmation of life:

> Wo uns das 'Naïve' in der Kunst begegnet, haben wir die höchste Wirkung
> der apollinischen Cultur zu erkennen: welche [. . .] durch kräftige
> Wahnvorspiegelungen und lustvolle Illusionen über eine schreckliche Tiefe der
> Weltbetrachtung und reizbarste Leidensfähigkeit Sieger geworden sein muss.
> (KGA 3.1, 33)

The nature of art, for Nietzsche and Simmel, is to be both serious and frivolous at
once. Great works of art do not shy away from either of these extremes, and *Felix
Krull* wears its frivolity with pride.

(ii) Art as Necessity

> Wir meinen, das Märchen und das Spiel gehöre zur Kindheit: wir Kurzsichtigen!
> Als ob wir in irgend einem Lebensalter ohne Märchen und Spiel leben
> möchten!
> NIETZSCHE (KGA 4.3, 129)

(a) *Müller-Rosé: the need for semblance*

In this section I will concentrate on what I regard as the heart of the novel, namely
the Müller-Rosé episode. Significantly, it is the very first section of the novel which
Mann decided to publish — as early as 1911.[64] This episode is critical because it
illustrates, in paradigmatic terms, Mann's view of the way in which art operates. It
reveals that people have a deep psychological need for semblance, and it defines art
as a reciprocal interaction between artist and public. The scene is brief but effective.
Felix Krull is taken by his father to see an operetta starring the actor Müller-Rosé,
who plays a devastatingly handsome and elegant man-about-town. Müller-Rosé
impresses the audience with his clothes, which are immaculate, and with his
manners, which are impeccable. He holds the audience in raptures by his portrayal
of a high life towards which they aspire. When Felix Krull is taken by his father
to visit the star backstage after the show, however, a different scene awaits him.
The dressing-room reeks of sweat and greasy make-up, and Müller-Rosé himself
is pallid, red-eyed and red-haired, and covered from head to toe with the most
revolting sores and suppurating, pustulous boils. The contrast between the image of
attractive celebrity and a kind of medieval vision of the bubonic plague could not
be more striking. Müller-Rosé, like his friend Engelbert Krull's brand of *Sekt*, is
marked by the stark contrast between fair appearance and degenerate substance. Just
as the pretty Lorley extra cuvée is formed of dubious ingredients, Müller-Rosé's
attractive surface is belied by the moral decrepitude beneath, and his dressing-room
resembles an alchemist's laboratory with its bowls, crucibles, and unholy stench,
formed of 'Schweißgeruch [. . .] Ausdünstungen der Näpfe, Tiegel und farbigen
Fettstangen' (292). In these contrasts we cannot fail to see a reflection of Nietzsche's
ambivalence about the artist. It becomes clear how much Mann's decision to write
a picaresque novel about an artist is informed by the work of Nietzsche, when we
examine two conflicting passages from *Die fröhliche Wissenschaft*. The first text
approves of the artist-rogue:

> Und gerade weil wir im letzten Grunde schwere und ernsthafte Menschen
> und mehr Gewichte als Menschen sind, so thut uns Nichts so gut als
> die *Schelmenkappe*: wir brauchen sie vor uns selber — wir brauchen alle
> übermüthige, schwebende, tanzende, spottende, kindische und selige Kunst,
> um jener *Freiheit über den Dingen* nicht verlustig zu gehen, welche unser Ideal
> von uns fordert. (KGA 5.2, 141)

The second text explicitly links the artist to the actor and the classical picaro Gil
Blas, but in a harshly critical way. Nietzsche begins by saying that the artist is in fact
a dangerous figure, motivated by the basest of instincts. He then continues:

> Die Falschheit mit gutem Gewissen, die Lust an der Verstellung als Macht
> herausbrechend, den sogenannten 'Charakter' beiseite schiebend [. . .]. Ein
> solcher Instinkt wird sich am leichtesten bei Familien des niederen Volkes
> ausgebildet haben, [. . .] bis zum Schluss dieses [. . .] Vermögen herrisch,
> unvernünftig, unbändig wird, [. . .] und den Schauspieler, den 'Künstler' erzeugt
> (den Possenreisser, Lügenerzähler, Hanswurst, Narren, Clown zunächst, auch
> den classischen Bedienten, den Gil Blas). (KGA 5.2, 290–91)

In this way, Nietzsche both criticizes artists and extols the virtues of art. Nietzsche
often sees the artist as akin to the criminal; both are endowed with attributes which
set them apart from other men; neither of them, however, is sufficiently noble and
spiritual for what he has in mind. But he still takes them as a model: in the section
of *Also sprach Zarathustra* entitled 'Von den Dichtern', Zarathustra says that he too is
a 'Dichter' (KGA 6.1, 159). In other words, for all his ambivalence about the artist,
Nietzsche regards art as a basic function of existence. Hence, art, for Nietzsche, is
a vital function of life.[65] Art, as Eagleton points out, is 'Nietzsche's theme from
beginning to end'.[66] This means that the will to power, which Nietzsche sees as
underlying everything, is essentially an aesthetic drive. Nietzsche thus implies that
the urge to shape and to create is the ultimate aim of life itself. More specifically,
art, for Nietzsche, is a means of overcoming the tragedy of existence and achieving
a divine exuberance. Nietzsche claims that both the strong and the weak have a
need for art:

> *Was man von der Kunst will.* — Der Eine will vermittelst der Kunst sich seines
> Wesens freuen, der Andere will mit ihrer Hülfe zeitweilig über sein Wesen
> hinaus, von ihm weg. Nach beiden Bedürfnissen giebt es eine doppelte Art von
> Kunst und Künstlern. (KGA 4.3, 161)

Nietzsche's analysis here is concerned with distinguishing between a 'high' art
for those who are noble and strong, and a 'low' art for those who are tired of
themselves and weakened by 'Selbstverdruß' (KGA 4.3, 83). What is important for
our purposes, however, is that Nietzsche defines the highest function of art as ludic:
art enables people to enjoy their own being: 'sich seines Wesens freuen' (KGA 4.3,
161).[67] Furthermore, Nietzsche's use of the word 'Bedürfnisse' ('needs') and his
description of a need for art are highly significant, because the same word appears
at the culmination of the Müller-Rosé episode. Reflecting upon the scene he has
witnessed, Felix Krull asks himself if the audience was taken in by this illusion.
Surely they must have known it wasn't real — these people were 'erwachsen' and
'lebenskundig', after all (294). Perhaps, then, there was a tacit agreement on the part

of the audience to play along with the fiction, to suspend their disbelief: 'Achteten sie in stillschweigendem Einverständnis den Betrug nicht für Betrug? Letzteres wäre möglich' (294). Very well then, supposing such an agreement exists, why does the audience collude in this way? The narrator decides that art must satisfy a basic human need ('Bedürfnis'):

> Hier herrscht augenscheinlich ein allgemeines, von Gott selbst der Menschennatur eingepflanztes Bedürfnis, dem die Fähigkeiten des Müller-Rosé entgegenzukommen geschaffen sind. Hier besteht ohne Zweifel eine für den Haushalt des Lebens unentbehrliche Einrichtung. (294)

It seems, then, that Müller-Rosé's fiction succeeds because there is a tacit agreement ('Einverständnis') on the part of the audience to credit his performance, to lend it a measure of belief. Coleridge famously described this as the 'willing suspension of disbelief' in his *Biographia Literaria*.[68] As Michael Beddow says, the audience's delight in Müller-Rosé is a 'delight in fiction *as* a fiction, pleasure created by the interaction of an unabating knowledge of what "prosaic reality" is like with the sight of an imaginative suspension of that reality'.[69] In other words, the audience is simultaneously aware of both fiction *and* 'prosaic reality'. It colludes with the artist out of self-interest, and the agreement is binding, although unspoken: Müller-Rosé's audience is composed of willing victims, who allow themselves to be seduced. This crucial insight had already appeared in Mann's story 'Das Wunderkind' (1903),[70] but in the Müller-Rosé episode it is developed much more fully. Now we enter into the psychology of the relation between artist and audience. The narrative considers Müller-Rosé's motivation, and concludes that he is motivated by the will to please. In his dressing-room, Müller-Rosé repeatedly questions Engelbert Krull about the public's reaction: he wants to know the precise degree to which he pleased the audience. The incessant nature of these questions shows this is more than professional curiosity. Instead, Müller-Rosé has invested a lot of emotion in the performance. The chapter culminates in a description of the artistic experience as an emotionally charged exchange in which each party satisfies the other:

> Beachte doch, wie der Mensch nicht satt hören kann an der Versicherung, daß er gefallen, daß er wahrhaftig über die Maßen gefallen hat! Lediglich der Hang und Drang seines Herzens zu jener bedürftigen Menge hat ihn zu seinen Künsten geschickt gemacht; und wenn er ihr Lebensfreude spendet, sie ihn dafür mit Beifall sättigt, ist es nicht ein wechselseitiges Sich-Genüge-Tun, eine hochzeitliche Begegnung seiner und ihrer Begierden? (295)

He wants to please — *they* want to be pleased. *He* wants to deceive — *they* want to be deceived, and so they become partners. Members of the public participate by lending credence to what they see, even if it beggars belief. In doing so, they become actors too.

There is a very similar configuration of the relationship between artist and audience in Heinrich Mann's 1905 novel *Professor Unrat*, which Thomas Mann may well have had in mind when he wrote this passage.[71] Rosa Fröhlich, the heroine of *Professor Unrat*, is only a second-rate cabaret artist, but when she is presented as a high-class demi-mondaine, the public chooses to accept this image. This in turn increases her feeling of self-worth:

> Zwischen ihr und ihrem Publikum, der Stadt, hatte augenscheinlich eine
> Art von gegenseitiger Beschwindelung stattgefunden. Sie hatte sich als
> repräsentative Schönheit gebärdet, war allmählich dafür angesprochen worden
> und hatte es selbst wieder den Leuten geglaubt. (WA 194)[72]

The key word in both these passages is 'reciprocal' ('wechselseitig', 'gegenseitig').
As Martin Travers points out, the actor and the audience are bound together in a
bond of mutual dependence.[73] Furthermore, the more each party commits to the
fiction, the more successful it becomes. Thus the success of an artwork depends
upon the willingness of the audience to accept the conventions of the artistic game.
Roland Barthes discusses this contractual arrangement in a brief but fascinating
passage. Barthes compares the artistic contract to Rousseau's social contract, but
points out that both contracts remain unspoken or concealed. Although in fact
they are highly regulated, they are usually taken for granted and assumed to be
natural.[74] If we accept Barthes's argument, then we must accept the existence of
an implicit linguistic contract and an implicit aesthetic contract as adjuncts to the
social contract. All successful communication requires that the parties involved
adopt a number of conventions, and indeed that they bring a measure of good faith
into the equation. This is especially true in the appreciation of an artwork, where
the conventions are often even more rigorous, and where a knowledge of tradition
is often required. Because these implicit contracts are so demanding, they have a
socializing capacity. And by calling these contracts into being, art can bind people
into a community of mutual appreciation. If culture is the repository of social
values, then semblance becomes the sign of a common humanity. Schiller says as
much in the twenty-sixth letter on aesthetic education:

> Und was ist es für ein Phänomen, durch welches sich bey dem Wilden der Eintritt
> in die Menschheit verkündigt? [. . .] es ist dasselbe bey allen Völkerstämmen,
> welche der Sklaverey des thierischen Standes entsprungen sind: die Freude am
> *Schein*, die Neigung zum *Putz* und zum *Spiele*. (NA 20, 399)

Thomas Mann, however, goes further than Schiller, regarding the aesthetic
experience under the aspect of Eros. The narrator of *Der Tod in Venedig* refers to a
'geheime Verwandtschaft' between artist and audience, a relationship of 'Sympathie'
(VIII, 452). The discussion of 'Sympathie' in that *Novelle* implies that Mann's aim
is to tune in to the deepest currents of his age. The Müller-Rosé episode in *Krull*
goes further, however, defining the artist–public relationship as a meeting of minds,
a marriage of desires between artist and audience: 'eine hochzeitliche Begegnung
seiner und ihre Begierden' (295).[75] This marriage metaphor is superimposed upon
an even more striking image, comparing Müller-Rosé to a flame, and the audience
to moths drawn to the flame: 'diesen Riesenschwarm von armen Motten und
Mücken, der sich still und toll in die lockende Flamme stürzte!' (294). The central
intertext here is with Goethe's poem 'Selige Sehnsucht', the final poem of 'Der
Buch des Sängers' in the *West-östlicher Divan*. In 'Selige Sehnsucht', the image of the
butterfly consumed by the flame conveys the idea that death and creative rebirth
are necessary aspects of life. I will discuss this intertextual relationship in more
detail in Chapter 3(ii). What is important here is that in terms of metaphorical
logic, it is no longer Schopenhauerian illusion but Goethean Eros which is being

privileged. Of course, Schopenhauer is present too. One of Mann's early work notes clearly alludes to Schopenhauer:

> 'Die Welt schreit von Ewigkeit danach, betrogen zu werden' — sehr gut. Aber auch seine [Krulls] Sehnsucht nach der Welt ist das Werk eines Betruges vonseiten der Welt, das *Blend*werk des Schleiers der Maja. [. . .] Es ist ein erotisches Betrugsverhältnis auf Gegenseitigkeit.[76]

'Maja' is a concept that Schopenhauer borrowed from Vedic philosophy, where it is used to define worldly appearance as an illusion.[77] But even this early note suggests that Felix Krull will not only deceive, he will be deceived, and he will even fall in love with the world of appearances. In other words, there is a strong element of Eros which relegates the Schopenhauerian doctrine of illusion to second place. As we have seen, Müller-Rosé's admirers are not deceived, they are willing victims. Indeed, if Müller-Rosé is a type of glow-worm, and the members of the audience are like moths attracted by his light, then we can envisage the scene as a kind of insects' mating dance. The appearance is a sexual lure, and art is a process of seduction — but one which requires the willing consent of the addressee.[78] The Müller-Rosé episode describes art as a ludic, even erotic relationship ('eine hochzeitliche Begegnung' (295)). After all, mental stimuli and imaginative inspiration can cause an almost physical pleasure. Aristotle's theory of catharsis seems a little too mechanical. Isn't art pure pleasure in mimesis, the pleasure of imaginatively subjecting the self to a series of forms?[79] This is what the narrative of *Felix Krull* seems to be saying when it depicts the eagerness with which the audience witnesses the contortions of Müller-Rosé. What we have here is an artistic justification of art itself. The narrative which describes the need for art is itself couched in artistic terms and metaphorical language. Nevertheless, the argument is a powerful one: why do certain art forms have an almost universal appeal? Why do people go to the theatre or to the cinema? The psychologist Abraham Maslow proposes the existence of a need for art: not a basic physiological need of the same order as eating, and drinking, but a deep-seated one nonetheless.[80] Felix Krull is quite aware of this need, and admits that it is his *raison d'être*. In Book III, when Zouzou accuses him of having a need for devotion ('Bedürfnis nach Devotion'), he replies that he has a need for beautiful form, not for devotion ('Nicht nach Devotion. Nach schöner Form' (593)).

What makes the defence of art in the Müller-Rosé episode so poignant is that it does not spare the artist. The text presents the reader with both sides of the argument. It celebrates art as a miracle, and it condemns art as a shabby deception, a veil used to cover up the ugliness of real life. What is wonderful about the text is that it refuses to decide. Instead, it allows both possibilities to coexist. Indeed, the narrator even tells the reader not to make an overly hasty decision ('Hüte dich, darüber zu entscheiden!' (294)). It offers two completely opposed visions of Müller-Rosé: on stage in all his glory, and off-stage, submerged in filth. This antithesis between stage persona and backstage hideousness even extends to Müller-Rosé's name and the language he uses. His name combines the banal everyday German of 'Müller' with the cheap exoticism of the French-sounding, obviously fake 'Rosé'.[81] What is more, his coarse colloquialisms and regional accent backstage ('Was, zum Deibel!' (291)) strongly contrast with the finesse of his onstage language. We are justified in assuming a moral corruption to accompany the physical one; indeed, one is reminded of Wilde's *The Picture of Dorian Gray*. And yet the narrator is touched by Müller-Rosé, and he urges the reader to beware of saying which one of these two faces is the real one: 'Wann zeigt der Glühwurm sich in seiner wahren Gestalt [. . .]? Hüte dich, darüber zu entscheiden!' (294). The narrator is making a crucial point here. He is telling the reader to beware of using fixed categories, and to shy away from such simplistic oppositions. Is the artist a questionable outsider or is he a noble, useful member of society? The answer is that he is both. The *Künstler* does not exist in opposition to the *Bürger*; rather, he colludes with him. Art may be a semblance, but it is still of value because it fulfills a basic human need ('Bedürfnis'), spreading joy and satisfaction, and bringing people together. Krull's claim is that there is an authenticity inherent in the aesthetic experience which lies beyond simple truth claims. The implication is that, in creating these grand fictions, the artist is doing more than trying to cover up his own morally dubious character. He is attempting to rise above temporal, messy, contingent nature by producing something ideal and beautiful. What does it matter if Müller-Rosé's entire body is covered in boils, if he can succeed in getting the audience to adore him as a vision of beauty? His foul body becomes the conduit for something greater than himself: a union of minds, a 'hochzeitliche Begegnung'. Nietzsche expresses this duality in his usual wry fashion: 'Gewiss, man findet Perlen in ihnen [den Dichtern]: um so ähnlicher sind sie selber harten Schalthieren. Und statt der Seele fand ich oft bei ihnen gesalzenen Schleim'.[82] The epigram could justly be applied to Müller-Rosé: beauty on the outside, slime on the inside. But Mann's vision of the artist is gentler and more humanistic: from this humble slime, greatness emerges. There is a further echo of this theme in a passage which Mann added in the 1950s, reflecting upon the miraculous nature of the human eye. Here, once again, a soft, slimy, rather disgusting physical body (the eye) becomes the vehicle for something higher:

> Welch eine wundersame Bewandtnis hat es, eindringlich betrachtet, mit dem menschlichen Auge, [. . .] — mit diesem kostbaren Gallert, der aus ebenso gemeiner Materie besteht wie alle Schöpfung und auf ähnliche Art wie die Edelsteine anschaulich macht, daß an den Stoffen nichts, an ihrer geistreichen und glücklichen Verbindung aber alles gelegen ist; — mit diesem in eine Knochenhöhle gebetteten Schleim, welcher, entseelt, dereinst im Grabe zu modern, in wässerigen Kot wieder zu zerfließen bestimmt ist, aber, solange der Funke des Lebens darin wacht, über alle Klüfte der Fremdheit hinweg, die zwischen Mensch und Mensch gelagert sein können, so schöne, ätherische Brücken zu schlagen versteht! (348)

For 'ätherische' here, one could so easily read 'ästhetische'. The general argument is clear: artistic performance and human contact rise above the contingent world, creating images of perfection and eternity from out of the flux of life. These images may be fragile, they may be illusory, but they give life meaning.[83]

(b) *The palaeontology museum*

> Wenn einer nur das Schöne, der andere nur das Nützliche befördert, so
> machen beide zusammen erst einen Menschen aus. [. . .] das Schöne muß
> befördert werden, denn wenige stellen's dar, und viele bedürfen's. — GOETHE
> (HA VII, 552)

The Müller-Rosé episode is the central chapter of Book I and it forms the
spiritual core of the first section of the novel. Book II centres upon Felix Krull's
own virtuoso performances in the *Musterungsszene* and in the hotel. Book III's
centre of gravity is the encounter with Professor Kuckuck and the visit to the
'Museu Sciências Naturaes' in Lisbon, based in part on Mann's visit to the Field
Museum of Natural History in Chicago in October 1951.[84] Since *Felix Krull* is
on one level an ethnological study of society, one could argue that the museum
scene is a self-referential moment, a moment of meta-narrative in which the novel
reflects upon itself. It is, at the same time, a charming scientific and philosophical
excursus. Professor Kuckuck himself is a complex figure. Hans Wysling has shown
that Kuckuck's doctrines combine the teachings of Goethe, Schopenhauer, and
Nietzsche.[85] His residence, high in the hills surrounding Lisbon, is reached by cable
car: a reminder of his affinity with the Olympian Goethe ('erhöhte Gegend' (581)).
He was even born in Gotha in Germany (535). The professor explains to Felix Krull
his place within the great chain of being, the cosmic continuum of life and death,
and invites him to expand his notion of sympathy until it includes the entire cosmos,
becoming 'Allsympathie' (548). As Michael Beddow has shown, the central point of
Kuckuck's lecture on the transience of the cosmos is to undercut 'the notion that the
enduring has a better claim to reality and truth than the transient'.[86] By offering a
cosmic perspective from which all substance becomes chimerical, Kuckuck provides
a philosophical justification for Krull's own mercurial being. The scientifically
informed humanism of the Kuckuck chapters has been extensively analysed in a
recent study by Malte Herwig.[87] Herwig points out that the arrangement of the
museum reinforces the Darwinian theory of evolution. The physical layout of the
museum presents the visitor with a narrative in which humanity is regarded as the
pinnacle of creation.[88] It is therefore hardly surprising that Felix Krull considers
himself to be the end result of this process, a triumph of evolution. His observation
that 'gar zu deutlich lief es bei ihnen allen schließlich auf mich hinaus' (577) might
appear egotistical, but it is a direct consequence of the museum's arrangement.
The design of the museum proves that Professor Kuckuck is an artist as well as
a scientist: assembling a collection demands aesthetic criteria as well as scientific
ones. In effect, Kuckuck has orchestrated Krull's visit to the museum, without even
being there. Furthermore, Professor Kuckuck's revelations are not some radical
departure from the spirit of the earlier novel. The museum episode might have a
wider cosmological import than the Müller-Rosé scene, but the basic narratological
function is the same: both scenes offer a metaphysical justification of art. In my
view, the museum scene restates and expands the significance of the Müller-Rosé
episode. Let us recall that Müller-Rosé satisfies a deep-rooted metaphysical need
('von Gott selbst der Menschennatur eingepflanztes Bedürfnis' (294)). Even the

theatre in which he performs appears to Felix Krull as a place of religious worship: 'Eine solche Vereinigung von Menschen in hohem, prunkvollem Kronensaal hatte ich bis dahin nur in der Kirche gesehen, und in der Tat erschien mir das Theater [. . .] als eine Kirche des Vergnügens' (287).

Thus, very early in the novel, the narrator establishes a link between art and religion. The museum scene in Book III expands upon this theme, endowing art with a cosmic significance. This argument is, at least in part, Nietzschean. Nietzsche, in *Die Geburt der Tragödie*, calls upon art to bear the weight of metaphysical longings in the absence of Christianity. He turns to Greek antiquity as to a model which could revitalize art by returning it to its origins in pagan myth. While Nietzsche's account stresses discontinuity, however, Mann's shows continuity. The museum scene in Lisbon reflects Mann's studies of myth and the origins of culture in the 1930s and 1940s, showing that art and religion have always been intertwined. Art, in its earliest forms, and for most of human history, has been an adjunct to the sacred. It is only in the last few centuries that art and religion have become separated.[89]

When Felix Krull descends into the basement of the museum, he symbolically descends into the dawn of human history. Awaiting him are life-size models which present him with the spectacle of his own origins ('kleine Theater, plastische Szenen' (578)). Humanity begins with cavemen crouching around a fire; we are introduced to the patriarchal head of the clan, to the mother and child. The next tableau reveals the first artist, the cave-painter; Felix Krull feels drawn to this figure as to a kindred spirit, twice calling him a 'Sonderling' (579). He seems strangely removed from reality, while his comrades hunt outside ('Seine Gesellen betrieben wohl draußen die Jagd in Wirklichkeit, er aber malte sie mit bunten Säften' (579)). Is he isolated, unique? Apparently not, since the very next figure is a sculptor, busily carving in stone. But if the artist has his colleagues, that gives the lie to the romantic myth of the isolated genius, of the artist as outsider. If the artist has colleagues, he is part of a group, and his vocation must somehow be a useful one.

The museum's final exhibit is an enclosure of stone pillars in which a prehistoric man presents a bouquet of flowers to the rising sun. The tableau is one of metaphysical affirmation — it is the culmination of the narrative's arguments in favour of art.[90] Admittedly, the man holding the flowers seems to be more of a priest than an artist. However, his decision to endow a bunch of flowers with a higher symbolic meaning seems inherently creative. At this stage of human development, art and religion are not yet distinct from one another. The line of stone pillars creates a sacred space. The stones could serve no possible utilitarian purpose; here is a structure that is removed from pragmatic concerns. The fact that the pillars are uncovered seems to imply a relation to the heavens ('es war wie ein Säulensaal, nur mit dem Himmel als Decke' (580)). The enclosure is not built for a functional purpose; functionality is 'unter seinem Sinn' (580). Religion requires a defined ritual space; privileged moments require a depragmatized context in which revelation may occur. Similarly, art requires the establishment of an aesthetic space, a framework in which disinterested contemplation may occur. It is noteworthy that the figure offering flowers is 'von kräftigem Gliederbau' (580) — in other words, he is healthy and in his prime; this is no Christian ascetic denial of life, but an affirmation of it. The narrator thinks that for some reason the man has been specially selected for this position, in other words, he performs a sacred office ('Er und die mit ihm lebten und ihn aus irgendwelchen persönlichen Gründen für sein Amt ausgesondert hatten', 580). This is a religious act, but it also has a creative, aesthetic dimension. As the text proceeds, it soars into a register of high affirmation: 'Schlupf und Brut hatten mit ihm nichts zu tun, sie waren unter seinem Sinn, der, abgelöst von gewitzter Bedürftigkeit, sich aufschwang zu noblem Bedürfnis' (580). The key word 'Bedürfnis' takes us right back to the 'eingepflanztes Bedürfnis' of the Müller-Rosé episode. The implicit argument, couched in terms that are just as lyrical as in the earlier episode, is to assert the existence of a primal need for beauty, a need which distinguishes humanity and which constitutes the crown of human endeavour. Once again, the intertextual allusions are Goethean. The rhythms of Mann's prose look back to the third stanza of Goethe's 'Selige Sehnsucht' ('Und dich reißet neu Verlangen, | Auf zu höherer Begattung' (HA II, 19)). The image of the rising sun also recalls the opening scene of *Faust* II ('Anmutige Gegend'), another metaphysically charged scene of bodily and spiritual awakening. The scene allows Faust to cast off the horrors of the Gretchen tragedy, and puts him on the road to moral recovery. Feeling the presence of nature, Faust feels a yearning for the summit of existence:

> Du regst und rührst ein kräftiges Beschließen,
> Zum höchsten Dasein immer fortzustreben.

Faust next turns his attention from the earth to the rising sun and then to the rainbow, a symbol of human life. The mood in both scenes (Thomas Mann's prehistoric man and Goethe's Faust) is primal; both scenes assert the yearning for a higher form of existence to be humanity's birthright. The brightly coloured flowers held out to the sun may even correspond to the rainbow witnessed by Faust. If so, then both texts speak of the desire to appreciate life as it reveals itself. The yearning for light and colour, warmth, beauty, and semblance are seen as natural instincts. *Felix Krull* thus affirms art as a vital condition of human existence.

(iii) Art as Exploitation

(a) *Rozsa*

In the previous sections we have looked at art's capacity to build consensus and to bind a community together. In this section we will see how art can sometimes be misused, to damaging effect. Part of the greatness of *Felix Krull* is that, despite its largely affirmatory tone, it recognizes this negative potential of art — it admits the fact that art can function as a tool of oppression, as propaganda. Mann shows us how art can sometimes manipulate the human psyche, producing an effect similar to brainwashing. Thus, while the general thrust of the narrative in *Felix Krull* is towards extolling the virtues of art, there are several more caustic moments in the novel which make it perfectly clear that art can form part of an oppressive praxis. These moments enable us to be critical about Felix Krull and make us doubt his claim that his activities are entirely harmless. The fact is that Felix Krull does exploit people, sometimes quite shamelessly. Of course, he wants us to forget that his fine fictions cover up some pretty unsavoury, illegal activities. Perhaps the prime example of this is the section in which he becomes Rozsa's pimp in Frankfurt in Book II.

There is no need to debate the ethics of prostitution here, except to point out that legislating against prostitution drives it underground, while more sympathetic legislation at least has the advantage of safeguarding the rights of those involved in it. In any case, it seems clear that most pimps are violent and exploitative, and that even if Felix Krull presents himself as removed from that type, he is nevertheless living parasitically from Rozsa's labour as a prostitute — a capitalism of the worst kind. Throughout the chapter, Felix Krull's aesthetic representations clearly serve to play down the seriousness of what he is doing. The whole business of prostitution is likened to the theatre, and it is striking how many similarities there are between the description of the prostitutes and the description of the singer Müller-Rosé. Like Müller-Rosé, the prostitutes wear a thick layer of make-up, designed to work well in relative darkness, and like him, they wear the most elegant costumes, although their diamonds are fake. The effect of all this is to portray prostitution as a harmless game, rather like the theatre.[91] Various phrases further link the prostitutes' activity to the artistic vocation. When they negotiate with their clients, what they seek is an 'Einverständnis' (376) — exactly the same word employed to characterize Müller-Rosé's relationship with the audience. And their cry of invitation, 'Komm mit!' (375), can be seen as paralleling Felix Krull's narrative, which constantly invites us to enjoy and play along with the fictions we are being offered, as if saying 'Mach mit!' ('play along', 'do likewise'). When one also considers that both Felix Krull and the prostitutes trade on their good looks, it seems only natural that they should treat him as a comrade ('kameradschaftlich'). But this is to gloss over and obscure the real differences between their activities. In the same way, Felix Krull's extensive and circumlocutory description of the professions ('Gewerbe') of prostitution and pimping somehow manages to leave out the key words prostitute ('Prostituierte') and 'pimp' ('Zuhälter'), preferring instead to rely on euphemisms such as 'anrüchige Schwesternschaft' and 'Freudenmädchen' for prostitutes and 'Kavaliere', 'Galane' for pimps. This is all part of a wider strategy of self-justification, which is to evade the cold, hard facts of reality by replacing them with beautiful fictions, by privileging the poetic over the prosaic.

At the end of the chapter, Felix Krull carries out a kind of modernist 'Sprachkritik', a pointed declaration of the limitations of language similar to those which we find in Nietzsche ('Über Wahrheit und Lüge im außermoralischen Sinn') or Hugo von Hofmannsthal ('Ein Brief'). But this rather abstract reflection serves an all-too concrete purpose, namely to make a crime seem harmless. Just as earlier, when Felix Krull defended his shoplifting by claiming that the word 'theft' ('Diebstahl') couldn't adequately represent reality (309),[92] so now he asserts the limitations of language in order to reject being labelled as a pimp. It is indeed highly ironic that Felix Krull should instrumentalize modernist *Sprachkritik* in order to paint his exploitation of Rozsa in a more appealing light. He begins with the po-faced, philosophical stance that one should not confuse words with deeds ('die Warnung

[. . .], eine Tat doch ja nicht mit ihrem Namen verwechseln' (383)). He then admits
that it would be possible to interpret his behaviour badly, that one might be tempted
to describe his conduct in the most disgusting terms:

> wenn sie zahlende Kundschaft bei sich empfing [. . .] und mir eine mäßige
> Teilhaberschaft an dem Gewinne nicht mißfallen ließ, so könnte man wohl
> versucht sein, meine damalige Existenz mit einem anstößigen Namen zu
> belegen. (383)

but he immediately adds that it would be mistaken to give him such a negative label.
Epithets such as 'degenerate' would, in his opinion, be out of place when applied
to him:

> Ich für mein Teil halte es mit der volkstümlichen Weisheit, daß, wenn
> zweie dasselbe tun, es mitnichten dasselbe ist: ja ich gehe weiter und meine,
> daß Etikettierungen wie etwa 'ein Trunkenbold', 'ein Spieler' oder auch
> 'ein Wüstling' den lebendigen Einzelfall nicht nur nicht zu decken und
> verschlingen, sondern ihn unter Umständen nicht einmal ernstlich zu berühren
> imstande sind. (383)

In other words, despite all appearances to the contrary, Felix Krull uses the
philosophy of language to assure us that he is not a cad. However, he only ever
shows off this conscientious distrust of words when it suits him. He has no qualms
about portraying his relations with Rozsa to be nothing more than a harmless game;
hence he refers to her as his opponent ('Gegenspielerin' (382)), and to their relations
as a mere interlude ('Zwischenspiel' (384)).

What makes Felix Krull's narrative even more suspect at this point is the fact
that Rozsa is never allowed to speak. Her voice, like that of the maid Genovefa,[93]
remains unheard. It is worth noting the variety of reasons enounced by Felix Krull
in order to explain why he does not intend to report anything that Rozsa has said.
First he claims that the coarse language of prostitutes is in general unsuitable for
public consumption: 'Solche Personen, am Rande bemerkt, sollten nicht sprechen'
(377). Then he makes reference to the explicit nature of Rozsa's discourse, saying it
was too wild and free to be reported politely: 'Unser Gespräch — das einzuschalten
ich Anstand nehme, da ich billig genug denke, um einzusehen, daß seine Freiheit
sich der gesellig mitteilenden Feder versagt' (380). He adds that his first conversation
with Rozsa seemed to take place as if in a dream, almost as if she was a part of
him. But he then goes on to say that despite this effortless intimacy which he has
just portrayed, he actually had some difficulty understanding her, since because she
was Hungarian, she could hardly speak German anyway: 'Sie [sprach] gebrochen
und fehlerhaft, ja konnte eigentlich überhaupt kein Deutsch' (381). The dreamlike
quality of Felix Krull's affair with Rozsa is actually very convenient, because it
excuses him from having to describe the actual — presumably squalid — conditions
in which Rozsa lives, leaving him free to abandon himself to his overriding
emotion, which is one of 'enthobene und entbundene Unverantwortlichkeit'. In
this condition, Rozsa seems almost a creation of his own unconscious: '[im Traum],
wo unser Ich mit Schatten ohne gültiges Eigenleben, mit Erzeugnissen seiner selbst
verkehrt' (380). The narrative strategy here effectively minimizes Rozsa's presence,
reducing her to almost an extension of Felix Krull.

In the face of all this poetic mystification it is extremely difficult for the reader to discern what Rozsa may actually be feeling. She is denied a voice, and one recalls the irritation of Charlotte Kestner in *Lotte in Weimar* at being put in a book without being asked. Neither can give her version of events, but Rozsa is exploited financially as well. We are denied any signs that might contradict Felix Krull's version of events — except perhaps the lingering expression on Rozsa's face: 'Namentlich aber und besonders ist anzumerken, daß ihr Verhalten bar jeder leichtfertigen Heiterkeit war; sondern unter allen Umständen [. . .] bewahrte sie strengen, fast finsteren Ernst' (381). Does the seriousness of Rozsa's face indicate her commitment to the 'game', or does it instead express her sullen dissatisfaction with her fate?

(b) *Diane Houpflé*

Rozsa is a bedroom artist whose voice remains unheard, but Diane Houpflé is an artist of a different sort, with a personality forceful enough to rival Felix Krull's. It is perhaps possible to trace the birth of Madame Houpflé back to a document which Thomas Mann collected in 1910 when he began work on *Felix Krull*. Ola Alsen's 'Die Dame im Hotel' describes the rise of the modern luxury hotel and connects this to an increase in independent female travellers.[94] These ladies have grown accustomed to a high standard of service. Thomas Mann highlighted the paragraph which describes the uniformed boys who surround the female traveller as soon as she enters the hotel: 'Wiederum ist es fraglos erfreulich, daß sich unzählige Diener regen, wenn man seinen Einzug hält. Die kleinen uniformierten Boys reißen die Türen auf, das Gepäck ist mit rasender Geschwindigkeit in den Zimmern'.[95] Alsen's article of 1910 even manages subtly to blur gender distinctions. Modern women have even become experts at giving the correct tip, a field of knowledge in which they have acquired a *masculine* expertise: 'Selbst in diesem Punkt bringen sie es jetzt zu einer männlichen Ueberlegenheit'.[96] Diane Houpflé is thus, among other things, a figure of female emancipation. She is also an accomplished author, adept at the manipulation of discourse. Her mastery of the spoken word gives her a power to reshape reality in a way which is denied to Rozsa. Diane Houpflé is even more eloquent than Felix Krull, and proves to be a match for him. He may be able to exploit her by taking her jewellery, but she in turn exploits him, insulting and humiliating him, and turning him into a tool of her sexual fantasy. We clearly have a moment here when Felix Krull encounters a will which is just as persuasive as his own. The fact that he is receptive to this, that he does to a certain extent fall under Diane Houpflé's spell, is further indication of the fact that he is not simply a blind narcissist.[97]

The Diane Houpflé episode explores what happens when two opposing narratives collide. The scene contains a complex web of literary allusions. Critics have noted the resemblance to Bruno Frank's novel *Die Fürstin* (1915),[98] as well as echoes of the love scene between Siegfried and Brünnhilde, allusions to Diane Houpflé as Helena in *Faust* and Felix Krull as Mignon in *Wilhelm Meister*. Houpflé expresses herself in the Alexandrine verse of Victor Hugo's *Hernani*,[99] and there is a similar seduction scene in Gore Vidal's *The City and the Pillar*. However, in my opinion, by far the most relevant literary model for this scene is to be found in Strindberg's *Miss Julie*, with its battle of wills between the self-destructive heroine and the servant with whom she has just slept. As in Strindberg's drama, the crux of the Diane Houpflé episode lies in the degrading nature of Diane's fantasies. These fantasies are not only masochistic but also sado-masochistic, since she seems almost as eager to humiliate Felix Krull as she is to abase herself. This episode clearly shows that art, like the humanity which creates it, has negative as well as positive potential. Some fictions tap into and cater for the human appetite for destruction; art often draws upon primal, destructive instincts. We will see this again in the bullfight episode, but first let us consider Diane Houpflé in more detail.

Diane Houpflé is a match for Felix Krull because she is just as much of an artist as he is, and just as skilled in the production of aesthetic semblance. As artists they both operate under assumed names. Felix Krull has the alias of 'Armand' given to him by the hotel director, something which causes him intense pleasure: 'Es macht mir die größte Freude [. . .] meinen Namen zu wechseln' (416). Diane Houpflé uses her maiden name, Diane Philibert, as a pen-name. She despises her own married name, since it reminds her of her husband and the fact that he manufactures toilet bowls (448). Thus both Felix and Diane are happy to ditch their legal names and operate under 'stage-names'.

From the start of their encounter in the hotel, Felix Krull is thrilled by the sight of Diane Houpflé. At first this is because he knows she doesn't recognize him as the man who stole her jewels. He loves the fact that she is so close to him without realizing this. But he also finds her highly attractive, despite her age (forty) and her nervous tic — her habit of suddenly opening her eyes very wide (419). He decides to impress her, and spends all his time practising his charms as a liftboy, in honour of her alone. However, when he finally does get her alone in his lift, the bold nature of the compliments she pays him quickly makes him realize that *she* is the one doing the seducing, not him. *She* is the one playing with *him*, asking him to take her coat off and teasing him coyly when he does so: 'Du entkleidest mich, kühner Knecht?' (438). She calls him bold (kühn), when she is in fact the bold one. This 'mere' phrase is enough to keep him spellbound: '"Kühner Knecht" hatte sie mich genannt — eine Frau von Poesie! [. . .] Das packende Wort lag mir den ganzen Abend im Sinn, diese ganzen sechs Stunden' (439). But the phrase does not just entrance him; it remoulds him, so that he becomes as bold as she claimed he was. The boldness she imputed to him has become reality; the word has called a reality into being. At the same time, the appellation 'Knecht' sets up a hierarchy between them, as Diane Houpflé assumes the role of 'mistress' in both social and sexual senses of the word. Thus, despite Felix Krull's enjoyment, he uneasily registers the fact that he has suddenly been assigned the role of subordinate:

> Es kränkte mich etwas, das Wort, und erfüllte mich doch auch wieder mit Stolz — sogar auf meine Kühnheit, die ich gar nicht besessen, sondern die sie mir einfach unterstellt und zudiktiert hatte. Jedenfalls besaß ich sie nun im Überfluß. Sie hatte sie mir eingeflößt. (439)

Diane Houpflé has breathed boldness into him, like a goddess breathing life into mortal clay. But just as she emboldens him through her fictions, she can also demean him and bring him low. She does this by her constant, patronizing references to his inferior social position. At first she is subtle and poetic, calling him 'Mignon in Livree', 'süßer Helot', and he is only slightly irritated: 'Leicht gekränkt, wie ich zugebe, durch ihre immer wiederholte Erwähnung und Betonung meines niedrigen Standes — was hatte und wollte sie nur damit?' (441). Despite this, Felix Krull is still in awe of her ('Nie gab es eine ausdrucksvollere Frau!' (442)). In effect, she is giving him a lesson in poetry. Soon, however, she gets much ruder, calling him a 'nichtigen Knaben' (443) and a 'Dümmling' (443). Being insulted in such a way is definitely not appealing to him. But when he asks her politely to stop taking him for an idiot ('für gar so auf den Kopf gefallen solltest du mich nicht halten' (444)), her apology sounds hollow ('Ich wollte nicht sagen, daß du besonders dumm bist. Alle Schönheit ist dumm' (444)). It soon becomes apparent that she enjoys insulting him because this adds to her own degradation, which she is fixated upon. In fact, she longs for him to whip her with his braces: 'Wenn du mich etwas schlügest? Derb schlügest, meine ich? [. . .] Da liegen deine Hosenträger, nimm sie, Liebster, drehe mich um und züchtige mich aufs Blut!' (447). What motivates Diane Houpflé to play these games? She is only too eager to confess her rather eccentric sexual proclivities. There are two aspects to her perversity. Firstly, there is the masochism. Bored with her own intelligence, she longs for degradation, she longs for the 'Wollust der Selbstentsagung, Selbsterniedrigung' (444). Secondly, there is the fact that she only falls for younger men, preferably no older than eighteen. The fact that Felix is twenty makes him almost too old for her. These two aspects are perhaps linked; guilt about her desire makes her long for punishment.

This theme of the degradation of the artist is only too common in Mann, and features in such major works as *Der Tod in Venedig* and *Doktor Faustus*. But unlike Aschenbach and Leverkühn, Diane Houpflé has no problem confessing her desire; on the contrary, she is only too eager to confess and be punished. She knows that this is all perverse, but doesn't really care ('Es ist mir auch gleichviel' (446)). Most interesting are the words she uses to justify herself. In terms which are clearly influenced by Freudian psychoanalysis, she claims that all love is in fact perverse, because of the underlying element of incest: 'Ist es nicht die Mutterliebe, die ihr unerlaubterweise im Weibe liebt? Verkehrtheit! Die Liebe ist verkehrt durch und durch, sie kann gar nicht anders sein als verkeht' (445). This same word 'Verkehrtheit' ('wrong-way-round-ness', 'perversion') crops up in Dr Krokowski's lecture on love in *Der Zauberberg*. Krokowski too is clearly inspired by Freudian theory when he claims that the very nature of love means that it is forever inclined towards perversion: '[Die Liebe] sei [. . .] von Grund aus zur Verirrung und heillosen Verkehrtheit geneigt' (III, 179). It is in the same spirit, later on in the novel, that Hans Castorp tells Clawdia Chauchat that true love is crazy, an adventure in evil ('une aventure dans le mal' (III, 475)). When we consider the fact that Thomas Mann lets so many of his characters pronounce these romantic, Freudian-inspired phrases (noting also his praise of Freud in his essay 'Freud und die Zukunft') we can conclude that Freudian theory has obviously left a big impression on his work. It is worth bearing in mind, though, that when Mann inserts Freudian theory into his novels, he utilizes narrative structures which tend to suggest an irony or ambivalence about the value of such theorizing. In the case of *Der Zauberberg*, the psychoanalytical explanation for the disease is overshadowed by the historico-political narrative.[100] And in the case of Diane Houpflé, the grotesque, comic nature of the scene means that we perceive the Freudian theory as the ramblings of a deranged woman.

This does not, however, disprove the fact that Mann obviously thought that psychoanalysis was a powerful tool for understanding human behaviour. Indeed, in light of Freud's view that the masochist wants to be treated like a helpless, naughty child,[101] it is particularly apt that Felix Krull addresses Diane Houpflé as 'liebes Kind' (444), and that she perceives this as a wonderful, thrilling insult. However, there is a divergence here. For Freud, masochism is the wish to be beaten by the father, and to enter into a passive sexual relation with him.[102] Diane Houpflé, however, has no intention of being passive — she wants to remain fully in control of the situation. Felix Krull is no father-figure for her, but rather a lowly servant, a nothing ('nichtigen Knaben' (443)). In fact, Diane Houpflé is a sado-masochist, since she gets her kicks by insulting him, and she is glad to sacrifice his personal pride for her own pleasure. For her, he is merely an object — a piece of biddable flesh. Even his confession that he stole her jewels does not distress her, for she is intent on keeping him in his subordinate role. The confession only provides her with another way to insult him and call him inferior: now he is a common thief ('ein ganz gemeiner Dieb!' (448)). And so, although Felix Krull began his encounter with Diane Houpflé with a sense of triumph and superiority, he leaves her more humbly, sneaking out like a common thief, and filled with a sense of wonder. He has been stunned, amazed, and for the first time, lost for words. It is an experience he will not forget: 'Es war [. . .] ein Erlebnis fürs Leben' (451). He may be her divine idol, her 'Hermes' (444), but he is also her little fool ('Närrchen' (450)). In fact, seen in a certain light, it is all pretty degrading for him. With Rozsa, he played the role of pimp; here, he plays the role of prostitute or toy boy. The 'Liebes-Diebesgut' (450) which Diane Houpflé encourages him to 'steal' is, in everything but name, his wage as a rent-boy, the wage paid to a servant.

(c) *The bullfight*

The liaison between Felix Krull and Diane Houpflé begins with an invitation to dance: '[Sie] sah lächelnd meiner [. . .] Verbeugung zu, die etwas von einer Aufforderung zum Tanze hatte' (436), but soon becomes a kind of artistic combat. The bullfight is another kind of dance, though of a more deadly nature. The bullfight as a form of public entertainment is one of the most violent spectacles that modern Europe has to offer. Here we find a public performance in which the participants risk death, and in which the bull is certain to die. The bullfight is death as spectacle. It also has erotic nuances. The narrator makes this clear by describing the sexual arousal of his hostess, Dona Maria Pia, as she regards the bullfight:

> Ihr strenges, südbleiches Gesicht im Schatten der Mantilha war unbeweglich, aber ihr Busen hob und senkte sich in Beschleunigung, und ich sah, ihrer Nichtacht-ung gewiß, dies Gesicht, diesen in unvollkommener Beherrschtheit wogenden Busen öfter an als das [. . .] etwas von Blut beronnene Opfertier. (652)

Of course, the connection between love, sex, and death is familiar from German romanticism — one thinks for example of the *Liebestod* from Wagner's *Tristan*. And there is something operatic about this bullfight: one thinks of the costumes, the virtuosity of the principal, the rapture of the audience, of Bizet's *Carmen*. The bullfight, like a Wagnerian opera, has a solemn, almost religious character. The faces of the waiting onlookers are composed, restrained by a mood of consecration ('gezügelt von einer gewissen Weihe' (650)). The bull looks like a divine animal ('Gott-Tier', 'Tiergott' (651)). When one of the capeadors is injured by the bull and carried off, Maria Pia briefly interrupts her clapping in order to cross herself and murmur a short prayer for the man.

Meanwhile, the interest which Felix Krull derives from looking at Maria Pia is only matched by his interest in one of the bullfighters, the strikingly handsome Ribeiro: 'Achtzehn- oder neunzehnjährig, war dieser Ribeiro in der Tat bildhübsch' (653). The sight of Ribeiro reminds Felix Krull of himself and the fact that he too once posed as a bullfighter for his godfather Schimmelpreester. Ribeiro stands alone and erect like a tree against the bull, and only moves away at the very last instant, as the horns are tearing his jacket. Felix Krull describes it as a thing extremely graceful to watch: 'Etwas äußerst Graziöses, sanft Überlegenes' (654). This feat draws a huge burst of applause from the crowd, and as Felix applauds, his eyes dart between Maria Pia at his side and Ribeiro and the bull below, until they all seem to merge into one:

> Die Zuschauermenge sprang jubelnd auf, rief 'Ribeiro!' und 'Toiro!' und klatschte. Ich selbst tat dies und neben mir die Rassekönigin mit dem wogenden Busen, die ich anblickte, abwechselnd mit der rasch sich auflösenden tier-menschlichen Schaugruppe, da die gestrenge und elementare Person dieser Frau mir mehr und mehr eins wurde mit dem Blutspiel dort unten. (654)

Felix then devotes his attention entirely to Ribeiro's 'Duett' (654) with the bull, and becomes aware that Ribeiro is essentially a performing artist, whose job it is to deliver splendid set pieces ('Glanzstückchen' (654)), and whose aim at all times is to pose gracefully while in danger, and to combine violence with elegance.

When Ribeiro leaves, the bullfight loses its interest and quickly ends. After the bullfight, Professor Kuckuck provides a gloss on the religious, pagan origins of the festival. The central mystery of this ritual seems to have consisted in the union of the killer and the killed ('Einheit [. . .] von Töter und Getötetem' (656)). Kuckuck also connects the spilling of sacrificial blood to Christian communion. This fails to interest Felix Krull, who is more concerned with Maria Pia.

How should one interpret this episode? Let us note first of all the extreme psychological realism of the scene. At first, Felix Krull had serious misgivings whether he would enjoy the bullfight. But then, as he enters the arena, he becomes fascinated by the solemn procession. He notices the rapturous effect which the bullfight has on the crowd, and especially on his hostess, Maria Pia. Then he starts to enjoy the actual bullfight, and before long, he is carried along by the energy of the crowd, cheering along with them. This is analogous to what happens to the narrator in Mann's short story *Mario und der Zauberer*. The two texts are similar in many ways, and I will discuss *Mario und der Zauberer* in the concluding section of this chapter. That story deals with fascism, and, since the bullfight takes place in a huge stadium, it too could be seen as alluding to the mass rallies of fascism. Both texts thus deal with the disturbing potential of art, the fact that it can become an instrument of cruelty and violence. But while *Mario und der Zauberer* pays special attention to the psychology of fascism, the bullfight episode in *Felix Krull* deals with the sexual and religious components of artistic violence. Both of these aspects must be taken into consideration.

The first question which presents itself is: why does the bullfight have an aphrodisiac effect on Maria Pia? Perhaps a brief comparison with another novel will help provide an answer. *L'histoire de l'oeil* (1928) by Georges Bataille shows exactly the same configuration of sex and violence in the context of the bullfight.[103] For Bataille, violence acts as an aphrodisiac not only because the physical symptoms of fear and arousal resemble each other, but because death, like sex, represents a kind of limit experience, in which the frontiers of the mind are transgressed. Thus Bataille suggests that the repetitive thrusts of the bull into the matador's cape call to mind the act of lovemaking, at the same time making one aware of the proximity of death. Bataille claims that these repetitive attack sequences can sometimes excite female members of the audience so much that they experience orgasm.[104] It is also seen as important that bullfighters should be young and handsome. Bataille underlines this erotic aspect by describing the young matador as a 'prince charmant' and pointing out that the matador's skin-tight trousers mould the bottom exactly.[105]

Sigmund Freud has a more technical explanation for sadism. According to him, the task of the libido is to counter the death instinct ('Todestrieb'). It does this by diverting the destructive instinct outwards, towards objects in the external world, where it becomes the instinct for mastery or will to power.[106] Part of that destructive instinct is then placed directly in the service of the sexual function, where it becomes sadism. Freud notes that sadism has an important part to play in the sexual function, although he does not specify what part exactly.[107] Thus for Freud as well, sex, death, and aggression are closely linked.

There is also the mythological and religious aspect of the bullfight to consider. As Professor Kuckuck points out, the bullfight is related to both pagan and Christian religion. As in *Joseph und seine Brüder*, it seems that a transformation of mythical thought has overcome animal-worship and human sacrifice. The new religions, however, are clearly marked by vestiges of the old. The bullfight is in many respects structurally similar to the myth of the Torn God Tammuz/Adonis, which has so much significance for Joseph. If one accepts Freud's view (in *Das Unbehagen in der Kultur*) that civilization is a result of repression of instinctual savagery, then the attractions of these violent myths become all too clear.

Indeed, if we wanted to play the psychoanalytical-mythological game favoured by so many commentators on *Felix Krull*, we could say that what we are witnessing here is a classic oedipal scene. The bull would represent the father, since in ancient Cretan myth the bull was worshipped as a father-god (this is reflected in the myth of the Minotaur, which was born of the union between a bull and Pasiphae, queen of Crete). Freud clearly links the totem animal to the father, and to the fear of being eaten up by the father.[108] Hence, from a Freudian perspective, the bullfight would represent the son's murder of the father. Meanwhile, since the bullfighter Ribeiro serves as a double for Felix Krull (who once posed as a matador), and since Professor Kuckuck is a father-figure to Krull, Maria Pia's arousal becomes even more heavily laden with oedipal significance. However, one could challenge this interpretation and say that Maria Pia identifies with the bull to some extent — experiencing perhaps an intimation of her own death in that of the bull.

Thomas Mann's narrative is adept at suggesting such interpretations and then discarding them ironically. As for Felix Krull, he is clearly uninterested in such abstractions — he prefers to devote himself to the sensual aspect of the experience. Thus the narrative reflects a fundamentally ambivalent attitude towards myth, which, according to T. J. Reed, Thomas Mann derived from Nietzsche, or rather from Ernst Bertram's reading of Nietzsche. Mann appears to have been fascinated by Bertram's opinion that Nietzsche was torn between the urge to analyse myth and the instinct to preserve its mysteries by rejecting knowledge.[109] Thus we can say that while Mann's narrative offers a psycho-historical analysis of the bullfight, it surrounds such explanations with a playful irony, choosing finally to represent the bullfight as a savage but fascinating enigma. Perhaps the ultimate reason for the attraction of the bullfight is its sheer irrationality.

The bullfight episode thus powerfully evokes the darker side of human nature as expressed in art. But it seems to me that it can also be read as a veiled commentary on fascism. The bullfight is an example of the pagan savagery of prehistory, which, as Thomas Mann pointed out in 'Deutsche Ansprache' in 1930, the Nazis were trying to bring back.[110] And it is worth noting that in the early 1950s both Spain and Portugal were still under fascist rule. Thus the episode alludes to the potential use of art as an instrument of mass control. When Felix Krull remarks that Maria Pia seems to have 'become one' with the scene below, this bears witness to the power of the mass spectacle — the power to reduce individuals into parts of a faceless crowd. The bullfight episode is thus Thomas Mann's final exploration of the fascination of violent irrationalism.

In our survey of *Felix Krull* we have seen that the novel suggests that art and society, far from being separate domains, are interrelated in a number of ways. *Felix Krull* is a novel about the contribution that art makes to social collectivity, but it is aware of both the benign and malign potentialities of that input. Felix Krull himself is an ultimately benign presence. He might occasionally break the law, but his art includes an ethical concern for his audience. Indeed, as the novel progresses, its humanism becomes ever more apparent: the art of the later *Felix Krull* is an art of conversation and dialogue.

(iv) Continuity with Other Works: Art in the Service of Democracy

In this section, I will consider one of Thomas Mann's central preoccupations: namely, the way in which art can make a positive contribution to society. I will show that the thematics of *Felix Krull*, far from being unique, extend throughout Mann's work. In order to do this, I will consider five works by Mann: *Königliche Hoheit, Der Zauberberg, Joseph und seine Brüder, Lotte in Weimar*, and *Mario und der Zauberer*. By examining these other works, I hope to demonstrate that the themes and problems which Mann addresses in *Felix Krull* are by no means isolated issues: rather, they form part of a development that spans the entire oeuvre. In my view, *Felix Krull* represents a watershed in terms of Mann's perception of the relations between art, society, and politics. It reflects Mann's awareness that art is not always necessarily benign. Even so, the novel is a major breakthrough because it demonstrates, with the utmost clarity, that art is deeply implicated in the forms and allegiances of a society. Mann's first serious engagement with politics takes place during the First World War. His defence of democratic politics begins in the early 1920s. In my view, however, these political engagements would not have been possible without the insight which Mann gained in writing *Felix Krull*: the insight that art depends upon the conscious, knowing assent of the audience, and, in consequence, the refusal of any art or politics based upon coercion. In order to work most richly and fully, art, like rhetoric, requires an audience that is completely free to make up its own mind. Since art depends upon assent, it is therefore on an ontological level deeply sympathetic to democratic politics. As Sartre pointed out in 1948, every literary work is an appeal to the existential freedom of the reader.[111] Mann had a similar insight, although formulated in different terms: the Müller-Rosé episode describes the understanding or agreement ('Einverständnis' (294)) which is necessary for the work of art to succeed. In other words, the artist has to court the free assent of his audience. This implies a bond which has an ethical dimension. Of course, one might argue that the insight occurred even earlier, during the composition of *Königliche Hoheit*, a novel which also demonstrates the artist's reliance on the public. In any case, once Mann had realized his ethical obligation to his audience, he never forgot it. The subsequent analysis will seek to show how Mann developed the idea that art might play a positive role in the public life of the nation. While his essays and speeches are often programmatic and polemical, it is above all in his fiction that we can trace the careful unfolding of this thought. I will therefore begin with the much-maligned *Königliche Hoheit*.

(a) *Königliche Hoheit*

Königliche Hoheit is admittedly a minor novel. According to Frithjof Trapp, Mann's *Fürstenroman* is too optimistic, a celebration of Wilhelmine Germany that fails to problematize the dangers of absolute power.[112] Nevertheless, this is the novel in which Mann begins to explore the collusion between *Bürger* and *Künstler*, and the many threads that bind them. Perhaps for the first time in his work, art is portrayed as something positive, with a definite social role. As early as 1910, Mann claimed that *Königliche Hoheit* articulated a 'geistige Wendung zum Demokratischen' (XI, 571).[113] At the heart of the novel is the young prince Klaus Heinrich's growing realization that his life serves a useful purpose: 'Sein Verdienst war, daß er [. . .] sich still der Form überließ, die um ihn waltete' (II, 50). For artists and princes do serve a purpose. Trivial though it may seem, they do bring beauty and dignity to public occasions; and they can delight people because they symbolize an ideal existence (II, 84). *Königliche Hoheit* presents the artist, as well as the monarch, as having a predominantly symbolic function.[114] In other words, the job of a prince is to embody an ideal of national unity and cohesion, and more than that: to symbolize the better qualities of human nature. The prince represents the people spiritually, not financially: 'Das Volk will sein Bestes, sein Höheres, seinen Traum, irgend etwas wie seine Seele in seinen Fürsten dargestellt sehen, — nicht seinen Geldbeutel. Den zu repräsentieren sind andere Leute da. . .' (II, 23). Unlike his elder brother Albrecht who despises the people, Klaus Heinrich is aware of his duty to the public and is happy to give them a good show. Refusing to disdain his audience, he performs his role with a sense of civic pride. His function is rather like that of the popular soubrette Mizzi Meyer, who is said to represent 'die Verklärung des Volkes selbst' (II, 172). Like Klaus Heinrich, Mizzi Meyer functions as a symbolic representation of the people, providing a focus for communal celebration: 'das Volk beklatsche sich selber, indem es sie beklatschte, und darin ganz allein beruhte Mizzi Meyers Macht über die Gemüter' (II, 172).[115]

At this point, one might ask: to what extent does this affectionate portrayal of the aristocracy really represent an inclination towards democracy on the part of Thomas Mann? Doesn't the novel really celebrate a pre-democratic society? At first glance, Mann's principality seems rather politically backward, governed as it is by royally appointed officials rather than by elected representatives. However, the people's representatives do have the power of veto on financial questions ('Da nämlich die Volksvertretung für nichts in der Welt zur Bewilligung neuer Steuern zu bewegen gewesen wäre' (II, 288)). And it soon becomes apparent that the power of the monarchy is pretty limited, and that the princes really are to a large extent bound by their duty to the people. For example, Albrecht II knows it would be fruitless for him to oppose the sale of palace 'Delphinenort' to the millionaire Spoelmann, since the people have already decided in favour of the sale. The royal family council is thus revealed to be (in this instance) a sham, a mere formality:

> Schließlich hatte Albrecht mit niedergeschlagenen Augen erklärt, der ganze Familienrat sei im Grunde 'Affentheater'. Das Volk habe längst entschieden, seine Minister drängen auf den Verkauf, und es bleibe ihm gar nichts anderes übrig, als wieder einmal auf den Bahnhof zu gehen und zu winken. (II, 194)

In other words, the function of the royal family is shown to be largely symbolic. *Königliche Hoheit* gives us a version of the monarchy which is spiritually very close to the British monarchy — in other words, not an absolute monarchy, but one very much bound by a democratic, parliamentary tradition. Thomas Mann is serious about assigning his princes a representative function rather than a political one. Like the British monarch, Klaus Heinrich opens parliament and then lets the commons get on with it, remaining as impartial as possible:

> Er eröffnete als Vertreter seines Bruders den Landtag, nahm aber keinen Anteil
> an den Vorgängen dortselbst und vermied jedes Ja und Nein im Zwiespalt der
> Parteien, — unentschieden und ohne Überzeugungswärme wie einer, dessen
> Angelegenheit höher ist, als alles Parteiwesen. Jeder sah ein, daß seine Stellung
> ihm Zurückhaltung auferlegte. (II, 170)

Albrecht must sell his castles when his ministers tell him to, and Klaus Heinrich
shows his willingness to break with tradition by marrying an outsider and by
studying economics. This is a monarchy prepared to adapt to the conditions of
modernity; an enlightened monarchy which knows it must embrace reform if it is
to survive.

Put simply, the novel shows little interest in preserving the political influence of
the monarchy; the narrative makes it abundantly clear that the value of princes lies
in the aesthetic aura which they generate. Mann's prince does not stage his own
political power, since in practice he has little real power. What he does is stage
something that is both imaginative and institutionally real; a way of doing things,
a *geistige Lebensform*. The central chapter 'Der hohe Beruf' makes this quite clear,
showing that Klaus Heinrich's function is to maintain a kind of bizarre fiction:
'Zuweilen schien es ihm, als habe er beständig mit großem Aufgebot an Spannkraft
etwas aufrecht zu erhalten, was eigentlich nicht, oder doch nur unter günstigen
Bedingungen, aufrecht zu erhalten war' (II, 163). Of course one can read this rather
Kafkaesque sentence as an allusion to artistic endeavour in general, but it also
refers to the immense energy and concentration which goes into ensuring that a
public occasion runs smoothly. An impression of polite cordiality and dignity can
be a worthy but difficult thing to maintain. There is of course something camp
about all of this. Like the Queen, Klaus Heinrich has had to work long and hard in
order to perfect his body language, in particular his smile and farewell wave: '[Er]
begleitete den ehrerbietigen Rückzug des Dichters mit Lächeln und jener ein wenig
theatralischen, gnädig grüßenden Handbewegung von oben nach unten, die nicht
immer gleichmäßig schön gelang, aber in der er es zu hoher Vollendung gebracht
hatte' (II, 180). In one telling scene, Klaus Heinrich even asks the press office to send
newspaper cuttings, so that he can see what the papers have been saying about him.
He does this in the same way as an artist checks his reviews — in order to make
sure that he has had a positive response from his audience (II, 167).

We are shown a very clear insight into the duties of prince and performer in the
scene where Klaus Heinrich goes to the small town of Knüppelsdorf in order to
unveil a statue of his late father. Long before the event, he has undertaken research
in order to ensure that his speech goes well. The speech is crammed with references
to local history which convey the impression that Klaus Heinrich has always been
passionately interested in Knüppelsdorf:

> Als er [. . .] die Enthüllung des Johann Albrechts-Standbildes zu Knüppelsdorf
> vollzog, hielt er auf dem Festplatze [. . .] eine Rede, in der alles untergebracht
> war, was er sich über Knüppelsdorf notiert hatte, und die allerseits den schönen
> Eindruck hervorrief, als habe er sich Zeit seines Lebens vornehmlich mit den
> historischen Schicksalen dieses Mittelpunktes beschäftigt. (II, 162)

By the time the speech is over, Klaus Heinrich has said all he knows about the town.

But he doesn't really have to be an expert; he just has to say complimentary things about the place. In doing so, he puts Knüppelsdorf on the map. It is not just that he appeals to the collective imaginary, bringing lustre and a sense of occasion. It is more the fact that he *says* Knüppelsdorf to itself and to the outside world. It is almost as if reality isn't quite real until it has been imaginatively endorsed as having reality. The prince gives style to the town, but more than that, he stages its apotheosis through his praise. After he has gone, the town will probably commemorate his visit with a plaque. This will not just reflect honourably upon the prince, however, but upon the town itself, which will draw substance from its royal patronage. This is not just an allegory of the artist. Mann is showing us what public figures and heads of state really do — they act out a kind of spiritual wholeness which secular modernity lacks. There is a theatrical aspect to all of this:

> Eine seltsame Unechtheit und Scheinbarkeit herrschte auf den Stätten seiner Berufsübung, eine ebenmäßige, bestandlose Ausstattung, eine falsche und herzerhebende Verkleidung der Wirklichkeit aus Pappe und vergoldetem Holz, aus Kranzgewinden, Lampions, Draperien und Fahnentüchern war hingezaubert für eine schöne Stunde. (II, 159–60)

This artistic effect has all the falsity of artistic semblance, but if it is uplifting ('herzerhebend'), isn't it valuable? After all, as Klaus Heinrich points out, the people must know what they are doing when they shout and cheer: 'da die Leute Juchhe rufen, wenn sie mich sehen, so müssen sie doch wohl wissen, warum' (II, 145). This is an important point and worth thinking about. Are those who cheer the royal family merely dupes, victims of some ideological swindle? Isn't it rather that they are celebrating themselves, their own lives? Mann certainly believes that people enter willingly into the ceremony because it gives them a chance to express their own joy, their own togetherness: 'Die "Hoch" riefen, meinten sich selbst damit, wie man deutlich sah, und riefen freudig aus, daß sie selbst hoch lebten und an hohe Dinge glaubten in diesem Augenblick' (II, 60). The public accepts the form because it sanctions a display of collective enthusiasm. As long as the majority continues to sign up to it, then perhaps the continuation of the monarchy is justified.

In this way, Thomas Mann's prince is utterly dependent on the will of the public. He cannot get married without the people's say-so; the fact that they approve of his marriage is the decisive factor in the granting of permission.[116] Klaus Heinrich is aware of the fact that he is a public servant, and that any power which he may have is invested in him by the people. Thus he must be accessible; he has to grant a private audience to any member of the public who wishes to see him. And he has to work hard at all times to earn the respect of the public, by carrying out the official duties which they expect of him. At no point does the text mention the concept of divine right, but it does constantly stress the fact that the prince must continually seek the assent of the public.

Thus, if Klaus Heinrich does stage power, he stages it in its democratic fragility, aware that his power is conditional and can be restricted or removed. However, in actual fact he does little to govern; his main concern is to encourage the 'team spirit' of the nation — he acts as a sort of mascot. Mann's fictional monarch is more emblem than ruler.[117] In the context of the time it was written *Königliche Hoheit* was doubtless too optimistic, but there is something very important and suggestive in the way that Thomas Mann is trying to adapt to the new while conserving what is good about the old.

(b) *Der Zauberberg*

A detailed discussion of *Der Zauberberg* is beyond the scope of this book. Nevertheless, Mann's great sanatorium novel deserves some consideration because it takes up issues of art and society that were already present in *Felix Krull*, developing them further. Like *Felix Krull*, it employs an anthropological perspective. The Berghof is a microcosm of pre-war Europe, but it is also a distinct community with norms and customs of its own. One important dimension of the novel is the anthropological concern with how a community functions, with the forms and rituals which hold it together. Of course, *Der Zauberberg* is conceived on a much broader thematic canvas than *Felix Krull*: it deals with philosophy and politics on a grand scale. Even so, the two works share a sense of art as a powerful force in society, both for good and for ill. Both works, too, were originally planned as satirical *Novellen*, but grew in scale as a result of their author's broadening concerns. The composition of *Der Zauberberg* can be divided into three main phases. Before 1914, it was a satire; between 1914 and 1915, it was an allegory for Mann's conservative viewpoint, soon abandoned in favour of the *Betrachtungen*; and in the early 1920s it assumed its definitive shape as a Bildungsroman.[118] Mann's defence of democracy began in 1922, and by the time he finished the novel in 1924 it bore the imprint of his new political convictions. The richness of *Der Zauberberg* derives from its attempt to mediate between two very different views of the world, between Enlightenment humanism and romantic asceticism, as represented by Settembrini and Naphta. Hans Castorp's allegorical vision in the snow brings these two modes of being together — sunny Mediterranean humanism and Romantic darkness — and shows that both are necessary aspects of existence. In other words, conciliation is at the heart of *Der Zauberberg*: each perspective remains limited as long as it lacks an ironic awareness of the other. Just as the Müller-Rosé scene in *Felix Krull* tells us to beware of the simplistic 'either–or' definition ('Hüte dich, darüber zu entscheiden!' (35)), so the narrator of *Der Zauberberg* tells us that love is great precisely because it hesitates between the physical and the metaphysical, excluding neither: 'Schwankender Sinn? Aber man lasse in Gottes Namen den Sinn der Liebe doch schwanken! Daß er schwankt, ist Leben und Menschlichkeit' (III, 832). One of Hans Castorp's great insights is that it must be possible to mediate between the two tendencies or 'Geistesrichtungen' (III, 409) that Settembrini and Naphta represent:

> Alles stellten sie auf die Spitze, diese zwei [. . .] während ihm doch schien, als ob irgendwo inmitten zwischen den strittigen Unleidlichkeiten, zwischen rednerischem Humanismus und analphabetischer Barbarei das gelegen sein müsse, was man als das Menschliche oder Humane persönlich ansprechen durfte.[119]

How does this relate to *Felix Krull*, and to the social function of art? The answer is: form. If there is one thing that the disputants on the magic mountain agree on, it is the importance of form. The debate on the mountain is also a debate about aesthetic form, since each of the competing 'schools' has its own aesthetic. As a humanist, Settembrini promotes the eloquence of the orator: he is an exponent of rhetoric. Naphta, on the other hand represents the romantic appetite for destruction at its most virulent. The gory, grotesque pietà in his study is a warning indication of his tastes (III, 544).[120] Hans Castorp seems to represent a middle point between these two. In the novel's early phases, he is concerned with the aesthetics of mourning and grief, an interest which leads him to visit those who are seriously ill. These bedside scenes in *Der Zauberberg* develop the insight (from *Königliche Hoheit* and *Felix Krull*) that art can have a positive social function, even a corporate, democratic one. One of the principal forms discussed in *Der Zauberberg* is the ritual of mourning, which is shown to be socially empowering and potentially democratic. The aesthetic of grief can have a benevolent social function: I am thinking of Hans Castorp's bedside visits to the terminally ill inhabitants of the Berghof in the 'Totentanz' section. It is worth noting that Castorp's interest in the dying is clearly set apart from the intellectual, programmatic nihilism of Naphta, who does not even appear until later in the novel. Castorp's motives for making the visits are admittedly ambiguous. They certainly excite him ('Gefühl der Abenteuerlichkeit' (III, 419)) and form part of his investigation into mortality ('das Bedürfnis seines Geistes, Leiden und Tod ernst nehmen und achten zu dürfen' (III, 412)). Crucially, however, there is also a humanitarian impulse at work here: the concept of charity is invoked several times ('Hans Castorps Antrieb und charitativer Unternehmungsgeist' (III, 422), 'charitative Teilnahme' (III, 438)). In other words, these visits may be formal, but they are far from being emptied of content. Hans Castorp's humane concern is evident throughout the chapter. At times he is almost overcome with emotion, for example, during his visit to Leila Gerngroß, when he is on the point of kneeling before the dying girl: 'Es fehlte nicht viel — der innere Antrieb dazu war jedenfalls vorhanden — , daß er sich vor dem Bett auf ein Knie niedergelassen hätte' (III, 420). And, as he sits at the bedside of Anton Karlowitch Ferge he listens to a lengthy description of Russian life ('Lebensstil') with anthropological interest ('[er] lauschte mit anthropologischem Anteil' (III, 434)). The anthropological perspective is reinforced at the end of the chapter when Castorp, Joachim, and Karen Karstedt go to the cinema. The programme ends with a documentary: a montage of images from all over the world. From European politics, the film moves to India, Borneo, Japan, Siberia, and Hebron. The final image is of a Moroccan woman with half-bare breasts, waving at the public.[121] These references place Hans Castorp's bedside visits in a broadly humanist context. Castorp's justification for the visits, that they are a 'Protest gegen den herrschenden Egoismus' (III, 422), is thus highly significant: he is impelled by a humane concern that is far removed from Naphta's cynical nihilism. Naphta might claim to have a pious attitude towards death, but in fact he has the bad taste to use Joachim Ziemßen's death as an occasion to score points off Settembrini — Joachim's dead body seems beneath his attention (III, 745). Hans Castorp's attitude to the deaths of his fellow patients is a world away from this. As Martin Swales has pointed out, when Castorp and Joachim visit Leila Gerngroß, Fritz Rotbein, and the son of Tous-les-deux, they provide human companionship, comfort that keeps death at bay.[122] Fritz Rotbein, for example, sheds tears of gratitude for their visit ('[er] zeigte sich zu Tränen dankbar' (III, 423)).

The visits bring consolation not only to the patients, but to their families as well. Earlier in the novel, Castorp wonders if he should have trained as a priest (III, 155). Now, in the absence of a priest, it is up to him to hear the confession of Frau Gerngroß, who blames herself for the congenital weakness that she has passed on to her daughter ('von ihr allein komme es' (III, 421)). In other words, Castorp assumes the function of secular ministrant. He gives no sermon, but provides a community service, filling an uneasy gap in the life of the Berghof. We must recall that most of the inhabitants of the sanatorium refuse to talk about death, living in a state of permanent denial. Quite simply, the topic is taboo, and Castorp's attempt to mention it meets with universal opprobrium ('einmütige und [. . .] verstockte Ablehnung' (III, 407)). It seems that in this modern, secular institution, most people are unable to cope with death. Castorp decides to reject this attitude, which he describes as 'Das egoistische Nichts-wissen, Nichts-sehen-und-hören-Wollen' (III, 406). His human concern is allied to the recognition that something has to be done to maintain human dignity in the face of death. Every death is a caesura, a miniature crisis in the life of the community, one which calls for ritual and symbol. What Castorp offers to the tuberculosis sufferers and their families is an aesthetic form, a respectfulness that somehow helps to contain their overwhelming sense of grief. He knows that the rituals of the flowers and the greeting cards give a form to that which dissolves form, a structure to that which is beyond structure. The moments when Castorp meets the dying and looks them in the eye are not personally cathartic, but formal and meta-individual. The formulae of condolence tap into grief and acknowledge it, but they contain it as well, holding pain at the level of the bearable. In a secular world, lacking metaphysical guarantees, only these corporate expressions of grief can be relied upon. These rituals may be conventional, but that does not make them superficial or vacuous. Indeed, the secularized ceremony gives more people the chance to speak. It is more democratic, because it implies that, in the absence of divine authority, everybody has to 'do it themselves', everybody has to come together and take part in the ritual. Later in the novel, when Joachim Ziemssen dies, it is agreed that the funeral will take place in his home town (III, 744). The mourners in the Berghof thus have to find their own ways to express their grief. When the coffin arrives, Hans Castorp insists on helping to prepare the body for the lying-in-state, against the wishes of the funeral assistant. Eventually, though, he accepts that the body must be handed over to the professionals; the farewell kiss he places on Joachim's forehead is a rejection of 'eingeborene Sittensprödigkeit' (III, 746). At this point, the corporate takes over from the individual. Joachim's death, although it affects Hans Castorp on the most personal level, needs to be given a corporate expression. Thus the aesthetic of mourning brings about a symbolic reaffirmation of the entire community.

To reiterate, then: Hans Castorp's attitude to death is opposed to Naphta's. While Naphta represents unbridled Romantic decadence, Castorp is impelled by humane, anthropologically informed concern. Castorp knows that the formality is there for a reason: to help people cope with suffering. His innate tact means that he knows when formality is appropriate, and when it is not. Like Felix Krull, he has a sense of balance which prevents him from venturing too far into wrongdoing. Ultimately, both Hans Castorp and Felix Krull aim at a classical idea of wholeness, which would reconcile facile oppositions such as body and mind, self and world. According to this viewpoint, death is not opposed to life, but a necessary part of it; something to be recognized, but not hypostasized or reified; something to be acknowledged with dignity as one part of the whole. It must be balanced by the communal perspective which transcends individual mortality. As Hans Castorp says to Joachim: 'Das muß sich vereinigen lassen, Mann, und wenn du das nicht glaubst, dann treibst du Weltentzweiung, und so was zu treiben, ist immer ein großer Fehler, will ich dir mal bemerken'. (III, 536)

(c) *Joseph und seine Brüder*

The most important link between Joseph and Felix Krull is their consciousness of the way in which social behaviour is dependent upon language, ritual, and aesthetic form. With an instinctive grasp of anthropology, they share the insight that ethics and linguistics go hand in hand (as Settembrini puts it: 'Die Sprache ist die Gesittung selbst' (III, 715)). Joseph's career shows that it is only a small step from artistry to social responsibility. At the start of the novel, he is obviously a selfish brat. Even so, he understands a basic truth of human nature: that people love stories. He learns this from his father Jaakob, who likes nothing better than trading anecdotes. The German term for it is 'schönes Gespräch', which very roughly translates as 'nice chat'. This highly ritualized conversation serves no immediate practical purpose and resembles a duet:

> Ein 'schönes Gespräch', das hieß: ein solches, das nicht mehr dem nützlichen Austausch diente und der Verständigung über praktische oder geistliche Fragen, sondern der bloßen Aufführung und Aussagung des beiderseits Bekannten [. . .] und ein redender Wechselsang war, wie die Hirtenknechte ihn tauschten des Nachts auf dem Felde am Feuer und anfingen: 'Weißt du davon? Ich weiß es genau.' (IV, 116)

Of course on one level such fine conversations have a delimiting function: they serve to confirm and reinforce social norms. But Mann's point is that such conversations do more than just transmit culture. They are culture itself. Such conversations rise above the satisfaction of basic needs; in them, the partners of the dialogue come together in play. Culture is centrally made up of conversations ('welche das menschlich Würdige, nämlich das mehr als Natürliche und also Gesittete eigentlich ausmachen' (IV, 162)). The idea is an old one. It draws on humanism and the Enlightenment, on anthropology, on Fontane, Freud, and Simmel. At the same time, it is not far removed from the structuralist view of the 1950s which sees civilization as the superstructure of signs that emerges as basic needs are sublimated and tamed. Thus the narrator of *Joseph* tells us that culture is our most natural element, and we are shocked, even horrified, whenever raw, primitive emotion bursts through it. The narrator talks of: 'jenes Grauens, das entsteht, wenn das Urtümliche die Schichten der Gesittung durchbricht, an deren Oberfläche es nur noch in gedämpften Andeutungen und Gleichnissen fortwirkt' (IV, 633). Joseph understands this right from the start. Since he has grown up in a culture of telling stories, he knows that culture *is* essentially telling stories. And if Joseph makes his way in the world, it is because he is finely attuned to the rituals, signs, and stories which make up civilized life. One important aspect of this is the fact that people are always willing to suspend their disbelief in the interests of a good story. This is evident from the adventures of Joseph's father Jaakob. When Jaakob (penniless after his encounter with Eliphas) goes about telling the story of the riches he has lost, he finds crowds who are only too eager to listen. The audience knows that his tale could be mere boasting, but since it is enthralling, the question of whether it is true or false is disregarded: 'Zuhörer, die wohl wußten, daß man aufschneiden könne, aber einmütig darauf verzichteten, zwischen dem gut Aufgeschnittenen und der Wahrheit einen Unterschied zu machen' (IV, 219). And such is the appeal of a good rumour that, later on, local farmers are all too eager to believe Jaakob's exaggerations about his sheep, to the extent that they willingly let themselves be deceived ('[Die Leute] ließen sich sogar wissentlich von ihm betrügen' (IV, 281)). In *Der junge Joseph*, we soon find that Joseph has inherited his father's understanding of ritual and the suspension of disbelief. Thus he can explain to his brother Benjamin how, every year, the worshippers of Tammuz (Adonis) re-enact the drama of the god's death and resurrection. They hide the statue of Tammuz in the bushes, and then pretend to look for it: 'Einige von ihnen haben die Gestalt versteckt im Gebüsch, aber auch sie suchen mit, sie wissen, wo sie ist, und wissen es nicht, sie verwirren sich absichtlich' (IV, 447). The worshippers suspend their disbelief and knowingly devote themselves to their roles in the drama. And Benjamin, though still only eight years old, shows that he has learned this most important of dramatic conventions, for when Joseph agrees to tell him his dream, Benjamin states his willingness to suspend his disbelief: '[ich] will vergessen, daß es ein Traum ist, damit ich mich recht ergötze' (IV, 460).[123]

This idea of a contract between artist and audience is, in fact, a kind of variation on the social contract. Both are implicit agreements between people which indicate a pattern of civilized interaction. And the one often leads to the other. Thus, alone in Egypt, Joseph quickly finds that the best way to make friends with people is to tell them stories. His understanding of how the artistic contract works makes it easier for him to form lasting social bonds. While his ancestor Abraham formed a mutually beneficial bond with God (IV, 319), Joseph applies the very same principle to the people he meets in Egypt. To a greater or lesser degree he manages to bond with nearly everyone he encounters there. He manages to charm the good dwarf Gottlieb or Schepses-Bes, Potiphar, and the servant whose position he takes. It is with Mont-Kaw and Pharao, however, that he forms the most solemn bonds. The pact between Joseph and Mont-Kaw to love and to serve Potiphar is touching because Mont-Kaw is in effect trusting Joseph to take over his life's work: '[wir] wollen ein Bund schließen um seines Dienstes willen' (IV, 903). And when Joseph calls Mont-Kaw 'Vater' (IV, 903) this is no mere flattery: Joseph is truly inspired by Mont-Kaw's selfless dedication. What we have here is an echo of Abraham's pact with God the father, but the model has been secularized. Joseph will no longer serve

God directly, but a mortal man instead. God has withdrawn; he no longer demands direct tribute; instead he authorizes love between human beings. The situation also recalls the moment in *Der Zauberberg* when Hans Castorp makes a pact with Clawdia Chauchat to love Peeperkorn. In both cases, notions of charity and service predominate. In *Der Zauberberg*, the pact is sealed with a kiss, and we find the same motif in *Joseph, der Ernährer* when Amenhotep is so impressed by Joseph's integrity that he kisses him (v, 1468). The motif is repeated yet again, when Pharao's mother Teje asks Joseph to promise that he will serve Pharao (v, 1469). And the bargain is sealed one more time, when Pharao gives Joseph his ring to wear (v, 1479). This recurring motif of bonds and contracts runs right through the novel and it forms a vital part of Mann's humanist argument.

The motif of the bond shows that bonds between people in society are not simply natural or instinctual; they are constructed through dialogue and they are sealed with ritual. In other words, the novel shows how society is composed out of a multitude of ritualized contracts between people. These bonds operate according to various conventions, which are usually taken as given by the partners in a dialogue. However, just because these conventions are constructed or assumed, it does not mean that they should be dismissed as false. These conventions are in fact the result of thousands, maybe millions of years of evolution. Indeed, these polite conventions are part of what makes us human. Human culture is made up of conventions: these are the very things which enable people to communicate with one another. But the reality of convention does not necessarily make social interaction false. Thomas Mann is trying to correct the deep-rooted German prejudice against convention, a prejudice of which Nietzsche was well aware:

> Die Form gilt uns Deutschen gemeinhin als eine Convention, als Verkleidung und Verstellung und wird deshalb, wenn nicht gehasst, so doch jedenfalls nicht geliebt; noch richtiger würde es sein, zu sagen, dass wir eine ausserordentliche Angst vor dem Worte Convention und auch wohl vor der Sache Convention haben. (KGA 3.1, 271)

Of course, it is possible for convention to become emptied of meaning. This occurs whenever political absolutism renders individual actors powerless or idle. The *Joseph* tetralogy illustrates this problem all too clearly, in the figure of the courtier Potiphar (Peteprê). Potiphar, like Klaus Heinrich in *Königliche Hoheit*, has a purely formal existence (II, 84). His whole life revolves around appearance, and lacks substance. But Potiphar's situation is even worse than Klaus Heinrich's. At least Klaus Heinrich's duties keep him constantly busy, while Potiphar's duties are minimal, leaving him with nothing to do. In contrast to Joseph (and to Klaus Heinrich), Potiphar cannot combine his artistic, symbolic existence with real action. He knows that this is not very manly of him ('Zierlichkeit, Form ohne Gegenstand und elegante Schnörkelrede [. . .] sind Höflings Sache, und insofern kann man sagen, daß [er] näher den Frauen steht' (v, 1036)); but he also knows it is the only thing he is capable of ('Denn reine Förmlichkeit ist meine Sache und Zier ohne Zweck' (IV, 1037)). Potiphar spends most of his time overcome by apathy, but surprisingly, when crisis does threaten at the end of *Joseph in Ägypten*, he copes with it quite well. His knowledge of courtly show turns out to be useful after all, and he finds the correct and dignified tone which saves the day. It seems that art and formality serve a valuable purpose after all. It is the task of Joseph, in the final volume, to use art in a way which is beneficial to society. Like the narrator, he has come to the insight that matters of art, taste, and politics are in fact linked because they are related modes of human development:

> Das Weltganze [. . .] redet noch [. . .] durch die Bildungen des Geschmacks, der Geschicklichkeit und des Weltschmucks, die für eine ganz eigene Sache zu erachten, welche aus der Welteinheit fiele und mit Religion und Politik nichts zu schaffen hätte, [. . .] närrisch wäre. (V, 1377)

Joseph, der Ernährer tries to show that political problems can sometimes be solved by aesthetic negotiation. Joseph's government of Egypt is presented as an artistic balancing act, bolstering the power of the state while at the same time guaranteeing individual freedom. His version of the New Deal safeguards social justice by attempting to reconcile the needs of the one with the needs of the many: 'eine überraschende Verbindung von Vergesellschaftung und Inhaberfreiheit des einzelnen' (V, 1766). Admittedly, one can only talk of democracy in *Joseph* in a limited sense. Egypt remains a monarchy, and Joseph's politics are somewhat paternalistic. Nevertheless, there are in fact very solid checks on his power. He has no control over foreign policy or the justice system (V, 1498–99). This is vital: in Mann's Egypt, executive power is divided strictly between ministers; the monarch withdraws from government, and the people even have a say in religion (IV, 691).[124] This might fall short of democracy, but in the context of the ancient world it is progressive to the point of anachronism. Finally, the novel also depicts aesthetic negotiation on the level of family politics. The entire process of reconciliation between the brothers is carefully stage-managed from beginning to end by Joseph. What is the purpose of the trickery with the silver in the sacks, the play-acting, and the accusations of theft? Is Joseph just getting his own back on his brothers? Not really. The trickery is a way for him to test his brothers, and to ensure that his beloved brother Benjamin will also be present when all is forgiven. Joseph knows that what happened in the past was so terrible that something out of the ordinary is required to put things right: a grand gesture, a big scene. When the brothers meet again, strong emotion must be shown, and tears will have to be shed — but they will be tears of joy. Joseph is the most perfect synthesis of *Bürger* and *Künstler* that Mann ever created. The novel tries to show that artistic self-consciousness does not always end in narcissism or solipsism. It can instead be employed in the service of others, and in doing so, find full expression.

(d) *Lotte in Weimar*

Lotte in Weimar, like *Joseph*, is a novel about the socially committed artist. In these later works, the artist, far from being an outsider, has become the working centre of society. The whole of Weimar revolves around Goethe. Goethe, as portrayed by Mann, combines the roles of artist and statesman, *Bürger* and *Künstler*, with consummate ease. Thus *Lotte in Weimar* carefully traces the interface between art and life, *Geist* and *Leben*. This aspect of the novel has, in my view, received

insufficient attention. Other aspects have been covered in detail. Gerhard Lange
has looked at the novel's intertextuality;[125] Yahya Elsaghe has viewed it from a
psychoanalytical perspective;[126] Reinhard Baumgart and Elsbeth Wolffheim have
dealt with the book's eroticism.[127] But though these studies are often excellent, they
say little about what I regard as the crux of the book: the contextualizing of Goethe,
the way in which he is seen as being enmeshed in the social world around him. The
structure of the novel, by delaying the appearance of Goethe, does not only increase
dramatic effect; it allows Goethe to emerge slowly out of the environment to which
he belongs, as if he had taken root there. By depicting Goethe through the eyes of
others, the novel allows us to see Goethe as the public phenomenon that he was.

Lotte in Weimar takes a backstage look at Goethe as literary institution in his own
lifetime, and shows the enormous supporting cast which was necessary to maintain
that institution. This perspective serves to dispel the notion that the life of a genius
is a solitary one, made up of a continual stream of epiphanies and poetic creations.
Mann's novels continually make the point that the genius is rarely an isolated figure;
on the contrary, the genius is constantly surrounded by others — muses, confidants,
assistants — whose lives he draws upon and impacts upon. Even the solitary Adrian
Leverkühn needs his Zeitblom, and in the case of Goethe, the whole of Weimar is
mobilized as a stage-setting for the great man. Goethe himself was well aware of the
importance of context, and he continually asserted it in his scientific studies, which
are still noteworthy today for their remarkable methodological acuity. In the short
essay 'Der Versuch als Vermittler von Objekt und Subjekt' (1793), Goethe writes
that a phenomenon must be studied in its immediate context (HA XIII, 18).[128] In
his autobiography, too, he insists that self-understanding emerges from an analysis
of the subject within its context (HA IX, 9). This is precisely the technique adopted
by Mann, who studies Goethe via the milieu which surrounds him. A number of
different witnesses are called, each one presenting Goethe in a different light. The
first witness is Mager, the butler at the inn at which Lotte stays. He is the first to
recognize that Lotte is a celebrity, and he is the one to decide which visitors she will
receive: which guests to admit and which ones to turn away. He also has the famous
last words of the novel: 'Es ist buchenswert' (GKFA 9.1, 446).[129] Helmut Jendreiek
regards Mager as a Mephistophelian figure,[130] but in my opinion, the all-knowing
Mager bears more than a passing resemblance to P. G. Wodehouse's Jeeves. He is
more of a Hermes, a *schelmischer Diener* along the lines of Joseph and Felix Krull.
His presence is not a malign one. Indeed, he is capable of his own creativity, stage-
managing the entrances and exits of Lotte's visitors. He is well aware that Lotte's
stay in Weimar needs to be correctly orchestrated — like Krull, he has a fine sense
of occasion. As for Miss Cuzzle, who travels around Europe making sketches of
famous people, her cheerful intrusiveness suggests that of the modern paparazzo
of which she is a clear forerunner. Next we have the confessions of Riemer. As
Goethe's secretary, Riemer is privy to the great man's daily routine, but this has only
made him more aware of the unbridgeable gap which separates him from Goethe's
genius. His description of Goethe, while it seems dispassionate, is in fact distorted
by his own subjective concerns. Riemer is ambivalent about Goethe, perceiving
him as both an inspiration and a threat. Despite his deep attachment to Goethe,

he feels that the great man may be stifling his own career and, quoting the jealous Cassius from *Julius Caesar*, asks why Goethe should be the one to be gifted with genius (GKFA 9.1, 84). It is easy to interpret this passage as Mann's confession of his own ambivalence towards Goethe. But when Riemer launches into a discussion of Goethe's irony, it suddenly seems that we are no longer analysing Goethe but Thomas Mann's own literary technique. If Goethe's inhuman irony somehow becomes moral thanks to his sympathy with humanity (GKFA 9.1, 93–94), this is to invoke Mann's own key concept of 'Sympathie'. And when Riemer compares Goethe to the self-transforming Proteus, the affinity with Felix Krull becomes even more pronounced (GKFA 9.1, 95). Goethe's genius derives from the fact that he exists in a state of endless becoming; at the same time, he fulfils an important need. Riemer comments that in a secular society, since the belief in God is lacking, the burden of mystery falls upon a few select people. People need mysteries to adore and this explains their need for the great man: 'Ohne Mysterien kommt offenbar der Mensch nicht aus; hat er an den christlichen den Geschmack verloren, so erbaut er sich an dem heidnischen oder Natur-Geheimnis der Persönlichkeit' (GKFA 9.1, 75). Goethe's art thus fulfils the metaphysical longings of a secular age. His art is seen as Olympian, the expression of a divine mystery, and he himself has come to represent the potential for greatness which rests within all humanity. In an increasingly secular society, art continues to signify divinity, offering privileged moments of cognition. Divine revelation has been transformed into artistic epiphany.

Adele Schopenhauer and August von Goethe are more critical of Goethe. Adele feels that her friend Ottilie von Pogwisch is being manipulated by Goethe into a disastrous marriage with his son. As for August, he is painfully conscious of his own inadequacy compared to his father ('Ich bin nur ein beiläufiger, mit wenig Nachdruck begabter Abwurf seiner Natur' (GKFA 9.1, 233)); he sincerely admires his father's work, but is less enamoured of Goethe the man. August presents his father as an adept literary operator who is not above exploiting the fashions of the age, referring pointedly to the calculated populism of *Hermann und Dorothea* (GKFA 9.1, 263).[131]

Chapter 7 is written from Goethe's perspective, in the form of a richly allusive interior monologue, interspersed with sections of dialogue. It soon becomes apparent that Goethe is deeply grounded in the sensual, practical world. As the chapter begins, we find him lying in bed with an erection. His ruminations continue for a few pages before he calls for his secretary Carl to bring the coffee. Goethe's love of food now comes to the fore, and he questions Carl extensively about the stocks of rusk biscuits ('Offenbacher Zwiebacken' (GKFA 9.1, 298–99)). Then Goethe begins to dictate his correspondence to Carl in a scene reminiscent of *Egmont*. After the dictation, Goethe returns to the topic of food; he plans inviting some guests to lunch and he orders that the roast goose be well stuffed with chestnuts (GKFA 9.1, 306). This is a Goethe who is attuned to mundane concerns and amenable to receiving guests. After Carl leaves, Goethe's thoughts articulate the unity of *Geist* and *Leben*: 'Geist — ein Product des Lebens, — das auch wieder in ihm erst wahrhaft lebt. Sind auf einander angewiesen' (GKFA 9.1, 309). In other words, Goethe can synthesize the duality which had plagued Mann's early characters. Then the barber arrives and we see Goethe putting his wig on. This passage shows that Goethe is highly conscious of the importance of conveying the correct visual image:

> 'Sorg' aber fürs Haar, ich will's gepudert, und auch ums Eisen magst du es hier und hier ein bischen [sic] legen, man ist ein ganz anderer Mensch, wenn das Haar aus der Stirn und den Schläfen ist und seinen Sitz hat' (GKFA 9.1, 319)

Thomas Mann's Goethe, like Felix Krull, is thus a consummate *Lebenskünstler*, one who can easily adapt to convention. Like Krull, he has a sense of his intrinsic worth. His 'Bin aus dem Holz, aus dem Gott mich geschnitzt hat' (GKFA 9.1, 321) clearly recalls Krull's own comment that he is 'aus feinerem Holz geschnitzt' (273). Like Krull, too, Goethe is a sort of acrobat, achieving a balancing act between difficulty and insouciance: 'Ich — ein Balance-Kunststück genauer Not, knapp ausgewogener Glücksfall der Natur, ein Messertanz von Schwierigkeit und Liebe zur Fazilität' (GKFA 9.1, 323). Again, like Felix Krull, Goethe knows the humane value of a little harmless deception:

> Das Leben wäre nicht möglich ohne etwelche Beschönigung durch wärmenden Gemütstrug, — gleich drunter aber ist Eiseskälte. Man macht sich groß und verhaßt durch Eiseswahrheit und versöhnt sich zwischenein, versöhnt die Welt durch fröhlich-barmherzige Lügen des Gemüts. (GKFA 9.1, 324–25)

What we have here is a statement to the effect that superficiality, even the odd lie, may sometimes be of more service to humanity than the strident insistence upon truth. From this perspective, human identity is seen as a matter of ironic compromise with life. The perfect host must know how to sparkle, and Goethe can do just that, as we see during the dinner at the Frauenplan. As Goethe enters the room, Lotte remarks upon the overall 'Koketterie und Zweideutigkeit' of his appearance (GKFA 9.1, 388). At the dinner-table Goethe displays his skill as a master raconteur, able to guide the conversation in any direction he sees fit. Lotte senses the attempt at control but can't help taking pleasure in his anecdotes (GKFA 9.1, 403). She soon comes to realize that Goethe somehow manages to incarnate both artist and bourgeois simultaneously:

> Das Seltsame war [. . .], daß sich in seinem Falle das Geistige [. . .] mit dem Gesellschaftlich-Amtlichen vermischte; daß der Dichter [. . .] zugleich ein großer Herr war, und daß man diese zweite Eigenschaft nicht als etwas von seinem Genie verschiedenes, sondern als dessen weltlich-repräsentativen Ausdruck empfand. (GKFA 9.1, 407–08)

In this passage, the dignity of Goethe's poetic genius not only *merges* with his role as bourgeois host, but the two qualities are seen as being intrinsically linked. In other words, Goethe's genius as a subjective artist is linked to the way he can express the more impersonal, general functions of the public sphere. Goethe is not a figure of romantic isolation; on the contrary, his genius consists in the way he is able to interact with his community and articulate its concerns.

What makes Mann's treatment of Goethe so important is the fact that it shows Goethe to be deeply enmeshed in the court society of Weimar. Goethe, of course, had already indicated that the opposition between artist and public could be subverted in the play *Torquato Tasso* (1790). *Tasso* is ostensibly about the conflict between the poet Tasso and the statesman Antonio, but the play ends with a measure of reconciliation. Although Tasso is apparently at odds with the courtly society of Ferrara, he is nevertheless shown to be carrying out a vital function, that of putting Ferrara on the map, expressing it to the world. In the world of Renaissance Italy, art was a source of great prestige, intimately involved with trade and politics. Thus, in both *Tasso* and *Lotte*, we are made to see the mutual interdependence of artist and public. In both texts there is a sense that a culture doesn't exist fully unless it is expressed and represented in art. Every culture has a need to say itself to itself, and artistic representation helps to define community. Goethe's works put Weimar on the map, just as Tasso did for Ferrara, just as Dante did for Florence, just as Mann did for Lübeck, just as Joyce did for Dublin. Goethe, in fact, represented the community in both senses of the word: he represented it as artist and as politician. The two activities were complementary. Goethe's presence in Weimar defined it as a centre of culture, and, on a national level, the success of Goethe's works promoted a sense of national culture, a vital step on the road to the creation of the modern nation-state, which at that time was still to come. Thus, although he withdrew from politics in his later years, Goethe's works gave added momentum to the burgeoning democratic movement of the 'Vormärz' period.

Lotte in Weimar also reminds us that Goethe's own work is often intimately bound up with the work of his contemporaries. This is related to Goethe's wish to become the representative poet of his age and to enter into a dialogue with his peers. Indeed, part of Goethe's genius was his ability to attract supporters, and it is clear that he saw his literary work as a project which required collaborators. He was also well aware of the need to create not only a new literary movement but also a new kind of audience to appreciate it.[132] His partnership with Schiller, although exemplary in this respect, is only the most famous element in a series which includes Herder, Wieland, and Grillparzer, to name but a few. In conversation with Frédéric Soret, Goethe showed that he was well aware of this synthetic aspect of his work:

> Das größte Genie würde nicht sehr weit kommen, wenn es alles aus sich schöpfen wollte. Was ist denn ein Genie, wenn es nicht die Fähigkeit besitzt, alles, was ihm nahe kommt, sich nutzbar zu machen? [. . .] Alles, was ich gesehen, gehört und beobachtet, habe ich gesammelt und ausgenutzt. Meine Werke sind von unzähligen verschiedenen Individuen genährt worden, [. . .] alle haben mir ihre Gedanken entgegengebracht; [. . .] ich habe oft geerntet, was andere gesät haben, mein Werk ist das eines Kollektivwesens, das den Namen Goethe trägt.[133]

This statement by Goethe shows an awareness of his debt to others, and *Lotte in Weimar* lends voice to some of those individuals who dedicated their lives to Goethe, doomed to become mere supporting characters to his genius. Many of them, such as Riemer, August, and Adele (on behalf of Ottilie) complain of sacrifice, and even Lotte feels that she has been exploited. But the feeling is also prevalent that somehow these sacrifices were worth it — the sacrifices were justified in light of Goethe's genius. In Chapter 8, Goethe tells a Chinese proverb to the effect that the great man is a public misfortune (GKFA 9.1, 411), but although the guests' laughter suggests agreement, Lotte disagrees: 'Nur gute Menschen wissen die Größe zu schätzen. Die Chinesen, wie sie da hüpfen und zirpen unter ihren Glockendächern, sind alberne, böse Menschen' (GKFA 9.1, 427). In other words she is, in the final analysis, glad to have been used by Goethe as material for his *Werther*. And the community which gathers around Goethe, despite its occasional griping, shows itself to be ultimately grateful.

At the finale of *Lotte in Weimar*, the notion of sacrifice is given symbolic expression, and metaphysical inflection, through the allusion to the poem 'Selige Sehnsucht'. The image of the butterfly consumed by the flame is central to *Felix Krull*, too, as I have shown in my discussion of the Müller-Rosé episode. The underlying message is that art, through transformation and sacrifice, somehow leads to a higher metaphysical union, to communion. Life demands sacrifice, demands transformation, since being is becoming. Goethe tells Lotte that he too is a sacrifice — in the burning light of sacrifice, all becomes fused together:

> Du handelst vom Opfer, aber damit ist's ein Geheimnis und eine große Einheit wie mit Welt, Leben, Person und Werk, und Wandlung ist alles. Den Göttern opferte man, und zuletzt war das Opfer der Gott. [. . .] Willst Du denn, daß ich diese [Flamme] sei, worein sich der Falter begierig stürzt, bin ich im Wandel und Austausch der Dinge die brennende Kerze doch auch, die ihren Leib opfert, damit das Licht leuchte, bin ich auch wieder der trunkene Schmetterling, der der Flamme verfällt. (GKFA 9.1, 444)

In other words, artist, muse, collaborators, and public, all come to experience the work in terms of sacrifice and painful transformation. Helmut Jendreiek points out that those around Goethe experience their proximity to him as both an intensifying ('Steigerung') and a cancelling-out ('Aufhebung') of their own existence.[134] While Goethe's poem calls this meeting a 'höhere Begattung', the narrator of *Felix Krull* calls it a 'hochzeitliche Begegnung'. What Mann is describing here is essentially a type of secular communion. After all, the climax of *Lotte in Weimar* is not some melodramatic *Liebestod*, but a meeting in a carriage between two old friends. In the absence of metaphysical guarantees, people turn to aesthetics and language as a means to constitute community, via the more humble epiphanies of art. If we lack access to the divine, we can still enjoy a good book and a good chat.

As with Fontane's *Der Stechlin* or Joyce's *Ulysses*, the great charm of *Lotte in Weimar* is that virtually nothing happens. There is no 'plot' in the traditional sense. Instead, through a series of conversations, the image of an entire world is conjured up. It is almost as if community is essentially created through language. In *Lotte in Weimar*, Mann shows himself to be a true disciple of both Goethe and Fontane. *Lotte in Weimar* is an eloquent demonstration of the fact that the substance of social cohesion is dialogue: dialogue which ranges from the urbane to the sublime and back again, and, all the while, patiently enacts society.

(e) *Mario und der Zauberer*

In this chapter I have mainly focused on the benign potential of art, but Thomas Mann was also aware of the countervailing argument: the fact that art can corrupt. The three works in which Mann gives fullest rein to his bad conscience about art are probably *Der Tod in Venedig*, *Mario und der Zauberer*, and *Doktor Faustus*. In all of these works, the critique of art highlights the dangerous political consequences of a culture based on Romanticism, and the ways in which art can cause the intellectual and sexual degradation of the individual. Here, as in Mann's other works, the personal and philosophical is intensely bound up with the political. Cavaliere Cipolla is probably the least sympathetic of all the artist figures created by Mann. He is a demonic hunchback akin to Richard III, a baleful, malevolent hypnotist. The fact that he is a magician immediately aligns him with Klingsor, Hagen, and other evil wizards of German Romanticism. Where other artists would seek to enchant or edify, Cipolla goes further and deliberately uses his art to control the minds of others, willing them to humiliate and debase themselves. Like Felix Krull, Cipolla is out to seduce his audience, but while Krull seeks the willing consent of his public, Cipolla favours a bullying, domineering approach. Cipolla's 'seduction' of Mario is aggressive, degrading, and in very bad taste, since it is carried out in public. It is a seduction that verges on rape. This is not just art as exploitation, but as domination, subjugation, and the parallels with fascism are obvious. However, *Mario und der Zauberer* does not deal with fascism directly; instead it examines the psychological phenomena associated with fascism, and therein lies its greatness.

A glance at Thomas Mann's speech 'Deutsche Ansprache — Ein Appell an die Vernunft' should help to confirm the underlying significance of *Mario und der Zauberer*, since the speech was written immediately after the short story's publication in 1930. The speech contains an analysis of the National Socialist movement, which, according to Mann, expresses itself as an irrational, vitalist atavism, promoting the dark forces of the unconscious.[135] National Socialism thrives on wild, confusing, intoxicating impressions ('wilder, verwirrender und zugleich nervös stimulierender, berauschender Eindrücke'). In other words, as Martin Travers says, the central appeal of Nazism is its irrationality.[136] The theme of the speech is thus rationality versus irrationality. The 'tree of reason' of the Enlightenment has been shaken by Romanticism and buffetted by the works of Nietzsche; the Nazis, however, want to uproot the tree and do away with it altogether, and this is wrong.[137] Why is irrationality so attractive? Thomas Mann's answer, echoing Freud, is that irrationality appeals to the most private fantasies and fears of the individual. Both fascism and art relate to the darker, more turbulent side of human nature (and Mann later likened Hitler to the artist). But while art seeks to entertain or to convey an experience, fascism seeks to harness instinct and desire for its own purposes (perhaps 'hijack' would be more accurate). While art excites in the play of desire, fascism uses aesthetic semblance in order to instrumentalize desire for destructive purposes. *Mario und der Zauberer* thus deals with the siren song of irrationality and its attractions for the liberal mind.

Let us now turn to a closer examination of the text, and in particular, to the unnamed narrator. Several commentators have drawn attention to the crucial role of the narrator, who appears to represent the type of humanist intellectual (rather like Serenus Zeitblom in *Doktor Faustus*).[138] The narrator quickly realizes that Cipolla's show is based upon humiliation and victimization, but he finds himself being fascinated by what he knows is morally wrong. He justifies his decision to remain seated (and his decision to remain in Torre di Venere) by saying that he hopes to learn something from these very strange events:

> Wir blieben auch deshalb, weil der Aufenthalt uns merkwürdig geworden war, und weil Merkwürdigkeit ja in sich selbst einen Wert bedeutet, unabhängig von Behagen und Unbehagen. Soll man 'abreisen', wenn das Leben sich ein bißchen unheimlich, nicht ganz geheuer oder etwas peinlich und kränkend anläßt? Nein doch, man soll bleiben, [. . .] gerade dabei gibt es vielleicht etwas zu lernen. (VIII, 669)

The narrator's decision to stay reflects the willingness of the liberal mind to entertain various viewpoints, even questionable ones. Thus the narrator falls prey to his own openness to the strange and exotic. He knows that Cipolla is manipulating the audience; he knows that the magician is deliberately trying to confuse people: 'Man mußte zugeben, daß er seine Worte nicht besser hätte wählen können, um die Wasser zu trüben und seelische Verwirrung anzurichten' (VIII, 689). But this very clouding of the faculty of reason seems to be, on one level, deeply appealing to him. The dilemma of the liberal narrator is similar to that of the young gentleman from Rome. Both succumb to Cipolla despite their critical sense, because their resistance is negative rather than positive: they kick against the threat but lack a strong alternative with which to oppose it: 'Verstand ich den Vorgang recht, so unterlag dieser Herr der Negativität seiner Kampfposition. Wahrscheinlich kann man vom Nichtwollen seelisch nicht leben; eine Sache nicht tun wollen, das ist auf die Dauer kein Lebensinhalt' (VIII, 702). Meanwhile, the rest of the audience undergoes a similar process. Right from the start, everyone senses that something is not right about Cipolla ('Die Vermutung regte sich schon, daß der Mann unter falscher Flagge segelte' (VIII, 681)). Even when this intuition develops into a feeling of stubborn resistance, this feeling remains for the most part unexpressed. The audience is under Cipolla's spell, despite the feeling that his triumph is their humiliation: '[Das Publikum war], wie mir wenigstens schien, nicht ohne widerspenstiges Gefühl für das eigentümlich Entehrende [. . .], das für den Einzelnen und für alle in Cipollas Triumphen lag' (VIII, 697). But isn't this humiliation the reason why Cipolla succeeds? What if the audience actually *wants* to be dishonoured and degraded? This is in fact the case. Cipolla's art targets the sado-masochistic impulses of the audience, who soon find that they enjoy seeing people humiliated and that they enjoy bowing to the pressure of his will. One young man in particular takes great pleasure in his bondage: 'Auch schien er in der Hörigkeit sich ganz zu behagen und seine armselige Selbstbestimmung gern los zu sein' (VIII, 701). This young man seems to enjoy his servitude partly because it enables him to produce his own theatrical effort ('schauspielerische Leistung' (VIII, 686)) and partly thanks to the Dionysian intoxication caused by his loss of self-control. Indeed, when Cipolla commands the audience to dance, they obey willingly, and whip themselves into a Dionysian frenzy, one which has little to do with reason and everything to do with instinct ('eine trunkene Auflösung der kritischen Widerstände' (VIII, 700)). This frenzy even affects the most respected members of the community, such as Frau Angiolieri. Frau Angiolieri, like Dona Maria Pia in *Felix Krull*, is the hostess of the narrator, and like her, she seems only too eager to abandon herself to the mood of the crowd. What we have here is an allusion to the violence unleashed by fascism, and the fact that Mario takes his revenge upon Cipolla does little to dispel the reader's feeling of unease.

In effect, *Mario und der Zauberer* revisits the central theme of the pre-war *Krull*, namely, the reciprocity between artist and audience. As Joyce Crick has shown, this relationship forms the crux of *Mario und der Zauberer*.[139] In the Müller-Rosé episode, Mann explored the relationship between artist and public, presenting it in terms of a contract, an agreement to respect certain conventions and rules. *Mario* returns to this idea. However, while in *Krull* the contract was regarded as something mutually beneficial, in *Mario* the contract has become corrupted and exploitative — it has become a *Teufelspakt*. Like Müller-Rosé's, Cipolla's relation with the audience is a kind of symbiosis. Yet Cipolla describes this symbiosis in terms that are reminiscent of Nazi ideology:

> Die Fähigkeit, sagte er, sich selbst zu entäußern, zum Werkzeug zu werden, [. . .] zu gehorchen, sei nur die Kehrseite jener anderen, zu wollen und zu befehlen, es sei ein und dieselbe Fähigkeit; [. . .] wer zu gehorchen wisse, der wisse auch zu befehlen, und ebenso umgekehrt; der eine Gedanke sei in dem anderen einbegriffen, wie Volk und Führer ineinander einbegriffen seien. (VIII, 691)

Here, the tacit agreement of the Müller-Rosé scene (between artist and audience) has degenerated into the union of the leader and the all-too-easily-led: a sort of fascist, sado-masochistic communion. The reciprocity of pleasure implied by the Müller-Rosé section has become a reciprocity of subjugation and obedience. It is easy enough to derive a moral from this story: what starts as harmless fun, artistic licence, can end in violence and degradation. Every game has the potential to spiral out of control.

At this point I want to consider the contribution that psychoanalysis can make to our understanding of *Mario und der Zauberer*. It seems reasonable to do so, since Thomas Mann's analysis of fascism was clearly influenced by Freud — as can be seen from the references to the unconscious ('Unbewußte') in the 1930 speech 'Deutsche Ansprache — Ein Appell an die Vernunft'. Freud's principal text on mass movements, 'Massenpsychologie und Ich-Analyse', was published in 1921 in the early days of modern fascism, a year before Mussolini came to power. Striking here is the fact that Freud describes the relation between leader and follower as characterized by both love and hypnosis: 'Von der Verliebtheit ist offenbar kein weiter Schritt zur Hypnose. [. . .] Dieselbe demütige Unterwerfung, Gefügigkeit, Kritiklosigkeit gegen den Hypnotiseur wie gegen das geliebte Objekt' (SA IX, 107). According to Freud, the leader of the group takes the place of the ego-ideal ('Ichideal') for all the members of the group, thereby providing them with a means of identification, as well as a direction: 'Eine [. . .] primäre Masse ist eine Anzahl von Individuen, die ein und dasselbe Objekt an die Stelle ihres Ichideals gesetzt und sich infolgedessen in ihrem Ich miteinander identifiziert haben' (SA IX, 108). Freud explains the power of hypnosis as deriving from the regression to a passive relation with the father, in which the father is perceived as a powerful godlike figure, just as in primitive times (SA IX, 117–18). Hartmut Böhme, commenting on *Mario und der Zauberer*, claims that Freud's explanation for mass control is a little too simple, tending to reduce people to mindless automata.[140] Perhaps Freud recognized this, because in 'Das ökonomische Problem des Masochismus' (1924) he offers an explanation of masochism, one which can easily be applied to the context of fascism. Freud regards masochism as a regression of the libido in which the subject wishes to be treated as a naughty child by the father (SA III, 346). This leads to an 'unconscious sense of guilt' ('das unbewußte Schuldgefühl') which in turn leads to a need for punishment ('Strafbedürfnis'). Whether one accepts this theory or not, the idea that the individual gains gratification from suffering and the postulate of a need for punishment seems highly persuasive. Freud mentions cases where mental problems suddenly vanish in the face of personal crisis, such as the start of an unhappy marriage or the onset of a serious disease. In these cases, what matters to the individual is not the type of suffering, but that a certain level of suffering should be maintained.[141] Applying this theory to *Mario und der Zauberer*, we are now better placed to understand that the audience complies with Cipolla because it derives an immense psychological pleasure from its own suffering. In the words of Hartmut Böhme: 'Cipolla herrscht, weil er gegen die Rationalisierungs-Potenzen des Ich die latenten masochistischen Bedürfnisse des Publikums entfesselt und den kollektiven Selbstverlust als Lustgewinn umzustilisieren versteht'.[142] Of course it is also possible to discard the Freudian theory and see the audience's desire for dissolution as resulting from what Nietzsche in *Die Geburt der Tragödie* calls the Dionysian drive, the joy of self-surrender. Indeed, Mann's text favours this interpretation when it employs such phrases as 'drunken dissolution' ('trunkene Auflösung'). Whether one reads the story with Freud or with Nietzsche in mind, Thomas Mann's warning about the instrumentalization of desire in *Mario und der Zauberer* remains highly topical. Cipolla's 'victims' were to a certain extent his partners; some were only too willing to be deceived. We need to remember that Cipolla is only a metaphor for a dictator; he does not use physical violence like a true fascist. But like Hitler, his success derives from the fact that he appeals to the baser instincts of his audience. As Hermann Kurzke puts it: 'Das Volk [. . .] wird nicht einfach hypnotisch vergewaltigt, sondern in seinem tiefsten Wesen angesprochen'.[143] *Mario und der Zauberer* thus demonstrates the insufficiency of the critical intellect, if unaided by the heart.[144] As Alan Bance says, the underlying message of the story may well be that reason and passion ought to augment each other in resistance to political evil.[145]

Mann's critique of art and its social function in *Mario* comes close to that of Walter Benjamin, who famously remarked that fascism operates 'eine Ästhetisierung des politischen Lebens', which is to say that it turns politics into a sinister pantomime, designed to conceal what is really going on. It offers the masses a theatre in which to express themselves (the political rally), but in fact the only real policy that it has to offer is war.[146] In response, Benjamin called for the politicization of art (GS I.2, 469). But perhaps Benjamin was wrong to reject the aestheticization of politics. Thomas Mann offers us a different perspective. In *Felix Krull* and elsewhere, art is shown to be an intrinsic part of society, something that makes society what it is. If society always has an aesthetic dimension, then it follows that politics too contains an aesthetic dimension. This is the conclusion which Thomas Mann reached in his mature writings. He expressed this view succinctly in 1934: 'Es ist schwer, zwischen künstlerischen und politisch-sozialen Ereignissen eine scharfe Trennungslinie auszumachen' (XIII, 325);[147] and again in 1938: 'Die Grenze zwischen Kunst und Leben, die Grenzen überhaupt zwischen den Bezirken des Menschentums sind fließend geworden' (XI, 466). If Mann is correct, if — contra Benjamin — aesthetics is an a priori category of politics, then it follows that politicians must take aesthetics into account. If the artist ignores politics at his peril, then maybe the politician ignores aesthetics at his peril. And perhaps aesthetics can be mobilized in a benign way as well as in a malign one. Novels such as Der Zauberberg and Joseph und seine Brüder demonstrate that art and aesthetics can be mobilized in the service of democratic politics, without compromising that cause. Roman Luckscheiter points out that both Thomas Mann and Georg Simmel see an underlying affinity between art and politics. The two domains are structurally related, because they both endeavour to give form to an existing social reality:

> Sowohl Simmel als auch Mann gehen davon aus, daß Politiker wie Ästheten darum bemüht sein müssen, sozialen Gegebenheiten eine strukturierende Form zu geben, wobei beim Politiker der Gedanke, durch die Formgebung auch zum sozialen Fortschritt beizutragen, bindender ist [. . .]. Aus beiden Blickwinkeln ist aber auch wichtig hervorzuheben, daß die beiden Sphären nicht einander bedienen, sondern aus sich heraus strukturelle Ähnlichkeiten erzeugen: Die Politik ist allein durch ihr originäres Handeln auch ästhetisch, die Kunst ist allein durch ihr ordendes Wesen auch politisch.[148]

According to Jacques Rancière, politics is intrinsically involved with aesthetics, because both practices entail the delimitation of spaces and times.[149] Felix Krull is a novel that knows all about the profound affinity between art and politics. The further up the social scale Krull travels, the more aesthetics he encounters. Political power is intimately bound up with its aesthetic representation. But the aestheticization of politics can be benign and even democratically liberating. The successful politician must be able to give expression to the thoughts and feelings of his public, much like the artist. Mann's political speeches of the 1920s, 1930s, and 1940s were persuasive because of their aesthetics — not in spite of them. In their own different but related ways, both politician and artist represent the community. This is something Thomas Mann makes plain in Joseph und seine Brüder. But the roots of this knowledge are already there in the early Felix Krull.

Notes to Chapter 2

1. Pamela Reilly, 'Die Synthese des Bürgers und des Künstlers bei Thomas Mann' (unpublished doctoral thesis, University College Dublin, 1949).
2. Reilly, 'Die Synthese', pp. 8, 73–74.
3. 'Man täte unrecht, über dem Feuerflüssig-Vulkanischen, dem Dämonischen und Genialen in seiner [Wagners] Produktion das altdeutsch-kunstmeisterliche Element zu übersehen, — das Treublickend-Geduldige, Handwerksfromme und Sinnig-Arbeitsame [. . .] Bürgerliches Künstlertum, ein verwickeltes Paradoxon, ein Paradoxon immerhin, eine Doppelheit und Zwiespältigkeit auf jeden Fall, trotz der Legitimität, die diese geistige Lebensform gerade in Deutschland besitzt.' (XII, 108–09) This description derives from Mann's reading of Nietzsche

(*Nietzsche contra Wagner*, KGA 6.3, 416) and is related to Mann's development of the technique of 'doppelte Optik', which I will discuss in section III(vii) below.

4. Jürgen Habermas, *Strukturwandel der Öffentlichkeit. Untersuchungen zu einer Kategorie der bürgerlichen Gesellschaft* (Berlin and Neuwied: Luchterhand, 1969), p. 48.

5. Habermas, *Strukturwandel*, pp. 50–51.

6. Hans Wysling notes that in 1909 Mann's principal concern was to go beyond this antithesis, but does not explore the topic in great detail. Cf. Scherrer and Wysling, TMS I, p. 234: 'der allzu schematische Bürger-Künstler-Dualismus der Tonio-Kröger-Zeit mußte gelockert [. . .] werden'.

7. In the *Betrachtungen* Mann also prides himself on having anticipated Weber's study of the Protestant work ethic in *Buddenbrooks* (XII, 145–46).

8. At this point I should define the terminology used. Ethnography, or 'Ethnologie' in German, is the empirical study of cultures based on fieldwork. It is also known as social anthropology in Britain and cultural anthropology in America. Ethnography is often simply referred to as anthropology *tout court*. Anthropology, however, also refers to the study of the origins of human culture using archaeological data. In contrast, the German word 'Anthropologie' designates a field of philosophical inquiry grounded in human experience, developed by Kant in the eighteenth century and continued by Helmuth Plessner in the twentieth century.

9. Cf. Alan Kuper's review of Michael Young, *Malinowski: Odyssey of an Anthropologist 1884–1920* (London: Yale University Press, 2004), in *LRB*, 7 October 2004, p. 29.

10. I do not propose at this stage to investigate the depth of Thomas Mann's knowledge of a science which was still developing throughout his lifetime. It is evident from his studies for *Joseph und seine Brüder* and his correspondence with Karl Kerényi that he was no stranger to anthropological inquiry.

11. Richard L. Anderson, *Art in Primitive Societies* (Englewood Cliffs, NJ: Prentice-Hall, 1979), pp. 28, 36, 49.

12. Bronislaw Malinowski, *Argonauts of the Western Pacific* [1922] (New York: Dutton, 1961).

13. Marcel Mauss, *The Gift* [1925] (London: Routledge, 1990).

14. Malinowski, *Argonauts*, pp. 83, 175.

15. Mauss, *The Gift*, p. 72.

16. Georges Bataille, 'La notion de dépense', in Bataille, *La part maudite* (Paris: Minuit, 1967), pp. 25–45 (p. 32).

17. When Goethe's Mephistopheles creates paper money at the Holy Roman Emperor's court (HA III, 188–89), he doesn't suddenly destroy a primordial authenticity, but accelerates an already existing process. Speculation and usury had already existed, but increased rapidly following the introduction of paper money.

18. Tb 29 September 1918: 'Graf Ed. Keyserling und Georg Simmel sind gestorben, beide Anfang der Sechziger. Habe ich noch 20 Jahre?'.

19. Georg Simmel, 'Soziologie der Mahlzeit', in Simmel, *Soziologische Ästhetik* (Bodenheim: Philo, 1998), pp. 183–90 (p. 184).

20. Simmel, 'Soziologie', pp. 186–87.

21. Simmel, 'Soziologie', p. 188.

22. Simmel, 'Soziologie', p. 188.

23. Incidentally, it is remarkable how much Engelbert Krull resembles Mynheer Peeperkorn in *Der Zauberberg*: they are akin in their carousing, in their fine gestures (Peeperkorn's 'Kulturgebärden' and Engelbert Krull's 'ausgesuchte Bewegungen'), and in the manner of their demise — suicide. They both seem to represent the charm and ultimate defeat of the obsessive pursuit of conviviality.

24. Pierre Bourdieu, *La Distinction: critique social du jugement* (Paris: Minuit, 1979) (English: *Distinction: A Social Critique of the Judgement of Taste*, London: Routledge, 1986).

25. Cf. Norbert Elias, *The Civilizing Process* [1939] (Oxford: Blackwell, 2000), pp. 424–26.

26. Ola Alsen, 'Die Dame im Hotel', *Die Woche*, 12.28, 9 July 1910, pp. 1181–87; 'Beim Fünfuhrtee', *Die Woche*, 12.50, 10 December 1910, pp. 2129–32. TMA: Mat. 3/135–38, 3/140–41, Dossier: 'Hotel. Reise. (Dandy. Gartenarbeit) Heimat. Zuchthausaufseher'.

27. 'Der Beruf eines Hotelkellners', source unknown. TMA: Mat. 3/381, Dossier: 'Allgemeines'.

Wysling states that the dossier was gathered before 1914, with only a couple of exceptions (TMS 5, p. 395). 'Der Beruf eines Hotelkellners' refers to events in the 1890s and in 1906, suggesting that it appeared some time between 1907 and 1914.

28. Alsen, 'Die Dame im Hotel', pp. 1186–87 (underlining by Mann).

29. Alsen, 'Beim Fünfuhrtee', p. 2129.

30. Alsen, 'Beim Fünfuhrtee', p. 2132.

31. Alsen, 'Beim Fünfuhrtee', pp. 2131–32 (underlinings by Mann).

32. Alsen, 'Beim Fünfuhrtee', p. 2132.

33. 'Der Beruf eines Hotelkellners'. TMA: Mat. 3/381 (underlinings by Mann).

34. One thinks of Nietzsche: 'Und wer von uns Dichtern hätte nicht seinen Wein verfälscht? Manch giftiger Mischmasch geschah in unsern Kellern, manches Unbeschreibliche ward da gethan' (Nietzsche, *Also sprach Zarathustra*, 'Von den Dichtern' (KGA 6.1, 160)).

35. Barthes, OC 1, p. 607: 'comme tout totem vivace, le vin [. . .] est avant tout une substance de conversion, capable de retourner les situations et les états, et d'extraire des objets leur contraire: de faire, par exemple, d'un faible un fort, d'un silencieux, un bavard; d'où sa vieille hérédité alchimique, son pouvoir philosophique de transmuter ou de créer *ex nihilo*.'

36. Barthes, OC 1, p. 608.

37. The periodicity of *Felix Krull* roughly coincides with that of structuralism. Saussure's *Cours de linguistique générale* was first published in 1916, but structuralism did not take off as a movement until the early 1950s. This almost corresponds with the hiatus in the composition of *Felix Krull*.

38. Barthes, OC 1, p. 1471: '[La langue] est essentiellement un contrat collectif, auquel, si l'on veut communiquer, il faut se soumettre en bloc'.

39. Harold W. Scheffler, 'Structuralism in Anthropology', in *Structuralism*, ed. by Jacques Ehrmann (New York: Anchor, 1970), pp. 56–77 (p. 58).

40. Barthes, OC 1, p. 609: 'Manger le bifteck saignant représente donc à la fois une nature et une morale'.

41. Barthes, OC 1, p. 707: 'les choses perdent en lui [mythe] le souvenir de leur fabrication'.

42. Barthes, OC 1, p. 655: 'La nouvelle Citroën tombe manifestement du ciel dans la mesure où elle se présente d'abord comme un *objet* superlatif'.

43. Nietzsche, *Menschliches, Allzumenschliches*, KGA 4.2, 143: 'Der Künstler weiss, dass sein Werk nur voll wirkt, wenn es den Glauben an eine Improvisation, an eine wundergleiche Plötzlichkeit der Entstehung erregt; und so hilft er wohl dieser Illusion nach und führt jene Elemente der begeisterten Unruhe [. . .] beim Beginn der Schöpfung in die Kunst ein, als Trugmittel, um die Seele des Schauers oder Hörers so zu stimmen, dass sie an das plötzliche Hervorspringen des Vollkommenen glaubt.'

44. 'Kur- und Lustorte. Intérieurs. Elegante Festlichkeiten. Weiblichkeit. Sport. Hôtel. Reise (Dandy. Gartenarbeit). Heimat. Zuchthausaufseher. Reisen. Coups Carlsson. Streiche. Gefangenschaft. Allgemeines. Nebendinge'. Cf. Wysling, TMS 5, pp. 395–97, 476–81. The dossiers are in the TMA.

45. Andrew Leak, *Barthes: Mythologies* (London: Grant & Cutler, 1994), p. 15.

46. Barthes, OC 1, p. 717: 'si l'on veut libérer le mythe, c'est la communauté entière dont il faut s'éloigner'.

47. Michael Neumann, 'Der Reiz des Verwechselbaren. Von der Attraktivität des Hochstaplers im späten 19. Jahrhundert', *TMJ* 18 (2005), 71–90 (p. 87).

48. Evelyn Waugh, *Brideshead Revisited* [1945] (London: Penguin, 2000), p. 8.

49. T. J. Reed, *Thomas Mann: The Uses of Tradition*, 2nd edn (Oxford: Oxford University Press, 1996); Peter Pütz, *Kunst und Künstlerexistenz bei Nietzsche und Thomas Mann* (Bonn: Bouvier, 1963).

50. Terry Eagleton, *The Ideology of the Aesthetic* (Oxford: Blackwell, 1990), p. 242: 'The aesthetic as self-actualization is in conflict with the aesthetic as social harmony, and Nietzsche is recklessly prepared to sacrifice the latter to the former'. Cf. also p. 254: 'The aesthetic as model or principle of social consensus is utterly routed by this radical insistence on autonomy'.

51. Rüdiger Görner, *Nietzsches Kunst. Annäherung an einen Denkartisten* (Frankfurt a.M.: Insel, 2000), p. 207.

52. Görner, *Nietzsches Kunst*, p. 198.

53. 'Daß sie mein Leiden eigentlich ernst nahm, glaube ich nicht; aber [. . . sie] brachte es nicht über das Herz, sich vom Spiele auszuschließen, sondern ging mit wie im Theater und fing an, mir bei meinen Darbietungen zu sekundieren' (300).

54. In this context it would be interesting to compare *Felix Krull* to Goethe's *Iphigenie*. At first glance, they seem poles apart. Felix Krull lies, Iphigenie tells the truth. However, they are both concerned with persuasion, with establishing a peaceful, happy consensus, with getting everyone to agree. The means they employ are radically different, but they both strive for the same end. Perhaps they are two sides of the same coin, two aspects of the same socializing impulse? (In Goethe's time one could still believe that a discourse could be entirely true. Since then, we late moderns have become aware of the innate duplicities of language. Nevertheless, language remains the best tool for communication we have. Felix Krull could thus be seen as a symbol of the modernist bad conscience about language.)

55. Simmel, *Soziologische Ästhetik*, p. 193.

56. Simmel, *Soziologische Ästhetik*, p. 196.

57. Simmel, *Soziologische Ästhetik*, p. 198.

58. Although it is worth bearing in mind that later events in the novel give an ironic slant to this sentence, since relationships between the Israelites and the people of Schekem end in a massacre.

59. Simmel, *Soziologische Ästhetik*, p. 194.

60. Simmel, *Soziologische Ästhetik*, p. 199.

61. Simmel, *Soziologische Ästhetik*, pp. 201–02.

62. Simmel, *Soziologische Ästhetik*, pp. 203–04.

63. Simmel, *Soziologische Ästhetik*, p. 205.

64. The chapter was first published as 'Bekenntnisse des Hochstaplers Felix Krull: Bruchstück aus einem Roman', in *Das fünfundzwanzigste Jahr. Almanach des S. Fischer Verlages* (Berlin: Fischer, 1911), pp. 273–88.

65. Pütz, *Kunst und Künstlerexistenz*, p. 15.

66. Eagleton, *Ideology*, p. 252.

67. This ludic quality of art should not be underestimated. Thomas Mann's narrator agrees: 'Müller-Rosé verbreitete Lebensfreude' (31).

68. Samuel Taylor Coleridge, *Biographia Literaria* (London: Everyman, 1965), ch. 14, p. 169.

69. Michael Beddow, 'Fiction and Meaning in Thomas Mann's *Felix Krull*', *Journal of European Studies*, 10 (1980), 77–92 (p. 87).

70. In 'Das Wunderkind' the point is that the audience is willing to believe that the child prodigy is younger than he really is. The audience contributes 'ein bißchen guten Willen [. . .] fünf gerade sein zu lassen' (VIII, 340). The phrase also occurs in the essay 'Der alte Fontane' (1910), where Mann quotes Fontane to much the same effect: 'Man muß den Künstlern gegenüber, wenn es wirkliche Künstler sind, Verzeihung üben und Fünfe gerade sein lassen' (IX, 18).

71. In a recent study, Helmut Koopmann examines the works of the brothers Mann as instances a complex literary dialogue, and presents *Felix Krull* as being, in part, a riposte to Heinrich Mann's novel *Im Schlaraffenland* (Helmut Koopmann, *Thomas Mann — Heinrich Mann. Die ungleichen Brüder* (Munich: Beck, 2005), pp. 464–83).

72. Thomas Mann picked up on this idea and developed it in *Königliche Hoheit*. The acclaimed soubrette Mizzi Meyer succeeds because she symbolizes her public, much like Klaus Heinrich (II, 170). See my discussion of *Königliche Hoheit* later on in this chapter.

73. Martin Travers, *Thomas Mann* (Basingstoke: Macmillan, 1992), p. 119.

74. Barthes, OC III, p. 140: '*Le signe, le récit, la société fonctionnent par contrat*, mais comme ce contrat est le plus souvent masqué, l'opération critique consiste à déchiffrer l'embarras des raisons, des alibis, des apparences, bref tout le naturel social, pour rendre manifeste *l'échange réglé sur quoi reposent la marche sémantique et la vie collective*'. (my italics)

75. This phrase 'hochzeitliche Begegnung', which indicates the existence of an erotic dimension to the relationship between artist and audience, may allude to a novel by Heinrich Mann, *Die kleine Stadt* (1909), in which the conductor Dorlenghi describes his audience as 'tausend Geliebte' (WA 117).

76. Cf. Wysling, TMS 5, p. 417.

77. Cf. Arthur Schopenhauer, *Sämmtliche Werke*, 5 vols (Leipzig: Insel, 1905), I, pp. 38–39 [*Die Welt als Wille und Vorstellung*, I, end of paragraph 3]. The text might also contain an echo of August Strindberg's *A Dream Play*, which is based upon the following Hindu creation myth: ' In the morning of time, before the sun shone, Brahma, the divine primal force, allowed Maja, the world mother, to induce him to multiply himself. This contact between the divine element and the earthly element was heaven's sin. Thus it is that the world, life, and mankind are but a phantom, an illusion, a dream vision. (Strindberg, *The Plays*, II, trans. by Michael Meyer (London: Secker & Warburg, 1975), p. 628)

78. Roland Barthes, similarly, points out that the artist is close to the prostitute because he acts out the fantasies of the bourgeois in return for money (OC III, p. 140).

79. As they leave the theatre, many young men try to imitate Müller-Rosé's gestures (290–91). Art also involves cognition. We recognize ourselves in the figures of art — for example, the older men in the audience recognize Müller-Rosé as the representative of their most cherished dreams: 'die Träume ihrer eigenen Jugend verwirklicht' (290).

80. Abraham Maslow, *Towards a Psychology of Being*, 3rd edn (New York: Wiley, 1998).

81. The name, with its suggestion of *vin rosé*, also implies Dionysian intoxication, as Eric Wilson ('*Felix Krull*', p. 112) points out.

82. Nietzsche, *Also sprach Zarathustra*, 'Von den Dichtern' (KGA 6.1, 161).

83. This passage was written in the 1950s, long after the Müller-Rosé episode. Its scientific register is reminiscent of Professor Kuckuck and appears, at first glance, to be far removed from the early *Felix Krull*, and closer to the short text 'Lob der Vergänglichkeit', written in early 1952 (X, 383–85). Thematically, however, this meditation on the human eye is very close to the Müller-Rosé episode, because Müller-Rosé's physical decay is redeemed by his art, just as the eye is redeemed by what it sees. In other words, the celebration of organic matter in all its fallibility and mortality does not begin in the 1950s. It is already there, forty years earlier, in the apotheosis of Müller-Rosé.

84. Tb, 4 October 1951 and 6 October 1951.

85. Hans Wysling, 'Wer ist Professor Kuckuck? Zu einem der letzten "großen Gespräche" Thomas Manns', in Wysling, *Thomas Mann heute. Sieben Vorträge* (Bern: Francke, 1976), pp. 44–63.

86. Beddow, 'Fiction and Meaning', p. 88.

87. Herwig, TMS 32, pp. 57–59, 266–76.

88. Herwig, TMS 32, p. 256.

89. Of course, the move towards monotheism was accompanied by the prohibition of images which we find in Judaism, in Protestantism during the Reformation, and in Islam. Nevertheless, even in those cultures which supposedly prohibit images, art never goes away; it is simply kept on a particularly tight rein, subordinated to religious doctrine, and limited to architecture and decoration.

90. One might compare the museum scene to Hans Castorp's famous vision in the snow in *Der Zauberberg*, where a golden, Arcadian scene soon gives way to the sacrificial violence of a ritual murder. The vision clearly indicates the Apollonian and Dionysian potentialities as being implicated in human civilization. Book III of *Felix Krull* presents the same two possibilities, but dissociated from one another. The offering of flowers to the rising sun and the bullfight present two distinct versions of primeval humanity. The underlying implication might be that two distinct versions of culture are possible, although one version will always retain the potential to transform into its other.

91. Another similarity: Rozsa's name faintly recalls the name Müller-*Rosé*.

92. 'das Wort, insofern es Taten bezeichnen soll, einer Fliegenklatsche gleicht, die niemals trifft' (309).

93. Felix Krull claims that, for Genovefa, satisfying his needs is a duty ('[meine] Zufriedenstellung [war] für sie gewissermaßen eine häusliche Pflicht' (313)) — but we never get to hear her side of the story.

94. Alsen, 'Die Dame im Hotel', pp. 1181–87.

95. Alsen, 'Die Dame im Hotel', p. 1184.

96. Alsen, 'Die Dame im Hotel', p. 1184.

97. It is highly ironic that the critical literature describes Felix Krull as the most narcissistic of

Thomas Mann's heroes, when he is in fact the most promiscuous. He is far closer to the type of Casanova or Don Juan, especially in his later conversations with Zouzou in Book III.

98. For a summary of intertextual references in this episode, see Schulz, *Identitätsfindung*, p. 623.

99. Cf. Anthony W. Riley, 'Three Cryptic Quotations in Thomas Mann's *Felix Krull*', *Journal of English and Germanic Philology*, 65 (1966), 99–106 (p. 101).

100. As T. J. Reed argues convincingly, psychoanalysis provides only one of many possible explanations for Hans Castorp's illness (Reed, *Uses of Tradition*, pp. 234–35).

101. SA III, 346: 'Der Masochist [will] wie ein kleines, hilfloses und abhängiges Kind behandelt werden, besonders aber wie ein schlimmes Kind'.

102. SA III, 353: 'Nun wissen wir, daß der in Phantasien so häufige Wunsch, vom Vater geschlagen zu werden, dem anderen sehr nahesteht, in passive (feminine) sexuelle Beziehung zu ihm zu treten'.

103. Bataille was a writer for whom, like Mann, the early reception of Nietzsche was critical. The young Bataille was a devout Catholic, until the discovery of Nietzsche's writings led him to adopt a violent paganism. Bataille would have agreed with the Blakean axiom that 'only the road of excess leads to the palace of wisdom'. However, another major influence on Bataille was the Marquis de Sade, who often links sexual arousal with the spectacle of violence.

104. Bataille, *L'Histoire de l'oeil* (Paris: Pauvert, 1979), p. 70: 'Ces suites de passes heureuses sont rares et déchainent dans la foule un véritable délire, les femmes, à ces moments pathétiques, jouissent, tant les muscles des jambes et du bas-ventre se tendent'.

105. Bataille, *L'Histoire*, p. 73: 'Le costume de matador [. . .] accuse une ligne droite, érigée raide et comme un jet (il moule exactement le cul)'.

106. SA III, 347: ' [Die Libido] hat die Aufgabe, diesen destruierenden Trieb unschädlich zu machen, und entledigt sich ihrer, indem sie ihn zum großen Teil [. . .] nach außen ableitet, gegen die Objekte der Außenwelt richtet. Er heiße dann Destruktionstrieb, Bemächtigungstrieb, Wille zur Macht.'

107. SA III, 347: 'Ein Anteil dieses Triebes wird direkt in den Dienst der Sexualfunktion gestellt, wo er Wichtiges zu leisten hat. Dies ist der eigentliche Sadismus'.

108. SA III, 348: 'Die Angst, vom Totemtier (Vater) gefressen zu werden, stammt aus der primitiven, oralen Organisation'.

109. Reed, *Uses of Tradition*, pp. 327–28; Ernst Bertram, *Nietzsche. Versuch einer Mythologie* (Berlin: Bondi, 1918).

110. (XI, 877–78): 'Wenn man aber bedenkt, was es, religionsgeschichtlich, die Menschheit gekostet hat, vom Naturkult, von einer barbarisch raffinierten Gnostik und sexualistischen Gottesausschweifung des Moloch-Baal-Astarte-Dienstes sich zu geistigerer Anbetung zu erheben, so staunt man über den leichten Sinn, mit dem solche Überwindungen und Befreiungen heute verleugnet werden.'

111. Jean-Paul Sartre, *Qu'est-ce que la littérature?* [1948] (Paris: Gallimard, 1990), p. 53: 'Tout ouvrage littéraire est un appel. [. . .] Ainsi, l'écrivain en appelle à la liberté du lecteur pour qu'elle collabore à la production de son ouvrage'.

112. Frithjof Trapp, 'Artistische Verklärung der Wirklichkeit', in *Stationen der Thomas-Mann-Forschung. Aufsätze seit 1970*, ed. by Hermann Kurzke (Würzburg: Königshausen & Neumann, 1985), pp. 25–40.

113. Two years later he had changed his mind and backtracked on his statement, claiming it should be understood ironically. Cf. Letter to Martin Havenstein, 9 May 1912 in DüD I, p. 258: 'Alles in Allem kann man sagen, daß "K.H." ein Buch mit demokratischer Tendenz ist, aber mit so viel ironischen Vorbehalten, daß die Tendenz fast *umschlägt*'.

114. One could argue that in modern times, the popular symbolic function of the monarch (personifying the life of the nation) is increasingly diffused between several figures, including politicians (presidents, prime ministers) and artists (writers, musicians, film stars).

115. My analysis here is in part indebted to an article by Roman Luckscheiter, 'Das Mizzi-Meyer-Prinzip. Zur Politik der Form bei Thomas Mann', in *Man erzählt Geschichten, formt die Wahrheit. Thomas Mann — Deutscher, Europäer, Weltbürger*, ed. by Michael Braun and Birgit Lermen (Frankfurt a.M.: Peter Lang, 2003), pp. 103–15.

116. 'Aber das [. . .] für die Zukunft Entscheidende bei alldem war, daß [. . .] die tausendstimmige

Erörterung bei aller Erregtheit durchaus im Sinne der Billigung und des Einverständnisses geführt wurde' (II, 294).

117. It is worth noting that towards the end of the novel we see Klaus Heinrich trying to transcend his 'Scheinexistenz' by studying economics. This may be read as a concession to the demands of reality, an admission that aesthetic appearance can never be entirely self-sufficient.

118. For detailed accounts of the compositional process, see Reed, *Uses of Tradition*, pp. 228–29, 236–46, and Heinz Saueressig, *Die Entstehung des Romans 'Der Zauberberg'* (Biberach an der Riss: Wege und Gestalten, 1965).

119. GKFA 5.1, 788. The thirteen-volume edition of Mann's *Gesammelte Werke* mistakenly prints 'versönlich' instead of 'persönlich' (III, 722).

120. For a detailed study of Naphta, see Wisskirchen, TMS 6, pp. 46–52. Naphta has also been linked (by Judith Marcus) to Georg Lukács, and (by Helmut Koopmann) to Oswald Spengler: Judith Marcus, *Georg Lukács and Thomas Mann: A Study in the Sociology of Literature* (Amherst: University of Massachusetts Press, 1987); Helmut Koopmann, 'Der Zauberberg und die Kulturphilosophie der Zeit', in *Auf dem Weg zum 'Zauberberg'*, TMS 16, ed. by Thomas Sprecher (Frankfurt a.M.: Klostermann, 1997), pp. 273–98.

121. The Moroccan woman is not only an avatar of Clawdia Chauchat, she is also a kind of primal earth-mother, rather like Dona Maria Pia in *Felix Krull*.

122. Martin Swales, *Mann: Der Zauberberg* (London: Grant & Cutler, 2000), p. 40.

123. Hermann Bausinger pointss out that although listening is often thought of as something passive, it is in fact highly active. The attitude and the gestures of the listener strongly affect the performance of what is being said. Storytelling is thus a 'Wechselspiel' or 'Zusammenspiel' between storyteller and public. Cf. Bausinger, 'Kannitverstan. Vom Zuhören, Verstehen und Mißverstehen', in *Über das Hören: einem Phänomen auf der Spur*, ed. by Thomas Vogel (Tübingen: Attempto, 1998), pp. 9–26 (p. 19).

124. Dierk Wolters, *Zwischen Metaphysik und Politik: Thomas Manns Roman 'Joseph und seine Brüder' in seiner Zeit* (Tübingen: Niemeyer, 1998), p. 142.

125. Gerhard Lange, *Struktur- und Quellenuntersuchungen zur 'Lotte in Weimar'* (Bayreuth: Tasso, 1970).

126. Yahya Elsaghe, 'Lotte in Weimar', in *The Cambridge Companion to Thomas Mann*, ed. by Ritchie Robertson (Cambridge: Cambridge University Press, 2002), pp. 185–98.

127. Reinhard Baumgart, 'Joseph in Weimar — Lotte in Ägypten', *TMJ* 4 (1991), 75–88; Elsbeth Wolffheim, 'Das Abenteuer der Verwirklichung des "Goethe-Mythos"', in *Heimsuchung und süßes Gift. Erotik und Poetik bei Thomas Mann*, ed. by Gerhard Härle (Frankfurt a.M.: Fischer, 1992), pp. 103–25.

128. HA XIII, 18: 'so kann man von einem jeden Phänomene sagen, daß es mit unzähligen andern in Verbindung stehe [. . .] so können wir nicht sorgfältig genug untersuchen, was unmittelbar an ihn grenzt, was zunächst auf ihn folgt'.

129. Because of the unreliable quality of earlier editions of *Lotte in Weimar*, quotations from this novel are taken from the GKFA.

130. Helmut Jendreiek, *Thomas Mann: Der demokratische Roman* (Düsseldorf: Bagel, 1977), p. 406.

131. (GKFA 9.1, 263): 'man solle doch die Zeit-Konjunctur der gegenwärtigen vaterländischen Erhebung nutzen, um ein Gedicht, das so artig damit harmoniere wie "Hermann und Dorothea", buchhändlerisch kräftiger zu propagieren'.

132. T. J. Reed, *The Classical Centre: Goethe and Weimar 1775–1832* (London: Croom Helm, 1980), pp. 34–35.

133. Frédéric Soret, *Goethes Unterhaltungen mit Friedrich Soret*, ed. by C. A. H. Burkhardt (Weimar: Böhlau, 1905), p. 146.

134. Jendreiek, *Thomas Mann*, p. 403.

135. (XI, 877): 'Eine neue Seelenlage der Menschheit [. . .] drückte sich philosophisch als Abkehr von Vernunftglauben [. . .] aus, als ein irrationalistischer, den Lebensbegriff in den Mittelpunkt des Denkens stellender Rückschlag, der die allein lebenspendenden Kräfte des Unbewußten, Dynamischen, Dunkel-schöpferischen auf den Schild hob.'

136. Travers, *Thomas Mann*, p. 76.

137. Mann also claimed in this speech that the Nazi movement is alien to German culture, but he

soon changed his mind about this. In *Deutschland und die Deutschen* he argues against the idea that there were 'two Germanies', one good and one bad.

138. J. P. Stern, *Thomas Mann* (Columbia: Columbia University Press, 1967), p. 25; Martin Swales, *Thomas Mann: A Study* (London: Heinemann, 1980), p. 79; Hartmut Böhme, 'Mario und der Zauberer. Position des Erzählers und Psychologie der Herrschaft', in *Stationen der Thomas-Mann-Forschung. Aufsätze seit 1970*, ed. by Hermann Kurzke (Würzburg: Könighausen & Neumann, 1985), pp. 166–89 (p. 167).

139. Joyce Crick, 'Thomas and Heinrich Mann: Some Early Attitudes to their Public', *MLR* 77 (1982), 646–54 (p. 652).

140. Karl Werner Böhm, *Zwischen Selbstzucht und Verlangen: Thomas Mann und das Stigma Homosexualität* (Würzburg: Königshausen & Neumann, 1991), p. 187.

141. SA III, 350: 'Eine Form des Leidens ist dann durch eine andere abgelöst worden, und wir sehen, es kam nur darauf an, ein gewisses Maß von Leiden festhalten zu können'.

142. Böhme, *Zwischen Selbstzucht*, p. 183.

143. Kurzke, *Thomas Mann*, p. 231.

144. If critical reason fails in a particular instance, that is not sufficient justification for abandoning it.

145. Alan Bance, 'The Political Becomes Personal: *Disorder and Early Sorrow* and *Mario and the Magician*', in *The Cambridge Companion to Thomas Mann*, ed. by Ritchie Robertson (Cambridge: Cambridge University Press, 2002), pp. 107–17 (p. 117).

146. Benjamin, GS 1.2, 467: 'Alle Bemühungen um die Ästhetisierung der Politik konvergieren in *einem* Punkt. Dieser eine Punkt ist der Krieg'.

147. The German original of this text, 'Literatur und Hitler', is lost. It was first published in English in *The Modern Thinker and Author's Review*, 5.2, August 1934, and then translated back into German by Peter de Mendelssohn. The English version of the phrase reads: 'It is difficult to distinguish any strong line of demarcation between artistic and political-social events' (XIII, 321). Mann says much the same thing in 'Problem der Freiheit' (1939): 'das Politische und Soziale [sind] Teilgebiete des Menschlichen, und es [ist] nicht möglich, sie vom Geistigen und Kulturellen reinlich zu trennen' (XI, 964).

148. Luckscheiter, 'Das Mizzi-Meyer-Prinzip', p. 105.

149. Jacques Rancière, *The Politics of Aesthetics*, trans. and intro. by Gabriel Rockhill (London and New York: Continuum, 2006), p. 13.

CHAPTER 3

Narrative Performance in *Felix Krull*

> Den Autor angehend, so ist er willig genug, sich durch freundliche
> Teilnahme, die das Fragment etwa finden mag, zur Fortführung und
> Beendigung anspornenzu lassen.
>
> Thomas Mann, postscript to the 1923 edition of *Felix Krull*[1]

(i) Narrative Voice and Temporality

So far I have considered *Felix Krull* thematically. However, it is only possible to assess the full effect and scope of the novel by examining how it operates on a stylistic level. I therefore intend to analyse the novel from the point of view of technique, in order to show how the novel's formal elements reinforce its exploration of art's contribution to both individual identity and community. Formally, the most remarkable aspect of *Krull* is the way in which the narrator continually pauses to address the reader. At the heart of this chapter is therefore section (iv), which analyses the narrative address to the reader. This aspect of the work is, however, closely related to questions of narrative voice, genre, and style, which require precise definition. Since *Felix Krull* is a novel written in the first person, it makes sense to begin with an analysis of the narrative voice and its temporality.

All first-person narrative implies a distinction between the time of the story and the time of the narration. *Felix Krull* respects this convention. Right from the start, we are dealing with two fictional Krulls, who inhabit two different fictional time zones. There is the younger Krull whose story is being told, and the older Krull who narrates the story. The former is known as the narrated or experiencing self (*erzähltes* or *erlebendes Ich*), and the latter is known as the narrating self (*erzählendes Ich*). While Krull the protagonist is consigned to a fictional past, Krull the narrator is able to adopt the present tense, and to address the reader directly.[2] Throughout the novel, and especially in the opening chapters, there is a continual switching between these two personae.

Like most traditional first-person narratives, *Felix Krull* begins in the present tense. In an imagined present, the aged Krull steps forward to introduce both himself and his neat, elegant handwriting to the reader:

> Indem ich die Feder ergreife, um in völliger Muße und Zurückgezogenheit —
> gesund übrigens, wenn auch müde, sehr müde (so daß ich wohl nur in kleinen
> Etappen und unter häufigen Ausruhen werde vorwärtsschreiten können),
> indem ich mich also anschicke, meine Geständnisse in der sauberen und

> gefälligen Handschrift, die mir eigen ist, dem geduldigen Papier anzuvertrauen, beschleicht mich das flüchtige Bedenken, ob ich diesem geistigen Unternehmen nach Vorbildung und Schule denn auch gewachsen bin. (265)

This first sentence introduces several important narrative issues. We are given a good deal of information about the narrator. We learn that he is independent, idle, and withdrawn from the world; healthy, but very tired. He is so tired that he will only be able to tell his story in fits and starts, with frequent pauses. This signals to the reader that there will be frequent interruptions in the narration; and these moments of caesura will give Felix Krull ample opportunity to address the reader directly, in an extradiegetic present tense. Despite being addressed in the present tense, the reader is not named, except indirectly and metonymically, via 'the patient paper' ('dem geduldigen Papier'). The reader is linked to the paper by a metonymic chain of association: both reader and paper will henceforth function as the willing recipients of Krull's confessions. Implicitly, this association asks the reader to assume the submissive posture of paper. Since paper is usually white, it suggests naïvety and uncritical acceptance. At the same time, the narrator's reference to his pleasing handwriting is a first attempt to establish his credentials as storyteller, to assert his mastery of style. The concern ('Bedenken') expressed at the end of the sentence, however, serves to question his reliability as narrator. Meanwhile, the use of the term 'enterprise' ('Unternehmen') refers to the act of narration itself as an adventure and a performance. Thus the very first sentence already places the narrator firmly in the foreground and invites reflection on the narrative voice.

Let us briefly widen our focus and consider how this opening sentence relates to traditional first-person narrative. At first glance, the opening sentence of *Felix Krull* seems to indicate that it belongs to the realist tradition that was so dominant in the nineteenth century. According to Jean-Paul Sartre, the realist novel usually begins with the appearance of the narrator, who tends to be a middle-aged man of the world. He is old enough to be detached from the passions of his youth, and he relates his previous exploits with calm indulgence. The milieu is reassuring and bourgeois: the after-dinner conversation, the fireside chat (Sartre cites Maupassant as an example). In other words, realist fiction is narrated from the perspective of a prevailing social order, and the reader, it is implied, is also part of that order. In Sartre's view, then, the narrative framework tends to confirm a social order by relegating uncomfortable events to a distant past which has been overcome.[3] Now, *Felix Krull* might initially appear to conform to Sartre's model. The narrator has, it seems, retired from his life of crime in order to write his confessions at a leisurely pace. His concern that his memoirs should be written in the correct manner already implies that he is primarily addressing a bourgeois public. And yet the reader already suspects that he is being led up the garden path. After all, the title of the novel informs us that the narrator is a confidence man.

This takes us back to a commonplace of the secondary literature on Thomas Mann: namely, the apparent traditionalism of his novels. Generally speaking, the novels present an ornate façade to the reader, the apparent order of which is soon undermined by aporias in the text, such as an ironic ambiguity which makes authorial intention almost impossible to pin down. In the case of *Felix Krull*, this ironic ambiguity is especially marked, because the narrator — traditionally considered as the author's alter ego — is suspect. Thus the text taunts the reader with its own unreliability from the outset. While nineteenth-century naturalists such as Zola tried to lay claim to a scientific method for fiction, *Felix Krull* is a text which flaunts its own fictional quality. The narrator makes it clear right from the start that this is a show, a narrative performance ('schriftlichen Auftreten' (266)).[4] The above points are general ones about the quality of the narration. I now wish to analyse in more detail the relationship between the two narrative selves in *Felix Krull*. We have just noted that the distinction between the older, narrating self (*erzählendes Ich*) and the younger, experiencing self (*erlebendes Ich*) is a classical one. The narrating self often addresses the reader in the present tense; on the other hand, the experiencing self, as character, remains firmly embedded in the preterite, the standard tense of realist narrative. The narrating self is mature and reflective, while the experiencing self is often passionate and impetuous. At first, Mann's novel seems to conform faithfully to this traditional distinction. Thus we learn that, having reached the age of forty, Felix Krull no longer feels impelled by the desire to live in society, as he did when he was a young man ('Jetzt nämlich, wo ich, obgleich erst vierzigjährig, gealtert und müde bin, wo kein gieriges Gefühl mich mehr zu den Menschen drängt' (270)). The narrator's passions are spent, and the underlying implication is that he has already drunk the cup of life to the full. However, despite the narrator's oft-repeated claim that he is tired (265, 270, 287, 295, 328), the tone of the narration is in fact never jaded and lacks bitterness. Even the fact that he spent several years in prison is presented in a positive light: he slept comfortably, and had plenty of time for reading and daydreams (271, 296, 355). So the difference in tone between older and younger self is negligible — both share the same enthusiasm. Indeed, we soon find that it is virtually impossible to distinguish the two narrative selves. Two pages into the novel and the narrator is identifying so strongly with his younger self that he puts words in his mouth. As the young Felix Krull apostrophizes the bottles in his father's cellars, the narrator retrospectively imputes to him a highly sophisticated vocabulary:

> Da liegt ihr, dachte ich bei mir selbst (wenn ich auch meine Gedanken natürlich noch nicht in so treffende Worte zu fassen wußte), da liegt ihr in unterirdischem Dämmerlicht, und in eurem Innern klärt und bereitet sich still der prickelnde Goldsaft, [. . .] um [. . .] Rausch, Leichtsinn und Lust unter den Menschen zu verbreiten. Ähnlich sprach der Knabe; [. . .] (267)

Guido Stein calls such instances 'retrospektive Stilisierungen' and cites them as evidence for the interplay between the two narrative selves.[5] Another critic, Werner Frizen, has also picked up on the complicity between narrator and hero. According to Frizen, this leads to a parody of the autobiographical form. In a traditional autobiography, the older, wiser, narrator tends to comment in a moralizing fashion on the wayward exploits of his youth. There is often repentance or regret, or at the very least contrast between impetuous youth and reflective maturity. The narrator of Felix Krull is, however, completely unrepentant, and often gets carried away: the telling of his past exploits causes him almost as much pleasure as the deeds themselves.[6] It therefore comes as no surprise that, as the novel progresses, the narrator's references to his tiredness become less and less frequent. In fact, for the last two thirds of the novel, his tiredness is not mentioned again. Thus, the narrator's function is not to criticize or to offer moral judgement; instead, he is far more interested in courting the reader. This is clear from the large number of sentences in the present tense (what Genette calls the extradiegetic mode) in which the narrator comments upon his own performance and invites the reader's assent and complicity. This occurs right from the start of the novel. Introducing himself to the reader, Felix Krull attempts to establish his credentials — his competence as a narrator — as being impeccable, despite the fact that he is a confidence man. He insists that he has complete control of his material: 'da [. . .] ich also meinen Stoff vollkommen beherrsche' (265). His account will be worth reading because of his own innate talent ('natürliche Begabung' (265)) and because it will relate his own most immediate experiences ('unmittelbarsten Erfahrungen' (265)). This is boasting, but with a purpose. Krull asserts his own value in order to sell himself to his readership. This is also a narrator who obviously enjoys teasing his audience: on the one hand, he tells us that he is a master of deception; on the other hand, he keeps insisting that he is in fact a reliable narrator. There is a strong sense of irony in his assurances that he will tell the truth: 'Welcher moralische Wert und Sinn wäre auch wohl Bekenntnissen zuzusprechen, die unter einem anderen Gesichtspunkt als demjenigen der Wahrhaftigkeit abgefaßt wären!' (266). This is a fiction which draws attention to itself as fiction, a narrative which admits its own unreliability and which nevertheless invites the reader to play along. This strategy brings the reader's own role and motivation sharply into focus. As Michael Beddow puts it, an important aspect of *Krull* is the way in which it offers readers a 'comprehensive self-unmasking of the narrative as a fabrication'.[7] In other words, *Felix Krull* is a self-aware narrative game in which the reader is a vital player.[8]

I will now turn to a discussion of temporality in the novel. The organization of time is a vital characteristic of every novel and is linked to questions of narrative voice. Like most realist novels, *Felix Krull* takes the form of a recollection of past events (analepsis). It begins with a mention of a time and a place: the narrator says he was born in the Rhineland, a few years after 1871 ('wenige Jahre nur nach der glorreichen Gründung des deutschen Reiches' (266)). From then on, dates are absent, until we learn that Felix Krull's ship will sail on 15 August (524). A little later, his letter to the Marquise of Venosta is dated 25 August 1895 (595). The novel's chronology was worked out in detail by Thomas Mann in a note of 1951, which gives Felix Krull's birthdate as 1875 and the time of narration as 1915.[9] Krull is thus aged nineteen when he arrives in Paris and twenty when he embarks on his *Weltreise*. Generally speaking, then, the conventions of realism are adhered to. Thus, some temporal periods are left out (ellipsis), while some scenes are described in inordinate detail. The length of scenes and the amount of description tend to increase in the second half of the book, which slows down narrative time. The structure of the novel is a loose sequence of episodes, which corresponds not only to picaresque novels but also autobiographical fiction in general. The ordering principle that selects which episodes to narrate and which ones to omit is highly subjective and may therefore seem arbitrary. The novel itself, however, spells this out. In an early moment of self-consciousness, Krull tells us that while some events have been highlighted, others are barely touched upon or simply left out:

> Bei Erfahrungen und Begegnissen, denen ich eine besondere Belehrung und Aufklärung über mich und die Welt verdanke, verweile ich lange und führe jede Einzelheit mit spitzem Pinsel aus, während ich über anderes, was mir weniger teuer ist, leicht hinweggleite. (293)[10]

In fact, this is a general feature of narrative fiction. All first-person narratives accord different emphases to the various phases of the life being recalled, all narratives skip events. By explicitly stating an agreed convention the text displays a high degree of self-consciousness about narrativity. The result is to make the reader aware that this novel is, like any other, on one level a formal game. But this insight is not permitted to disrupt the reader's pleasure; the narrator, having alerted the reader, quickly resumes his tale and the onward momentum is regained.

Use of the future tense in the novel is very rare, and is mostly limited to organizing units of narrative ('von dem an gehörigem Orte noch zu sprechen sein wird' (270); 'ich werde etwas weiter unten erklären' (287); 'dessen Schilderung ich hier [. . .] einrücken werde' (279)). An important exception to this is Felix Krull's comment that Müller-Rosé's image will live on forever in his memory: 'sein Bild wird ewig in meinem Gedächtnis fortleben' (287). In my view, this rare use of the future tense indicates a strong emotional attachment; it is echoed in Diane Houpflé's passionate declaration at the end of Book II: 'Armand, tu vivras dans mes vers et dans mes beaux romans' (450). In the case of Felix Krull's attraction to Andromache, the depth of feeling is indicated by switching to the present rather than the future tense: 'Noch heute träume ich von ihr' (458). These examples show that if Felix Krull knows how to be a star, it is because he long ago learned what it means to be an admirer, and to yearn for an unattainable object of desire.

One final aspect of temporality in the novel is prolepsis (also known as 'flash-forward'). These are the moments when the narrator skips ahead of himself in order to allude to later events. The narrator drops titbits of information and then says 'we must save that for later, I must proceed in the correct order'. As a strategy, it seems designed to tantalize the reader and to excite his curiosity. Thus Felix Krull makes frequent references to his time in prison (271, 296, 355, 435) and teasing allusions to his future love affairs (270, 391, 451). He pointedly drops the names of two fine clarets (Château Margaux, Château Mouton Rothschild (278)) which he later learns to enjoy. At the opening of Book II, he mentions the time he impersonated a Belgian aristocrat and had a conversation with a police chief about confidence men; he also talks of the details of his 'first arrest' ('meiner ersten Verhaftung' (323)) — thus implying he has been arrested more than once. He continually teases the reader with allusions ('der Leser wird sehen' (335)). One future episode will feature his return to his home town in order to show off his acquired riches (335–36); another episode will tell of his final reunion with Schimmelpreester (336). The effect of all these allusions is of course to set up a mood of eagerness and anticipation in the reader. The beginning of the 'Musterungsszene' uses a similar technique: Felix Krull creates suspense by refusing to reveal the secret of how he avoided conscription (349, 351) until the end of the chapter. Later he excites curiosity by alluding to the 'verblüffende Bekundungen' which he will receive from Zouzou (559), and by giving information about the hosts who await him in Argentina, the Meyer-Novaros (587). This simple technique is very effective at making the reader hungry for more, and it is still being used in the final chapter of the novel as the narrator flashes forward to a description of the bullfight, only to backtrack and tell the events leading up to it (645). The frequent use of prolepsis puts the emphasis firmly on to the telling of the story, onto the act of narration itself. It does so however, not in order to provoke criticism but in order to induce self-conscious, knowing assent on the part of the reader. *Felix Krull* thus turns a spotlight upon those narrative conventions (the reliability of the narrative voice, the novelistic treatment of time, the collusion between narrator and reader) which usually remain implicit. In the novel, pleasure and self-awareness are not mutually exclusive, but complementary.

(ii) Genre and Intertextuality

It is evident that Thomas Mann, like his hero, was light-fingered and eclectic in his choice of literary borrowings. Commentators on the novel from Hans Wysling onwards have shown that it contains a multitude of intertextual references. The problems of genre and intertextuality in *Felix Krull* have been dealt with so extensively in the secondary literature that it would be of little value to repeat them here.[11] Such a recapitulation would be beyond the scope and the intention of this thesis. The vital question for our purposes is: *how* does the novel interact with tradition, and to what purpose? In other words, a critical approach is required to assess the novel's relation to tradition. The problem of genre here is crucial. When we try to situate *Felix Krull* within the literary tradition, it soon becomes apparent that the novel is a hybrid: it deliberately juxtaposes a wide variety of genres. The narrator himself is aware of this problem and admits that this contemplative text sits uneasily under the rubric of 'crime novel':

> [ein Schriftwerk], das sich durch seine Aufschrift den Kriminalromanen und Detektivgeschichten an die Seite zu stellen scheint, — während doch meine Lebensgeschichte zwar seltsam und öfters traumähnlich sich anläßt, aber der Knalleffekte und aufregenden Verwicklungen gänzlich entbehrt! (322)[12]

On further examination, it seems that *Felix Krull* contains elements from many different genres: from the thriller on the one hand and the philosophical novel on the other, and also from the Bildungsroman and the picaresque novel or 'Schelmenroman'. How do these genres interact? Does the novel create a successful stylistic unity out of these widely disparate elements? I will argue that the strength of this novel is the way in which it holds a number of different genres in suspension and allows them to interact with one another. It is this interaction which makes the work so rich. *Felix Krull* represents a broadening of range within Thomas Mann's oeuvre, and Mann himself was well aware that the novel contained these divergent tendencies. Initially, however, he saw these tendencies as antagonistic and irreconcilable. In this early phase he perceived the novel as a parody, a satire revealing a fundamental lack of unity. This is evident from the introduction he gave to a reading from *Krull* at the Berliner Sezession in November 1916, in which he claims that the novel registers the collision between the Bildungsroman and the type of politically progressive, satirical 'Gesellschaftsroman' favoured by his brother Heinrich.[13] The sharp polemical dichotomies are familiar to readers of the *Betrachtungen*: the 'unpolitical', humanist individualism of German culture is under threat from the dehumanizing politics of the West,[14] and this development can also be seen in the literary domain, as the German Bildungsroman becomes supplanted by the social satire of the French novel. *Felix Krull* is now described as a symptom of this very process:

> Was Wunder nun, wenn [. . .] unter der Einwirkung dieses Prozesses, die ursprünglich nationale Form der deutschen Prosa-Epopöe, der individualistische deutsche Bildungsroman, der Zersetzung anheimfiele? [. . .] Der deutsche Bildungsroman [. . .], parodiert und der Schadenfreude des Fortschritts ausgesetzt als Autobiographie eines Hochstaplers und Hoteldiebes —, das wäre also der melancholisch-politische Zusammenhang, in den ich dies Buch zu stellen hätte? (XI, 703)

This fascinating polemic needs qualification, however.

At this period, still strongly influenced by the Romantic reception of Goethe, Mann sees the Bildungsroman as socially naive and unpolitical. Only thus can he view the Bildungsroman and the Gesellschaftsroman as being mutually exclusive. In fact, the relation between the two has always been more complementary. The Bildungsroman describes the process of growing up, the process whereby the individual comes to terms with the world. It therefore acknowledges and engages with the social world, while still retaining an important philosophical dimension. It is however true that the Bildungsroman's focus upon the inner life of the individual does at times entail a corresponding paucity of social treatment. The narrator of *Wilhelm Meisters Lehrjahre* is aware of this dilemma and comments that those who concentrate on their own development tend to do so at the expense of their understanding of society.[15] As T. J. Reed points out, since German society in the eighteenth century was relatively underdeveloped, the German writers of the time made 'an artistic virtue out of necessity' and concentrated on 'the inner riches of the individual'.[16] This emphasis, however, was soon challenged by developments abroad. In the nineteenth century the idea of the Bildungsroman was taken up by French novelists and merged with the Gesellschaftsroman. At the hands of Flaubert, however, the Bildungsroman is stripped of its focus on the inner life: in *L'Éducation sentimentale*, the word 'education' is deeply ironic, since Frédéric Moreau neither progresses nor learns from his mistakes. Worse still, his inner life is often overwhelmed by a flood of *idées reçues*. This tendency continues in the novels of Émile Zola and Heinrich Mann, where the wide-ranging social perspective is achieved at the expense of the inner life of the characters. It was the lack of interiority in his brother's novels that Thomas Mann was keen to avoid. While seeking to rival his brother's artistic achievements, he wished to conserve the German intellectual tradition of individual development. And so, in comparison with Andreas Zumsee, the hero of Heinrich Mann's *Im Schlaraffenland* whose appetite for luxury ruins him, Thomas Mann's hero is far more intelligent and self-aware. In contrast to the young *arrivistes* featured in the novels of Heinrich Mann, Balzac, and Flaubert, who immediately squander their wealth, Felix Krull is clever enough to bank his money with the Crédit Lyonnais:

> Mit Beifall und dem Gefühl der Beruhigung wird der Leser von diesem Verhalten Kenntnis nehmen. Leicht wäre ein junger Fant vorzustellen, der, durch Fortunens versucherische Gunst zu solchen Mitteln gelangt, sofort seinen unbezahlten Arbeitsplatz verlassen, sich eine hübsche Junggesellenwohnung genommen und sich in dem alle Genüsse anbietenden Paris gute Tage gemacht hätte — bis zur freilich absehbaren Erschöpfung seines Schatzes. (452)[17]

This intertextual allusion shows that Felix Krull is a cut above the Parisian dandy of the Gesellschaftsroman; he possesses a degree of reflective self-awareness which those other heroes simply lack. *Felix Krull* was thus a daring attempt to combine two literary traditions: its two main intertextual sources are the Bildungsroman and the Gesellschaftsroman. These two novel genres are brought together under the common heading of autobiography (Goethe's *Dichtung und Wahrheit* and Manolescu's memoirs). The juxtaposition is a scandalous one.[18] But does the comparison really occur to the detriment of Goethe? In my view, the reverse happens: the lowly figure of the trickster is elevated by association with Goethe; even the act of deception gains a higher justification when placed in the context of Goethe's 'Selige Sehnsucht'. Before I discuss this intertextual moment in detail, however, let us return to the problem of genre.

We have seen that, when Thomas Mann in 1916 opposes the Bildungsroman to the Gesellschaftsroman, he is essentially posing the question of whether the modern novel will focus mainly on the individual or on society at large. This tension is not by any means a new one: it harks back to the origins of the novel. In the sixteenth century, for example, the flourishing of the picaresque novel in Spain (*La Vida de Lazarillo de Tormes*, 1554) brought a new social realism to prose fiction which had not been seen since the classic Roman novel *The Golden Ass* by Lucius Apuleius. It is possible to contrast the socially conscious genre of the picaresque with the other great prose tradition: the tradition of confessional literature which charts the spiritual progress of the individual. The genre's founding text is of course St Augustine's great spiritual autobiography, the *Confessions* (AD 397).[19] Now, as T. J. Reed has pointed out, the German Bildungsroman, with its concern for individual development, is directly descended from this tradition of confessional literature.[20] In other words, the modern tension between Bildungsroman and Gesellschaftsroman exactly reproduces the earlier tension between confessional and picaresque modes of narrative. The great merit of *Felix Krull* is the way in which it deliberately sets out to blend these two traditions, the way it tries to be both exalted spiritual adventure and picaresque odyssey. It was a bold experiment in terms of range, and one which was to pay dividends, since it paved the way for *Der Zauberberg*, a novel whose richness lies precisely in the way that it successfully merges the two traditions.[21] In order to understand why this development was such a creative watershed for Thomas Mann, it is necessary to recall the antithesis between *Leben* and *Geist* which had dominated his earlier creative output. As a young writer, Mann had been obsessed with the thought that life and art, *Bürger* and *Künstler* were incompatible. The years 1906–09 are however marked by a new optimism and hope in the possible reconciliation of these opposing pairs. What occurs in both *Königliche Hoheit* and the early *Felix Krull* is a deliberate blending of popular genres with the more exalted genre of the Bildungsroman.[22] This phenomenon has already been described under the rubric of 'doppelte Optik',[23] but what has not been brought out is the way in which Mann is working out his own philosophical problems (the perceived antithesis between *Geist* and *Leben*) through his own fiction, on the page, at the level of genre. Just as the genres interact and intermingle in *Königliche Hoheit* and *Felix Krull*, so too do the social categories of *Bürger* and *Künstler* and the philosophical categories of *Leben* and *Geist*.

How conscious was this process in the composition of *Felix Krull*? Mann's decision to adapt Manolescu's memoirs shows that, right from the start, *Felix Krull* was to be a popular hero. Even at this early stage, however, Mann was aware that Manolescu's work had earlier antecedents in the picaresque novel. Hans Wysling has shown that Thomas Mann's preoccupation with the 'Schelmenroman' dates back to the years 1908–09: precisely the time in which Mann was starting to write *Felix Krull*. N 51 for the (planned, unfinished) essay 'Geist und Kunst' deals with the modern artist's desire for popularity ('Ehrgeiz der Volkstümlichkeit'), and describes Manolescu's memoirs as 'Ein *wirklicher* Schelmenroman!'[24] So already, at the initial conception of the novel, Thomas Mann viewed it as being constituted by a fundamental tension: the tension between Bildungsroman and 'Schelmenroman'.[25] Bildungsroman here implies a profoundly metaphysical dimension. The word 'Bekenntnisse' in the title evokes the confessions of Augustine and Rousseau, and 'Bekenntnisse einer schönen Seele' in *Wilhelm Meister*.[26] A confession is also a declaration of religious faith, and the narrative of *Felix Krull* continually strives to give art and semblance a higher metaphysical justification. Indeed, it is on one level a philosophical novel. Here is a narrator who muses on the nature of fiction, who is continually weaving philosophical reflection into the realist narrative. In many chapters, the events related provide the springboard for a general philosophical reflection, and the narrative shifts, as I have already indicated, from the past tense into the extradiegetic present tense.[27]

In this section I have shown that there are a multiplicity of genres at work (or: at play) in *Felix Krull*. In my view, this play of genres contributes immensely to the richness of the reading experience. By allowing different genres to coexist upon the page, *Felix Krull* opens up the possibility of a dialogue between them. This dialogue between genres is also a dialogue between different views of the world. The juxtapositions create a kind of dissonance or interpretative gap which provokes reflection in the reader. According to Wolfgang Iser, it is this asymmetry in a text which stimulates the reader. Iser uses the example of Fielding's *Tom Jones*, where the different characters all represent different social norms and attitudes to life. The discrepancies between the different perspectives demand an effort on the part of the reader to make sense of them all.[28] In *Felix Krull*, this creative asymmetry between perspectives is not produced through characters, but through genres. In the gaps between the genres is the locus of interaction with the reader. Through the agency of the reader, these genres are permitted to enter into a debate with each other. One might even call it a democratic cohabitation of genres, since no one genre manages to predominate or gain ascendancy. Instead, there is a measure of reconciliation implied in the insight that these genres, and the different spheres of human experience they represent (spiritual, intellectual, artistic, social, sensual, etc.), can and do interact with one another. Thus, despite its sometimes scandalous moments, *Felix Krull* moves (on a formal level) towards reconciliation between self and world and towards the ideal of wholeness which is implied in the notion of 'Bildung'.[29]

To conclude this section I will briefly look at three types of intertext in the novel, namely, allusions in *Felix Krull* to Goethe, Nietzsche, and to other works by Thomas Mann. I believe these intertextual references are particularly significant because they help to situate the novel both in terms of tradition and in terms of Mann's own oeuvre.

(a) *Allusions to Goethe*

Thomas Mann himself described *Felix Krull* as a parody of *Dichtung und Wahrheit*, but a great deal of the secondary literature fails to point out just how affectionate this parody actually was. In 1915, Mann certainly viewed the novel as a parody, but as one with positive intentions: '"Bekenntnisse des Hochstaplers Felix Krull", — ein grundwunderliches Unternehmen, die Karrikatur der großen Autobiographie und im Styl selbst eine Parodie auf "Dichtung und Wahrheit", aber positiv endlich doch in seiner verzerrten Lyrik'.[30] It seems evident that Thomas Mann gradually moved from a youthful period of rivalry with Goethe to a mature period of admiration and deliberate imitation. Hans Wysling points out that this shift towards Goethe begins relatively early — around the time Mann was working on the early section of *Felix Krull*. Wysling shows that the shift towards Goethe is linked to a reaction against Wagner.[31] In a letter of 26 August 1909, Mann expresses his disenchantment with Wagner and proposes Walt Whitman as an alternative role model.[32] Two years later, the alternative to Wagner is no longer Whitman, but Goethe.[33] Nevertheless, Wysling remains unsure whether to read the early *Felix Krull* as a mocking parody or as a sign of a new allegiance to Goethe.[34] He describes Mann's relationship to Goethe at this early stage as one of ambivalence, and contrasts this with the later section of the novel which he describes as being much closer to Goethe.[35] When Thomas Mann returned to *Felix Krull* in the early 1950s, the analogy with Goethe's *Faust* II seemed obvious. As with *Faust*, work on *Krull* had been interrupted for decades. While *Dichtung und Wahrheit* had served as a model for the early *Krull*, Mann now turned to *Faust* II, reading studies of the drama by Wilhelm Hertz and Konrat Ziegler.[36] Wysling has shown that the latter half of *Felix Krull* draws heavily on Goethe, especially the Kuckuck episode and the mass of intertextual allusions to the *Klassische Walpurgisnacht*.[37] Thomas Mann even feared that, like *Faust* II, *Felix Krull* could spill over into the episodic ('ins Faustische entarten'),[38] and both works conclude with the adoration of the feminine principle. In this section, however, I will argue that even the early section of *Felix Krull* reveals an admiration for Goethe. The text is not simply satirical, it actually represents a move towards Goethean optimism and towards the imagery of the poem 'Selige Sehnsucht'. Even in this early phase of the work, Goethe is partly an object of parody and partly a motivating, structuring force.

The use of Goethean style in *Felix Krull* has been well documented by Christian Grawe[39] and Thomas Sprecher,[40] and so I will not go into detail here. According to Sprecher, the use of an exalted style is another aspect of Felix Krull's social climbing: it acts as a signal to the reader that he deserves a place in the upper echelons of society.[41] Sprecher notes the reproduction of many stylistic tics, such as the disappearance of the definite article to tighten constructions, the variety of conjunctions employed to link relative clauses, often in pairs,[42] and the omission of auxiliary verbs.[43] There is also the frequent use of certain adjectives such as 'anmutig' and 'trefflich',[44] and the use of compound adjectives.[45] Sometimes, even very specific vocabulary is reproduced; Goethe describes the advice of older, more experienced men as a 'Fingerzeig' (HA IX, 163), and the word is also used to describe Schimmelpreester's plans for the young Felix Krull (330). As a student in Strasbourg Goethe calls himself a 'Pflastertreter' (HA IX, 376) and Felix Krull recalls his own days in Frankfurt as 'der einsame junge Pflastertreter' (558–59). The word 'Leidwesen' also crops up in both texts (297; HA IX, 33). And Mann even had to prevent a well-meaning proofreader from correcting his use of the archaic 'hiemit' to 'hiermit'.[46] The use of classical style in *Felix Krull* is closely bound up with the question of hyperbole and I will examine this in the next section.

I will now turn to a more significant intertextual knot: the allusion to Goethe's 'Selige Sehnsucht' from the *West-östlicher Divan*, which takes place at the climax of the Müller-Rosé episode. This is the crucial moment in Book I of *Krull* because it describes the human need for art and appearance. The central image in Goethe's poem is that of a butterfly consumed in a candle flame; it is an image of transformation. The final stanza of the poem communicates the importance of change in life, even though change implies the death of what has gone before:

> Und solang du das nicht hast
> Dieses: Stirb und werde!
> Bist du nur ein trüber Gast
> Auf der dunklen Erde. (HA II, 19)

Thus the poem is an incitement to live and to become, even though in that becoming there is an element of death. The poem is also related to artistic creation, as is evident from the fact that Goethe placed it at the end of the 'Buch des Sängers'. Words like 'Liebesnächte', 'zeugte', and 'Verlangen' imply that there is something inherently erotic about creation and transformation.[47] The German phrase 'wie Mücken ins Licht' is common and actually occurs twice in Manolescu's memoirs, where he uses it to describe the effects of his own assumed identity as a young aristocrat — the fact that his wealthy appearance made him irresistible:

> Vom stolzen Kaufmann bis zum biederen Droschkenkutscher, vom hochmütigen Kavalier bis zum flinken Lift-boy, — sie alle fliegen wie die Mücken ins Licht und lassen sich durch jeden Humbug blenden. [. . .] Die Mücken flogen in Scharen in das Licht.[48]

The phrase is reproduced in Mann's early work notes for *Krull*: 'Alle fliegen wie

Mücken ins Licht'.[49] Perhaps it was even this remarkable conjunction, the use of the same basic metaphor by both Goethe and Manolescu, which inspired Mann to combine the two figures in his novel. Of course the image is used differently: while Manolescu wonders at the ease with which people let themselves be deceived, Goethe conjures up the image of erotic and metaphysical self-sacrifice. Nevertheless, both writers are dealing with themes of desire and transformation. Mann's first use of the image — to describe the audience's yearning ('Sehnsucht' (289)) for Müller-Rosé — falls somehow between the two. On the one hand, the plurality of the image, the fact that it refers to a swarm of insects, is closer to Manolescu's usage; on the other hand, the presence of the word 'selig' ('blissfully') is a clear allusion to Goethe: 'Ja, diese ganze beschattete Versammlung glich einem ungeheuren Schwarme von nächtlichen Insekten, der sich stumm, blind und selig in eine strahlende Flamme stürzt' (290). A few pages later, the second use of the image develops the theme. The insistent use of the personal pronoun ('du') clearly echoes Goethe's poem, but there is a slight modulation here. While Goethe's poem stresses a metaphysical dimension, only subtly implying the theme of artistic creation by its location in the 'Buch des Sängers', in Mann's text metaphysical yearning is explicitly given an artistic dimension. Here, the human need for artistic semblance is described as coming directly from God himself:

> Rufe dir vielmehr das Bild zurück, das du vorhin zu sehen glaubtest: diesen Riesenschwarm von armen Motten und Mücken, der sich still und toll in die lockende Flamme stürzte! Welche Einmütigkeit in dem guten Willen, sich verführen zu lassen! Hier herrscht augenscheinlich ein allgemeines, von Gott selbst der Menschennatur eingepflanztes Bedürfnis [. . .] (294)

In my view, this moment is an important step away from the Schopenhauerian doctrine of illusion. But it is an important step away from Nietzsche as well. The dominant category here is neither Apollo nor Dionysus, but Eros. Instead of being 'will to power', this is 'good will': it comes from God, and it is a will that *knowingly* lets itself be deceived. The need for aesthetic play is defined, not in Nietzschean, but in Goethean terms as a universal, organic principle (and note the Goethean plant metaphor here too: 'eingepflanzt'). The desire to be transfigured by and through art is seen as a universal phenomenon, a constitutive feature of life ('Das Lebendige' of Goethe's poem). Of course, a shift has occurred: whereas Goethe's poem expresses the desire for transformation in terms of a philosophy of intense experience, Mann's post-Nietzschean text places a greater emphasis upon art. But art, in this passage, remains just one element in an ontology which still seems to have room for both God and nature.

The moth or butterfly is of course the perfect leitmotif for *Felix Krull*, since it goes through a series of transformations, from egg to caterpillar to chrysalis to winged creature. The image occurs twice more in the novel: at the circus, the clowns' costumes are covered in silver butterflies (457), and later, Zouzou compares Felix Krull to a butterfly and he is pleased by this poetic image (586).[50] There are other echoes of 'Selige Sehnsucht' too in the novel. When, at the very end of their love-scene, Diane Houpflé swears Felix Krull to secrecy — 'verrat der Welt es nie!'(450) — this recalls the prohibition at the beginning of 'Selige

Sehnsucht' ('Sagt es niemand, nur den Weisen'). And the central motif of aesthetic-metaphysical yearning returns once more — significantly — in the Palaeontology Museum sequence in Lisbon. I have already analysed the Goethean implications of this scene in Chapter 2(ii) above: the climax of Krull's visit to the museum is the primal scene of a man holding flowers to the sun, described in terms which allude to the opening scene of *Faust* II ('Anmutige Gegend'). Both the museum scene and 'Anmutige Gegend' convey a sense of cosmic awakening, transporting the reader to the dawn of creation. And there, at the beginning of life, we have colour (the flowers, the rainbow). The underlying message here is that nature loves art, loves decoration. The museum scene concludes, then, with an act of reverence: a Goethean affirmation of art and life.

(b) *Allusions to Nietzsche*

The significance of Nietzsche for Thomas Mann's work in general and for *Felix Krull* in particular is not to be underestimated. It was Nietzsche's psychology of the artist in particular that interested Mann, and it is with this intertextual link that Hans Wysling chooses to begin his study of *Felix Krull*.[51] The Nietzschean aspect of *Krull* is also considered in a recent study by Sabine Appel. Appel argues that Felix Krull is a highly Nietzschean figure because he rejects the pessimistic form of knowledge favoured by Schopenhauer, preferring naivety and optimism, which, according to Nietzsche, are the preconditions for creative action.[52] Appel quotes the preface to *Die fröhliche Wissenschaft*, where Nietzsche, in Apollonian mood, maintains that the Greeks were 'superficial out of profundity' because they chose to keep at bay the dark truth of existence:

> Oh diese Griechen! Sie verstanden sich darauf, zu *leben*: dazu tut not, tapfer bei der Oberfläche, der Falte, der Haut stehen zu bleiben, den Schein anzubeten, an Formen, an Töne, an Worte, an den ganzen Olymp des Scheins zu glauben! Diese Griechen waren oberflächlich — *aus Tiefe!* (KGA 5.2, 20)[53]

As I have shown in the previous section, this passage is certainly relevant to *Felix Krull*, but in the Müller-Rosé episode it is relativized by the erotic force of the intertext with Goethe. Appel concludes her study with an analysis of the links between *Felix Krull* and *Also sprach Zarathustra*, and she finally asserts that Mann's novel achieves a successful mediation between naivety and critical reflection.[54] Overall, Appel's analysis is excellent, although she dwells too long on Felix Krull's naivety, barely mentioning his high degree of knowingness. She is correct, however, when she discerns a playful dialectic between naivety and reflection in the novel. Indeed, as I have shown, the mediation occurs on the level of narrative itself, since the text encourages the reader to move continually between belief and scepticism. The knowing narrative often provokes critical thought, but this is never allowed to disrupt the story to a significant degree. *Felix Krull* achieves this balancing act, since the reflections are never allowed to impede the grace and flow of the narrative. This, however, is precisely where Appel's comparison between *Krull* and *Zarathustra* breaks down. *Zarathustra* may be a novel, but it is dominated by philosophy at the expense of character and plot. Mann's late essay 'Nietzsches Philosophie im Lichte unserer Erfahrung' is particularly critical of Zarathustra, calling him a shapeless monstrosity ('gestaltlose Unhold', 'Unfigur' (IX, 683)). And J. P. Stern has pointed out that while both works describe aesthetic ways of living, the scale of *Felix Krull* is modest and human, far from the overblown rhetoric of Nietzsche's work.[55]

In fact, Thomas Mann had been differentiating himself subtly from a certain reception of Nietzsche as early as *Tonio Kröger*. Tonio Kröger deliberately rejects daemonic hubris, preferring the charms of everyday life. Even in the conservative *Betrachtungen*, Mann distances himself from an overly simplistic interpretation of Nietzsche, from 'jener Ruchlosigkeits- und Renaissance-Ästhetizismus, jener hysterische Macht-, Schönheits- und Lebenskult, worin eine gewisse Dichtung sich eine Weile gefiel' (XII, 25). In this passage, Mann offers his own revision to the Nietzschean conception of 'life': 'life', in Mann's view, is no longer simply a violent struggle for power; it can also be pleasant and sedate.[56] These important differences come more sharply into focus when we compare Felix Krull to Zarathustra. Krull is an artist, not a prophet. Zarathustra prizes solitude and preaches to an elite, a few select individuals. Krull, on the contrary, loves society and is eager to show his accomplishments to the public at large. While Zarathustra is a hermit, Felix Krull is gregarious. With these fundamental contrasts in mind, the intertextual allusions to Nietzsche in the early section of *Felix Krull* appear playful and ironic, rather than indicative of a programme. Thus the young Felix Krull's intention to study the workings of the human will is described as 'grillenhaft'.[57] A little later, he describes his own achievement of self-mastery, his overcoming of his fragile constitution, as 'eine sittliche Leistung' (299): Here, the Nietzschean category of self-overcoming is given a moral inflection.[58] And when we find Müller-Rosé described as a kind of higher being ('dieses höheren Wesens' (288)), we know that this is deeply ironic since he is about to be revealed as a fake.

In my view, the most significant intertextual allusion to Nietzsche in the novel occurs during Felix Krull's visit to the Circus Stoudebecker. There, the aerial feats of the acrobats approach the boundaries of human possibility ('an die Grenze des Menschenmöglichen' (455)). The basic model is the *salto mortale* or leap of death. There, the acrobat Andromache is described as inhuman, androgynous, incapable of love because of her total dedication to her art:

> denn zu wohl erkannte man, daß dieser strenge Körper das, was andere der Liebe geben, an seine abenteuerliche Kunstleistung verausgabte. Sie war kein Weib; aber ein Mann war sie auch nicht und also kein Mensch. Ein ernster Engel der Tollkühnheit war sie [. . .] eine unnahbare Amazone des Luftraums. (460)

The Andromache episode contains several allusions. Andromache's title 'la fille de l'air' recalls Calderon's play *La hija del aire* (*Daughter of the Air*) about Semiramis, the tyrannical queen of Assyria — a play that Goethe criticized for its attempt to imbue irrationality with an artistic purpose.[59] Fontane likens his Effi Briest to a daughter of the air. In my view, however, the most significant allusion is to the opening scene of Nietzsche's *Zarathustra*, where Zarathustra proclaims the Übermensch against the background of an acrobat or 'rope-dancer' ('Seiltänzer'). The acrobat becomes a symbol of the Übermensch because of his grace and the fact that he makes danger into a profession. Zarathustra announces that man is a rope-bridge between animal and Übermensch: 'Der Mensch ist ein Seil, geknüpft zwischen Tier und Übermensch, — ein Seil über einem Abgrunde' (KGA 6.1, 10). Krull echoes this statement when he reflects that man stands between animal and angel, and that the chaste Andromache is closer to the angels:

> Herrliche Tierleiber, zwischen Tier und Engel, so sann ich, stehet der Mensch. Näher zum Tiere stehet er, das wollen wir einräumen. Sie aber, meine Angebetete, obgleich Leib ganz und gar, aber keuscher, vom Menschlichen ausgeschlossener Leib, stand viel weiter hin zu den Engeln. (461)

Andromache, then, is clearly a figure of Nietzschean self-overcoming, but she is also cold and inhumanly chaste. Risking death, she scorns the public ('Sie verschmähte jedes Liebäugeln mit dem Publikum' (459)) as much as she appears to scorn life and death. Andromache is fascinating, but also strangely repellent. Her violent asceticism parallels that of Nietzsche, as seen by Thomas Mann in 'Nietzsches Philosophie im Lichte unserer Erfahrung'. There Mann describes Nietzsche's attempt to achieve the stylistic cheerfulness and grace of an acrobat as a failure:

> Der 'Akt des sich selbst Überspringens' [. . .], dieser 'Akt' nun (einen Artisten- und Akrobatenausdruck) hat bei Nietzsche so gar nichts Übermütig-Gekonntes und Tänzerisches. Alles 'Tänzerische' in seinem Gehaben ist Velleität und im höchsten Grade unangenehm. Sondern es ist ein blutiges Sich-ins-eigene-Fleisch-Schneiden. (IX, 693)

It seems that Andromache, like Leverkühn in *Doktor Faustus*, is a means for Thomas Mann to express both his admiration and his pity for the tragic figure of Nietzsche. The circus acrobat Andromache hints strangely at Leverkühn's fate. Like Leverkühn, she sacrifices her life to her art; like him, she is cold. In her disdain for the public and for the trappings of humanity she remains an uncanny figure. As for Felix Krull, he has little interest in tragedy: he welcomes knowledge, but not if it is to be bought at the price of terrible suffering. In general, this is a more healthy attitude: less grandiose, but more humane. Mann himself summed up his relationship to Nietzsche rather neatly in 1940 when he said that he had toned Nietzsche down to a more human scale.[60]

(c) *Self-parody*

Felix Krull features numerous instances of self-parody, and it is full of allusions to Thomas Mann's other works.[61] The seeds of the novel — the artist as confidence man — go back to *Tonio Kröger*. In that story, Tonio Kröger is mistaken for a confidence man and questioned by the police. He sees a certain poetic justice in this event (VIII, 318). *Tonio Kröger* also uses the motif of Schiller's *Don Carlos* to express the loneliness of the artist, and the metaphor is continued in both *Königliche Hoheit* and *Felix Krull*. As a child, Felix Krull enjoys pretending to be the Kaiser, demanding that people bow to him (271–72), and such fantasies continue in his teenage years, when he imagines that he is an eighteen-year-old prince called Karl (272). The Schillerian theme of self-overcoming, so familiar from the short story 'Schwere Stunde', is also present in the early *Krull* ('Selbstüberwindung' (299)).

However, despite Felix Krull's resemblance to Tonio Kröger and Klaus Heinrich, there is an important difference: he is no wallflower — he knows how to enjoy life. In this he is one step closer to his model Goethe, that great *Lebenskünstler*. What we have here, in effect, is a restatement of Mann's earlier characters but with a lighter and more humorous inflection: the tragic illness of Hanno Buddenbrook becomes in *Felix Krull* a trick, a means to avoid school (302–06). And the perennial theme of the relation between genius and sickness reaches a miniature climax in the feigned attack of epilepsy in the *Musterungsszene*. There, the army doctor is so impressed by the one-man version of a witches' sabbath that he likens epilepsy to a mystically heightened state.[62]

In many ways, *Felix Krull* acts as a bridge between the early and the later work. In the pre-war *Krull*, the narrator describes his love of holidaying by the water, recalling Hanno Buddenbrook. There is a difference, however: his gaze is no longer directed at the endless sea, but (anticipating Aschenbach) at the bodies of his fellow holidaymakers.[63] Felix Krull also anticipates Hans Castorp in several ways. Like Castorp, Krull loves smoking ('Zigarette' (340, 509)), and admires the pious formality of funerals (324). They both seem to have an affinity with the sly god Hermes. In the latter half of *Felix Krull*, written in the early 1950s, the drawing of Zouzou's naked body (591) recalls the portrait of Clawdia Chauchat which plays such an important role in *Der Zauberberg*. Krull's dalliance with the prostitute Rozsa has a happier outcome than Adrian Leverkühn's brothel visits. And, in the later *Krull*, Schiller's *Don Carlos* crops up once again, in Krull's encounter with the King of Portugal. Tonio Kröger, particularly moved by the play, had once remarked to Hans Hansen: 'Da ist zum Beispiel die Stelle, wo der König geweint hat, weil er von dem Marquis betrogen ist' (VIII, 277). Book III of *Krull* offers a miniature pastiche of *Don Carlos*, only this time the Marquis von Posa has been replaced by Krull (alias the Marquis de Venosta), and this time the King is moved to laughter, rather than to tears: 'Der König hielt sich die Seiten vor Lachen' (614). In this way — as Eric Wilson remarks — Mann's final novel sometimes appears as the antidote to his earlier fiction.[64] It recapitulates and reprises many of Mann's earlier themes under a more pleasant aspect.

There is also a distinct feeling of autobiographical allusion. For example, Krull seems to share his creator's own strong ambivalence towards the public. Like Thomas Mann, he sometimes seems torn between his scorn for popularity and his desire for it: 'In dieser Zeit wurde die Neigung zur Weltflucht und Menschenscheu weiter ausgebildet, die von jeher meinem Charakterbilde angehaftet hatte und mit werbender Anhänglichkeit an Welt und Menschen so einträchtig Hand in Hand zu gehen vermag' (328). The novel also contains references to Mann's technique of montage, his habit of adapting other texts to suit his own purposes. T. J. Reed has shown that the disarmingly elegant traditional mode of Mann's narrative mode often conceals the modernist use of montage.[65] Krull's comment upon his research into epilepsy can be read as a self-conscious justification of the technique of montage:

> Gleichwie das Schiff der Sandlast, so bedarf das Talent notwendig der Kenntnisse, aber ebenso gewiß ist, [. . .] daß wir nur auf solche eigentlich ein

Anrecht haben, nach denen unser Talent im brennenden Einzelfalle verlangt und die es hungrig an sich rafft, um sich die nötige Erdenschwere und solide Wirklichkeit daraus zu schaffen. (350)

And Krull continues to ape Mann's own use of montage by repeating the *bons mots* which he hears. Having heard about Hermes from Diane Houpflé (444), he mentions the name in order to impress Professor Kuckuck (540); then, in turn, he uses the knowledge that he has gained from Kuckuck in order to impress Hurtado (572–73) and the King of Portugal (612–14). He also manages to bluff Herr Stürzli into thinking he is a linguist (414–16) and to bluff his way through a game of tennis in Lisbon (616–19). In all these cases, Felix Krull's basic strategy is the same: he strings a few scraps of knowledge together and he covers over the gaps with as many fine gestures as possible. He manages thereby to create the impression of virtuosity from what are actually quite limited resources. Here, then, this slightly kleptomaniac novel comments upon its own eclectic and light-fingered borrowings. And literary theft is nearly always a compliment — one only takes what one wants. Perhaps we should agree with Thomas Mann's argument that talent is entitled to borrow, as long as the desire and the feeling of affinity is there. It is worth remembering that the technique of literary adaptation has a long and distinguished pedigree that includes Shakespeare, Goethe, Flaubert, and Joyce, to name but a few. There is nothing wrong with using tradition, especially if it is used well.

(iii) Style, Hyperbole, Continuity

Style is something that Felix Krull has in abundance, and as a narrator he uses it to full effect. Although he uses Goethe as a model, the novel sometimes exceeds *Dichtung und Wahrheit* in terms of baroque elegance. Stylistically, *Felix Krull* is an act of seduction intended to win our admiration. The stately progression of the long sentences and the unfurling of relative clauses is a pleasure to behold. Sometimes the narration is lyrical, as when Krull apostrophizes the bottles of *Sekt* in the opening section of the book: 'da liegt ihr in unterirdischem Dämmerlicht, und in euerem Innern klärt und bereitet sich still der prickelnde Goldsaft, der so manchen Herzschlag beleben, so manches Augenpaar zu höherem Glanze erwecken soll!' (267). At other times it is pathetic or disingenuous: 'Ich ermangelte in jenem zarten Alter jeder geschäftlichen Einsicht' (318). At other times it is swaggering and self-assured: 'Hiermit verlasse ich diese Materie, bei deren Bearbeitung ich den Kanon des Schicklichen keinen Augenblick durchbrochen zu haben glaube' (315).

The narrative disports itself like an acrobat among the higher registers of language, scintillating with *bons mots*. The more disreputable the events which are being described, the higher the register seems to go: 'Ich ließ schon weiter oben eine Anspielung einfließen auf die Störungen, welche durch die Anwesenheit des Fräuleins aus Vevey in unser Familienleben getragen wurden' (276); '[ich] sah auch, wie wohlgekleidete Herren [. . .] mit der unzüchtigen Führerin beschwingten Schrittes entschwanden' (376). Does the narrator employ this exalted register in order to give his account a solidity, and a legitimation, which it might otherwise lack? This is Hans Wysling's view.[66] Many of the novel's critics have interpreted its high style as a trick, and one that fails: Wysling, Sprecher, and Stein maintain that Felix Krull overreaches himself, that his style is overstretched, and that it reveals his bad education.[67] In my view, these comments miss the point; Mann intended *Felix Krull* to be a happy text ('positiv endlich doch'):[68] he did not want his hero to fall flat on his face. Surely the narrative is taking pleasure in sending itself up. In my view, this effervescent novel deliberately thematizes it own hyperbole. Its style may be hyperbolic, overreaching and exaggerated, but if this is a 'trick', it is one that reveals itself as trick: an honest trick because it signals its own nature to the reader. From the beginning, the narrator presents himself as a product, one whose value is above the norm:

> Das ist mir ganz einerlei, ob dieser oder jener mich der Selbstgefälligkeit anklagt, denn ich müßte Dummkopf oder Heuchler sein, wollte ich mich für Dutzendware ausgeben, und der Wahrheit gemäß wiederhole ich, daß ich aus dem feinsten Holze geschnitzt bin. (273)

Here, the narrator is, in effect, haggling with the reader over his own value and it is in this sense that he is a 'Hochstapler', since the word 'hochstapeln' means to talk up the value of one's wares — it derives from the expression 'hoch aufstapeln' (to set something up high). 'Hochstapeln' is thus closely related to exaggeration and hyperbole: as 'Hochstapler', the narrator will make himself appear larger than life. In order to sell himself to the reader, he will continually talk himself up, hype himself. But this is the essence of art itself, this is what art does: it makes things seem important. Art is frequently affirmatory; the use of aesthetic representation tends invariably to glorify any subject matter. The earliest forms of art once had a sacral function (cf. the palaeontology museum in Lisbon), and even modern art retains this dimension of glorification. In this way, *Felix Krull* is a novel about art itself and about the way aesthetics can thrill us. The novel's use of hyperbole is a deliberate strategy: it shows that an element of exaggeration is the vital ingredient of any good yarn. The narrative continually makes use of the adverbs 'perfectly' and 'completely' in order to elevate itself. The most popular adverb in the novel is 'völlig', occurring thirty-three times (265, 298, 300, 315, 316, 319, 320, 330, 331 (twice), 334, 338, 339, 340, 349, 365, 366, 367, 377, 382, 387, 433, 459, 470, 476, 495, 561, 613, 629, 639, 640, 641, 643). Almost as frequent is 'vollkommen', occurring thirty-three times, often occurring as an adjective as well (265, 268, 275, 276, 281, 288, 301, 303, 305, 326, 327, 343, 349, 352, 357, 358, 397, 400, 409, 435, 488, 497, 503, 513, 514, 537, 552, 566, 622, 623, 629, 637, 641) and also giving rise to related nouns such as 'Vollkommenheit' (280, 294, 297, 540) and 'Vollkommen' (289). Also common are 'vortrefflich' (285, 297, 332, 334, 371, 605, 653), 'vorzüglich' (266, 279, 296, 327, 344, 488, 519, 566, 580, 597, 648), and 'vollendet' (266, 411, 451, 487, 582).[69] There is also a frequent evocation of the extraordinary: the word 'außerordentlich' appears thirty times (270 (twice), 276, 288, 306, 328, 330, 352, 368, 369, 384, 405, 417, 425, 430, 438, 451, 469, 485, 537 (twice), 542, 546, 562, 565 (twice), 582, 596, 607, 614).[70] The systematic use of such adverbs ('completely', 'perfectly', 'extraordinarily') is camp, in the sense of being excessive and 'over the top', and it therefore corresponds to Susan Sontag's definition of camp.[71] This is, however — in my view — a knowing and ironic instance of camp. The excessive adverbs in *Felix*

Krull function as a self-reflective narrative gesture, by means of which the text both asserts its own uniqueness and trumpets its own use of hyperbole. The repetition of these adverbs enables the reader to become aware of hyperbole as an essential component of the narrative. The narrative becomes an extravagant gesture which the reader is free to accept or to reject.

This self-aware novel comments upon its own style in many other ways as well. The reactions of the various supporting characters anticipate possible reactions to the novel itself. The doctor (Oberstabsarzt) in the *Musterungsszene* is highly suspicious of Felix Krull's 'exalted' way of speaking ('exaltierte Redeweise' (369)); he senses that there is something excessive about this young conscript's style of delivery: ' "Sie reden fortgesetzt Überflüssiges! [. . .] Ihre Redeweise ist von einer gewissen Hemmungslosigkeit, die mir schon längst geradezu aufgefallen ist" ' (360). The doctor is right, of course: Felix Krull's style *is* over the top, and especially in this scene, where he milks the story of his father's death for every possible drop of sentimentality. On the other hand, the Marquise Victoria de Venosta's opinion of Felix Krull's style is much more generous: she finds it mannered, but polished.[72] Another self-referential moment in which the text alludes to its own narrative style is the scene in which Felix Krull practises imitating his father's signature. Engelbert Krull, a 'natural role model' for his son, has a wonderfully pretentious signature, full of decorative flourishes. The excessive grandeur of his father's signature is the visual equivalent of Felix Krull's use of language:

> Was den Namenszug 'E. Krull' betraf, [. . .] so umhüllte ihn eine Schnörkelwolke [. . .]. Die untere Hälfte des E nämlich lud weit zu gefälligem Schwunge aus, in dessen offenen Schoß die kurze Silbe des Nachnamens sauber eingetragen wurde. Von oben her aber [. . .] gesellte sich ein zweiter Schnörkel hinzu, welcher den E-Schwung zweimal schnitt und [. . .] nach unten verlief. Die ganze Figur war höher als breit, barock und kindlich von Erfindung (296–97)

The key words here are 'Schnörkel' (flourishes) and 'barock': two words often used by critics to describe the novel's style.[73] *Felix Krull*, then, is well aware of its use of superlative and hyperbole. Ironic and highly self-conscious, this is a narrative that continually signals what it is doing. These signals remain discreet, however: they fit elegantly into the story without causing narrative sclerosis. It was a difficult balance to maintain: Mann himself describes it as 'ein heikelstes Balancestück' (XI, 123), and one is reminded of the 'eleganten Strapazen' (289) of Müller-Rosé. In my view, this balance is a successful one: the novel can both charm readers and cultivate their critical awareness; it is engaged in producing a beautiful surface, and yet it knows of a human reality beyond words:

> das Wort [ist] so wesensfremd der heißen und stummen Sphäre der Natur [. . .]. Das sage ich, der, begriffen in dem Bildungswerk meiner Lebensbeschreibung, einem belletristischen Ausdruck gewiß die erdenklichste Sorgfalt zuwendet. Und doch ist mein Element die wörtliche Mitteilung nicht; mein wahrstes Interesse [. . .] gilt den äußersten, schweigsamen Regionen menschlicher Beziehung. (348–49)

Indeed, the emphasis upon surface appearance in the novel goes hand in hand with a rich subjectivity and interiority. Felix Krull has an imagination which sets him aside from the other young army recruits; caught before their gaze, he revels in his own inwardness ('innerlich zurückgeschlagen' (357)), and the novel's numerous references to dreams, fantasy, and fairytales are evidence of Mann's ongoing fascination with Romanticism. The word 'Traum' appears several times (290, 294, 302, 308, 310 (twice), 346 (thrice), 380, 441, 453, 522, 549, 550 (twice), 556, 633 (twice), 634), as does the the word 'träumerisch': (276, 280, 366, 528, 619, 659).[74] The adjective 'phantastisch' is very popular (271, 367, 495, 513, 516, 620, 636)[75] and there are several references to fairytales: 'Fee' (556, 562); 'Féerie' (636), 'märchenhaft' (294, 308, 341, 453), 'Märchen' (308), 'Märchenland' (343), and 'Märchenpracht' (636). Magic and wonder are also frequently evoked: 'bezaubernd' (287, 288, 457), 'verzaubert' (308, 453), 'Zauber' (584), 'wundervoll' (433, 448, 461, 564, 568, 644, 660), 'wunderbar' (458, 626, 641), 'wundersam' (348), 'wunderschön' (494, 577), and 'Wunderlichkeiten' (635).

Are these reiterated words there to give the impression of literary fireworks, are they ostentatious show, a 'Blendwerk' designed to fool the reader? The repetition of these adjectives clearly seems to destabilize the realism of the work. By continuously evoking the irreality of a dreamlike state, the narrative deliberately undermines its own realism. Thus, beneath its bravura style, there is a distinct note of scepticism suggesting lack of faith in reality. We can trace this scepticism back to the influence of Schopenhauer. However, if one can speak of the influence of Schopenhauer here, it is only in a limited sense. Although Felix Krull can recognize the ethical force of Schopenhauerian thought, he will not resign himself to morbid disenchantment with the world. On the contrary, Krull is in love with the world of appearances and throws himself headlong into it. His sympathy goes beyond Schopenhauerian pity ('Mitleid'), since he even sympathizes with the desires, dreams, and illusions of the people he encounters. Thus, in *Krull*, the Schopenhauerian discourse of illusion has been given a positive twist. In Mann's novel, illusions and dreams are — for better or for worse — considered as forming part of everyday life. This is a statement of fact, and not a doctrine of deceit. In the final phases of the novel, we learn that illusion must be guided by both 'Sympathie' (472, 476, 547 (twice), 548, 556, 573, 615, 641) and 'Allsympathie' (548 (twice), 573, 586, 646). In other words, illusion must remain more or less within the boundaries of decency, and it remains attached to a notion of human substantiality.

To conclude this section, I will briefly address the question of stylistic continuity between early and late sections of *Felix Krull*. Mann himself claimed in 1954 that he had tried to make the transition between the old and new portions of the text as seamless as possible. However, he also gradually wanted to reduce the feeling of parody and make the language more up to date:

> Sie werden gefunden haben, daß ich es mir angelegen sein ließ, genau in dem Tonfall des alten Fragments wiederanzusetzen, doch habe ich dann mit Vorsicht den zu ausgesprochen parodistischen Stil von damals allmählich verlassen und meinen Helden eine zwar immer humoristisch gewählte, aber doch kurrentere Schreibweise zugestanden.[76]

In fact, the later section of *Krull* is just as technically complicated and elevated in style as the earlier section, as Guido Stein points out.[77] What Mann really seems to be saying in this letter is that he no longer wishes to present the novel as a parody of Goethe. This is indicative of a shift in Mann's own perception of Goethe — a measure of his increased respect — rather than of any radical stylistic departure. In my view, the degree of stylistic unity in *Krull* is remarkable, given the forty-year gap in the process of composition. Donald F. Nelson has identified a number of linguistic traits which create an impression of stylistic unity in the novel as a whole, including the use of theatrical metaphors, genitive constructions, and the persistent use of oppositional conjunctions.[78] Michael Beddow, too, sees a metaphorical continuity between the early and the late *Krull* which transcends linear plot development.[79] One could also point to the leisurely, meandering style of narration in *Krull*, which in my opinion owes a great deal to Theodor Fontane. Even the surname 'Krull' itself is close to 'Kroll', the name of a well-known Berlin music hall mentioned in Fontane's novel *Die Poggenpuhls* (HF I.IV, 513). While the evidence for actual intertextual borrowing from Fontane in *Krull* is sparse,[80] the periodicity of Mann's two essays on Fontane (1910, 1954) almost precisely matches his work on *Krull*. To a certain extent, it seems that both halves of *Krull* were written — in part, at least — under the influence of Fontane. When, in 1910, Mann paused in his work on *Krull* in order to write 'Der alte Fontane', he seems to have hoped that reading Fontane's letters would help to maintain the exuberant style of *Krull*. As Hans Wysling puts it: 'Die Arbeit am *Hochstapler* hatte er [Mann] indes schon vorher unterbrochen zugunsten des Aufsatzes über *Fontane*, dessen Briefe ihm wohl helfen sollten, zum leichten Ton der Schwindlerbekenntnisse zurückzufinden'.[81] Close attention to 'Der alte Fontane' reveals a cluster of Krullian motifs. The quoted letters reveal that Fontane takes pleasure in praising, even exaggerating the qualities of beautiful people ('die schönen, lachenden Menschen [. . .], denen die Herzen ihrer Mitmenschen immer wieder und wieder zufallen' (IX, 19)); Fontane also believes that one should give artists the benefit of the doubt ('Man muß den Künstlern gegenüber [. . .] Verzeihung üben und Fünfe [sic] gerade sein lassen' (IX, 18)). At times, Mann's comments on Fontane seem to be moving in the direction of *Krull*, for example when he talks of Fontane's 'poetische Bedürfnisse' (IX, 24), and the fact that 'sein Causeurtum [. . .] besteht in einer Verflüchtigung des Stofflichen, die bis zu dem Grade geht, daß schließlich fast nichts als ein artistisches Spiel von Ton und Geist übrigbleibt' (IX, 24). If we now turn to the latter part of *Krull*, it seems that the epistolary ninth chapter of Book III was written at roughly the same time as Mann was reading a new edition of Fontane's letters to Georg Friedländer, in preparation for an article in the Zurich magazine *Die Weltwoche*.[82] Far from being coincidental, I believe that the simultaneity of the two Fontane essays with *Krull* indicates that Fontane acted as a sort of spiritual midwife for *Krull*, twice assisting at its birth, and lending a degree of stylistic unity to the whole.

Nevertheless, there are certain differences between the early and the later *Krull*. Donald F. Nelson argues that while the earlier fragment parodies the Goethean memoir, the later fragment can be read as a parody of lyricism. Nelson has found that in the second part of the novel, the use of duality and oxymoron is more impressively refined, while the structure of the syntax is more rambling and playful.[83] While both early and late *Krull* rely on effervescent word play, it is clear that there are significant differences between the two sections. The chapters of the novel written before 1914 are much shorter and tighter. The use of the narratorial present tense is more frequent and there are numerous asides to the reader. There are frequent philosophical digressions, and the style is more aphoristic, and thus closer to Goethe (as well as to Schopenhauer and Nietzsche). Overall, there is a strong feeling of Romantic isolation, and the supporting cast of characters is only briefly sketched in.

When he returned to *Krull* in the 1950s, Mann did not revise the earlier sections of the novel, except for Chapter 4 of Book II, as Eva Schiffer has shown. The effect of these changes was to tighten the episode thematically, and to provide it with a lyrical climax — a paean to the human eye.[84] Apart from these alterations, Mann continued from where he had left off. In the section of the novel written after 1950, the pace of the narrative is more leisurely and the conventions of realism are adhered to more closely. Krull leaves the family home and goes out into the world. In consequence, dialogues with other characters in the novel gain in significance and increasingly replace dialogue with the reader. Supporting characters now acquire more psychological depth. The joy of storytelling takes over; the narrative, now less tightly structured, revels in the baroque twists and turns of the picaresque travelogue. There is a greater feeling of verisimilitude and the descriptions of object and place become more extended. In the first half of the novel, the confidence tricks are mostly based on physical and technical skill. In the latter half, Krull does not so much rely on 'tricks' as on a general charm offensive in order to win over those he meets. His stunts are no longer physical but verbal, existing in the realm of discourse. From now on it will be the function of others to display physical virtuosity (Andromache, Ribeiro), while Felix Krull increasingly contents himself with verbal sophistication alone.[85]

(iv) Interaction with the Reader

In my analysis of the Müller-Rosé episode, I argued that the central thematic message of *Felix Krull* is that art sets up a relationship of knowing collusion, an agreement ('Einverständnis') between artist and audience. If we now examine the formal qualities of the novel, we will find that, on a stylistic level, the message is exactly the same. Time and time again in *Felix Krull*, the narrator addresses himself to his audience, often in the most intimate terms. This relationship between narrator and reader is one of the novel's main centres of gravity, as a number of commentators have pointed out.[86] Karl-Martin Kühner even goes as far as analysing the novel solely in terms of its continual gestures to the reader.[87] The narrator's attempts to instil a sense of collusion in his readership provide a formal parallel to the 'Einverständnis' (294) of the Müller-Rosé episode. Put simply: in *Felix Krull*, form mirrors content. This holds true for the very first sentence of the novel, which subtly figures the relationship between narrator and reader in a number of different ways.[88] It also applies to what Gérard Genette calls the 'paratexts' or 'thresholds' of the text, i.e. the devices chosen to frame the text. Thus the edition of *Krull* printed in 1923 contains an afterword in which Thomas Mann directly appeals to the readers for their approval. In effect, he wants a positive response from the public to encourage him to finish the novel: 'Den Autor angehend, so ist er willig genug, sich durch freundliche Teilnahme, die das Fragment etwa finden mag, zur Fortführung und Beendigung anspornen zu lassen'.[89] And Mann made similar appeals at two public readings of *Krull* in late 1916.[90] These formal appeals to the audience by Mann himself are echoed in the text by his fictional creation. Krull the narrator continually pauses in order to take the reader into his confidence and in order to enlist the reader's own confidence.

On a formal level, one might say that the principal feature of *Felix Krull* is its gesture to the reader. Despite his vanity, Krull as narrator never lapses into solipsism; on the contrary, he continually signals his awareness of the reader. In my view, Krull's desire is *not* narcissistic, since it is directed outwards, towards his public — Krull is, after all, 'zum Liebesdienste geschaffen' (381). This is a novel that plays with a constructed image of the reader, evoking and soliciting his or her desire through an array of textual cues. The reader is figured as silent accomplice, willing victim, and even (as in the works of Jean Genet) as voyeur. Ideally, the reader colludes with the narrator's artistry.

It is pertinent at this juncture to recall the fundamentals of the theory of reading, in order to analyse the treatment of the reader-figure in *Krull*. Although Sartre argued as early as 1948 in favour of an increased awareness of the reader,[91] it was not until the 1970s that Wolfgang Iser and Hans Robert Jauss developed a comprehensive theory of reading. Iser was the first to study in detail how literary texts tend to indicate the presence of an imaginary reader. According to Iser, texts of prose fiction often contain a series of cues which posit the reader as a character within the text — what he calls 'der implizite Leser'.[92] The notion of an implicit, or implied, reader is a useful one because it allows critics to examine the network of response-inviting structures or 'Wirkungsstrukturen' which impel the reader to understand the text in a particular way.[93] Another major contributor to reader-response theory is Hans Robert Jauss. Like Iser, Jauss analyses the aesthetic experience of the reader in terms of cognitive and affective functions (aisthesis, catharsis). Jauss divides the reader's identification with the hero into five main modalities (assoziativ, admirativ, sympathetisch, kathartisch, ironisch).[94] In my view, all five categories are at work in the reader's enjoyment of *Felix Krull*. The radical modernism of the novel comes most to the fore, however, when we consider the fifth category, what Jauss calls 'ironic identification'. For Jauss, this occurs when the text sets up the expectation of a conventional identification with the hero, only in order to confound that expectation. Since readers are denied a straightforward identification with the hero, they are thrown back upon themselves and forced to reflect upon the aesthetic and moral nature of the text, including the conventions which govern it.[95] In this respect, the narrative of *Felix Krull* is exemplary. The context of the intimate confession sets up the expectation of a narrator who wears his heart on his sleeve, but the fact that he is a confidence man completely undermines all sense of authenticity. Thus the text is both forthcoming and withholding — it both offers and denies access to the reader, who is led into a disturbing proximity to the ambiguous narrator. The narrative achieves this by a continual, intimate, insistent address to the reader as interlocutor, to the extent that, as in Diderot's *Jacques le fataliste*, the reader becomes a central character in the novel.

What kind of reader, then, is implied by *Felix Krull*? In general, the implied reader set up by the novel is nearly as polymorphous as the protean narrator himself. For example, there are the two key moments when the reader enters the scene and interacts with the hero. In the first of these moments, the reader is gendered as male and portrayed as a gentleman (346); in the second scene the reader is addressed as a woman ('du Kostbare' (373)). And if the reader's gender is ambiguous, so is the reader's attitude. Guido Stein has pointed out that Krull as narrator wavers between viewing the reader on the one hand as a moralist, to whom he must justify himself, and on the other hand as an avid consumer who must be titillated with the most lurid sensations.[96] In other words the novel figures a clear tension between the reader as highly moral, enlightened bourgeois and the reader as irrational consumer of mass culture — it tries to satisfy both the demand for intellectual argument *and* the desires of the reader.[97] The underlying implication is of course that the reader may well be just as multi-faceted as Felix Krull, both questioning and sympathetic, but also capable of transgression. It is precisely this collusion with the reader which the narrative seeks to establish and maintain. In order to show how this collusion is generated, I will now turn to a more detailed analysis of the text.

The principal technique involved in manipulating the reader's assent is the increasing intimacy of pronominal address. The first instance of informal address to the reader in the 'du' form occurs on page 294, roughly thirty-five pages into the novel. Before this form of address is used, however, the basis of intimacy is already carefully established, so that the use of the 'du' form seems natural and not intrusive. At the very beginning of the novel, the form of narratorial address to the reader is coy, polite, and reserved. At first, the reader is addressed gently, without the use of pronouns or substantives (except for oblique ones such as the reference to 'dem geduldigen Papier' (265)). The description of Felix Krull's earliest memories gives an impression of intimacy, which is bolstered by the chatty style, the numerous digressions into the present tense, and the instances of prolepsis which tempt the reader with things to come. The first mention of the public is indirect: Engelbert Krull announces 'ich gebe dem Publikum, woran es glaubt' (268); a little later, the 'Publikum' in question is not the reader, but the holidaymakers at Langenschwalbach (281). The first substantive mention of the readers as '[das] Publikum' comes in the Müller-Rosé episode (293), and even then it comes in the form of Krull's claim that he is writing his memoirs primarily in order to amuse himself and not the public. But this short lapse into the present tense is only the prelude to the astonishing climax of the chapter, which takes the form of a prolonged and intimate direct address to the reader. Initially this is presented as Krull's mental dialogue with himself ('so etwa gingen damals meine Gedanken' (293)). But somehow by the time he gets to 'Hüte dich, darüber zu entscheiden!' (294) one can sense that it is really the reader who is being addressed. A sleight of hand has occurred: while the narrative initially claimed the verisimilitude of a private self-dialogue, in fact the sudden flood of 'du' pronouns, combined with the flow of exclamation marks and question marks, cannot help but involve the reader.

The crescendo comes with a whole flood of 'du's and imperative verbs: 'Rufe dir vielmehr das Bild zurück' (294); 'Gebiete deinem Ekel und empfinde ganz [. . .]' (294); 'Empfinde noch mehr! Frage dich [. . .]' (295); 'brauchst du dich'; 'du weißt es gar wohl!' (295). This repeated address is highly charged; it almost seems as if the narrator has leaned over and grabbed the reader by the throat. The 'du' form draws us in and demands that we follow every step of the argument. Far from being a detached philosophical meditation, the text has become a loaded, emotive, personal appeal for us (as readers) to accept deceit as something wonderful. The Müller-Rosé episode is formally unique — nowhere else in Mann's work do we find such an intimate address to the reader. Furthermore, in the economy of the novel as a whole, the use of the 'du' form here is highly significant. Generally, Krull avoids the 'du' form, even when dealing with his accomplices. Although Stanko continually addresses him as 'du', Krull refuses to return the gesture and absolutely insists on addressing him as 'Sie' (401, 408). As Krull discusses exchanging roles with the Marquis de Venosta, he uses the 'Sie' form. At the end of the scene he finally agrees to use the 'du' form with the Marquis (520), but the novel never actually shows him addressing the Marquis as 'du'. In fact, Diane Houpflé is the only character in the novel — apart from the reader — whom he addresses as 'du'. This means that — with the exception of Diane Houpflé — Felix Krull seeks a greater degree of intimacy with the fictional *reader* than he does with any other character in the novel. And if the use of 'du' with Diane Houpflé signifies seduction, surely this implies that the narrator's interaction with the reader is also a seduction? This erotic aspect tends to be confirmed by the phrase 'hochzeitliche Begegnung' (295) which concludes the Müller-Rosé sequence. In this sequence, the intimacy of the address to the reader reaches an early peak of intensity which is without equal, despite two further (notable) instances of informal address to the reader (340, 373). From now on, addresses to the reader, although frequent, will be less insistent and more playful and teasing. It is as if the narrator already seems more certain of our assent.

The structure of the Müller-Rosé chapter provides a general model which will be used again and again in the course of the novel. The chapter opens with a narratorial aside to the reader. Then the scene is set; then an action or event is described, which in turn provides the occasion for a philosophical excursus. The chapter generally concludes with this moral or philosophical discourse, which often culminates in frequent direct addresses to the reader in order to add rhetorical force to the argument. Several chapters follow this structure, including Chapters 5–8 in Book I and Chapters 2–6 in Book II.[98] In this way, asides to the reader are principally found at the beginning and end of chapters, rather like a framing device. They are especially common at the end of chapters, whenever Krull attempts to explain or to justify his exploits. Book I, Chapter 7 deals with the actual crime of shoplifting and culminates in a long justification to the reader. The narrator begins humbly enough by saying that if anyone wants to accuse him of common theft, he can — far be it from him to stop anybody using a word (309). He then enlists Nietzschean 'Sprachkritik' in order to explain why the word 'theft' would not be appropriate. The use of the leading pronoun 'uns' invites the reader to identify further with him — always a good tactic of persuasion. The deferential tone continues, politely asking the reader to forgive the digression 'der etwaige Leser verzeihe mir diese Abschweifung ins rein Betrachtende' (309) — only, however, to end the paragraph rather rudely, telling the reader that if he doesn't like it, he can always stop reading: 'Allein ich erachte es für meine Pflicht, ihn nach Möglichkeit mit den Eigentümlichkeiten meines Lebens zu versöhnen, oder aber, wenn dies unmöglich sein sollte, ihn beizeiten vom Weiterblättern in diesen Papieren abzuhalten' (309–10). In other words, Krull is saying: 'Take it or leave it. Why carry on reading if you don't agree?' There is a slight element of coercion in this plea for understanding. The reader is being nudged into a complicity with the narrator. Next, in a further play for the reader's sympathy, the reader is encouraged to forget the crime and to share in Krull's joy at waking up and finding all those sweets (310). The plea for the defence ends with a gesture of dismissal ('man lege die Tatsache aus, wie man will — ich selbst hielt es nicht für meine Aufgabe, darüber nachzudenken' (310)). It is clear that the deferential narrator is playing games with the reader in order to get himself off the hook. If there is an element of manipulation in all of this, it is, however, gentle, playful, and relatively harmless. Stealing bonbons is, after all, a pretty minor offence. What the text is doing here, essentially, is asking the reader to be lenient, to accept the fantasy even though it is distinct from reality. Readers should, ideally, act like Krull's own mother when she found her son pretending to be sick. Her reaction was to play along, even though she knew the sickness was feigned:

> Daß sie mein Leiden eigentlich ernst nahm, glaube ich nicht; aber da ihre Empfindsamkeit bedeutend ihre Vernunft überwog, so brachte sie es nicht über das Herz, sich vom Spiele auszuschließen, sondern ging mit wie im Theater und fing an, mir bei meinen Darbietungen zu sekundieren. (300)

The reader, like Krull's mother, is asked to suspend his or her disbelief and join in the fun ('mitgehen'). Thus the true drama of the book becomes a drama of the reader's faith: Mann makes the reader reflect upon his or her own attitudes to Krull and to his message. *Felix Krull* presents the reader with a philosophical and literary justification of art and semblance, supported by a formidable array of narrative effects. The reader is free to agree or to disagree, but that choice probably reveals more about the reader than it does about Thomas Mann or Felix Krull. Above all else, however, Mann's novel allows the reader space for critical reflection. *Felix Krull* stimulates, but it does not bludgeon or coerce the reader.

At the beginning of Book II there is another key aside to the reader. The narrator now finally confesses that he was lying when he claimed to be writing for his own pleasure. Krull admits that he does write with his readers in mind ('daß ich [. . .] doch auch der lesenden Welt einige Rücksicht zuwende'); indeed, he hopes to elicit the 'Teilnahme' and 'Beifall' of his readers (322). I agree with Karl-Martin Kühner when he asserts that this 'Rücksicht auf die lesende Welt' is the guiding principle of Krull's narration.[99] As Kühner notes, however, there is also an educative purpose to the Krullian project: parts of the novel (the Müller-Rosé episode, the conversations with Kuckuck and Zouzou) seem almost to be constructed like Socratic dialogues.[100] Krull himself is acutely aware of the tension between education and entertainment in his narrative. He identifies his target audience as the readers of thrillers and murder mysteries, but immediately admits that his philosophical speculations often contravene the conventions of the genre (322).[101] There are compensations, however: his own physical beauty, which he is keen to stress (328, 411). At the same time, Krull as narrator is careful to spare the reader's sensibilities when it comes to omitting unpleasant details ('Ich [. . .] müßte besorgen, durch eine breite Schilderung unserer damaligen Umstände den Mißmut des Lesers zu erregen'. (336)).

One of the peaks of the relationship between narrator and reader occurs in the fourth chapter of Book II, which describes Krull's nocturnal promenades through Frankfurt and which contains his encounter with the 'Geschwisterpaar' (346).[102] As Krull enters the street, there is an apostrophe to the reader: 'Nun seht den unscheinbar gekleideten Jüngling, wie er, allein, freundlos und im Getriebe verloren die bunte Fremde durchstreicht!' (340). As Kühner points out, the sudden switch to third-person present here effectively creates solidarity between narrator and reader: the older Krull unites with the reader in considering his younger self.[103] The use of the present tense continues for a whole page, clearly signifying an appeal for the reader's sympathy. In order that the reader may share in the narrator's excitement at the beauty of Frankfurt's nightlife, the narrative provides a number of signals designed to establish a greater intimacy with the reader. These include a liberal scattering of punctuation marks (nine exclamation marks and seven question marks) which convey a feeling of enthusiasm. The narrator gets so excited that he stops himself in mid-sentence in order to address the reader (' — so einfach war es, ich entschuldige mich — ' (345); ' — ich rate nur — ' (345)). This patter with the reader reaches a climax towards the end of the chapter, when the reader enters into the text and addresses the narrator directly. In this remarkable passage, the reader has become so attuned to the narrator that he takes over the task of narration:[104]

> Schwärmer und Gaffer! höre ich den Leser mir zurufen. Wo bleiben deine Abenteuer? Gedenkst du mich durch dein ganzes Buch hin mit solchen empfindsamen Quisquilien, den sogenannten Erlebnissen deiner begehrlichen Schlaffheit zu unterhalten? Drücktest auch wohl, bis etwa ein Konstabler dich weitertrieb, Stirn und Nase an große Glasscheiben, um durch den Spalt crèmefarbener Vorhänge in das Innere vornehmer Restaurants zu blicken, — standest in verworrenen Würzdüften, [. . .] und sahst die feine Gesellschaft Frankfurts, bedient von geschmeidigen Kellnern [. . .]? (346)

There are two important points here. Firstly, the fictional reader is outraged because the narrator is not keeping his side of the arrangement — he demands more thrills from the narrative. The informality of the 'du' is striking: this reader has dropped his mask of bourgeois respectability and is avid for sensation. He is so intimate with the narrator that he seems to be standing right next to him and peering into the very same window.[105] Secondly, this doubling of the narrative voice occurs in the middle of the description of the mysterious pair of siblings ('Geschwisterpaar'). The narrative content (the fascination of unity in duality) is therefore reproduced on the level of narrative form. Once again, form mirrors content. Krull, for his part, is only too happy to give his assent to the reader's narrative interjection, although he disputes the accusation that he is lackadaisical:

So tat ich — und bin überrascht, wie treffend der Leser meine dem schönen
Leben abgestohlenen Schaugenüsse wiederzugeben weiß, gerade als hätte
er selbst seine Nase an den erwähnten Scheiben plattgedrückt. Was aber die
'Schlaffheit' betrifft, so wird er der Verfehltheit einer solchen Kennzeichnung
sehr bald gewahr werden und sie, als Gentleman, unter Entschuldigungen
zurücknehmen. (346)

Krull's affectionate, bantering tone underlines the fact that he considers the reader
to be an essential part of the narrative process. Karl-Martin Kühner regards the
reader-figure in *Krull* as a secondary narrator who performs important critical
functions.[106] While I think that Kühner overstates his case somewhat, his study has
the merit of demonstrating that the interplay between narrator and implied reader
is integral to the working of *Krull*. As Anthony Riley has shown, Krull wishes
to take the reader into his confidence at every turn. Krull imagines the reader's
reaction ('der Leser wird die Überzeugung gewonnen haben [. . .]' (305)) and at
one point Krull even looks directly into the reader's face: 'Allein ich gewahre in
des Lesers Miene die Sorge [. . .]' (349).[107] As for us, the real readers, it is difficult
not to be charmed by this bantering, hard to refuse this relation of complicity with
the narrator. Indeed, reading the novel can provoke an uncanny and ambiguous
reaction: one can find oneself distrusting Felix Krull and cheering him on at the
same time. The work clearly operates in this tension between moral dictates and
vicarious pleasure.

In the second half of the novel, the play with the reader continues. A flattering
address to the reader ('ernsthafter Leser' (383)) serves to introduce a philosophical
justification. Krull still enjoys teasing the reader, pointing out that at any time his
flow of confessions might dry up: 'daß ich [. . .] nach Belieben mit ihnen hinter
dem Berge halten könnte' (384). Krull is also bold enough to challenge his readers:
are they well-educated enough to know ('wie der Gebildete weiß' (392)) that the
rue de Rivoli is parallel to the rue Saint-Honoré? In general, the narrator now
takes the reader's sympathy for granted; he is now so sure of having won over the
reader that he addresses him as 'den um mich besorgten Leser' (420). Addresses
to the reader continue to occur at moments of heightened intensity, for example
in the circus sequence where they underline the importance of the Nietzschean
figure of Andromache. Here the rhetorical questions to the reader signal the
philosophical implications of the passage (457, 460). In the next chapter, dealing
with Lord Kilmarnock and Miss Twentyman, the narrative employs gestures to
the reader to comic effect. Felix Krull defends himself to the reader against the
charge of being a heartbreaker; ironically enough, he hopes that reader's image of
him will 'remain pure': 'Um das Bild rein zu halten, das diese Erinnerungen dem
Leser von meinem Charakter vermitteln' (473). Well-placed exclamation marks
add to the comedy (479, 485). From here on (apart from the odd exclamation mark
(494, 556) or question mark (498, 559–60)), however, interaction with the reader
is increasingly replaced by dialogue with other characters, such as the Marquis de
Venosta, Professor Kuckuck, and Zouzou. But the narrator can still spare a thought
for the now 'sympathetic' reader: 'Mitfühlender Leser!' (523). He can also indulge in
in-jokes with the reader who is in the know about his new identity as the Marquis

de Venosta ('unserem Namen' (527); 'meiner Heimat' (555)). The narrator is by now so confident of his rapport with the reader ('man wird es mir glauben' (548)) that he expects the reader to guess what he means and to understand the depth of his feeling for Professor Kuckuck without him having to spell it out: 'das verschweige ich, [. . .] weil der feinfühlende Leser (und nur für solche lege ich meine Geständnisse ab) es sich selber sagen mag' (549). As interlocutors, the Marquis de Venosta's mother and Zouzou act to a certain extent as surrogates of the reader, since they express the imagined criticism of the reader and give voice to the reader's own (still persisting) mistrust of Felix Krull. In particular, the sudden change to the epistolary form in the ninth chapter of Book III allows the Marquise to act as proxy for the reader by voicing the reader's concerns ('Das ist gewiß eine briefstellerische Fiktion' (622)). The distant figure of the Marquise enables the reader to view himself or herself at one remove. The reader can both approve of the Marquise's scepticism *and* delight as she is fooled. She is evoked again later on as a mouthpiece for the reader (643).

The final gesture to the reader comes two pages from the end of the novel, at the very moment of Felix Krull's long-awaited kiss with Zouzou. Zouzou, having resisted his advances for so long, finally gives in to him, and, as she kisses him, he cannot resist a triumphal, teasing aside to the reader (along the lines of 'don't you envy me?'): 'Ich küßte ihren bloßen Arm an meinem Halse, ich hob ihre Lippen auf zu mir und küßte die erwidernden [. . .] Wer wohl, dessen Auge diese Zeilen durchfliegt, wird mich nicht beneiden um so süße Sekunden?' (659).Even during this intimate climax, the reader is evoked and made present as a witness to the scene. It is a pledge of faithfulness to the reader — the reader as companion, as bosom friend, as intimate confidant.

To conclude, I have shown that the novel gestures continually to the reader, making explicit the reader's own role as the interpretative partner of the narrative. Indeed, a vital component of the pleasure of reading *Felix Krull* derives from the knowledge that the reader has become the narrator's own object of desire. In *Krull*, the reader's self-consciousness is deliberately invoked, *not* in order to alienate the reader from the text but in order to open up a space for reflection, for dissent and knowing assent. The sceptical position is assumed and discarded at will; it is one moment among many. The reader is not bludgeoned or forced but gently invited — through a series of knowing winks — to participate knowingly in the pleasure of the text.

(v) Narrative and Sexuality

In this section I will address the narrative treatment of sexuality in *Felix Krull*. This is distinct from the performativity of identity and gender, a topic which I have already discussed in Chapter I(v). My concern here is rather different; here I will examine the discourse of love and sex which runs throughout the novel. From Genovefa to Rozsa, Diane Houpflé and Maria Pia, Felix Krull has sexual relations with women of every type and social class. Love in the novel is never platonic and disembodied. It is on the contrary, physical and full-bodied. The narrator is fascinated by the human body and tells us early on that he loves to visit holiday resorts because of the wide variety of bodies on display ('Der Anblick wohlgeborener und gepflegter Menschen auf den Sportplätzen und in den Kurgärten entspricht meinen tiefsten Wünschen' (280)). And the eroticism of the tennis court features again, later on (583). Yet even while bathing, the bodies are not naked; they are well-groomed and fashionably, if scantily, dressed. This is not nature in the raw, but sexuality mediated through culture. As in *Der Zauberberg*, where Hans Castorp's infatuation with Clawdia Chauchat is mediated through images (painting, X-ray), Felix Krull's sentimental education occurs through images. His hotel room in Lisbon contains a tapestry of the rape of the Sabines ('einen sagenhaften Frauenraub' (552)), and some porcelain figures with rather prominent posteriors: 'Damen in Reifröcken [waren] zu sehen, von denen der einen das Kleid hinten zerrissen war, so daß ihre rundeste Blöße, nach der sie in größtem Embarassement sich umwandte, dort gar lustern zum Vorschein kam' (553). These kitsch figurines are just one example of a more universal phenomenon. We hear of a picture book, full of nudes, which he saw in a Parisian dentist's waiting room:

> 'Ich [habe] ein Album gesehen, ein Bilderbuch mit dem Titel 'La beauté humaine', das wimmelte von Ansichten all der Darstellungen des schönen Menschenbildes, die zu allen Zeiten mit Lust und Fleiß verfertigt worden sind in Farbe, Erz und Marmelstein'. (634)

The picture book testifies to humanity's enduring fascination with images of the body. The overall message is that human sexuality is aesthetically mediated, and it comes as no surprise that a drawing of Zaza/Zouzou assumes such an important function in the later stages of the novel. Time and time again, the novel shows us how sexuality becomes bound up with representations, with images and words.

The highly self-conscious eroticism of the text is evident throughout. The word 'Bekenntnisse' in the title promises intimate secrets, and the locations appear to guarantee titillation: the novel opens with ribald parties in the Rhineland, and soon moves to Paris, an iconic city, famous for romance. It is as if the text sets out to evoke disreputability in order to excite the reader, showing that the reader's desires are actively involved. The Genovefa episode in Book I, Chapter 8 is a case in point. Here, Krull relates his sexual experiences with the housemaid, a woman nearly twice his age. The chapter addresses notions of propriety and the problems involved in writing about sex — how far should one go? The opening of the chapter neatly reverses the usual roles of narrator and reader. Whereas Krull normally allows the reader the moral high ground, he now presents himself as honourable and the reader as prurient. He claims that his account of the affair will be dictated by a high moral seriousness — the reader who expects lewdness ('schlüpfrige Scherze' (311)) will be disappointed. This is a typical strategy of tabloid newspapers whose claims of moral sensibility often serve as an alibi for printing sensational stories. It is also a way to tease and embarrass the reader. By withholding the details of his affair with Genovefa, Krull deliberately frustrates the reader's own desire for explicit detail. The narrator continues to tease, condemning the coarse laughter of the mob ('Gewieher des Pöbels' (311)) and assuming that his readers ('das gebildete Publikum' (313)) will be above that sort of thing. After much preamble, he finally gives in and dishes the dirt, talking of 'das markverzehrende, wahrhaft unerhörte

Vergnügen, das ich an Genovefas weißer und wohlgenährter Brust erprobte [. . .]. Ich schrie und glaubte gen Himmel zu fahren' (314). But the narrator's attention is still focused on the reader and at once he feels he must excuse this lapse. He assures us that his desire was not selfish but based upon the wish to please Genovefa ('Und nicht eigennütziges Wesen war meine Lust' (314)). He quickly adds that he is no mere skirt-chaser — his notion of lovemaking is more spiritual than that. This is a prime example of narrative teasing, a kind of 'now you see it, now you don't': a game of concealing and revealing rather like the one Roland Barthes describes in *Le Plaisir du texte*. The question of propriety reappears in the Rozsa section, where Krull employs a formidable range of specious rhetoric in order to justify his activity as a pimp, as I have already shown in Chapter 2(iii), on art as exploitation. As for Diane Houpflé, tragically intelligent and yet ridiculously mannered, she expresses her own sexuality in alexandrine verse and poetic-mythical imagery. Dissatisfied with her husband, she has chosen fantasy and the brief encounter over reality (again, see Chapter 2(iii)).

Thomas Mann's interest in the figure of the seducer can be traced to an entry — written some time between 1906 and 1908 — in his ninth notebook. In a list of 'Gewünschte Bücher' Mann cites Kierkegaard's *Das Tagebuch des Verführers*, perhaps with *Krull* in mind (N II, 215).[108] If Krull is a seducer, however, his principal target appears to be the reader. The novel is, on one level, a love letter to the reader. Krull enjoys flirting with the reader, describing his own body in detail and presenting it to the reader's gaze (284, 328). He points out several times that men as well as women are sexually attracted to him (284, 328, 373, 404). The flirtation with the reader reaches its peak in Book II, Chapter 6. There, we return to the nightlife of Frankfurt and hear of the sexual advances made to Krull by older, richer men. The narrator says he is sure that the reader is experienced enough not to be shocked (373).[109] In the very midst of the ensuing discussion of homosexuality, we hear of the older women who also found him attractive. Suddenly there is a direct address to the reader, as if the reader was one of these female admirers. The sentence is long and lyrical; it lasts for half a page, making it the second longest in the novel.[110] In this sentence, the play of eyes becomes deeply erotic,[111] imbued with metaphors of penetration and liquidity (drinking, diving). The sentence becomes a seduction of the reader in miniature, and when the head of the woman (who is now the reader) tilts back it seems like a *petite mort*:

> Deine schwarzen Augen, du Kostbare im brokatenen Abendmantel [. . .] durchdrangen meine Lumpen, so daß ich ihre forschende Berührung auf meinem bloßen Leibe empfinden konnte, sie kehrten fragend zur Hülle zurück, dein Blick empfing den meinen, nahm ihn tief auf, indes dein Köpfchen sich wie beim Trinken ein wenig zurückneigte, er gab ihn wieder, tauchte mit süßem und unruhvoll-dringlichem Versuch der Ergründung in meinen, — und dann freilich mußtest du dich 'gleichgültig' abwenden, mußtest dein rollendes Heim erklettern, [. . .] (373–74)

This 'encounter' with the reader, though fleeting and anonymous, is highly charged erotically. The homodiegetic moment of narrative has been turned inside-out, and now the extradiegetic narrator stares the reader in the face. The hypnotic intimacy of the gaze, the metaphors of interpenetration and the insistent, repetitive use of the 'du' form all add to the effect. Another consequence of this enigmatic moment is to create an ambiguity about the gender of the implied reader. The reader, who was pictured as male two chapters previously, is suddenly addressed as female. And the implied androgyny of the reader mirrors the androgyny of the youthful Felix Krull, still standing as he does on the threshold of manhood ('nicht Frau [. . .], nicht [. . .] Mann, sondern etwas Wunderbares dazwischen. Und das Wunderbare war ich' (374)). The allusion is enough to implicate both reader and narrator in a suggestion of bisexuality, for, although the addressee is female ('du Kostbare'), the fact that the sentence is situated in the middle of a discussion about homosexuality sets up a clear association between the implied female reader and the male admirers referred to by the text. Thus here, as elsewhere in the novel, gender is portrayed in a way which suggests its fluidity and interchangeability.

The penultimate chapter of the book, which describes Felix Krull's wooing of Zouzou, is a linguistic tour de force — what Walter Berendsohn has called 'das größte Meisterstück der Felix Krullschen Beredsamkeit'.[112] In this sequence, the self-consciousness of the narrative reaches new heights. We have seen that Zouzou functions (to a certain extent) as a surrogate for the reader, representing the process whereby an initial mistrust is gradually overcome and transformed into erotic attraction. It seems clear that, on one level at least, Krull's seduction of Zouzou re-enacts his earlier seduction of the reader. If we understand the novel as a deliberate wooing of the reader, then the Zouzou sequence allows the novel to restate itself in miniature and at one remove, as a seduction within a seduction. Indeed, Krull's seduction of Zouzou affords a singular pleasure to the reader: the pleasure of witnessing his or her own downfall by proxy. The Zouzou sequence can thus be read as a masterful and accomplished staging of romantic discourse, one which ironically draws attention to itself as a product intended for consumption. As a highly self-aware compendium of romantic discourse, the text bears comparison with Roland Barthes's *Fragments d'un discours amoureux*.

Felix Krull's speech to Zouzou in defence of love is fantastically eloquent. But even as it sweeps us along with its romantic verve, it continually draws attention to its own nature as a textual construct. The speech is six pages long and it is divided into five paragraphs. What is remarkable is that these divisions into paragraphs are announced in the speech itself. Here, the text asserts itself as an artefact, as paragraphs upon a printed page: '[Ich] mache in der Rede, die ich eigens für Sie vorbereitet habe, einen Abschnitt' (639); 'Sie müssen entschuldigen, Zouzou, wenn ich [. . .] sozusagen einen neuen Paragraph beginne' (639–40); 'Das ist ein Paragraph meiner Rede, Zouzou, ich mache einen Abschnitt' (641); 'Ich tue es paragraphenweise' (642). This speech is full of signals to the reader which underline its own constructed quality. Thus Felix Krull swears three times that every word of his speech has been faithfully reproduced, a prodigious feat of narrative recall which stretches the boundaries of verisimilitude: 'Ich versichere und schwöre: so sprach ich' (632); 'Ich schwöre: so sprach ich' (634); 'Bei meiner Ehre schwöre ich: so sprach ich' (643). These narrative utterances give the text a special status. In a standard realist novel, such a long speech would have been presented without the question of reliability ever being raised. In most novels, the reader's suspension of disbelief is simply taken for granted. In contrast, this section of *Felix Krull* encourages the reader to adopt a sceptical attitude by continually asserting its own word-perfect veracity. Indeed, if the narrator didn't draw attention to his own feat of memory in this way, the reader would probably never notice or question it. And so the reader's scepticism is carefully aroused, only to be dispelled by the panache of the narrative performance. The narrative thus deliberately provokes the reader into self-consciousness, but these moments of critical detachment do not fragment the reading experience; instead, they add to its piquancy by inviting the reader's knowing assent. These gestures to the reader act as reminders of the reader's own vital contribution, the necessity of the reader's own readiness to make believe.

At the end of the novel, Zouzou finally gives in; she embraces her wooer and they kiss. In a final gesture to the reader, the narrator asks who would not envy him: 'Wer wohl, dessen Auge diese Zeilen durchfliegt, wird mich nicht beneiden? [. . .] Welche Schicksalswende nun aber! Welcher Wandel des Glücks!' (659). Of course, this is where the traditional romantic novel always ends — with a final, passionate kiss, a slow and discreet fade to black, and perhaps a brief epilogue which sets the seal on a happy end, along the lines of *Jane Eyre*'s 'Reader, I married him'. However, this being a novel by Thomas Mann, we are not going to be allowed to get off that easily. The idyll is immediately punctured, and we are left with one final blast of irony: the romantic fade-out is not with the pure young heroine Zouzou, but with her bloodthirsty goddess-like mother, Maria. Felix Krull's love affair with the reader and his journey of discovery finally tails off into post-Freudian farce and a cosmic vision of the eternal feminine. Overall, what stands out is the textual awareness of the constructedness of sexuality, and the way the narrator makes use of this insight, feeding it back into his own narrative performance. This teasing narrative plays with the expectations and desires of its readers, and, when it breaks off, it leaves them wanting more.

(vi) The Rhetoric of the Real

In this section I will investigate the nature of the representation of reality in *Felix Krull*. What kind of realism is at stake here? For Roland Barthes, the measure of a text's realism is given by descriptions of superfluous objects, ones which reveal no information about the characters and seem to be there for their own sake. Although these objects have no function in the plot, they tend to signify an independent reality, what Barthes calls the effect of the real ('l'effet de réel').[113] Because these objects resist interpretation they become part of the 'referential illusion' of the real world. However, in defining this effect, Barthes uses the example of Flaubert, a writer who was already moving beyond classical realism, towards texts which deliberately resisted interpretation through their use of *discours indirect libre* and their use of absurd description (Charles Bovary's hat, for example). In the classical realism of Balzac, however, description is never indifferent or impersonal, but always highly motivated, shedding moral light on the characters themselves. As Martin Swales has shown, classical German realism also avoids the Barthesian *effet de réel*, by metonymically embedding characters within an environment which conditions them morally, emotionally, and spiritually.[114] Turning now to the works of Thomas Mann, we find what I would call a polyvalent realism. By this I mean that while Mannian description retains the conceptual sophistication of German realism, his is a realism which has quietly adopted a variety of modernist techniques, including the use of montage and a new encyclopaedic dimension deriving from Flaubert (who was in turn inspired by Goethe's *Faust*). As Russell Berman points out, Mann incorporates scientific and documentary material into his narratives, thereby lending a new objectivity to his fiction.[115]

Felix Krull in particular problematizes the notion of reality, since it was originally conceived as a satirical application of Schopenhauer's doctrine of the world as a veil of illusion. But while Schopenhauer views the world as insubstantial, Thomas Mann remains attached to the project of realism. Despite his romantic tendencies, Mann as a novelist had a sense for practical reality. His novels try to avoid the simplistic dichotomy of body and mind, substantiality and insubstantiality; in them, we can witness the interaction of subjective desire and palpable reality. In *Felix Krull*, reality is intimately linked with desire, and desired objects have an insubstantiality because they point to something beyond themselves, an ethos of culture and taste. Thus the description of the delicatessen in Book I mingles reality and unreality. It is a painterly description, rather like a Flemish still-life. Forms, colours, and the play of light are rendered masterfully; nouns are heaped on top of each other.[116] But this is a realism carried to excess: the shop is dreamlike, Dionysian ('diesen schwelgerischen Ort' (307)). The description of the objects piled high in the Frankfurt shop windows in Book II has a similar quality. It, too, reads like an expensive catalogue, presenting a vertiginous pile of *objets de luxe*. These objects are valuable because they signify a whole social order; they are the essential stage props required to enjoy the good life. Whenever the description of objects peaks in *Felix Krull*, this has to do with subjective desire. Here, the novel shows us that human experience is never unmediated, but always informed by culture, desire, and the imaginary. Like a good post-Kantian, Krull perceives phenomena from an all-too-human perspective: his experience of the world is filtered through the pre-existing categories of his own background (that is to say, the cultural imagination of Wilhelmine Germany). Krull is a creature of his own society to such an extent that he seeks to inhabit the worlds of leisure, tourism, and high society as represented in the media of the time. As I have shown in Chapter II, Mann's preparation for the novel involved the creation of a dossier of newpaper cuttings and excerpts from the illustrated magazine *Die Woche*. Mann sorted this documentary material under several headings including 'Kur- und Lustorte', 'Intérieurs', 'Elegante Festlichkeiten', 'Weiblichkeit', 'Hôtel. Reise', and 'Sport'.[117] Here again the obvious literary precedent is Flaubert, a writer famous for his conscientious research. *Madame Bovary*, his masterpiece, is the tragedy of a woman whose imaginary life is conditioned by sentimental novels and Paris fashion magazines. Emma Bovary's reverie as she dreams of running off with Rodolphe to foreign climes (never to return) has all the exoticism of a modern travel brochure.[118] In the same way, there is a distinct, and, I would argue, deliberate unreality about the description of place in *Felix Krull*. Descriptions in the novel often read as if they have been culled directly from tourist guides, or from magazines. The importance of travel guides is apparent in Mann's earliest work notes. In these notes, written between 1910 and 1911, the exchange of roles with the Marquis de Venosta is sketched out in miniature, along with the idea of cobbling together a description of the *Weltreise* from Baedecker guides: 'Sie schreiben zusammen nach dem Bädecker die Briefe, Felix reist als Graf und giebt die Briefe an den betreffenden Stationen auf'.[119] The mediated description of reality is not just to be found in Felix Krull's letters to the Venostas, however; it is everywhere in the novel. The opening description of the Rhineland is a case in point. Although reminiscent of a passage from Goethe's *Dichtung und Wahrheit*, as Thomas Sprecher has shown,[120] the text also reads like the opening of a travel brochure:

> Der Rheingau hat mich hervorgebracht, jener begünstigte Landstrich, welcher, gelinde und ohne Schroffheit sowohl in Hinsicht auf die Witterungsverhältnisse wie auf die Bodenbeschaffenheit, reich mit Städten und Ortschaften besetzt und fröhlich bevölkert, wohl zu den lieblichsten der bewohnten Erde gehört. (266)

And if this opening is already comically overstretched, it soon gets worse. The pompous descriptiveness is sent up by the ending of the chapter, which degenerates into a description of Engelbert Krull's garden, replete with garden gnomes and other tacky ornaments. We are being served up a Rhineland as cultural object, as object of stereotypical discourse. This kitsch Rhineland is one of surface without substance — the textual equivalent of Engelbert Krull's gaudy bottles of sparkling wine. What Mann seems to be doing here is sending up the sentimental representations of nature which were prevalent at the time, e.g. the anodyne travelogues which he collected from the magazine *Die Woche*.[121] In the popular media of his day, Mann found a highly mediated, commodified portrayal of nature: nature repackaged as a tourist destination, as in the works of the Munich painter Zeno Diemer (1867–1939). At the turn of the century, Diemer was famous for his brightly coloured, romantic Alpine landscapes. The popularity of such images prompted Mann to reflect upon the triumph of kitsch over nature in his seventh notebook: 'Freude an der Natur, wenn sie ein gewisses kitschmalerisches Ideal erreicht. Man rechnet es ihr hoch an, wenn sie die Kunst verwirklicht: wenn der Gardasee Farben zeigt wie eine Postkarte von Zeno Diemer' (N II, 81). By the early twentieth century, the Romantics' cult of nature had become popularized and yoked into the service of the leisure and tourist industries. In *Felix Krull*, Mann satirizes this phenomenon, allowing the narrative to glide from one elegant snapshot to the next. For example, the narrator's description of his visit to Wiesbaden might have been lifted straight from a holiday brochure: '[ich] promenierte in den herrlichen Parkanlagen, welche den quellenreichen Badeort schmücken, vergnügte mich und bildete mein Auge an den prächtigen Kaufläden der Kurhauskolonnaden' (351). Later on, the description of Lord Kilmarnock's Scottish residences is pure Walter Scott, with rocky crags and the scent of heather, marvellously kitsch:

> Nach und nach erfuhr ich, daß er auf einem Schloß unweit der Stadt Aberdeen zu Hause sei, [. . .] daß er außerdem aber ein Sommerhaus an einem der Seen der Highlands besitze, in einer Gegend, [. . .] wo es sehr schön und romantisch

sei, die Berghänge jach und zerklüftet, die Luft mit würzigen Heidekrautdüften
erfüllt. (481)

And the description of the Marquis de Venosta's ancestral home also descends into
cliché. This is an utterly stereotypical castle, so generic that it exactly resembles the
English castles which feature on the plates of the Hotel Saint James and Albany:

> Er war in Luxemburg zu Hause, wo seine Eltern, 'mes pauvres parents', in der
> Nähe der Hauptstadt ein parkumgebenes Stammschloß aus dem siebzehnten
> Jahrhundert bewohnten, das nach seiner Angabe ganz so aussah wie die
> englischen Castles, die auf den Tellern abgebildet waren, worauf ich ihm seine
> zwei Bratenschnitten und sein Stück Eisbombe legte. (493)

Later on, when Felix Krull manages to get a private audience with the King of
Portugal, he charms the King with a description of the country's main tourist
attractions, despite the fact that he has never visited these places and is merely
echoing travel brochures: '"Wo gibt es denn auch sonst in der Welt ein Panorama,
dem zu vergleichen, das sich dem Betrachter von den Höhen der Königburgen
Cintras über die in Getreide, Wein und Südfrüchten prangende Estremadura hin
bietet?..."' (606). Whereas Barthes talks of an effect of the real, here one could even
talk of an effect of the unreal. In this respect, I am reminded of Peter Handke's
novel *Die Stunde der wahren Empfindung*, another novel which calls reality into
question. Gregor Keuschnig, the hero of that novel, comes to experience external
appearances as utterly false, and this may well be connected to his job, which
involves collecting press cuttings about Austria. Reality for Keuschnig becomes
pure show, uninterrupted exteriority ('ungebrochene Äußerlichkeit'),[122] and he
starts to feel trapped, as if he were a prisoner in Disneyland.[123] Handke's novel can
be seen (on one level) as a critical response to the omnipresence of modern media.
Begun over sixty years earlier, *Felix Krull* also deals with the alienation of modern
culture, but in a gentler and more conciliatory way.

The advent of modernity, experienced by Baudelaire and linked by Walter
Benjamin (in his famous 'Kunstwerk' essay) to the loss of aura owing to improvements
in technological reproduction, was accompanied by the erosion of old metaphysical
truths. Decades earlier, Nietzsche had proclaimed the death of God and called upon
art to bear the burden of humanity's metaphysical longings. Social theorists such
as Siegfried Kracauer, however, increasingly saw other leisure activities — such as
tourism and dance — as fulfilling a metaphysical function. In his essay 'Die Reise
und der Tanz', Kracauer analyses the theological dimension of modern tourism, and
argues that tourism, in a secular age, acts as a partial replacement for religion.[124]
Tourism can no longer offer a true experience of the exotic because modern visual
culture has disseminated images of even the most distant lands — even the most
exotic imagery has become familiar. Nevertheless, the mere fact of travelling from
one place to another allows people to experience a sort of spatial transcendence,
a hint of infinity. The mere change of spatial coordinates produces a freedom
which, however, cannot last: 'Wir gleichen Konquistadoren, die noch nicht Muße
gefunden haben, um die Bedeutung ihres Erwerbs sich zu kümmern'.[125]

The discourse of travel and leisure time in *Felix Krull* is, indeed, a remarkably
effective way of expressing unease about the modern condition. The novel is set at

a time when mass communication and transport meant that much of the otherness people witnessed while on holiday was already interpreted, culturally mediated otherness. Modern travel had already become so ritualized that it resembled some kind of religious pilgrimage, and indeed, travel guides have always been full of the iconography of the 'promised land', ever since the first appearance of Baedekers in the mid-nineteenth century. Clearly, the late-feudal aesthetic of the hotel harks back to an age of rigid social order and cognitive certainty. Hotels enable guests to play at being aristocrats, allowing themselves to be waited on in a world where everything is highly rehearsed and everyone knows their parts. The hotel is, in other words, the modern bourgeois equivalent of the chateau. But whereas for Kracauer the kitsch grandeur of the modern hotel is symptomatic of the spiritual poverty of modernity, Felix Krull quite simply adores it. Like Kracauer, he can see beyond the materialism and appreciate the metaphysical yearning which lies behind it. But while Kracauer mourns for a lost notion of community, Krull ultimately chooses to embrace the uncertainties of modernity. In this respect, the description of the grand hotel suite in Lisbon is a tour de force. Mann based it upon a photograph of the reception room in the German Embassy in Copenhagen, which he took from the magazine *Die Woche* in 1911.[126] From this tiny photograph, Mann elaborated a sumptuous array of details for the description of Krull's hotel suite. Nearly two pages long (552–53), it culminates in the longest sentence in the entire novel. This sentence, which is over half a page long, is a catalogue of fine things, full of nouns and adjectives heaped luxuriantly on top of each other. One might call it an apotheosis of materialism:

> Ein Vitrinenschränkchen, hinter dessen Scheiben allerliebste Porzellanfiguren, Kavaliere in galant geschraubten Stellungen und Damen in Reifröcken zu sehen waren, [. . .] eine stilvolle Ottomane mit Kissen und Sammetdecke vervollständigte eine Einrichtung, deren Anblick meinen bedürftigen Augen ebenso wohltat wie der Luxus des in Blau und Grau gehaltenen Schlafzimmers mit seinem Gardinenbett, [. . .] seinem hohen Standspiegel, dem Beleuchtungskörper aus Milchglas, dem Toilettentisch, den weißen breiten Schranktüren, deren Messingklinken blitzten . . . (553)

The sentence doesn't even clearly end but tails off langorously with three dots, as if to imply the endlessly sensual potential of the room itself. The inordinate length of this sentence seems to draw attention to the text as artefact: is this simply a list of indifferent clutter, an effect of the real? Or is it another instance of the novel's self-thematizing and playing with the conventions of mimesis? The godlike narrator seems to have an inexhaustible supply of items at his disposal to add to the list, he could go on at will, piling object upon object — the sentence need not end. It is as if the text is saying to the reader: 'How many more details would you like? I could go on . . .' This is a realism which knows — and plays with — the conventions upon which it relies.

Felix Krull is thus a kind of meta-novel: as a text, it is aware, in a postmodern sense, that human reality and fiction are constructs, ones that may be deconstructed. But the novel escapes the trap of an endlessly free-floating scepticism; it chooses ultimately to affirm these constructs and beliefs, since they are part of what makes us human. Felix Krull himself tells us that his deceptions only succeed because they are partially true, because each one is an elaboration of a truth which has 'not yet fully come into being' ('die Ausstattung einer lebendigen, aber nicht völlig ins Reich des Wirklichen eingetretenen Wahrheit' (298)). And despite Felix Krull's obsession with surface, he does in fact have a sense of underlying nature (for example, his tribute to the importance of origins and the power of *Heimat*, (335)). The play of identity and reality in *Felix Krull* is not endless, and neither is it detached from all notions of substance. Instead, there is an interaction between the domains of reality and rhetoric; the book tells us that there is no human reality without some kind of rhetoric informing it, or quickening it. Desire in the novel is not free-floating but structured and embodied; play is not simply a category of liberation, but a structured play which takes place within limits. To conclude: realism in *Felix Krull* is multi-layered and polyvalent, because although it clearly registers the disruptions of (post-)modernity, it has not lapsed into the enactment of failure; despite its artifice, it still remains linked to tradition. The novel has both critical meta-perspective and access to materiality: it shows that insubstantiality and human substance can, and do, coexist and coincide.

(vii) Continuity with Other Works: Narrative Community

In this chapter, I have analysed narratological performance in *Felix Krull*, and have sought to suggest that the novel's formal qualities are closely related to its content. In *Felix Krull*, narrative forms such as the play of genres, interaction with the reader, and polyvalent realism operate as a meta-commentary upon the thematics of the story. This is a novel in which the narrative mode functions as a correlative of the theme, and as a reflection of it and upon it. It offers a first-person narrative which is not only highly sophisticated but also unreliable, even dubious. Krull's narrative voice sets out to charm and to bamboozle the reader. As a narrator he continually gestures towards his readership, while simultaneously flaunting his unreliability as a narrator: he both offers and withdraws himself. This narrative voice admits that it is a performance, and yet seeks the willing consent of its readers, inviting them to collude knowingly with the performance. In doing so, it invites readers to be both emotionally engaged and critically detached, implying an attitude which is poised halfway between belief and disbelief. *Felix Krull* sets up a condition of reader assent that is both free *and* enthralled, knowing *and* beguiled. In theory and in practice it demonstrates how rational and competent human beings may freely choose to adopt the conventions of fiction. In reflecting upon the nature of art, Mann's novel shows that art is a social product, one which must seek the legitimation of an audience.[127]

Thanks to the work of Helmut Koopmann[128] and Eberhard Lämmert[129] it has long been established that Thomas Mann's works are constructed with a double perspective or 'doppelte Optik' in mind. The technique of 'doppelte Optik' implies that Mann wrote intentionally both for connoisseurs *and* for the general public. The idea stems from Mann's reading of Nietzsche, or rather Nietzsche's critique of Wagner. In *Der Fall Wagner*, Nietzsche had claimed that Wagner's music is degenerate because of 'die Unruhe ihrer Optik, die dazu nöthigt, in jedem

Augenblick die Stellung vor ihr zu wechseln' (KGA 6.3, 21). According to Nietzsche in *Nietzsche contra Wagner*, Wagner's preference for the grand gesture is a betrayal of his true nature, which thrives upon domesticity. For Nietzsche, this contradiction means that Wagner is trapped in an 'entgegengesetzte Optik' (KGA 6.3, 416). However, whereas Nietzsche regards this contradiction as detrimental to Wagner's music, Thomas Mann sees the creative potential implied in the tension. Thus, in a letter to Hermann Hesse of 1 April 1910, written in response to Hesse's review of *Königliche Hoheit*, Mann declares that his longing for popular acclaim is the result of Wagner's influence:

> Nietzsche spricht einmal von Wagners 'wechselnder Optik': bald in Hinsicht auf die gröbsten Bedürfnisse, bald in Hinsicht auf die raffiniertesten. Dies ist der Einfluß [Wagners], den ich meine, und ich weiß nicht, ob ich je den Willen finden werde, mich seiner völlig zu entschlagen. Die Künstler, denen es nur um eine Coenakel-Wikung[130] zu thun ist, war ich stets geneigt, gering zu schätzen. Eine solche Wirkung würde mich nicht befriedigen. (Br Hs 6)

While Nietzsche views Wagner's oscillating perspective as a weakness, Mann decides that this ability — to appeal simultaneously to a select few and to a wider audience — is a sign of artistic greatness. From now on, he adopts it as a conscious artistic strategy. By the time we come to the *Betrachtungen eines Unpolitischen*, Mann is no longer speaking about a 'wechselnde Optik', but a 'doppelte Optik', one which enables the artistic and the bourgeois perspectives to coexist: 'Wagners Einfluß [. . . ist] das, was Nietzsche die 'doppelte Optik' nennt, die artistische und die bürgerliche nebeneinander und auf einmal, den Instinkt [. . .] raffinierte und gutmütigere Bedürfnisse zugleich zu befriedigen, die Wenigen zu gewinnen, und die Vielen obendrein' (XII, 109). It is now generally recognized that much of Mann's work was written under the influence of the 'doppelte Optik'.[131] Indeed, Michael Minden has shown how much of Mann's success as writer is due to this mastery of a dual perspective, which offers readers both consumerist pleasure *and* the promise of redemption.[132]

The dual perspective is certainly there in *Felix Krull*, which provides both the sensation of a well-crafted tale *and* metaphysical speculation about the meaning of art. What holds that speculation in check, however, is the need to make it novelistic, to put it in the service of narrativity. As I have shown in Chapter 3(iv), much of the force of the novel derives from its rhetorical address to the reader. This is another example of the 'public' perspective at work in *Krull*. In this section I wish to show that the narrative gesturing to the audience is not unique to *Krull*. *Krull* may be the most outstanding example of it, but we find similar types of address to the reader in all of Mann's major works. Mann's narratives are famous (and justifiably so) for being intensely personal explorations of an austere and intellectually brooding self. However, they also have a highly public mode of address built into them, one which evokes a notion of plurality and community. In all of the great novels, and in many of the shorter works, the gesture to the readership is present — and often at the most crucial junctures.

In *Buddenbrooks*, the title itself sends a signal to the reader. Calling the novel *Die Buddenbrooks* would have implied a certain formality and distance; the fact that Mann chose to omit the definite article indicates that he wanted to inspire a feeling of familiarity in the reader, as if he or she were an acquaintance of the Buddenbrooks. Similarly, the first words of the novel, 'Was ist das', can be read as a challenge to the reader, a demand for interpretation and exegesis. In the opening scenes, the gradual arrival of the dinner guests signals that the Buddenbrooks are well-known pillars of the community. It also sets up an implicit parallel between the reader and the other guests: the reader is, so to speak, just another new arrival. Jochen Vogt has pointed out that Part I of *Buddenbrooks* functions as a kind of overture to the whole work, one that introduces the major themes of the novel in miniature.[133] The description of the Buddenbrook house opens up a symbolic space that discloses an entire social ethos, thereby immersing the reader in the family's world view.[134] In this opening section, the frequent use of the congenial pronoun 'man' serves almost imperceptibly to include the reader in the proceedings: 'Man saß im "Landschaftszimmer"' (I, 12); 'Man hatte zum Teil auf den Stühlen und dem Sofa Platz genommen' (I, 18); 'Man setzte sich gar nicht erst, sondern stand' (I, 19); 'Man blickte in seinen Teller' (I, 23); 'Man saß auf hochlehnigen, schweren Stühlen, speiste mit schwerem Silbergerät schwere, gute Sachen' (I, 31). This use of 'man' sets up a degree of intimacy, even complicity. Almost subliminally, then, the reader is invited to imagine that he or she is also part of this great patrician family. In this way, Part I of *Buddenbrooks* may justifiably be regarded as a masterclass in the art of engaging the reader. This 'public' dimension of *Buddenbrooks* is not, however, confined to the opening of the book. As the novel progresses, the use of free indirect discourse makes the reader ever more familiar with the central characters, despite the increasing emphasis upon interiority. Also, rhetorical devices such as exclamation marks are used to stress particularly important moments, e.g. 'Wirklich! Thomas Buddenbrooks Dasein war kein anderes mehr, als das eines Schauspielers' (I, 614). Even in the closing phase of the novel, when the final debilitating action takes place so much in the inner realm of the psyche, the narration still endeavours to render the private recesses of Hanno's mind publicly articulate. In this respect, the description of Hanno's piano solo is exemplary. Hanno's music is described less in terms of technicality than in terms of an existential drama. In the very midst of this drama, the reader is rhetorically invoked and asked to bear witness: 'Was geschah? Was war in Vorbereitung?' (I, 749); 'Was geschah? Was wurde erlebt? Wurden hier furchtbare Hindernisse bewältigt, Drachen getötet, Felsen erklommen, Ströme durchschwommen, Flammen durchschritten?' (I, 749). This repeated narrative address to the reader serves to make Hanno's extraordinary rhapsody publicly negotiable. Furthermore, the textbook definition of typhus which immediately follows introduces a corporate, objective style into the narrative. And finally, when the schoolmistress Sesemi Weichbrodt closes the novel with an imperious '*Es ist so!*' (I, 759), it is clear that she is doing so in an official capacity: the public dimension of *Buddenbrooks* is once more reaffirmed.

Der Zauberberg is even more formally conscious of the presence of the reader. Like *Buddenbrooks*, it has a masterful opening section which is designed to draw the reader slowly into the world of the novel. The harsh and confusing environment of the magic mountain is of course a world away from the Hanseatic comforts of the Buddenbrooks. Even so, the text offers a number of reassuring markers to its readers. *Der Zauberberg* even begins with a direct address to the reader. Thus, in the opening sentence of the 'Vorsatz', the disembodied narrator informs readers that they will soon get to know and like Hans Castorp: 'der Leser wird einen einfachen, wenn auch ansprechenden jungen Mann in ihm kennenlernen' (III, 9). At the same time, the narrative voice introduces itself in the first person plural, as a 'wir': 'Die Geschichte [. . .], die wir erzählen wollen, [. . .] die uns in hohem Grade erzählenswert scheint' (III, 9). There is of course a grandeur about this 'wir', one which seems firmly rooted in the bourgeois liberalism of the nineteenth century. At the same, the reader is allowed a way into the book through the humble perspective of Hans Castorp. Mann regarded Castorp as an identificatory figure for his German readers, as he explained in 'Lebensabriß' (1930).[135] But the 'Vorsatz' has another important function too: it anticipates the concerns of readers who may be put off by the size of the novel, and it provides a justification for its own length: 'Ohne Furcht [. . .] neigen wir vielmehr der Ansicht zu, daß nur das Gründliche wahrhaft unterhaltend sei' (III, 10).

Once the prelude is over, the novel opens with a pleasantly anodyne description of Castorp's journey, one which could almost have been taken from a travel brochure (the public dimension once again). As in *Buddenbrooks*, the repeated pronoun 'man' invites the sympathy of the reader:

> Beim Orte Rorschach, auf schweizerischem Gebiet, vertraut man sich wieder der Eisenbahn, gelangt aber vorderhand nur bis Landquart, einer kleinen Alpenstation, wo man den Zug zu wechseln gezwungen ist. Es ist eine Schmalspurbahn, die man [. . .] besteigt. (III, 11)

Only a few lines later, however, the text informs us that as one ascends into the mountains, the journey becomes less calm; now begins 'der eigentlich abenteuerliche Teil der Fahrt' (III, 11). From now on, the journey itself is described in terms that resemble a roller-coaster ride, and it starts to get confusing — however, by now the reader's perspective is anchored by the perspective of Hans Castorp, for whom the journey is also an adventure.

Hans Castorp makes an enjoyable companion for the reader of *Der Zauberberg*. Castorp's perplexity and sincere desire to make some sense of the conflicting ideologies which he encounters on the mountain are infectious, and readers soon find themselves sharing in Castorp's education — guided, of course, by the complex narrative perspective. If the gesture to the reader was in any doubt, it becomes evident at crucial moments, for example at the culmination of the section entitled 'Fülle des Wohllauts', where the narrative leaps into the present tense with a direct (if rhetorical) question: 'Will man glauben, daß unser schlichter Held [. . .] tief genug ins geistige Leben eingetreten war, um sich der "Bedeutsamkeit" seiner Liebe und ihres Objektes *bewußt* zu sein? Wir behaupten und erzählen, daß er es war' (III, 904–05). The narrative mode, the address to the reader, is all-important here. It is a signpost to the reader that serves to underline the significance of the passage. The final sentence of the novel ends with another rhetorical question: 'Wird auch aus diesem Weltfest des Todes [. . .] einmal die Liebe steigen?' (III, 994). This open-endedness makes an important gesture to the reader. By leaving the question open, the narrative invites readers to reflect upon what they have read, and indeed to reflect upon their own present, and their own future. The question raises issues of continuity and meaning: was Hans Castorp's time on the mountain spent in vain, was his life wasted? Or does the telling of the story have moral significance for the reader's own time?

Narrative gestures to the reader in *Der Zauberberg* are made by a detached, mysterious third-person narrator. In *Mario und der Zauberer*, the story is narrated in the first person, and the narrative addresses to the reader have a very different function. While narrative address in *Der Zauberberg* serves to promote a more general philosophical reflection, in *Mario* it is related to the narrator's own attempts to disassociate himself from the tragedy that has occurred. This is a narrator who is historically and politically implicated in the events of the story, and not merely a detached observer as Wolfgang Freese has claimed.[136] The unnamed narrator is a German holidaymaker, a well-educated bourgeois liberal. He is a concerned citizen, although not a very forthright one: for most of the story he fails to take a stand on anything. But he is also an accomplished and highly refined storyteller. The opening section of *Mario* is notable for the repeated use of the word 'man', which tends to create a sense of complicity between narrator and reader: 'Torre di Venere, wo man sich übrigens nach dem Turm [. . .] längst vergebens umsieht' (VIII, 658); 'man kennt das' (VIII, 659); 'man geht nicht mehr in das Weltbad, [. . .] man geht nebenan, nach Torre' (VIII, 659); 'Man findet kaum einen Tisch' (VIII, 660); 'Ernstlich, man soll im September nach Torre di Venere gehen' (VIII, 660). On numerous occasions, the narrator addresses the implied reader directly using the 'Sie' form, which increases the impression of lively conversation (despite the apparent formality of the 'Sie'). In these asides, the narrator's principal concern seems to be to explain or to excuse himself: 'Ich halte Ihnen keinen Vortrag' (VIII, 667); 'Sie begreifen unsere Nervosität' (VIII, 672); 'Sie verstehen, daß ich nur ein Beispiel seiner Arbeit gab' (VIII, 693). The narrative also contains a number of rhetorical questions to the reader. These questions do more than simply ask for assent, they also implicitly ask the reader to put himself in the narrator's shoes, to think what he or she would have done in that situation. The narrator appeals to the reader as an equal, as a friend or colleague: 'Mögen Sie das? Mögen Sie es wochenlang?' (VIII, 664); 'Hätten wir die Welle von Hohn, Anstoß, Widerspruch voraussehen müssen [. . .]?' (VIII, 667); 'Hätten wir nicht abreisen sollen?' (VIII, 668). This mode of dialogic interchange is also indicated by the way in which the narrator replies to an implied comment by the implied reader ('Sie haben recht' (VIII, 664); 'auch da haben Sie recht' (VIII, 665)). But he goes even further still, claiming to be able to anticipate the reader's comments. By drawing attention to this ability, the narrator has implicity aligned himself with Cipolla, suggesting an uncomfortable complicity: 'Die Gedanken der Menschen zu lesen, ist meistens nicht schwer, und hier ist es sehr leicht. Unfehlbar werden Sie mich fragen, warum wir nicht endlich weggegangen seien, — und ich muß Ihnen die Antwort schuldig bleiben' (VIII, 694). In this fascinating aside, the narrator admits that he cannot answer the question why he didn't leave during the interval; and the vocabulary here even suggests guilt ('schuldig bleiben'). The narrator is ashamed of his passive complicity with Cipolla, and seeks to justify himself by referring to his previous statement that he was drawn by what was strange and interesting ('weil Merkwürdigkeit ja in sich selbst einen Wert bedeutet' (VIII, 669)) — in other words, he stayed out of curiosity. Seemingly aware that this explanation does not fully get him off the hook, the narrator ends on a note of defiance: 'Nehmen Sie das als Erklärung unserer Seßhaftigkeit an oder nicht!' (VIII, 696). In a perceptive article, Alan Bance has shown that the narrator of *Mario und der Zauberer* chooses 'the interesting' rather than 'the good', thereby privileging aesthetics above morality.[137] For Bance, the brutal honesty of the tale lies in the fact that the narrator 'is a part of the malaise which he deplores'.[138] *Mario und der Zauberer* offers a much darker version of the reciprocity between artist and audience than that which Mann explored in the early *Felix Krull*. As I discussed in Chapter 2(iv), this is art as exploitation, art as degradation of the individual. Even so, the basic theme and the narrative treatment of it are remarkably similar in both works. Both describe the relationship between artist and audience. The difference is primarily a moral one: Krull and Müller-Rosé are (mainly) benign characters, Cipolla is irremediably malign. The basic mechanism is the same, however, since both Krull and Cipolla succeed by giving expression to the desires of their public. This kinship is reproduced on a formal level, since both works contain a high degree of narratorial address to the reader. This interaction between narrator and reader corresponds on a formal level to the interaction between artist and audience described in the text itself. In both works, we therefore have a double reciprocity. The narrators of both *Krull* and *Mario* deliberately set out to create a feeling of complicity with the reader. At the same time, both works present the relationship between artist and public as potentially suspect. The central difference is that in *Krull*, the complicity — and art itself — is ultimately vindicated. In *Krull*, art is shown to be a natural drive, a fundamental aspiration of humanity. In the context of the political crisis represented by Italian fascism, however, the situation is different, and thus *Mario* ends with a dire warning.

In *Doktor Faustus*, Serenus Zeitblom's narrative interjections summon the reader to act as a witness (or a member of the jury), while Adrian Leverkühn's life is weighed in the balance. Zeitblom's narrative asides have a crucial function: they contextualize Leverkühn's life historically, placing it against the background of the Second World War. The time of narration is wartime, and this perspective ensures that we read the story of Adrian Leverkühn through the lens of history. From the very first page of the novel, Zeitblom tells us that his mind is firmly fixed upon posterity, i.e. his eventual readership ('der zukünftige Leser' (VI, 9)). As in the opening section of *Krull*, Zeitblom wants to assure the reader that his credentials as narrator are adequate, although he admits that his statements may have the opposite effect and create doubt in the reader's mind ('gerade dadurch dem Leser Zweifel zu erwecken' (VI, 9)). As a narrator, Zeitblom has a concern for the general public which his friend Leverkühn lacks. Zeitblom talks of two distinct time periods — the time *in* which he writes, and the time *of* which he writes — before going on to mention a third time, the future time in which he will be read by an as yet unknown reader.

> Ich weiß nicht, warum diese doppelte Zeitrechnung meine Aufmerksamkeit fesselt, und weshalb es mich drängt, auf sie hinzuweisen: die persönliche und

> die sachliche, die Zeit, in der der Erzähler sich fortbewegt, und die, in welcher
> das Erzählte sich abspielt. Es ist dies eine ganz eigentümliche Verschränkung
> der Zeitläufe, dazu bestimmt übrigens, sich noch mit einem Dritten zu
> verbinden: nämlich der Zeit, die eines Tages der Leser sich zur geneigten
> Rezeption des Mitgeteilten nehmen wird, so daß dieser es also mit einer
> dreifachen Zeitordnung zu tun hat: seiner eigenen, derjenigen des Chronisten
> und der historischen. (VI, 335)

Russell A. Berman draws particular attention to this passage, pointing out that
the polyphony of independent voices in *Doktor Faustus* draws the reader in, as an
equal among the fictional personae.[139] Mann himself stated that the inclusion of
an implied reader in a text acts as a sort of beam of light, bringing a degree of
brightness to even the darkest subject matter. The statement occurs in the essay
'Dostojewski — mit Maßen' (1946), which Mann wrote during the composition of
Doktor Faustus, as he praises the discursive aspect of Dostoevsky's work:

> Das 'scheinbare' Sich-an-Leser-Wenden, das beständige Harangieren irgend-
> welcher 'Herren', mit denen der Redende sich herumstreitet, ist ebenfalls
> sehr vorteilhaft; denn es bringt ein Element des Diskursiven, Dialektischen,
> Dramatischen in den Vortrag, worin Dostojewski außerordentlich zu Hause
> ist, und das auch das Ernsteste, Böseste, Abgründigste in einem höchsten Sinn
> amüsant macht. (IX, 672–73)

In other words, the inclusion of the implied reader in a literary work has an
Apollonian function: it lends a certain critical distance, endowing the oppressive
mood of the tragedy with a moment of anagnorisis. Of course, as Martin Swales
has pointed out, the narrator Serenus Zeitblom is, in a most indirect way, complicit
in the tragedy of history, since he shares Leverkühn's fascination with the idea of
totality; he has what one might call 'totalizing' instincts.[140] Nevertheless, it is clear
that Zeitblom's testimony, his discursive appeal to the reader, helps to provide that
valuable dimension of recognition (*Erkenntnis*) which lends meaning to the novel.

It seems that whenever the public dimension is at stake in Mann's works, as is
especially the case in *Doktor Faustus*, *Mario und der Zauberer*, and — as I would argue
— *Felix Krull*, the work includes a narrative voice that is aware of speaking to the
public. The narrative voice may vary from work to work. Sometimes it is intimate
and in the first-person singular; at other times it is a more imperious first-person
singular or disincarnate third person. What is important here is that no matter which
mode is being used, there is a highly thoughtful form of address to the reader, which
figures the reader both as private individual and as a member of a wider public.
Even when Mann's narratives appear to have reached the most profound degree of
interiority, one may still discern the implied gesture to a broader readership. Mann's
fiction seems designed to cultivate a community of highly self-conscious readers.
As Russell A. Berman puts it: 'Even at his most impenetrable, Mann is involved
in an effort to produce a new reader who participates in a rational collective'.[141]
Mann certainly took his role as a public figure seriously and regarded it as his
mission to educate a generation of readers.[142] This applies to both his fiction and his
essays. Mann evidently regarded the two genres as complementary: 'Von deutscher
Republik' reflects upon the themes of *Der Zauberberg*, just as 'Deutschland und die

Deutschen' functions as a commentary on *Doktor Faustus*, and just as 'Geist und Kunst' and 'Lob der Vergänglichkeit' are important complements to, respectively, the early and the late *Krull*. In this chapter, however, I have concentrated on the fiction. In doing so, I have tried to show that the high degree of narratorial address in Mann's fiction proves that the interaction with a wider community was an essential aspect of his artistic project. In Mann's works, the reader is continually figured as an essential element of the narrative process. The ironic ambivalence of Mann's narrative implicitly invites the reader to join in the debate. Indeed, Mann's irony continually gestures to the reader; it cries out for exegesis. Mann himself was firmly of the opinion that he wrote in order to make contact with his public. In the short piece 'Politische Novelle', first published in 1928, he declared:

> Ein Kunstwerk ist nicht an sich und von vornherein gut oder schlecht; es ist keine Sache mit unleugbar feststehenden Eigenschaften, es ist vielmehr ein schwebendes Anerbieten an das Herz und den Geist des Menschen und erst zusammen damit wird es zur wirkenden Einheit, zum Wert. (x, 689)

In other words, Mann was aware that there was a fundamentally dialogic aspect to his work. At times, his works approach the intellectual beauty of the Socratic dialogue. We treasure Mann for this leisurely and teasing, affectionately cajoling, majestically ironic style. In the words of Marcel Reich-Ranicki: 'Was den Charme seiner [Thomas Manns] Prosa ausmacht [. . .]: [seine] makellose Gepflegtheit, seine elegante Umständlichkeit und Gelassenheit, seinen zärtlichen Spott und sein vielsagendes Augenzwinkern'.[143] This supple, highly gestural aspect of Mann's prose is one of his greatest achievements. It is both effortlessly sophisticated and generously humane. It is fitting that his work is bracketed by *Felix Krull*, because this novel, perhaps more than any other, is where Mann's gestural language and openness to the reader comes to the fore. It is a novel of all-too-human proportions, and as such it beautifully expresses the transition from the grandiosity of the nineteenth century to the self-problematizing temper of our own contemporary era. Yet that is not all. More important still is the way in which *Felix Krull* represents an attempt to mobilize art in order to produce a community of self-conscious readers. In all of his works, but especially in the greater works such as *Krull, Tod in Venedig, Zauberberg, Mario, Joseph*, and *Faustus*, Mann is trying to cultivate a sense of aesthetically motivated community among his readership. At the same time, he builds in an awareness of the limitations and dangers inherent in such a project. In other words, Mann both defends *and* criticizes the use of aesthetics as a means to cultivate and shape a community. Aesthetics cannot and should not replace politics, as Benjamin so rightly argued. What distinguishes Mann from Benjamin on this point is that Mann was still committed to art to the extent that he believed that it could have a civilizing effect, as an adjunct and complement to the political life of a nation. The fact that Mann only came to this insight in later life bears witness to the fact that it was the fruit of long and hard experience. Mann memorably expressed his conviction in 'Rede zur Gründung der Sektion für Dichtkunst der Preussischen Akademie der Künste' (1926):

> [Der Dichter] entdeckt, zuerst mit Unglauben, dann mit wachsender Freude und Rührung, daß seine Einsamkeit und Beziehungslosigkeit eine *Täuschung*

war, eine *romantische* Täuschung, wenn Sie wollen. Er entdeckt, [. . .] daß er für
viele sprach, als er für sich, nur von sich zu sprechen glaubte. Er entdeckt, [. . .]
daß Kunst- und Geisteswerke nicht nur sozial *genossen*, sondern auch schon
sozial *empfangen, konzipiert* werden [. . .] Mit einem Worte, er entdeckt [. . .] daß
Kunst [. . .] ein Organ des nationalen Lebens ist [. . .]. Der deutsche Dichter
entdeckt seine Sozialität. (x, 213)

As a writer, Thomas Mann never forgot his audience; he never forgot his representative function. He regarded his life's work as a contribution to the self-awareness
of his nation, and to the self-understanding of humanity in general. It is in this sense
that one is justified in talking about 'narrative community' in the works of Thomas
Mann.

Notes to Chapter 3

1. Mann, *Bekenntnisse des Hochstaplers Felix Krull. Buch der Kindheit* (Stuttgart, Berlin, and Leipzig: Deutsche Verlagsanstalt, 1923).
2. Gérard Genette classifies these two narrative time zones of past and present by using the terms 'homodiegetic' and 'extradiegetic'. The terms derive from 'diegesis', the word used by Aristotle in the *Poetics* to denote narrative. While the main body of prose fiction describes a 'homodiegetic' past, the framing device of first-person narrative is 'extradiegetic' because it is a moment when the fictional narrator pauses in order to address the reader directly. Genette, *Figures III* (Paris: Seuil, 1972), p. 239.
3. Sartre, *Qu'est-ce que la littérature?* [1948] (Paris: Gallimard, 1990), pp. 143–47 [English: Sartre, *What is Literature?*, trans. by Bernard Frechtman (London: Routledge, 1993), pp. 103–06].
4. Felix Krull gives his account while ironically withdrawing it; he is personal and intimate at the same time as being impersonal and distant. Like other modernist novels, this one retains the traditional conventions of realist narrative while, at the same time, questioning those conventions.
5. Guido Stein, *Thomas Mann. Bekenntnisse des Hochstaplers Felix Krull: Künstler und Komödiant* (Paderborn and Munich: Schöningh, 1984), p. 92. Incidentally, Stein's claim (pp. 92, 94) that the narrator is sitting in prison is incorrect. The novel itself makes it clear that the prison period predates the time of narration ('vormals im Zuchthause' (12)). Indeed, as is shown in a worknote of 1910 and a letter of 15 April 1955, Felix Krull is narrating his story while enjoying a comfortable retirement in his London residence. See Wysling, *Dokumente und Untersuchungen: Beiträge zur Thomas-Mann-Forschung*, TMS 3 (Bern: Francke, 1974), p. 149.
6. Werner Frizen, *Thomas Mann: Bekenntnisse des Hochstaplers Felix Krull* (Munich: Oldenbourg, 1988), p. 80.
7. Michael Beddow, 'Fiction and Meaning in Thomas Mann's *Felix Krull*', *Journal of European Studies*, 10 (1980), 77–92 (p. 80).
8. I will discuss the theme of interaction with the reader more fully in section III(iv) following.
9. Cf. Wysling, TMS 3, p. 150.
10. Krull says something similar at the beginning of Book II, Chapter 4: 'Geschwind schlüpfe ich über die ersten, verworrenen Tage hin, [. . .] denn nur ungern erinnere ich mich der kümmerlichen Rolle, die wir [. . .] zu spielen verurteilt waren' (336).
11. The most notable contributions to the problematic of genre in *Felix Krull* are the following: Oskar Seidlin, 'Picaresque Elements in Thomas Mann's Work', *Modern Language Quarterly*, 12 (1951), 183–200; Rainer Diederichs, *Strukturen des Schelmischen im modernen deutschen Roman: Eine Untersuchung an den Romanen von Thomas Mann 'Bekenntnisse des Hochstaplers Felix Krull' und Günter Grass 'Die Blechtrommel'* (Düsseldorf: Diederichs, 1971); Michael Beddow, 'Thomas Mann's "Bekenntnisse des Hochstaplers Felix Krull" and the Traditions of the Picaresque Novel and the Bildungsroman' (unpublished doctoral thesis, Cambridge, 1975); Karl L. Schneider, 'Thomas Manns "Felix Krull": Schelmenroman und Bildungsroman', in *Untersuchungen zur*

Literatur als Geschichte. Festschrift für Benno von Wiese, ed. by V. J. Günther and others (Berlin: Schmidt, 1973), pp. 545–58; Karl L. Schneider, 'Der Künstler als Schelm. Zum Verhältnis von Bildungsroman und Schelmenroman in Thomas Manns *Felix Krull*', *Philobiblon*, 20 (1976), 2–18. Michael Beddow's thesis is particularly good at unpacking the contradictions in *Krull* between Gesellschaftsroman and Bildungsroman. Recently, Friedrich Gaede explores *Krull* in the light of Grimmelshausen's *Simplicissimus*. Friedrich Gaede, 'Gewinn und Verlust des "Selbst". Simplicius und Krull', *TMJ* 18 (2005), 107–21.

12. This self-awareness about problems of genre is repeated a little later on: 'so täte ich Unrecht, wenn ich mich nicht den hauptsächlichsten Regeln und Maximen unterwürfe, von denen die Kunstverfasser, um Neugier und Spannung zu erzeugen, sich leiten lassen' (349).

13. Mann repeats this assessment of *Felix Krull* in the *Betrachtungen* when he claims that it contributes to 'der intellektualistischen Zersetzung des Deutschtums' (XII, 101). On this point, see also Wysling, TMS 5, p. 144 and Walter Berendsohn, 'Thomas Manns "Bekenntnisse des Hochstaplers Felix Krull". Struktur- und Stilstudien', *Stockholm Studies in Modern Philology*, n.s. 2 (1964), 57–115 (pp. 62–63).

14. 'die Politisierung [. . .], Radikalisierung Deutschlands [. . .] ist seine "Vermenschlichung" im westlich-politischen Sinne und seine Enthumanisierung im deutschen' (XI, 702).

15. HA VII, 552: 'Er wußte nicht, daß es die Art aller der Menschen sei, denen an ihrer innern Bildung viel gelegen ist, daß sie die äußeren Verhältnisse ganz und gar vernachlässigen'.

16. T. J. Reed, *The Classical Centre: Goethe and Weimar 1775–1832* (London: Croom Helm, 1980), p. 108.

17. Krull's responsible attitude to money is quite consistent with Mann's early work notes: 'Seine moralische Distanz zu den leichtsinnigen Leuten, die das Geld ohne Arbeit haben und in den Händen von Wucherern sind. Er ist solid in Geldsachen' (Wysling, TMS 5, p. 418).

18. It prepared the way for *Der Tod in Venedig*, which on one level is a sly critique of the aged Goethe's infatuation for Ulrike von Levetzow.

19. Mann acquired a copy during the early work on *Krull*, and his copy remains in the TMA. St Augustine, *Die Bekenntnisse des heiligen Augustin*, trans. by J. E. Poritzky (Munich: Müller, 1911).

20. Reed, *The Classical Centre*, p. 108: 'The religious metaphor [. . .] is apt in earnest for the goal of the German novel-hero, "Bildung", which though secularized has traces still of the religious preoccupations it derived from'.

21. The union is so successful that *The Oxford Companion to German Literature* (1986) is unsure whether to classify *Der Zauberberg* as a Bildungsroman or a Gesellschaftsroman. In fact it is both. The key to the picaresque element in the novel is the way in which the deceptively simple Hans Castorp bears a family resemblance to Grimmelshausen's Simplicius Simplicissimus.

22. The importance of 'Bildung' in the novel has been disputed in the secondary literature, but Felix Krull himself is happy to acknowledge Müller-Rosé, Schimmelpreester, Rozsa, and Kuckuck as mentors. When Krull asserts that 'Bildung wird nicht in stumpfer Fron und Plackerei gewonnen, sondern ist ein Geschenk der Freiheit und des äußeren Müßigganges' (339), his point is that 'Bildung' cannot be forced. Even so, the phrase 'äußeren Müßigganges' actually implies that while the body appears idle, the mind may well be active.

23. For a detailed discussion of Mann's technique of 'doppelte Optik', see section (vii) of this chapter.

24. The note deals primarily with Frank Wedekind's play *Musik* and that author's desire for popularity. Mann affirms that Wedekind's provocative play deserves a place in the literary tradition. See Wysling, TMS 5, pp. 41–42; and Scherrer and Wysling, TMS 1, p. 176.

25. Most of the discussion of *Felix Krull* as 'Schelmenroman' centres on the later section of the novel, since Mann only explicitly linked the two for the first time in 1947; see letter to Agnes Meyer, 10 October 1947 (DüD 1, pp. 320–21). It is also true that Oskar Seidlin's 1951 essay on the picaresque in *Felix Krull* was highly influential on the second phase of the novel; see letter to Oskar Seidlin, 10 October 1951 (DüD 1, pp. 328–29). Book III even comments upon its own picaresque origins: Felix Krull dreams that he is mounted on the skeleton of a tapir, a sort of primeval ass (549). Even so, the 'Schelmenroman' was already in place as a category of *Felix Krull* as early as 1908, as N 51 for 'Geist und Kunst' shows.

26. The title may also be an allusion to one of the key texts of German romanticism, Schlegel's *Lucinde*, whose subtitle is 'Bekenntnis eines Ungeschickten'.

27. See in particular chapters 5–8 in Book I and chapters 2–6 in Book II.

28. Wolfgang Iser, *Der Akt des Lesens: Theorie ästhetischer Wirkung* (Munich: Fink, 1976), pp. 307–15 [English: Iser, *The Act of Reading: A Theory of Aesthetic Response* (Baltimore: Johns Hopkins, 1994), pp. 198–203].

29. *Felix Krull* represents a watershed in Mann's ability to portray a number of world-views or Welt-anschauungen held in suspension. While in *Felix Krull* this occurs through genre, in *Der Zauberberg* this occurs through character, through the different mentors encountered by Hans Castorp during his stay at the Berghof. We also witness a kind of perspectivism in *Doktor Faustus*, where the 'totalizing' interpretations of Leverkühn and Zeitblom — their tendency to see everything in terms of a higher symptomatology — is put into question by the juxtapositions of the narrative. Of course, another word for perspectivism is irony: the creative juxtaposition of different views. One might say that Thomas Mann's irony is inherently democratic because it allows other views to be heard.

30. Letter to Paul Amann, 3 August 1915 (A 30; DüD 1, 305).

31. Wysling, TMS 5, p. 215. For Wysling, the turn towards Goethe is a turn away from the 'Dreigestirn' of Mann's youth (from Wagner, Schopenhauer, and Nietzsche).

32. Letter of 26 August 1909 to Walter Opitz (Br 1, 78): 'Aber ob es [Wagner] noch Zukunft hat? Ob es als Stimmung, Tendenz, Geschmack nicht schon etwas Historisches ist? Auf die jungen Welt hat Walt Whitman, glaube ich, mehr Einfluß, als er. . .'.

33. Letter of 14 September 1911 to Julius Bab (Br 1, 91); see also Wysling, TMS 5, p. 215.

34. Wysling, TMS 5, p. 176: 'Es ist schwer auszumachen, inwieweit solche Anlehnung Bekenntnis zu Goethe, inwieweit sie Anmaßung, inwieweit sie Verulkung ist. Wird Goethe geliebt, wird er verspottet, wird er verhaßt? [. . .] Daß in Thomas Mann selbst um 1910 alle diese Möglichkeiten angelegt waren, wird sich zeigen'.

35. Wysling, TMS 5, pp. 222–23.

36. Wysling, TMS 5, p.286; cf. also Herwig, TMS 32, p. 243.

37. Wysling, TMS 5, pp. 288–99.

38. Letters of 11 March 1952 to Emil Preetorius and 20 March 1952 to Karl Kerényi (Br III 246, 250; DüD 1, 337–38).

39. Christian Grawe, 'Die Sprache in Goethes *Dichtung und Wahrheit* gesehen durch Thomas Manns *Die Bekenntnisse des Hochstaplers Felix Krull*', in Christian Grawe, *Sprache im Prosawerk. Beispiele von Goethe, Fontane, Bergengruen, Kleist und Johnson* (Bonn: Grundmann, 1974), pp. 9–24.

40. Thomas Sprecher, *Felix Krull und Goethe. Thomas Manns 'Bekenntnisse' als Parodie auf 'Dichtung und Wahrheit'* (Bern: Peter Lang, 1985).

41. Sprecher, *Felix Krull und Goethe*, p. 49.

42. Sprecher, *Felix Krull und Goethe*, p. 62.

43. Sprecher, *Felix Krull und Goethe*, p. 71.

44. Sprecher, *Felix Krull und Goethe*, pp. 74–75.

45. Sprecher, *Felix Krull und Goethe*, pp. 79–80.

46. Stein, *Thomas Mann*, p. 88.

47. It is interesting to note that Walter Benjamin uses a related image in his famous essay on narration, 'Der Erzähler': 'Der Erzähler — das ist der Mann, der den Docht seines Lebens an der sanften Flamme seiner Erzählung sich vollkommen könnte verzehren lassen' (GS 2.2, 464–65).

48. Georges Manolescu, *Der Mann mit dem blauen Gehrock: Memoiren eines Hochstaplers* (Frankfurt a.M.: Fischer, 1987), pp. 80, 155. Cf. Wysling, TMS 5, p. 417.

49. Wysling, TMS 5, p. 417.

50. A further source for the butterfly motif may well be the article by Anna Pavlova which forms part of the dossier for *Felix Krull*, 'Aus meinem Leben', pp. 1128–33 [TMA: Mat. 3/25–26, 43–44]. In her memoir, Pavlova compares herself to a butterfly: 'Diese Nacht träumte ich mein Leben als Ballerina und wie ich, gleich einem Falter, nach der Musik Tschaikowskys tanzen würde' (p. 1129). She also likens happiness to a butterfly: 'Das Glück ist ein Schmetterling, der einen Augenblick entzückt und dann weiterfliegt' (p. 1133).

51. Wysling, TMS 5, pp. 21–23. I have already discussed this in my analysis of the Müller-Rosé episode.

52. Sabine Appel, *Naivität und Lebenskunst: Die Idee der Synthese von Leben und Geist in Thomas Manns Hochstapler-Memoiren* (Frankfurt a.M.: Peter Lang, 1995), p. 16: 'Das Vergessen bildet bei Nietzsche die Voraussetzung aller plastischen Kraft der Gestaltung und Erneuerung, die Voraussetzung zu allem Handeln'.

53. Cf. Appel, *Naivität*, p. 121.

54. Appel, *Naivität*, p. 139: 'die Idee des zwischen Naivität und Reflexion vermittelnden und heiter/harmonischen Künstlertums'.

55. J. P. Stern, 'Living in the Metaphor of Fiction', *Comparative Criticism*, 1 (1979), 14: 'In the end, the philosophy of Thomas Mann's con man is a thing more modest than the grand aesthetic justification of the world and being which Nietzsche had envisaged. It is, and it is acknowledged to be, an artifact, part of a larger, non-aesthetic world.'

56. (XII, 25): 'In meinem Falle wurde das Erlebnis der Selbstverneinung des Geistes zugunsten des Lebens zur Ironie, — einer sittlichen Haltung [. . .] wobei unter dem 'Leben', ganz wie beim Renaissance-Ästhetizismus, nur in einer anderen, leiseren und verschlagenen Gefühlsnüance, die Liebenswürdigkeit, das Glück, die Kraft, die Anmut, die angenehme Normalität der Geistlosigkeit, Ungeistigkeit verstanden wird.'

57. 'Erstens war ich auf eine grillenhafte Manier verfallen, die menschliche Willenskraft, diese geheimnisvolle und oft fast übernatürlicher Wirkungen fähige Macht, an mir zu üben und zu studieren' (274).

58. 'Was ich da sage, ist bezeichnend für meine Natur, die von jeher im tiefsten Grunde leidend und pflegebedürftig war, so daß alles, was mein Leben an tätiger Wirksamkeit aufweist, als ein Produkt der Selbstüberwindung, ja als eine sittliche Leistung von hohem Range zu würdigen ist. (299)'

59. HA XII, 304. The Andromache episode might allude to an interview in Mann's dossier in which the ballerina Anna Pavlova confesses that she has sacrificed the pleasures of a normal life to her art: 'Warum ich nicht heirate? Nach meiner Meinung muß die wahre Künstlerin sich ganz ihrer Kunst opfern. Ich kann nicht das Leben führen, das die meisten Frauen ersehnen [. . .] nicht nach einem Leben voll friedlichen Glückes am häuslichen Herd verlangen wie andere Frauen. ('Aus meinem Leben', p. 1133)'

60. 'Mochte doch die persönliche Verwandlung, die Nietzsche in mir erfuhr, Verbürgerlichung bedeuten. Diese Verwandlung schien mir und scheint mir noch heute tiefer und verschlagener als aller heroisch-ästhetische Rausch, den Nietzsche sonst wohl entfachte' (XIII, 143)

61. On this point, see Eckhard Heftrich, 'Der unvollendbare *Krull* — Die Krise der Selbstparodie', *TMJ* 18 (2005), 91–106.

62. 'Es ist bemerkenswert, daß noch heute im Bewußtsein vieler Epileptiker etwas von der mystisch-religiösen Auffassung lebendig scheint, die das Altertum von dieser Nervenkrankheit hegte.' (369)

63. 'Ich habe stets den Aufenthalt an Badeorten geliebt [. . .] der Anblick wohlgeborener und gepflegter Menschen auf den Sportplätzen und in den Kurgärten entspricht meinen tiefsten Wünschen' (280).

64. Eric Wilson, 'Felix Krull: Thomas Mann's Comic Artist' (unpublished doctoral thesis, Stanford University, 1966), p. 270.

65. T. J. Reed, *Thomas Mann: The Uses of Tradition*, 2nd edn (Oxford: Oxford University Press, 1996), p. 417: 'His techniques turned out to have been a way of keeping up appearances, "die Dehors wahren", in the Buddenbrook phrase'.

66. Wysling, TMS 5, p. 64.

67. Wysling (in Scherrer and Wysling, TMS 1, p. 247) describes Felix Krull's narrative style as 'das gezielte Fehlen des richtigen Ausdrucks, mit dem der Autor Krulls Unbildung entlarvt; jenes Zu-hoch-Greifen im Ton, dem immer wieder ein jähes Absacken in die plumpe Handgreiflichkeit folgt; die sonderbare Mischung von Direktheit und Umschreibung, von Plattheit und preziösem Schnörkel.' Cf. Sprecher, *Felix Krull und Goethe*, pp. 49–50; Stein, *Thomas Mann*, pp. 82–84.

68. Letter to Paul Amann, 3 August 1915 (Br A, 30; DüD 1, 305).

69. Other related adjectives include 'vollendetste' (266, 574), 'ausgezeichnet' (285, 430), 'vollends' (441), and 'vollbracht' (455, 456). Related nouns include 'Vollendung' (287, 439, 458), 'Vorzüglichkeit' (310) and 'Vortrefflichkeit' (636). There is also the verb 'vollenden' (318, 411, 437).

70. Related words are 'äußerst' (272, 349, 350, 369, 480, 485, 582, 636 (twice), 639, 645, 654, 656, 657), 'außergewöhnlich' (627, 649), 'nicht [. . .] durchschnittsmäßig' (362), 'widernatürlich' (366), 'übernormale' (370), 'Unvergleichlichkeit' (309), and 'Äüßerste' (321, 352, 636 (twice), 641).

71. Susan Sontag, 'Notes on "Camp" ', in A Susan Sontag Reader, intro. by Elizabeth Hardwick (New York: Farrar, Straus, Giroux, 1982), pp. 105–19.

72. 'Deine Schrift, mein guter Loulou, ließ immer zu wünschen übrig und ist nach wie vor nicht ohne Maniertheit, aber Dein Stil hat gegen früher entschieden an Gepflegtheit und angenehmer Politur gewonnen' (622).

73. See Sprecher, Felix Krull und Goethe, p. 53: 'Schnörkelwolken'; Stein, Thomas Mann, p. 90: 'barocke Schnörkel'.

74. The word also appears in various compounds such as 'Traumgüter' (310), 'Liebesträume' (346 (twice)); traumähnlich' (322); 'Traumgefühl' (357); 'traumverloren' (476); 'Kindertraum' (636). We also find related words such as 'Träumereien' (306); 'Träumer' (315, 528), 'Traumhaftigkeit' (381) and 'traumhaft' (349). Felix Krull does actually have a dream, in which he features as Don Quixote riding on a skeletal tapir (549–50).

75. Other references to fantasy include 'Phantasie' (293), 'Phantasiesteine' (343), 'Phantastischen' (456, 513 (twice)), 'phantasieweise' (522), 'phantastique' (619), 'Phantastereien' (619) and 'Phantastik' (620).

76. Letter to Hermann Stresau of 3 October 1954 (DüD I, 365).

77. Stein, Thomas Mann, p. 90.

78. Donald F. Nelson, 'Stylistic Unity and Change in Thomas Mann's Felix Krull: A Study of Style as the Reflection of Perception and Attitude' (unpublished doctoral thesis, University of Minnesota, 1966), pp. 196–97.

79. Beddow, 'Fiction and Meaning', p. 90.

80. The beautiful pair of siblings is definitely borrowed from Fontane; see section I(v) of this work.

81. Scherrer and Wysling, TMS I, p. 239.

82. Mann completed Book III of Krull in April 1954, while 'Noch einmal der alte Fontane' was published on 2 February 1954.

83. Nelson, 'Stylistic Unity and Change', pp. 198–203.

84. Eva Schiffer, 'Changes in an Episode. A Note on Felix Krull', Modern Language Quarterly, 24 (1963), 257–62.

85. Cf. Wysling, 'Archivalisches Gewühle', in Scherrer and Wysling, TMS I, pp. 234–57.

86. Anthony W. Riley, 'Die Erzählkunst im Alterswerk von Thomas Mann mit besonderer Berücksichtigung der Bekenntnisse des Hochstaplers Felix Krull' (unpublished doctoral thesis, Universität zu Tübingen, 1958), pp. 197–99; Eric Downing, Artificial I's: The Self as Artwork in Ovid, Kierkegaard, and Thomas Mann (Tübingen: Niemeyer, 1993), pp. 184–95.

87. Karl-Martin Kühner, 'Wer liest den Roman? Zur Interpretation der Leserfigur in Thomas Manns Hochstapler-Roman', in Hommage à Maurice Marache (Paris: Les Belles Lettres, 1972), pp. 287–301.

88. For my analysis of this sentence, see the beginning of this chapter.

89. Mann, Bekenntnisse des Hochstaplers Felix Krull: Buch der Kindheit (Stuttgart, Berlin, and Leipzig: Deutsche Verlagsanstalt, 1923).

90. The two public readings in question occurred in Berlin in autumn 1916 and in Munich on 5 October 1916. In both cases, Mann ends the introduction to his reading from Krull with an implicit demand for positive feedback from the audience. The Berlin preamble ends: 'Ich beginne zu lesen . . . und bin neugierig, ob Sie (und ich) den Eindruck haben werden, daß es sich lohnen würde, das vor Jahren begonnene Werk in Zukunft einmal fort- und zu Ende zu führen' (XI, 703). And in Munich, Mann states: '[Ich bin] neugierig, ob Sie und ich den Eindruck haben werden, daß es sich lohnen würde, das wunderliche Unternehmen zu Ende zu führen' (DüD I, 307).

91. Sartre, 'Qu'est-ce que la littérature?', p. 53: 'la création ne peut trouver son achèvement que dans la lecture [. . .] tout ouvrage littéraire est un appel [. . .] au lecteur'.

92. Iser, *Der Akt des Lesens*, p. 60: 'Der implizite Leser [besitzt] keine reale Existenz; denn er verkörpert die Gesamtheit der Vororientierungen, die ein fiktionaler Text seinen möglichen Lesern als Rezeptionsbedingungen anbietet. Folglich ist der implizite Leser nicht in einem empirischen Substrat verankert, sondern in der Struktur der Texte selbst fundiert.'

93. Iser, *Der Akt des Lesens*, p. 61.

94. Hans Robert Jauss, *Ästhetische Erfahrung und literarische Hermeneutik 1* (Munich: Fink, 1977), p. 220.

95. Jauss, *Ästhetische Erfahrung*, p. 250: ' Unter ironischer Identifikation soll eine Ebene ästhetischer Rezeption verstanden werden, auf der dem Zuschauer oder Leser eine erwartbare Identifikation nur vorgezeichnet wird, um sie hernach zu ironisieren oder überhaupt zu verweigern. Solche Verfahren der ironisierten Identifikation und der Illusionszerstörung dienen dazu, den Rezipienten aus seiner unreflektierten Zuwendung zum ästhetischen Gegenstand zu reißen, um seine ästhetische und moralische Reflexion hervorzurufen.'

96. Stein, *Thomas Mann*, p. 93: 'Welcher Leser ist der wahre in Felix Krulls Vorstellung, der strenge Zensor oder der sensationslüsterne Leser — oder vielleicht beide?'.

97. This is a hallmark of Mann's fiction, as Michael Minden has pointed out. See Minden, 'Mann's Narrative Techniques', in *The Cambridge Companion to Thomas Mann*, ed. by Ritchie Robertson (Cambridge: Cambridge University Press, 2002), 43–63 (p. 60).

98. The structure is followed precisely with two slight alterations: Chapter 6 of Book I contains an extra paragraph which serves to introduce the next chapter; Chapter 3 of Book III does not begin with an address to the reader.

99. Kühner, 'Wer liest den Roman?', p. 291.

100. Kühner, 'Wer liest den Roman?', p. 290.

101. On this rare occasion when Krull expresses some disdain for the public at large, he makes sure to enlist the reader's complicity by using the identificatory pronoun 'man'. The reader is thereby excluded from Krull's criticism of 'die Gunst eines Publikums, welches man sich durch so krasse Kunsterzeugnisse nicht übersättigt und abgestumpft genug denken kann' (322).

102. Originally published in 1937, this chapter was revised considerably for the edition of 1954, as Eva Schiffer has shown. Schiffer, 'Changes in an Episode', pp. 257–62.

103. Kühner, 'Wer liest den Roman?', p. 294.

104. We know that the implied reader here is male, since Krull calls him a 'Gentleman' (346).

105. In this respect, I would reject Karl-Martin Kühner's claim that the figure of the reader is sober ('nüchtern'; Kühner, 'Wer liest den Roman?', p. 297). In this passage, the reader (as constituted by the text) has abandoned his moral scruples and become Krull's accomplice, egging him on.

106. Kühner, 'Wer liest den Roman?', pp. 296–99.

107. Riley, 'Die Erzählkunst im Alterswerk', pp. 197–99. Other instances cited by Riley are: 'zur Beruhigung des Lesers' (386), 'das Lächeln des Lesers' (393), and 'Mit Beifall und Beruhigung wird der Leser von diesem Verhalten Kenntnis nehmen' (452).

108. Cf. also Wysling, TMS 5, p. 483, and Downing, *Artificial I's*, p. 128.

109. 'bei unwillkommenen Vorschlägen, die meiner Jugend — nicht zur Überraschung des in der vielfältigen Welt der Gefühle erfahrenen Lesers — [. . .] von gewisser männlicher Seite unterbreitet wurden' (373).

110. I will discuss the longest sentence in the novel, which is a lavish description of a hotel room (552–53), in section III(vi) below.

111. The *Augenspiel* motif also occurs later in the novel in the description of Zaza (494–95).

112. Berendsohn, 'Thomas Manns "Bekenntnisse"', p. 88.

113. Barthes, 'L'effet de réel' [1968] (OC II, pp. 479–84).

114. Martin Swales, *Epochenbuch Realismus* (Berlin: ErichSchmidt, 1997), pp. 51–53.

115. Russell Berman, *The Rise of the Modern German Novel: Crisis and Charisma* (Cambridge, MA: Harvard University Press, 1986), pp. 284–85.

116. One critic who has drawn attention to the highly determined, painterly realism of *Krull* is Viktor Lange. Cf. Viktor Lange, 'Betrachtungen zur Thematik von "Felix Krull"', in Viktor

Lange, *Illyrische Betrachtungen: Essays und Aufsätze aus 30 Jahren* (Bern: Peter Lang, 1989), pp. 365–79 (p. 368).

117. Wysling, TMS 5, pp. 395, 476–81. For a selection of notes from the 'Reisen' dossier, see pp. 428–44

118. Flaubert, *Madame Bovary* (Paris: Gallimard, 1972), pp. 258–59: 'Souvent, du haut d'une montagne, ils apercevaient tout à coup quelque cité splendide avec des dômes, des ponts, des navires, des forêts de citronniers et des cathédrales de marbre blanc, dont les clochers aigus portaient des nids de cigognes. [. . .] Et puis ils arrivaient, un soir, dans un village de pêcheurs, où des filets bruns séchaient au vent le long de la falaise et des cabanes. C'est là qu'ils s'arrêteraient pour vivre.'

119. Wysling, TMS 5, p. 409.

120. Sprecher, *Felix Krull und Goethe*, pp. 57–60; cf. Stein, *Thomas Mann*, pp. 88–89, 91.

121. Cf. Mann's dossier 'Kur- und Lustorte' in the TMA. For a description, see Wysling, TMS 5, p. 476.

122. Handke, *Die Stunde der wahren Empfindung* (Frankfurt a.M.: Suhrkamp, 1975), p. 64.

123. Handke, *Die Stunde*, p. 23: 'Er kam sich vor wie der Gefangene von Disneyland'.

124. Siegfried Kracauer, *Das Ornament der Masse* (Frankfurt a.M.: Suhrkamp, 1977), pp. 40–49.

125. Kracauer, *Das Ornament*, p. 49.

126. 'Die deutsche Gesandtschaft in Kopenhagen', *Die Woche*, 13. 27, 8 July 1911, pp. 1137–41 (p. 1138). TMA: Mat. 3/278–80, Dossier: 'Intérieurs'.

127. Every artwork implies an audience, even those works created for the select few; even those works which appear to seek oblivion, such as Kafka's.

128. Helmut Koopmann, *Die Entwicklung des 'intellektualen Romans' bei Thomas Mann. Untersuchungen zur Struktur von 'Buddenbrooks', 'Königliche Hoheit' und 'Der Zauberberg'* (Bonn: Bouvier, 1962), pp. 28–36.

129. Eberhard Lämmert, 'Doppelte Optik. Über die Erzählkunst des frühen Thomas Mann', in *Literatur, Sprache, Gesellschaft*, Dialog Schule-Wissenschaft, Deutsche Sprache und Literatur 3, ed. by Karl Rüdinger (Munich: Bayerischer Schulbuch-Verlag, 1970), pp. 50–72.

130. 'Coenakel' means an intellectual elite; the term derives from the group 'le Cénacle' in Balzac's novel *Illusions perdues*. Honoré de Balzac, *Illusions perdues* (Paris: Flammarion, 1990), pp. 238–44.

131. Cf. Kurzke, *Thomas Mann*, p. 115.

132. Minden, 'Mann's Narrative Techniques', p. 60.

133. Jochen Vogt, *Thomas Mann: 'Buddenbrooks'* (Munich: Fink, 1983), p. 13. Vogt also offers a close reading of Part I of the novel, pp. 13–28.

134. The initiation of the reader also takes place via the references to Thomas's yellowish teeth, Christian's indigestion, and the fate of the Ratenkamps; these details announce the leitmotifs of illness and decline.

135. 'Ja, gewiß, der deutsche Leser erkannte sich wieder in dem schlichten, aber "verschmitzten" Helden des Romans; er konnte und mochte ihn folgen' (XI, 134).

136. Wolfgang Freese, 'Thomas Mann und sein Leser. Zum Verhältnis von Antifaschismus und Leseerwartung in *Mario und der Zauberer*', *Deutsche Vierteljahrsschrift*, 51 (1977), 659–75. While Freese's article makes some interesting points, I strongly disagree with his basic argument, which defends an apolitical interpretation of *Mario*, claiming that such a reading would be more in line with the expectations of Mann's loyal readership in 1930. This fails to take into account the political aspect of Mann's publications from mid-1920s onwards, a change which Mann's readers would have been well aware of. Freese also erroneously claims that the narrator of *Mario* uses the 'du' form to address the reader (p. 669).

137. Alan Bance, 'The Narrator in Thomas Mann's *Mario und der Zauberer*', MLR 82 (1987), 382–98. While Bance's analysis is brilliant, I must take exception to his claim that aesthetics and morality are completely unrelated (p. 397). For Thomas Mann, it seems that aesthetics, morality, and politics *are* related spheres of human endeavour. I have tried to show this in my conclusion to Chapter II.

138. Bance, 'The Narrator', p. 398.

139. Berman, *Rise of the Modern German Novel*, pp. 283–84.

140. Martin Swales, 'The Over-representations of History? Reflections on Thomas Mann's *Doktor Faustus*', in *Representing the German Nation: History and Identity in Twentieth-Century Germany*, ed.

by Mary Fulbrook and Martin Swales (Manchester: Manchester University Press, 2000), pp. 77–90 (p. 83).

141. Berman, *Rise of the Modern German Novel*, p. 262. In my view, Berman's study of Mann relies rather too heavily upon the cultural criticism of Theodor Adorno, who adopts a theoretical position which Mann did not share. Nevertheless, Berman gives an excellent account of the way in which, for Mann, the individual and society are profoundly and intimately linked: 'Mann's fiction approaches the issue of the collective through a constant inversion of the analysis of the individual. [. . .] the contradictory structure of the individual is presented implicitly as the corollary to the social totality' (p. 263). Berman's argument is borne out by the following assertion of Mann's: 'In mir lebt der Glaube, daß ich nur von mir zu erzählen brauche, um auch der Zeit, der Allgemeinheit die Zunge zu lösen, und ohne diesen Glauben könnte ich mich der Mühen des Produzierens entschlagen' (XI, 571)

142. In terms of intellectual history, Mann marks an important phase in the reception of Nietzsche. He sought to rescue Nietzsche from his fascist (and aestheticist) admirers by emphasizing Nietzsche's qualities as a moralist and an ironist. Furthermore, from the early 1920s onwards, Mann was a highly influential advocate of German democracy.

143. Reich-Ranicki, *Die Wahrheit über Thomas Mann*, FAZ, 11 March 1978.

CONCLUSION

The main argument of this book is that, in *Felix Krull*, art and aesthetics are shown to be central to the life of the mind and to the life of society. The Müller-Rosé episode offers a paradigm of how art works: *not* as an imposed illusion, but as a mutually agreed, deliberate pretence.[1] The crucial point of this episode is that art is not a deception, but an imaginative exchange which relies upon an intersubjective arrangement. Müller-Rosé requires the 'stillschweigende[s] Einverständnis' (294) of his audience in order to succeed. Mann, like Coleridge, is advocating a willing suspension of disbelief,[2] in order that the aesthetic experience may take place. The climax of the Müller-Rosé episode is the address to the reader: 'wann zeigt der Glühwurm sich in seiner wahren Gestalt, [. . .]? Hüte dich, darüber zu entscheiden!' (294). This is an appeal to the reader to transcend the distinction between Müller-Rosé's on-stage persona and his off-stage ugliness. The reader is requested momentarily to suspend his or her judgement, and, for the sake of the experience, to adopt an attitude of mind which is midway between belief and disbelief.[3] According to Catherine Gallagher, this encounter between belief and disbelief is an important feature of the European novel as it develops in the eighteenth century. By focusing upon deceptions of various kinds, novels such as Fielding's *Joseph Andrews* and Diderot's *La Religieuse* pose questions of verisimilitude. For Gallagher, reading fiction requires a 'cognitive provisionality', defined as 'a competence in inverting contingent and temporary credit'.[4] In *Felix Krull*, then, Mann appears to be exploring the nature of the novel, and indeed of art itself, as an experiential category poised between fictionality and fact. We should not dismiss art as illusion, nor should we accept it as ultimate truth. It is a domain of human possibility, a mutually agreed performance, an essential part of what makes us human.

As a character, Felix Krull's foremost concern is to be free, to present an appearance of freedom in everything he does. As he puts it at the end of the *Musterungsszene*: 'so beruhte es [mein Leben] doch in erster Linie auf der Vor- und Grundbedingung der Freiheit' (372). Freedom means something very specific for Krull; it means being able to pursue his ideal of beauty, his 'Bedürfnis [. . .] nach schöner Form' (593). And so Krull associates beauty with freedom: 'Die Schönheit ist Freigut des Herzens' (591). In this, he distantly echoes Schiller, who defined beauty in his *Kallias* letters as 'Freiheit in der Erscheinung'.[5] In fact, there is something utopian about the character of Krull which recalls the argument of Schiller's famous 1795 treatise on aesthetics, *Über die ästhetische Erziehung des Menschen in einer Reihe von Briefen*. Krull's love of play appears justified when we consider Schiller's claim that: 'der Mensch [. . .] *ist nur da ganz Mensch, wo er spielt*' (NA 20, 359). Krull's lightness is the lightness of a person in whom duty and inclination coincide. This is because Krull considers it his foremost moral duty to be beautiful, to delight the world: 'Aus eingeborener Rücksicht auf die Welt, die mich erwartete, habe ich im Werden acht darauf gegeben, daß ich ihr Auge nicht kränkte. Das ist alles. Ich möchte es eine Sache der Selbstdisziplin nennen' (591). Krull is directed towards beauty by both inclination and duty, by both feeling and necessity. According to Schiller, when these two antitheses coincide, necessity loses its heavy seriousness and acquires lightness: 'indem es mit der Empfindung zusammentrifft, legt das Nothwendige den [Ernst] ab, weil es *leicht* wird' (NA 20, 357). No wonder, then, that Krull is light-hearted, since he has found his true calling, one in which duty becomes pleasure. And Krull himself approaches Schiller's definition of beauty in the fifteenth letter, since he is most definitely a 'lebende Gestalt' (NA 20, 355). Such speculations about the affinities between *Felix Krull* and Schiller's aesthetics might appear misconstrued, were it not for the fact that Thomas Mann's final essay, written between September 1954 and January 1955 (only a few months after the completion of Book III of *Krull* in April 1954), is an affectionate salute to Schiller.[6] Only recently have Thomas Mann critics begun to wake up to the significance of Schiller for our understanding of *Krull*: Christian Benne links the key Krullian concept of 'Sympathie' to Schiller's ode 'An die Freude',[7] and Karin Tebben sees traces of Schiller's letters *Über die ästhetische Erziehung des Menschen* in Krull's great speech to Zouzou.[8] Further evidence is offered by a letter of 17 October 1954 to Fritz Martini, which suggests that Mann himself associated *Krull* with Schiller:

> Schiller meinte, auch das Frivole habe in der Kunst seine Berechtigung, wenn die Form ihm zu Hilfe komme, — und dieser moderne Hermes ist im Grunde garnicht frivol, sondern hat eine gewisse komisch-versöhnende Weltandacht — so scheint mir.[9]

According to Schiller, aesthetics gives us a sense of the importance of freedom. Once we know this, we will respect the freedom of other people and things.[10] Now, the narrative technique of Mann's *Felix Krull* appears to be designed in order to provoke an attitude of freedom in the reader. As unreliable narrator, Krull continually asks for our assent, reminding us that we are free to grant it, or to withhold it, as we please. The narrative fireworks delight us but they also keep us cognitively alert. And so Mann's prose pays a humorous tribute to Schiller's aesthetics, showing how art can give us an education in freedom, and a sense of our own social being.

For all its levity, *Felix Krull* is a novel which endows art with great significance. It portrays art as an arbiter of the life of the mind and as being essential to the coherence of society. Because it accords supreme importance to art, it is possible to link *Felix Krull* to the great tradition of German philosophical aesthetics. The German aesthetic tradition has become justifiably famous, because it treats aesthetics with an intensity and a differentiation that is without parallel in European intellectual history. Kant, Schiller, Hegel, Schopenhauer, Nietzsche, and Walter Benjamin all made major contributions to aesthetics in the belief that aesthetics *mattered*, that art was a fundamental manifestation of human dignity. This is a tradition which has, if anything, gained in importance with the secularization of modern society. The Nietzsche who proclaimed the death of God also proclaimed that the world would only ever be justified as an aesthetic phenomenon. *Felix Krull* stands firmly in this tradition.

Yet even so, one problem remains: if *Felix Krull* really was intended as a justification of art, then why did Thomas Mann choose to make his protagonist a confidence man? Why did he not choose a more dignified figure? The narrator of *Krull* is not a major creative artist (and Thomas Mann does venture into that territory with Goethe and Adrian Leverkühn), nor is he an obviously 'civic' artist like an architect. He is a confidence trickster, albeit one who prefers to delight rather than to deceive. Why did Mann choose to express his justification of art through such a figure? The simple answer is that *Felix Krull* represents a lightening of the German aesthetic tradition, a relaxation from the high strenuousness of the nineteenth century.[11] Mann himself makes this clear in 'On Myself' (1940) when he remarks: 'Auf jeden Fall mag es [*Felix Krull*] das Persönlichste gewesen sein, denn es gestaltet mein Verhältnis zur *Tradition*, das zugleich liebevoll und auflösend ist' (XIII, 147; cf. XI, 122–23; Mann's italics). The fact that Felix Krull is a lovable rogue imparts a lightness and gaiety to the novel. It obliges us to realize that the novel is profound *because of* — and not in spite of — its good humour. Above all, the presence of the confidence trickster gives a vivacity to the reading experience. The virtuosic narrative voice keeps readers on their toes. We find ourselves reflecting on the claims that Felix Krull makes; we find ourselves assenting to and dissenting from his account. And in that interplay of assent and dissent is located a space for our cognitive freedom. *Felix Krull* is no monolithic validation of the place of art in society. Rather, the lightness, the sheer disreputability of the central figure continually problematizes the grand philosophical issues. Yet if we are persuaded to collude, to suspend disbelief, we do so with a sense of the profundity of all this lightness, of the richness of all this semblance. *Felix Krull* has in the past been regarded by some critics as lightweight, and by others as a work of profound seriousness. Both camps are right; but the crucial point is — and this has not always been recognized — that its profundity resides in its lightness.

Notes to the Conclusion

1. Felix Krull requires his audience to play along with him in order that they can enjoy what he calls (in Book I, Chapter 6) the 'Genuss[e] einer *vereinbarten* Illusion' (300, my italics). But if an illusion is *agreed*, then it is a *pretence*, not an illusion. Krull's art relies upon *agreed conventions*.
2. Samuel Taylor Coleridge, *Biographia Literaria* (London: Everyman, 1965), ch. 14, p.169.
3. Schiller seems to have had something remarkably similar in mind in his poem 'Die Kraniche des Ibycus', where he describes the attitude of a theatre audience in ancient Greece. The audience seems to hover between an attitude of belief and disbelief: 'Und zwischen Trug und Wahrheit schwebet | Noch zweifelnd jede Brust und bebet' (NA I, 389). Such an attitude implies the simultaneous working of the emotional *and* critical faculties, and therefore implies a degree of harmony within the individual. For this reference I am indebted to a recent article by Kevin Hilliard, '"Nicht in Person sondern durch einen Repräsentanten": Problematik der Repräsentation bei Schiller', in *Schiller: National Poet — Poet of Nations: A Birmingham Symposium*, Amsterdamer Beiträge zur neueren Germanistik, 61, ed. by Nicholas Martin (Amsterdam: Rodopi, 2006), pp. 89–105.
4. Catherine Gallagher, 'The Rise of Fictionality', in *The Novel: Volume I: History, Geography and Culture*, ed. by Franco Moretti (Princeton and Oxford: Princeton University Press, 2006), pp. 336–63; p. 347.

5. Schiller, letter of 8 February 1793 to Körner: 'Schönheit ist also nichts anders als Freiheit in der Erscheinung' (NA 26, 183).

6. For a detailed analysis of Mann's sources for 'Versuch über Schiller', see Hans-Joachim Sandberg, *Thomas Manns Schiller-Studien: Eine quellenkritische Untersuchung* (Oslo: Universitets forlaget, 1965).

7. Christian Benne, '"An die Freude"? Miszelle zum *Felix Krull* oder Thomas Manns Schillervariationen', *TMJ* 18 (2005), 277–93 (p. 285).

8. Karin Tebben, '"Du entkleidest mich, kühner Knecht?". Felix Krull und die Frauen', *TMJ* 18 (2005), 51–70 (p. 68).

9. DüD I, p. 368; Br III, 360.

10. Schiller, *Über die ästhetische Erziehung*, letter 27: 'Kein Vorzug, keine Alleinherrschaft wird geduldet, soweit der Geschmack regiert' (NA 20, 411). And does not Schiller, in the Kallias letter of 23 February 1793, partially anticipate the Krullian notion of 'Allsympathie' when he states that aesthetic judgement endows every natural organism with equal rights? As Schiller puts it: 'In der ästhetischen Welt ist jedes Naturwesen ein freier Bürger, der mit dem Edelsten gleiche Rechte hat' (NA 26, 212).

11. Cf. J. P. Stern, 'Living in the Metaphor of Fiction', *Comparative Criticism*, 1 (1979), 16.

BIBLIOGRAPHY

This bibliography is in no way intended to replace Hans Wysling's definitive
bibliography in TMS 5. Instead, it lists the works cited in this thesis and
a few of the other sources which I have consulted.
Volumes marked ★ are to be found in Thomas Mann's own library in the TMA.

Primary Sources

(i) Editions of Felix Krull

'Bekenntnisse des Hochstaplers Felix Krull: Bruchstück aus einem Roman' [Book I,
    Chapter 5], in *Das fünfundzwanzigste Jahr. Almanach des S. Fischer Verlages* (Berlin: Fischer,
    1911), pp. 273–88
'Schulkrankheit: Bruchstück aus dem unvollendeten Roman "Bekenntnisse des Hoch-
    staplers Felix Krull"' [Book I, Chapter 6], in *Das Kestnerbuch*, ed. by P. E. Küppers
    (Hannover: Böhme, 1919), pp. 7–17
Bekenntnisse des Hochstaplers Felix Krull: Buch der Kindheit [Book I] (Vienna, Leipzig, and
    Munich: Rikola, 1922)
Bekenntnisse des Hochstaplers Felix Krull: Buch der Kindheit [Book I] (Stuttgart, Berlin, and
    Leipzig: Deutsche Verlagsanstalt, 1923)
Bekenntnisse des Hochstaplers Felix Krull [Book I, Book II, Chapters 1–5] (Amsterdam:
    Querido, 1937)
★*Bekenntnisse des Hochstaplers Felix Krull. Der Memoiren erster Teil* [Books I–III] (Frankfurt:
    Fischer, 1954)
'Thomas Mann: Ein nachgelassenes Kapitel aus "Felix Krull"', *Die neue Rundschau*, 68.2
    (1957), 181–86

(ii) Unpublished sources

Felix Krull, Manuscript (TMA: Mp XI/12)
Documentary folders for *Felix Krull* (TMA: Mat. 3). [A very small selection of images from
    the folders has been published in *Bild und Text bei Thomas Mann: Eine Dokumentation*, ed.
    by Hans Wysling and Yvonne Schmidlin (Bern and Munich: Francke, 1975)]

(iii) Works and Letters by Thomas Mann

Gesammelte Werke, 13 vols (Frankfurt a.M.: Fischer, 1974)
Große Kommentierte Frankfurter Ausgabe: Werke — Briefe — Tagebücher, ed. by Heinrich
    Detering, Eckhard Heftrich, Hermann Kurzke, T. J. Reed, Thomas Sprecher, Hans R.
    Vaget, and Ruprecht Wimmer [38 vols planned] (Frankfurt a.M.: Fischer, 2002–)
Essays, 6 vols, ed. by Hermann Kurzke and Stephan Stachorski (Frankfurt a.M.: Fischer,
    1993–97)

Notizbücher, 2 vols, ed. by Hans Wysling and Yvonne Schmidlin (Frankfurt a.M.: Fischer, 1992)

Tagebücher 1918–1921, 1933–1955, 10 vols, ed. by Peter de Mendelssohn and Inge Jens (Frankfurt a.M.: Fischer, 1979–95)

Dichter über ihre Dichtungen, 3 vols, ed. by Hans Wysling and Marianne Fischer (Munich: Heimeran, 1975–81)

Briefe 1889–1955, 3 vols, ed. by Erika Mann (Fischer: Frankfurt a.M., 1961–65)

Briefe an Paul Amann 1915–1952, ed. by Herbert Wegener (Lübeck: Max Schmidt-Römhild, 1959)

Thomas Mann–Heinrich Mann, *Briefwechsel 1900–1949*, ed. by Hans Wysling (Frankfurt a.M.: Fischer, 1984)

Hermann Hesse–Thomas Mann, *Briefwechsel*, ed. by Anni Carlsson (Frankfurt a.M.: Suhrkamp, 1968)

Thomas Mann–Karl Kerényi, Gespräche in Briefen, ed. by Karl Kerényi (Zürich: Rhein, 1960)

Die Briefe Thomas Manns: Regesten und Register, 5 vols, ed. by Hans Bürgin and Hans-Otto Mayer (Frankfurt a.M.: Fischer, 1976–87)

Tonio Kröger, ed. and intro. by John J. White and Ann White (London: Bristol Classical Press, 1996)

Two Stories: Unordnung und frühes Leid; Mario und der Zauberer, ed. and intro. by William Witte (London and Edinburgh: Nelson, 1961)

(iv) Sources used by Thomas Mann

*AUGUSTINE, *Die Bekenntnisse des heiligen Augustin*, trans. by J. E. Poritzky (Munich: Müller, 1911)

*BALZAC, HONORÉ DE, *Glanz und Elend der Kurtisanen*, trans. by Ferdinand Hardekopf (Zurich: Buchergilde Gutenberg, 1950)

*BANG, HERMAN, *Exzentrische Novellen* (Berlin: Fischer, 1905)

*BERTRAM, ERNST, *Nietzsche. Versuch einer Mythologie* (Berlin: Bondi, 1918)

*FONTANE, THEODOR, *Der Stechlin* (Munich: Nymphenburger, 1954)

*FONTANE, THEODOR, *Briefe Theodor Fontanes*, 2 vols, ed. by Otto Pniower and Paul Schlenther (Berlin: Fontane, 1910)

FONTANE, THEODOR, *Werke, Schriften und Briefe*, 5 vols, ed. by Walter Keitel and Helmuth Nürnberger (Munich: Hanser, 1970–)

*GOETHE, J. W. VON, *Goethes Sämtliche Werke*, 30 vols (Berlin: Tempel, 1909–10)

——*Goethes Sämtliche Werke*, 45 vols, 4 supplementary vols (Munich: Georg Müller; Berlin: Propyläen, 1909–23)

*KERÉNYI, KARL, *Hermes der Seelenführer: Das Mythologem vom männlichen Lebensursprung* (Zurich: Rhein, 1944)

MANN, HEINRICH, *Werkauswahl in 10 Bänden* (Düsseldorf: Claassen, 1976)

MANOLESCU, GEORGES, *Ein Fürst der Diebe* (Berlin/Lichterfelde: Langenscheidt, 1905)

——*Gescheitert. Aus dem Seelenleben eines Verbrechers* (Berlin/Lichterfelde: Langenscheidt, 1905)

MAUPASSANT, GUY DE, *Bel-Ami* [1887] (Paris: Larousse, 2001)

*MUSIL, ROBERT, *Der Mann ohne Eigenschaften* (Berlin: Rowohlt, 1931–33)

*NIETZSCHE, FRIEDRICH, *Nietzsches Werke*, 20 vols (Leipzig: Naumann/Kröner, 1895–1926)

*SCHILLER, FRIEDRICH, *Schillers Sämtliche Werke*, 13 vols (Leipzig: Tempel, 1911–12)

*SCHOPENHAUER, ARTHUR, *Sämmtliche Werke*, 6 vols (Leipzig: Brockhaus, 1922)

VIDAL, GORE, *The City and the Pillar* [1948] (London: Abacus, 1997)

WILDE, OSCAR, *The Picture of Dorian Gray* [1890] (Harmondsworth: Penguin, 1949)

(v) Other primary texts

ANON., *The Life of Lazarillo de Tormes* (*La vida de Lazarillo de Tormes y de sus fortunas y adversidades*), trans. by David Rowland (Warminster: Aris & Phillips, 2000)

BALZAC, HONORÉ DE, *Illusions perdues* (Paris: Flammarion, 1990)

BARTHES, ROLAND, *Œuvres complètes*, 3 vols, ed. by Eric Marty (Paris: Seuil, 1993–96)

BATAILLE, GEORGES, *La part maudite* (Paris: Minuit, 1967)

—— *L'Histoire de l'oeil* (Paris: Pauvert, 1979)

BENJAMIN, WALTER, *Gesammelte Schriften*, ed. by Rolf Tiedemann and Hermann Schweppenhäuser (Frankfurt a.M.: Suhrkamp, 1972–89)

COLERIDGE, SAMUEL TAYLOR, *Biographia Literaria* (London: Everyman, 1965)

DÖBLIN, ALFRED, *Berlin Alexanderplatz: Die Geschichte vom Franz Biberkopf* [1929], in *Ausgewählte Werke in Einzelbänden*, ed. by Walter Muschg (Olten, Breisgau: Walter, 1961)

FIELDING, HENRY, *Tom Jones* (Harmondsworth: Penguin, 1978)

FLAUBERT, GUSTAVE, *Madame Bovary* (Paris: Gallimard, 1972)

FREUD, SIGMUND, *Studienausgabe*, 12 vols, ed. by Alexander Mitscherlich and others (Frankfurt a.M.: Fischer, 1982)

GOETHE, J. W. VON, *Goethes Gespräche*, ii: *1805–1810*, ed. by Woldemar Biedermann, (Leipzig: Biedermann, 1889)

—— *Werke, Hamburger Ausgabe*, 14 vols, ed. by Erich Trunz (Munich: C. H. Beck, 1981)

HANDKE, PETER, *Die Stunde der wahren Empfindung* (Frankfurt a.M.: Suhrkamp, 1975)

IBSEN, HENRIK, *Peer Gynt* (Oxford: Oxford University Press, 1998)

LEBLANC, MAURICE, *Arsène Lupin, gentleman-cambrioleur* (Paris: Lafitte, 1907)

MALINOWSKI, BRONISLAW, *Argonauts of the Western Pacific* [1922] (New York: Dutton, 1961)

MANOLESCU, GEORGES, *Der Mann mit dem blauen Gehrock: Memoiren eines Hochstaplers* (Frankfurt a.M.: Fischer, 1987)

MAUSS, MARCEL, *The Gift* [1925] (London: Routledge, 1990)

MELVILLE, HERMAN, *The Confidence-Man: His Masquerade* (London: Penguin, 1990)

MUSIL, ROBERT, *Gesammelte Werke in neun Bänden*, ed. by Adolf Frisé (Hamburg: Rowohlt, 1978)

NIETZSCHE, FRIEDRICH, *Werke, Kritische Gesamtausgabe*, ed. by Giorgio Colli and Mazzino Montinari (Berlin: Walter de Gruyter, 1967–)

SANTAYANA, GEORGE, *Soliloquies in England and Later Soliloquies* (London: Constable, 1922)

SARTRE, JEAN-PAUL, *Qu'est-ce que la littérature?* [1948] (Paris: Gallimard, 1990)

SCHILLER, FRIEDRICH, *Werke, Nationalausgabe*, ed. by Julius Petersen and others (Weimar: Böhlaus Nachfolger, 1943–)

—— *On the Aesthetic Education of Man in a Series of Letters, English and German Facing*, ed. by Elizabeth M. Wilkinson and L. A. Willoughby (Oxford: Oxford University Press, 1982)

SCHOPENHAUER, ARTHUR, *Sämmtliche Werke, Grossherzog Wilhelm Ernst Ausgabe*, 5 vols, ed. by Eduard Grisebach (Leipzig: Insel, 1905)

SERNER, WALTER, *Letzte Lockerung. Ein Handbrevier für Hochstapler und solche, die es werden wollen* [1927] (Munich: Renner, 1981)

SIMMEL, GEORG, *Soziologische Ästhetik* (Bodenheim: Philo, 1998)

SORET, FRÉDÉRIC, *Goethes Unterhaltungen mit Friedrich Soret*, ed. by C. A. H. Burkhardt (Weimar: Böhlau, 1905)

STRINDBERG, AUGUST, *The Plays*, vol. 2, trans. by Michael Meyer (London: Secker and Warburg, 1975)

VOIGT, WILHELM, *Wie ich Hauptmann von Köpenick wurde* (Leipzig and Berlin: Püttmann, 1909)

WAUGH, EVELYN, *Brideshead Revisited* [1945] (London: Penguin, 2000)

Secondary Sources

(i) Literature on Thomas Mann

APPEL, SABINE, *Naivität und Lebenskunst: Die Idee der Synthese von Leben und Geist in Thomas Manns Hochstapler-Memoiren* (Frankfurt, a.M.: Peter Lang, 1995)

BANCE, ALAN, 'The Narrator in Thomas Mann's *Mario und der Zauberer*', *MLR* 82 (1987), 382–98

—— 'The Political Becomes Personal: *Disorder and Early Sorrow* and *Mario and the Magician*', in *The Cambridge Companion to Thomas Mann*, ed. by Ritchie Robertson (Cambridge: Cambridge University Press, 2002), pp. 107–17

BAUMGART, REINHARD, 'Joseph in Weimar — Lotte in Ägypten', *TMJ* 4 (1991), 75–88

BEDDOW, MICHAEL, 'Thomas Mann's "Bekenntnisse des Hochstaplers Felix Krull" and the Traditions of the Picaresque Novel and the Bildungsroman' (unpublished doctoral thesis, University of Cambridge, 1975)

—— 'Fiction and Meaning in Thomas Mann's *Felix Krull*', *Journal of European Studies*, 10 (1980), 77–92

—— *The Fiction of Humanity: Studies in the Bildungsroman from Wieland to Thomas Mann* (Cambridge: Cambridge University Press, 1982)

BENNE, CHRISTIAN, '"An die Freude"? Miszelle zum *Felix Krull* oder Thomas Manns Schillervariationen', *TMJ* 18 (2005), 277–93

BERENDSOHN, WALTER, 'Thomas Manns "Bekenntnisse des Hochstaplers Felix Krull". Struktur- und Stilstudien', *Stockholm Studies in Modern Philology*, n.s. 2 (1964), 57–115

BERGMANN, CHRISTIAN, '"hübsch" und "schön": Zum Wortgebrauch in Thomas Manns *Bekenntnisse des Hochstaplers Felix Krull*', *Muttersprache*, 113 (2003), 66–76

BERMAN, RUSSELL, *The Rise of the Modern German Novel: Crisis and Charisma* (Cambridge, MA: Harvard University Press, 1986)

BERTHEAU, JOCHEN, *Eine komplizierte Bewandtnis: Der junge Thomas Mann und die französische Literatur* (Frankfurt a.M.: Peter Lang, 2002)

BISHOP, PAUL, 'The Intellectual World of Thomas Mann', in *The Cambridge Companion to Thomas Mann*, ed. by Ritchie Robertson (Cambridge: Cambridge University Press, 2002), pp. 22–42

BLUME, BERNHARD, *Thomas Mann und Goethe* (Bern: Francke, 1949)

BÖHM, KARL WERNER, *Zwischen Selbstzucht und Verlangen: Thomas Mann und das Stigma Homosexualität* (Würzburg: Königshausen & Neumann, 1991)

BÖHME, HARTMUT, 'Mario und der Zauberer. Position des Erzählers und Psychologie der Herrschaft', in *Stationen der Thomas-Mann-Forschung. Aufsätze seit 1970*, ed. by Hermann Kurzke (Würzburg: Könighausen & Neumann, 1985), pp. 166–89

BOLLACHER, OLIVER MICHAEL, *Geistiges Aristokratentum im Dienste der Demokratie: Thomas Mann und Paul Valéry* (Frankfurt a.M.: Peter Lang, 1999)

BRUFORD, W. H., *The German Tradition of Self-Cultivation: 'Bildung' from Humboldt to Thomas Mann* (Cambridge: Cambridge University Press, 1975)

CRICK, JOYCE, 'Thomas and Heinrich Mann: Some Early Attitudes to their Public', *MLR* 77 (1982), 646–54

CURTIUS, MECHTHILD, *Erotische Phantasien bei Thomas Mann* (Königstein: Athenäum, 1984)

DETERING, HEINRICH, 'Das Ewig-Weibliche. Thomas Mann über Toni Schwabe, Gabriele Reuter, Ricarda Huch', *TMJ* 12 (1999), 149–69

—— 'Juden, Frauen, Literaten. Stigma und Stigma-Bearbeitung in Thomas Manns frühen Essays (1893–1914)', in *Thomas Mann und das Judentum*, TMS 30, ed. by Manfred Dierks and Ruprecht Wimmer (Frankfurt a.M.: Klostermann, 2004), pp. 15–34

DIEDERICHS, RAINER, *Strukturen des Schelmischen im modernen deutschen Roman: Eine Untersuchung an den Romanen von Thomas Mann 'Bekenntnisse des Hochstaplers Felix Krull' und Günter Grass 'Die Blechtrommel'* (Düsseldorf: Diederichs, 1971)

DOTZLER, BERNHARD J., *Der Hochstapler: Thomas Mann und die Simulakren der Literatur* (Munich: Fink, 1991)

DOWDEN, STEPHEN D., ed., *A Companion to Thomas Mann's 'The Magic Mountain'* (Rochester, NY: Camden House, 2002)

DOWNING, ERIC, *Artificial I's: The Self as Artwork in Ovid, Kierkegaard, and Thomas Mann* (Tübingen: Niemeyer, 1993)

ELSAGHE, YAHYA, 'Lotte in Weimar', in *The Cambridge Companion to Thomas Mann*, ed. by Ritchie Robertson (Cambridge: Cambridge University Press, 2002), pp. 185–98

FEUERLICHT, IGNACE, *Thomas Mann und die Grenzen des Ich* (Heidelberg: Carl Winter, 1966)

FREESE, WOLFGANG, 'Thomas Mann und sein Leser. Zum Verhältnis von Antifaschismus und Leseerwartung in *Mario und der Zauberer*', *Deutsche Vierteljahrsschrift*, 51 (1977), 659–75

FRIZEN, WERNER, *Thomas Mann: Bekenntnisse des Hochstaplers Felix Krull* (Munich: Oldenbourg, 1988)

GAEDE, FRIEDRICH, 'Gewinn und Verlust des "Selbst". Simplicius und Krull', *TMJ* 18 (2005), 107–21

GAIER, KONRAD, 'Figur und Rolle des Erzählers im Spätwerk Thomas Manns' (unpublished doctoral thesis, Albert Ludwigs Universität zu Freiburg, 1966)

GERIGK, HORST-JÜRGEN, '"Die Reize des Inkognitos". Felix Krull in komparatistischer Sicht', *TMJ* 18 (2005), 123–39

GÖRNER, RÜDIGER, 'Der Zauber des Letzten: Thomas Mann im spätbürgerlichen Zeitalter', *TMJ* 10 (1997), 11–25

—— *Thomas Mann. Der Zauber des Letzten* (Düsseldorf: Artemis & Winkler, 2005)

GRAWE, CHRISTIAN, 'Die Sprache in Goethes *Dichtung und Wahrheit* gesehen durch Thomas Manns *Die Bekenntnisse des Hochstaplers Felix Krull*', in Christian Grawe, *Sprache im Prosawerk. Beispiele von Goethe, Fontane, Bergengruen, Kleist und Johnson* (Bonn: Grundmann, 1974), pp. 9–24

HÄRLE, GERHARD, 'Simulationen der Wahrheit. Körpersprache und sexuelle Identität im *Zauberberg* und *Felix Krull*', in *'Heimsuchung und süßes Gift.' Erotik und Poetik bei Thomas Mann*, ed. by Gerhard Härle (Frankfurt a.M.: Fischer, 1992)

HAYMAN, RONALD, *Thomas Mann: A Biography* (London: Bloomsbury, 1996)

HEFTRICH, ECKHARD, 'Der unvollendbare *Krull* — Die Krise der Selbstparodie', *TMJ* 18 (2005), 91–106

HELLER, ERICH, *The Ironic German: A Study of Thomas Mann* (London: Secker & Warburg, 1958)

HERMSDORF, KLAUS, *Thomas Manns Schelme: Figuren und Strukturen des Komischen* (Berlin: Rütten & Loening, 1968)

HERWIG, MALTE, *Bildungsbürger auf Abwegen: Naturwissenschaften im Werk Thomas Manns*, TMS 32 (Frankfurt a.M.: Klostermann, 2004)

—— '"Nur in der Jugend gestielt". Die langen Wurzeln des *Felix Krull*', *TMJ* 18 (2005), 141–58

HOFFMANN, MARTINA, *Von Venedig nach Weimar: Eine Entwicklungsgeschichte paradigmatischen Künstlertums* (Frankfurt a.M.: Peter Lang, 1999)

JANZ, ROLF-PETER, 'Schwindelnde Männer oder die Liebe zum Betrug. Krull, Schwejk, Gunten, "Rotpeter"', in *Schwindelerfahrungen. Zur kulturhistorischen Diagnose eines vieldeutigen Symptoms*, ed. by Rolf-Peter Janz, Fabian Stoermer, and Andreas Hiepko (Amsterdam: Rodopi, 2003), pp. 99–116

JENDREIEK, HELMUT, *Thomas Mann: Der demokratische Roman* (Düsseldorf: Bagel, 1977)

KOOPMANN, HELMUT, *Die Entwicklung des 'ntellektualen Romans' bei Thomas Mann. Untersuchungen zur Struktur von 'Buddenbrooks', 'Königliche Hoheit' und 'Der Zauberberg'* (Bonn: Bouvier, 1962)

—— *Der schwierige Deutsche: Studien zum Werk Thomas Manns* (Tübingen: Niemeyer, 1988)

—— 'Der Zauberberg und die Kulturphilosophie der Zeit', in *Auf dem Weg zum 'Zauberberg'*, TMS 16, ed. by Thomas Sprecher (Frankfurt a.M.: Klostermann, 1997), pp. 273–98

—— *Thomas Mann — Heinrich Mann. Die ungleichen Brüder* (Munich: Beck, 2005)

——, ed., *Thomas-Mann-Handbuch* (Stuttgart: Kröner, 1990)

KÜHNER, KARL-MARTIN, 'Wer liest den Roman? Zur Interpretation der Leserfigur in Thomas Manns Hochstapler-Roman', in *Hommage à Maurice Marache* (Paris: Les Belles Lettres, 1972), pp. 287–301

KURZKE, HERMANN, *Thomas Mann: Epoche-Werk-Wirkung* [1985] (Munich: Beck, 1997)

—— *Thomas Mann: Das Leben als Kunstwerk* (Munich: Beck, 1999)

LÄMMERT, EBERHARD, 'Doppelte Optik. Über die Erzählkunst des frühen Thomas Mann', in *Literatur, Sprache, Gesellschaft, Dialog Schule-Wissenschaft*, Deutsche Sprache und Literatur 3, ed. by Karl Rüdinger (Munich: Bayerischer Schulbuch-Verlag, 1970), pp. 50–72

LANGE, GERHARD, *Struktur- und Quellenuntersuchungen zur 'Lotte in Weimar'* (Bayreuth: Tasso, 1970)

LANGE, VIKTOR, 'Betrachtungen zur Thematik von "Felix Krull"', in Viktor Lange, *Illyrische Betrachtungen: Essays und Aufsätze aus 30 Jahren* (Bern: Peter Lang, 1989), pp. 365–79

LEHNERT, HERBERT, 'Heine, Schiller, Nietzsche und der junge Thomas Mann', *Neophilologus*, 48 (1964), 51–56

LUBICH, FREDERICK A., 'The Confessions of Felix Krull, Confidence Man', in *The Cambridge Companion to Thomas Mann*, ed. by Ritchie Robertson (Cambridge: Cambridge University Press, 2002), pp. 199–212

LUCKSCHEITER, ROMAN, 'Das Mizzi-Meyer-Prinzip. Zur Politik der Form bei Thomas Mann', in *Man erzählt Geschichten, formt die Wahrheit. Thomas Mann — Deutscher, Europäer, Weltbürger*, ed. by Michael Braun and Birgit Lermen (Frankfurt a.M.: Peter Lang, 2003), pp. 103–15

LUFT, KLAUS PETER, *Erscheinungsformen des Androgynen bei Thomas Mann* (New York and Berlin: Lang, 1998)

*LUKÁCS, GEORG, 'Das Spielerische und seine Hintergründe: Fragmentarische Bemerkungen zum ersten Teil der "Bekenntnisse des Hochstaplers Felix Krull"', *Aufbau*, 11 (1955), 501–24

—— *Essays on Thomas Mann* (London: Merlin, 1964)

MARCUS, JUDITH, *Georg Lukács and Thomas Mann: A Study in the Sociology of Literature* (Amherst: University of Massachusetts Press, 1987)

MINDEN, MICHAEL, 'Mann's Narrative Techniques', in *The Cambridge Companion to Thomas Mann*, ed. by Ritchie Robertson (Cambridge: Cambridge University Press, 2002), pp. 43–63

—— 'Popularity and the Magic Circle of Culture: Thomas Mann in the Twentieth Century', *Publications of the English Goethe Society*, 76.2 (2007), 93–101

NELSON, DONALD F., 'Stylistic Unity and Change in Thomas Mann's *Felix Krull*: A Study of Style as the Reflection of Perception and Attitude' (unpublished doctoral thesis, University of Minnesota, 1966)

—— '*Felix Krull* or: "All the World's a Stage"', *The Germanic Review*, 45 (1970), 41–51

—— *Portrait of the Artist as Hermes: A Study of Myth and Psychology in Thomas Mann's 'Felix Krull'* (Chapel Hill: University of North Carolina Press, 1971)

NEUMANN, MICHAEL, 'Der Reiz des Verwechselbaren. Von der Attraktivität des Hochstaplers im späten 19. Jahrhundert', *TMJ* 18 (2005), 71–90

NORTHCOTE-BADE, JAMES, 'Der Tod in Venedig and Felix Krull: The Effect of the Interruption in the Composition of Felix Krull caused by Der Tod in Venedig', Deutsche Vierteljahrsschrift, 52 (1978), 271–78

PRICE, MARTIN, 'Felix Krull and the Comic Muse', in Modern Critical Views: Thomas Mann, ed. by Harold Bloom (New York: Chelsea House, 1986), pp. 325–34

PÜTZ, PETER, Kunst und Künstlerexistenz bei Nietzsche und Thomas Mann (Bonn: Bouvier, 1963)

—— Thomas Mann und die Tradition (Frankfurt a.M.: Athenäum, 1971)

REED, T. J., 'Thomas Mann, Heine, Schiller: The Mechanics of Self-Interpretation', Neophilologus, 47 (1963), 41–50

—— 'Geist und Kunst: Thomas Mann's Abandoned Essay on Literature', OGS 1 (1966), 53–101

—— Death in Venice: Making and Unmaking a Master (New York: Twayne, 1994)

—— Thomas Mann: The Uses of Tradition, 2nd edn (Oxford: Oxford University Press, 1996)

REILLY, PAMELA, 'Die Synthese des Bürgers und des Künstlers bei Thomas Mann' (unpublished doctoral thesis, University College Dublin, 1949)

RIECKMANN, JENS, '"In deinem Atem bildet sich mein Wort": Thomas Mann, Franz Westermeier und Bekenntnisse des Hochstaplers Felix Krull', TMJ 10 (1997), 149–65

RIGGAN, WILLIAM, Picaros, Madmen, Naives and Clowns: The Unreliable 1st-Person Narrator (Norman, OK: University of Oklahoma Press, 1981)

RILEY, ANTHONY W., 'Die Erzählkunst im Alterswerk von Thomas Mann mit besonderer Berücksichtigung der Bekenntnisse des Hochstaplers Felix Krull' (unpublished doctoral thesis, Universität zu Tübingen, 1958)

—— 'Three Cryptic Quotations in Thomas Mann's Felix Krull', Journal of English and Germanic Philology, 65 (1966), 99–106

SANDBERG, HANS-JOACHIM, Thomas Manns Schillerstudien: Eine quellenkritische Untersuchung (Oslo: Universitets forlaget, 1965)

SAUERESSIG, HEINZ, Die Entstehung des Romans 'Der Zauberberg' (Biberach an der Riss: Wege und Gestalten, 1965)

SCHARFSCHWERDT, JÜRGEN, Thomas Mann und der deutsche Bildungsroman: Eine Untersuchung zu den Problemen einer literarischen Tradition (Stuttgart: Kohlhammer, 1967)

SCHERRER, PAUL, and WYSLING, HANS, Quellenkritische Studien zum Werk Thomas Manns, TMS 1 (Bern: Francke, 1967)

SCHIFFER, EVA, 'Manolescu's Memoirs: The Beginnings of "Felix Krull"?', Monatshefte für deutschen Unterricht, 52 (1960), 283–92

—— 'Changes in an Episode. A Note on Felix Krull', Modern Language Quarterly, 24 (1963), 257–62

SCHNEIDER, KARL L., 'Thomas Manns "Felix Krull": Schelmenroman und Bildungsroman', in Untersuchungen zur Literatur als Geschichte. Festschrift für Benno von Wiese, ed. by V. J. Günther and others (Berlin: Schmidt, 1973), pp. 545–58

—— 'Der Künstler als Schelm. Zum Verhältnis von Bildungsroman und Schelmenroman in Thomas Manns Felix Krull', Philobiblon, 20 (1976), 2–18

SCHÖLL, JULIA, '"Verkleidet also war ich in jedem Fall". Zur Identitätskonstruktion in Joseph und seine Brüder und Bekenntnisse des Hochstaplers Felix Krull', TMJ 18 (2005), 9–29

SCHONFIELD, ERNEST, 'Mann Re-Joyces: The Dissemination of Myth in Ulysses and Joseph, Finnegans Wake and Doctor Faustus', Comparative Critical Studies 3:3 (2006), 269-90

—— 'Civilization in the dining room: Table manners in Thomas Mann's Buddenbrooks', in Un-civilizing Processes: Excess and Transgression in German Society and Culture, ed. Mary Fulbrook (Amsterdam: Rodopi, 2007), pp. 160-76

SCHULZ, KERSTIN, *Identitätsfindung und Rollenspiel in Thomas Manns Romanen 'Joseph und seine Brüder' und 'Bekenntnisse des Hochstaplers Felix Krull'* (Frankfurt a.M.: Peter Lang, 2000)

SCHWARZ, EGON, 'Felix Krull', in *A Companion to the Works of Thomas Mann*, ed. by Herbert Lehnert and Eva Wessell (Rochester, NY: Camden House, 2004), pp. 257–69

SEIDLIN, OSKAR, 'Picaresque Elements in Thomas Mann's Work', *Modern Language Quarterly*, 12 (1951), 183–200

——, ★'Pikareske Züge im Werke Thomas Manns', *Germanisch-Romanische Monatsschrift*, 5 (1955), 22–40

SIEFKEN, HINRICH, *Thomas Mann. Goethe — 'Ideal der Deutschheit', Wiederholte Spiegelungen, 1893–1949* (Munich: Fink, 1981)

SPRECHER, THOMAS, *Felix Krull und Goethe: Thomas Mann's 'Bekenntnisse' als Parodie auf 'Dichtung und Wahrheit'* (Bern: Peter Lang, 1985)

——'"Ein junger Autor hat es begonnen, ein alter setzt es fort". *Felix Krull* im Gesamtwerk Thomas Manns', *TMJ* 18 (2005), 159–76

——'Das grobe Muster. Georges Manolescu und Felix Krull', *TMJ* 19 (2006), 175–200

STEIN, GUIDO, *Thomas Mann. Bekenntnisse des Hochstaplers Felix Krull: Künstler und Komödiant* (Paderborn and Munich: Schöningh, 1984)

STEINER, GEORGE, 'Thomas Mann's *Felix Krull*', in George Steiner, *Language and Silence: Essays 1958–1966* (London: Faber and Faber, 1967), pp. 297–307

STERN, J. P., *Thomas Mann* (Columbia: Columbia University Press, 1967)

——'Living in the Metaphor of Fiction', in *Comparative Criticism*, 1 (1979), 3–16

—— *The Dear Purchase: A Theme in German Modernism* (Cambridge: Cambridge University Press, 1995)

SWALES, MARTIN, *Thomas Mann: A Study* (London: Heinemann, 1980)

—— *Mann: Der Zauberberg* (London: Grant and Cutler, 2000)

——'The Over-representations of History? Reflections on Thomas Mann's *Doktor Faustus*', in *Representing the German Nation: History and Identity in Twentieth-Century Germany*, ed. by Mary Fulbrook and Martin Swales (Manchester: Manchester University Press, 2000), pp. 77–90

TEBBEN, KARIN, '"Du entkleidest mich, kühner Knecht?". Felix Krull und die Frauen', *TMJ* 18 (2005), 51–70

TRAPP, FRITHJOF, 'Artistische Verklärung der Wirklichkeit', in *Stationen der Thomas-Mann-Forschung. Aufsätze seit 1970*, ed. by Hermann Kurzke (Würzburg: Königshausen & Neumann, 1985), pp. 25–40

TRAVERS, MARTIN, *Thomas Mann* (Basingstoke: Macmillan, 1992)

VOGT, JOCHEN, *Thomas Mann: 'Buddenbrooks'* (Munich: Fink, 1983)

WIESE, BENNO VON, '"Die Bekenntnisse des Hochstaplers Felix Krull" als utopischer Roman', in *Thomas Mann 1875–1975. Vorträge in München-Zürich-Lübeck*, ed. by Beatrix Bludau, Eckhard Heftrich, and Helmut Koopmann (Frankfurt a.M.: Fischer, 1977), pp. 189–206

WILL, WILFRIED VAN DER, *Pikaro heute: Metamorphosen des Schelms bei Thomas Mann, Döblin, Brecht, Grass* (Stuttgart: Kohlhammer, 1967)

WILSON, ERIC, 'Felix Krull: Thomas Mann's Comic Artist' (unpublished doctoral thesis, Stanford University, 1966)

WIMMER, RUPRECHT, '*Krull I – Doktor Faustus – Krull II*. Drei Masken des Autobiographischen', *TMJ* 18 (2005), 31–50

WISSKIRCHEN, HANS, *Zeitgeschichte im Roman: Zu Thomas Manns 'Zauberberg' und 'Doktor Faustus'*, TMS 6 (Bern: Francke, 1986)

WOLFFHEIM, ELSBETH, 'Das Abenteuer der Verwirklichung des "Goethe-Mythos"', in *'Heimsuchung und süßes Gift.' Erotik und Poetik bei Thomas Mann*, ed. by Gerhard Härle (Frankfurt a.M.: Fischer, 1992), pp. 103–25

WOLTERS, DIERK, *Zwischen Metaphysik und Politik: Thomas Manns Roman 'Joseph und seine Brüder' in seiner Zeit* (Tübingen: Niemeyer, 1998)

WYSLING, HANS, 'Archivalisches Gewühle. Zur Entstehungsgeschichte des Hochstapler-Romans', *Blätter der Thomas Mann Gesellschaft*, 5 (1965), 23–43; [and, revised, in TMS 1, 234–57]

——*Dokumente und Untersuchungen: Beiträge zur Thomas-Mann-Forschung*, TMS 3 (Bern: Francke, 1974)

——'Wer ist Professor Kuckuck? Zu einem der letzten "großen Gespräche" Thomas Manns', in Hans Wysling, *Thomas Mann heute. Sieben Vorträge* (Bern: Francke, 1976), pp. 44–63

——*Narzißmus und illusionäre Existenzform. Zu den Bekenntnissen des Hochstaplers Felix Krull*, TMS 5 (Bern: Francke, 1982)

——*Ausgewählte Aufsätze 1963–1995*, ed. by Thomas Sprecher and Cornelia Bernini, TMS 13 (Frankfurt a.M.: Klostermann, 1996)

(ii) Other

ANDERSON, RICHARD L., *Art in Primitive Societies* (Englewood Cliffs, NJ: Prentice-Hall, 1979)

BAUSINGER, HERMANN, 'Kannitverstan. Vom Zuhören, Verstehen und Mißverstehen', in *Über das Hören: einem Phänomen auf der Spur*, ed. by Thomas Vogel (Tübingen: Attempto, 1998), pp. 9–26

BELL, VICKI, *Performativity and Belonging* (London: Sage, 1999)

BLACKBURN, ALEXANDER, *The Myth of the Picaro: Continuity and Transformation of the Picaresque Novel, 1554–1954* (Chapel Hill: University of North Carolina Press, 1979)

BOURDIEU, PIERRE, *La Distinction: critique social du jugement* (Paris: Minuit, 1979)

BUTLER, JUDITH, *Bodies That Matter: On the Discursive Limits of "Sex"* (New York and London: Routledge, 1993)

——*Gender Trouble: Feminism and the Subversion of Identity*, 2nd edn (New York: Routledge, 1999)

CULLER, JONATHAN, *Structuralist Poetics* (Ithaca, NY: Cornell, 1975)

DENNETT, DANIEL C., *Consciousness Explained* (London: Allen Lane, 1991)

EAGLETON, TERRY, *The Ideology of the Aesthetic* (Oxford: Blackwell, 1990)

ELIAS, NORBERT, *The Civilizing Process* [1939] (Oxford: Blackwell, 2000)

FAIRLEY, BARKER, *Goethe as Revealed in his Poetry* (London and Toronto: Dent, 1932)

FOUCAULT, MICHEL, *Histoire de la sexualité*, 3 vols, [I. *La volonté de savoir*, II. *L'Usage des plaisirs*, III. *Le Souci de soi*] (Paris: Gallimard, 1976–84)

GALLAGHER, CATHERINE, 'The Rise of Fictionality', in *The Novel. Volume I: History, Geography and Culture*, ed. by Franco Moretti (Princeton and Oxford: Princeton University Press, 2006), pp. 336–63

GENETTE, GÉRARD, *Figures III* (Paris: Seuil, 1972)

GOFFMAN, ERVING, *The Presentation of Self in Everyday Life* [1959] (London: Penguin, 1990)

GÖRNER, RÜDIGER, *Nietzsches Kunst: Annäherung an einen Denkartisten* (Frankfurt a.M.: Insel, 2000)

HABERMAS, JÜRGEN, *Strukturwandel der Öffentlichkeit: Untersuchungen zu einer Kategorie der bürgerlichen Gesellschaft* (Berlin and Neuwied: Luchterhand, 1969)

HILLIARD, KEVIN, '"Nicht in Person sondern durch einen Repräsentanten": Problematik der Repräsentation bei Schiller', in *Schiller: National Poet — Poet of Nations: A Birmingham Symposium*, Amsterdamer Beiträge zur neueren Germanistik, 61, ed. by Nicholas Martin (Amsterdam: Rodopi, 2006), pp. 89–105

HOBSBAWM, ERIC, *The Age of Empire 1875–1914* (London: Abacus, 1994)

ISER, WOLFANG, *Der Akt des Lesens: Theorie ästhetischer Wirkung* (Munich: Fink, 1976)

JAUSS, HANS ROBERT, *Ästhetische Erfahrung und literarische Hermeneutik 1* (Munich: Fink, 1977)

KERBY, ANTHONY P., *Narrative and the Self* (Bloomington, IN: Indiana University Press, 1991)

KRACAUER, SIEGFRIED, *Das Ornament der Masse* (Frankfurt a.M.: Suhrkamp, 1977)

LEAK, ANDREW, *Barthes: Mythologies* (London: Grant & Cutler, 1994)

LETHEN, HELMUT, *Cool Conduct: The Culture of Distance in Weimar Germany* (Berkeley, CA: University of California Press, 2002)

LYNX, JOACHIM JOE, *The Prince of Thieves: A Biography of George Manolesco alias H. H. Prince Lahovary alias the Duke of Otranto* (London: Cassell, 1963)

MACINTYRE, ALISDAIR, *After Virtue: A Study in Moral Theory* (Notre Dame, IN: University of Notre Dame Press, 1984)

MACRAE, DONALD G., *Max Weber* (London: Fontana, 1987)

MASLOW, ABRAHAM, *Towards a Psychology of Being* (New York: Wiley, 1998)

MATTHIAS, BETTINA, *The Hotel as Setting in Early Twentieth-Century German and Austrian Literature: Checking In to Tell a Story* (Rochester, NY: Camden House, 2006)

NEHAMAS, ALEXANDER, *Nietzsche: Life as Literature* (Cambridge, MA: Harvard University Press, 1985)

NICHOLLS, ANGUS, *Goethe's Concept of the Daemonic: After the Ancients* (Rochester, NY: Camden House, 2006)

RANCIÈRE, JACQUES, The Politics of Aesthetics, trans. and intr. by Gabriel Rockhill (London and New York: Continuum, 2006)

REED, T. J., *The Classical Centre: Goethe and Weimar 1775–1832* (London: Croom Helm, 1980)

——'Goethe and Happiness', in *Goethe Revisited: A Collection of Essays*, ed. by Elizabeth M. Wilkinson (London and New York: Calder, 1984), pp. 111–31

REUTER, HANS-HEINRICH, *Fontane*, 2 vols (Munich: Nymphenburger, 1968)

ROBERTSON, RITCHIE, 'Modernism and the Self 1890–1924', in *Philosophy and German Literature 1700–1990*, ed. by Nicholas Saul (Cambridge: Cambridge University Press, 2002), pp. 150–96

SCHEFFLER, HAROLD W., 'Structuralism in Anthropology', in *Structuralism*, ed. by Jacques Ehrmann (New York: Anchor, 1970), pp. 56–77

SONTAG, SUSAN, 'Notes on "Camp"', in *A Susan Sontag Reader*, intro. by Elizabeth Hardwick (New York: Farrar, Straus, Giroux, 1982), pp. 105–19

SPURLING, HILARY, *La Grande Thérèse, or, The Greatest Swindle of the Century* (London: Profile, 1999)

STAIGER, EMIL, *Goethe*, 3 vols (Zurich: Atlantis, 1956–59)

SWALES, MARTIN, *Studies of German Prose Fiction in the Age of European Realism* (Lewiston, NY: Mellen, 1995)

——*Epochenbuch Realismus* (Berlin: Erich Schmidt, 1997)

WHITE, JOHN J., *Mythology in the Modern Novel: A Study of Prefigurative Techniques* (Princeton, NJ: Princeton University Press, 1971)

INDEX